# Dying with Dignity

# Dying with Dignity

## A Legal Approach to Assisted Death

GIZA LOPES

*Global Crime and Justice*
Graeme R. Newman, Series Editor

 PRAEGER™

An Imprint of ABC-CLIO, LLC
Santa Barbara, California • Denver, Colorado

**Library of Congress Cataloging-in-Publication Data**

Lopes, Giza, author.
  Dying with dignity : a legal approach to assisted death / Giza Lopes.
    pages cm
  Includes bibliographical references and index.
    ISBN 978–1–4408–3097–6 (hardback) — ISBN 978–1–4408–3098–3 (ebook)
1. Euthanasia—Law and legislation—United States. 2. Euthanasia—Law and legislation—Europe.
3. Right to die—Law and legislation—United States. 4. Right to die—Law and legislation—Europe. 5. Assisted suicide—United States. 6. Assisted suicide—Europe. 7. Palliative treatment.
8. Terminal care—Moral and ethical aspects. I. Title.
K3611.E95L67   2015
344.7304'197—dc23          2014047689

ISBN: 978–1–4408–3097–6
EISBN: 978–1–4408–3098–3

19  18  17  16  15      1  2  3  4  5

This book is also available on the World Wide Web as an eBook.
Visit www.abc-clio.com for details.

Praeger
An Imprint of ABC-CLIO, LLC

ABC-CLIO, LLC
130 Cremona Drive, P.O. Box 1911
Santa Barbara, California 93116-1911

This book is printed on acid-free paper ∞

Manufactured in the United States of America

*For Andy, Sam, and Benji*

"History is irony on the move. Turns out that, by so bettering and extending our lives, we have re-achieved suffering."

Kent Russell

# Contents

## PART 3: CONCLUSION

# Tables and Figures

## FIGURES

# Series Foreword

*And death shall have no dominion.*
*Dead men naked they shall be one*

—Dylan Thomas, 1936

IN THE POSTMODERN ERA OF THE TWENTY-FIRST CENTURY, where everything is relative, is death included? For centuries now, death has been viewed, paradoxically, as the only absolute and at the same time the great leveler: a condition where everyone is at last made equal, the relativism of the postmodern era taken to its logical conclusion. This blustering demand for the reduction of justice to the equality of death has driven the postmodern countries of Europe to favor death over life. Their advocacy of birth and death control and the reduction of wages to a level that can support only childless families in the luxury they can afford have produced populations that decline with negative birth rates, their population growth saved by immigration. It is not surprising that the relentless logic of the postmodern era should take the final step to hasten death, removing barriers for those who want to die. The events of the twenty-first century appear to be overtaking Dylan Thomas's famous poem. Though the meaning of his poem is often argued, it appears that Death *is* the dominion.

Here is another strange paradox. In developed nations where the rule of law holds sway, the right to terminate life has remained entirely with the state, yet at the same time, especially during and after the Enlightenment, the sacred right of the individual as the sovereign owner of his or her body was embalmed in the laws of many Western countries, none greater than the worship of individual freedom written into the U.S. constitution, an attempt to put into practice the ideals expressed by the Enlightenment thinkers. If one were serious about individual sovereignty, suicide, no matter what kind, should not be a crime. And if we care about our loved ones, it should not be a crime to help an individual who freely expresses the desire to take his or her own life (regardless of the reason, mistaken or otherwise). Trouble is, there is a serious problem in ascertaining whether an individual is *freely* making a decision. In the extreme case obviously a fetus cannot decide whether to be aborted or not. But in many cases, individuals for whatever reason—fear, agony, misery, depression, any number of human conditions (including life itself) that would be *relieved* by death—may be thought by observers, whether loved ones or professionals or government officials, not to be capable of making such a decision.

It may be argued that the reason suicide has been and continues to be in many legal codes a crime is a hangover of the Judeo-Christian ethic, especially the Christian presumption that a Christian's life is owned by God and that it is only God who has the right to take it away. Indeed, the Christian religion, especially in its pre-Enlightenment forms, was entirely preoccupied with death and how to overcome it (again, paradoxically, it seems that in order to have everlasting life, one must first die). The many woodcuts of the middle ages by such masters as Holbein, Durer, and Cranach are ample evidence of this obsession, the pictures of Death personified as a vile, skeletal, nastily cloaked character hovering above the bed of the sick and dying, commonly with a priest, clergy, or angel sitting beside the bed.

While people and loved ones are shocked by a sudden, unexpected death, a slow death loses its shock value and instead turns into a process in which loved

**A dying man attended by Mary Magdalene and Saint Peter, angels, and the devil, Ars moriendi, Germany, 1466. (Library of Congress)**

ones sit helplessly by and watch the slow but sure onset of death, and in many cases—though just how many cases who knows—watch their loved ones suffer in discomfort, whether mental or physical, perhaps many in agony. But of these, the watchers and the dying, who would seek to hasten death's onset? The old woodcuts served to create an aura of horror that remains to this day and is celebrated in every horror movie, the modern ethos of which can be easily traced to Edgar Allan Poe's *The Masque of the Red Death*, which in turn inspired André Caplet's *Conte Fantastique,* the music that can be found in the majority of scary movies to this day.

It is likely that the postmodern deconstructionists have met their match with Death because it cannot, by their own definition, be deconstructed. What we do see, though, is that death was thoroughly *con*structed by Christianity and the rule of law expressed it. Lopes convincingly argues that not only have the clergy as the shepherds of Death been replaced by modern medicine's doctors and technologies, but that the rule of law has intervened to codify the ways and rights of helping people to die. She catalogues, with fascinating case studies and detailed historical observation, the quite different ways that the United States and European countries have tackled this problem of all problems. This is an erudite book that leaves no detail untouched; relentlessly unravels the moral, judicial, and political events that arguably precede—seen and unseen—not only every assisted death but arguably every single death on earth; and shows how these events have relentlessly set the stage for the coming movement to quicken the time it takes to die. In the twenty-first century, everything is quickened: Communication is reduced to 117 characters in Twitter, photos communicate quicker than do words, and videos, now universal, are reduced even to *vines* of six seconds. So if communication with multiple others can be reduced to seconds, why not dying? Adapting Murphy's Law, "If it can be done, it will be done."

Finally, what is so fascinating about this book is the grammar and vocabulary of Death. The full title of the book reveals its complexity: *Dying with Dignity: A Legal Approach to Assisted Death.* Is this book about dignifying death as the title implies? Or is it about actively killing people? A quick count of the language used in the book reveals that the word *dying* occurs 337 times and *death* 851 times. So death wins that prize. The subtitle of the book, *assisted death* (176 times), is a soft expression for the more action-oriented word *killing*, which occurs 121 times, and of these an undetermined number of usages of the word as a noun, such as *mercy killing*. The grammar suggests to me a subtitle hiding the purposive and intentional requirement of every assisted death: Someone has to actually do it. Lopes shows how different legal systems have answered this problem, especially the difficulty of determining or even assigning responsibility for the actual killing to an individual or individuals and the lengths to which the rule of law must go to justify their actions. Does this make dying more dignified? I would argue that there is nothing dignified about death; in fact, it is obviously an affront to life, so the idea of dying with dignity is a loser right from the start. It is this effrontery to life that the advocates of assisted dying at heart want to eradicate by speeding up the process of dying, because no matter how much you do to soften the pain or agony of the process of dying, the hard facts of dying reveal the very unhappy condition of all of life: that it is finite.

*Dying with Dignity* is a fitting capstone to the Global Crime and Justice series, even reaching beyond it, since Death most likely is not only global but also universal.

Graeme R. Newman
Albany, November, 2014

# 1

## Introduction

IN 1999, 2,391,399 PEOPLE DIED in the United States (Hoyert, Arias, Smith, Murphy & Kochanek, 2001). Half of them succumbed to heart disease or cancer. Most expired in hospital beds. Rick Miller, a 52-year-old resident of Portland, Oregon, was among those who died that year. Like many others, Miller had cancer—a particularly aggressive type that began in his lungs and quickly spread to other organs. But he did not die of cancer; neither did he die in a healthcare facility. Miller died in his living room recliner, after ingesting a lethal mixture of applesauce and Seconal—a drug he had obtained legally from his oncologist with the purpose of killing himself (Miller, 2005).

In 1999, 32 other Oregonians requested and received prescriptions for deadly doses of medication to end their lives. Besides Miller, 26 others actually took the drugs (Department of Human Services, 2000). Two years earlier, Oregon had become the first U.S. state where a competent, terminally ill adult could hasten his or her death with the help of a physician. Today, Washington and Vermont also afford their residents access to medical aid in dying. In two other states, court rulings also have opened the door to the practice. In Montana the state Supreme Court has ruled that physicians helping patients die are "shielded from criminal liability by the patient's consent," while in New Mexico a judge has determined that, under the state's constitution, terminally ill individuals who are mentally competent have the "right to aid in dying" (see Table 1.1 for a summary of the legal aspects related to assisted death domestically and abroad).

While most of these legal milestones were reached since the late 1990s, efforts to legalize assisted death have a much longer history, with ideological underpinnings unfolding from the Hippocratic Oath to Jack Kevorkian's *Mercitron*.[1] In the United States, they can accurately be said to date to 1906, when the first bills to legalize euthanasia were introduced in Ohio and Iowa. Since then, a variety of activists have pursued legalization through legislative lobbying, ballot initiatives, constitutional challenges to extant laws, and the more radical strategy of confessing to having precipitated the death of an invalid and inviting prosecution. Currently, concerted legal actions continue to be carried out in various states.

Abroad, the Netherlands, Belgium, and Luxembourg also permit individuals to control the manner and timing of their deaths with physicians' collaboration.

**Table 1.1 Summary of the Legal Aspects Related to Assisted Death in the United States and Europe**

| | The United States |
|---|---|
| Oregon | The Oregon *Death with Dignity Act*, first passed in 1994 but enacted in 1997, allows doctors to prescribe lethal medication upon request by competent, adult, terminally ill individuals. |
| Washington | The Washington State *Death with Dignity Act*, enacted in March 2009, allows doctors to prescribe lethal medication upon request by competent, adult, terminally ill individuals. |
| Vermont | Vermont's *Patient Choice and Control at the End of Life Act*, signed into law in 2013, allows doctors to prescribe lethal medication upon request by competent, adult, terminally ill individuals. |
| Montana | In *Baxter v. Montana* (2009), the Montana Supreme Court decided that state law protects doctors in Montana from prosecution for helping terminally ill patients die. |
| New Mexico | In 2014, a New Mexico lower court ruled that under the state's constitution, terminally ill individuals who are mentally competent have the "right to aid in dying" (*Morris v. Brandenberg*). This decision, currently under appeal, may apply statewide, if upheld. |
| | Europe |
| Netherlands | The *Termination of Life on Request and Assisted Suicide (Review Procedures) Act of 2002* allows Dutch doctors, upon patient's request, to prescribe or administer lethal medication to individuals whose suffering (physical or psychological) is unbearable and without prospect of improvement. Minors between 12 and 15 years of age may request assisted death but parental consent is required. 16- and 17-year-olds can make the decision for themselves, but parents must be involved in discussions. |
| Belgium | The *Act on Euthanasia of May 28th, 2002*, allows Belgian doctors, upon patient's request, to prescribe or administer lethal medication to individuals whose suffering is unbearable and without prospect of improvement. Suffering can be physical or psychological, but must result from illness or accident. Minors of any age who have the "capacity of discernment" can request assisted death if their suffering is somatic. |
| Luxembourg | The *Euthanasia and Assisted Suicide Law of 16 March 2009* allows doctors in Luxembourg to prescribe or administer lethal medication to terminally ill adults upon request. |
| Switzerland | Since 1942, the Swiss Criminal Code allows anyone to assist another in committing suicide, provided the assistor is not guided by selfish motives. |

In Switzerland, help can be given by anyone, provided those who assist are not selfishly motivated. In France, Canada, the United Kingdom, and Germany, several court cases have forced the issue to the forefront of public debate. This wide-reaching, ongoing discussion is unlikely to abate any time soon, especially as our living years progressively lengthen, thanks to the development of marvelous drugs and cutting-edge hospital machinery.

The debate as to whether *voluntary death*, with or without assistance, should be an acceptable, reasonable solution to the extension of life beyond what an individual deems meaningful living is at once captivating and polarizing. Science fiction writers have imagined a time when "Suicide Parlors" would be available to those wishing to be painlessly killed by "pretty," "tough-minded" six-foot tall hostesses while lying on a "Barcalounger" (Vonnegut, 1968). Loftier authors, particularly Enlightenment thinkers, also proposed that certain "misfortunes"—such as sickness and old age—can make life sufficiently miserable that continued existence is worse than death (Hume, 2005). Regardless of one's intellectual lineage, writings such as these have always sparked divisiveness. In the modern debate surrounding the legalization of assisted death, things are not different. On the one side of the argument, opponents subscribe fundamentally to the idea that "life is sacred." On the other, supporters appeal to the principle of autonomy and self-determination—"Whose life is it anyway?," they ask (Clark, 1993). Interestingly, they all agree, albeit tacitly, that pain and suffering are undesirable (see Battin, 2008a, for a discussion). Frequently pinned at the center is the physician, trapped between the professional duty to relieve suffering and the age-old vow to "first, do no harm."

This book is less preoccupied with *whether* assisted death should be legalized or not than it is concerned with retracing *how* and *why* the pleas for legalization of *euthanasia* in the beginning of the twentieth century in the United States and elsewhere were transmuted into the assisted-suicide laws we have today. Before we explore that history, in Chapter 2, I provide the reader with key concepts and definitions related to assisted death as well as with a brief overview of the notion of "medicalization of society" (Conrad, 2007). The latter offers a useful theoretical framework through which one can understand the expansion of the medical jurisdiction over human behavior, including dying. In this sense, I will show throughout the book that the increasing medicalization of death taking place over the past century has accompanied the redefinition of suicide from sin/crime to a decriminalized, secular solution to pain and suffering.

The remainder of this book is divided into two sections. The first concentrates on the American experience and recounts the key developments in the controversy over assisted death spanning the period from the early nineteenth century to the legal efforts of the present day. To that end, beginning with the invention of anesthesia in the 1830s, Chapter 3 charts physicians' accretion of control over pain and death. This shift was not only symbolic but also regulatory as anesthesia came to be widely practiced and controlled. Contemporary debates with clerical authorities on this shift are discussed in detail. The chapter culminates with the introduction of the bills to legalize physician-assisted death in Iowa and Ohio in 1906.

In Chapter 4, the issue of *mercy killing* by laypersons and physicians is discussed. The chapter highlights the case of Hermann Sander, one of the few doctors prosecuted for assisted death during the twentieth century. In 1950, he was charged with first-degree murder of a terminally ill patient, Abbie Borrotto, by injecting air into her bloodstream. Following a short trial that attracted intense curiosity by the national media, Sander was acquitted.

Chapter 5 shifts to the appellate courtroom. It describes two landmark cases —*Vacco v. Quill* and *Washington v. Glucksberg*—which first posed the question before the Supreme Court of the United States of whether there is a recognized right to physician's assistance in committing suicide.

Chapter 6 concludes the American experience by describing the legalization of physician-assisted death in the state of Washington through the passage of the "I-1000" ballot initiative. Led by popular and chronically ill former governor Booth Gardner, proponents' campaign prevailed over a concerted resistance by the Catholic Church and disability groups, consecrating the viability of medically assisted death in its neighbor state of Oregon.

The second part of this book takes us beyond the United States to assess the way assisted death became legal in the Benelux countries (Chapter 7) and in Switzerland (Chapter 8). The former represent an extremely medicalized model of assisted death, in that their doctors are allowed to go beyond prescription to actual injection of lethal drugs. In turn, the latter permits altruistic laypersons to provide aid in dying. In both instances, controversy seems to follow. Moreover, the law and practice of assisted death in each of these countries represent a comparison example that expands our ability to understand and appreciate the distinctiveness of the policies that were developed in the United States.

In Chapter 9, the book returns to the theme of *medicalization* and ends with a comparison of different models of assisted death adopted here and abroad. A discussion about the role of medical professionals at different stages of lawful aid in dying is also presented.

## NOTE

1. The Mercitron was a device built by Jack Kevorkian to help his *patients* die. Unlike the *Thanatron*, another one of his devices, which involved the self-administration of controlled substances (sodium thiopental and pancuronium bromide) through an IV, Kevorkian's Mercitron merely employed a gas mask fed by a canister of carbon monoxide. Other euthanasia devices have been developed in the past two decades or so.

Among the most popular are the Exit Bag (essentially a plastic bag equipped with a rubber band), the *Deliverance Machine* (a laptop fixed to a syringe driver, which can deliver a lethal injection at the touch of a button), and the *Co-Genie* (also based on the release of carbon monoxide). Recently, other DIY suicide strategies have gained notoriety. For example, Philip Nitschke, an Australian physician and director of a pro-euthanasia organization, began promoting the use of the barbiturate Nembutal to hasten death (Nitschke & Stewart, 2006). The drug, commonly used in veterinarian euthanasia, can be easily obtained from Mexico and Asia without regulation. As a result, Dr. Nitschke sells drug-testing kits that can be used to check the strength of these drugs obtained illegally. Kits sell for 35 pounds in the UK (Doward, 2009).

──────────────────────────────────

# 2

# Background

WORLDWIDE, CURRENT LAW ON AID IN DYING goes by many names. *Euthanasia, death with dignity,* and *assisted suicide* are but a few terms associated with the practice. Here, I distinguish between these and other terms, offering an explanation of each and drawing attention to the important legal boundaries that separate them.

As will become clear throughout this book, one of the most complex and persistent aspects of assisted death as it is presently implemented around the world is the connivance of medicine. Medical professionals are gatekeepers of lethal prescriptions or de facto assistors in expediting death in almost every context and country where it is permitted (see Table 2.1 for an overview).

Since 1906, when attempts to legalize assisted death in the United States began, however, the position of physicians relative to the dying process has changed considerably. Put simply, they now occupy a much more prominent role at the deathbed, alongside others such as clergy, whose presence there far predates that of the physicians (see Chapter 3 for an extended discussion). How, then, did death become a medical event? And how did medical assistors in death become increasingly legitimized? These and other questions are explored in this chapter through a discussion of *medicalization*—a useful framework to understand how dying has moved from a metaphysical phenomenon to a progressive concession to medical judgment.

## *GOOD DEATH*: A CONCEPTUAL DISCUSSION

"An easy, pleasant mode of death (from the Greek: *eu* = good, well; *thanatos* = death)"—this is how the 1904 edition of the *Chambers's Etymological Dictionary of the English Language* defines *euthanasia* (Chambers, 1904, p. 161).

The lucidity offered by the term's etymology vanishes as soon as one focuses on the *evaluative* aspect of the definition and its diachronic changes. Put simply, the idea of what constitutes a *good* death has changed in different cultures and throughout history, accompanying eventual shifts in societies' moral values. Dominated by religion in the past and by medicine nowadays, *euthanasia* is far from a monolithic term. This normative aspect of defining what *dying well*

**Table 2.1 Physicians' Role in Aid in Dying Where the Practice Is Legal**

| | Benelux countries | U.S. States | Switzerland |
|---|---|---|---|
| Assistance must be provided by a physician | Yes | Yes | No* |
| Physician may administer lethal drugs | Yes | No | No |
| Lethal drugs may be self-administered by the patient orally | Yes | Yes | Yes |
| Lethal drugs may be self-administered by the patient intravenously or through gastric tube | Yes | No | Yes |
| Physician determination of medical eligibility required** | Yes | Yes | No |

*However, as discussed in Chapter 8, in practice physicians are involved in that most elective deaths follow ingestion of lethal substances that must be prescribed by a doctor.
**Terminal prognosis* in some jurisdictions and *unbearable suffering* in others.

means and the many nuances built into the term over time are reflected in part in current dictionary entries, such as the following:

> Euthanasia—the act or practice of *killing* or *permitting the death* of *hopelessly sick or injured* individuals (as *persons* or *domestic animals*) in a *relatively painless* way for reasons of *mercy* (*Merriam-Webster Online*, 2009; my emphasis).

Evaluative aspects that speak to the historical changes associated with *euthanasia* are readily evident in this definition. For instance, the reference to a "relatively painless way" of dying is strikingly different from previous uses of the word. Between the late medieval era and well into the Enlightenment, *euthanasia* was mainly understood within the framework of *ars moriendi*, or the art of dying. Pain, the central pedagogical metaphor in Judeo-Christian doctrine, was not to be relieved. As a matter of fact, thirteenth-century Pope Innocent III decreed that until the spiritual needs of the moribund person had been met, no medical assistance was to be given (see Lewis, 2007, p. 199). Dying well, while once understood as having an opportunity for spiritual atonement with an emphasis on the redemptive character of pain and suffering, signifies something diametrically different today.

Other normative aspects transpire in the *Merriam-Webster* definition of *euthanasia*, particularly in regard to issues of motivation and eligibility. As discussed later in this book, the moral emotion sustaining modern understandings of *euthanasia* as "mercy" killings was at times transected by utilitarian purposes of social control. In such cases, *euthanasia* was not exclusively pursued for the "hopelessly sick or injured individuals." Furthermore, the conceptualization of *euthanasia* as inclusive of "domestic animals" is fairly recent. It was only in the 1950s that the discussion of *veterinary euthanasia* gained momentum, particularly as public debate on animal welfare issues increased and the roots for the modern animal rights movement were put in place.[1]

Additionally, and perhaps most important for the purposes of this section, by referring to issues of agency ("killing" and "permitting the death"), the *Merriam-Webster* description of *euthanasia* alludes to a taxonomy that, though ordinary nowadays, was not always employed. Despite the arguably artificial character of such distinction, the differentiation between *active* and *passive* euthanasia carries divergent legal implications and is used often enough to merit clarification. Let us turn to that.

Current understanding of *euthanasia* distinguishes between a *good death* achieved by direct action (commonly known as *active euthanasia*) *versus* one that results from omission (aka, *passive euthanasia*). Cases of *passive euthanasia* typically arise from the withholding of treatment (e.g., failure to perform cardiovascular resuscitation) and/or withdrawal of essential life support systems (e.g., discontinuation of mechanical respiration, forced nutrition and hydration, kidney dialysis, etc.) when death is imminent, thereby *allowing nature to follow its course.*

In contrast, *active euthanasia* involves hastening the death of a person through direct measures. As practiced in the Netherlands, Belgium, and Luxembourg, *active euthanasia* is legal when performed by physicians and is controlled by narrow guidelines designed to ensure patients' voluntariness and verify their competence (see Chapter 7 for details).

The issue of patients' voluntariness and competence is crucial not only in defining the boundaries surrounding the legality of active euthanasia within the cultures of the Benelux countries but also in cases of passive euthanasia as practiced in the United States. Besides the binary distinction based on positive or negative agency (*active* vs. *passive*), *euthanasia* is also commonly typified according to the extent of patients' exercise of autonomy.

*Voluntary euthanasia* thus occurs when patients' choice to hasten death is made freely, whereas *involuntary euthanasia* takes place when death is a result of actions carried out without consent. Alternatively, a third category has arisen from cases where patients' choice is unclear for one reason or another (e.g., pediatric patients, persons in permanent vegetative state) and the decision is made by a healthcare proxy. These cases of *non-voluntary euthanasia*, even in the context of a reasonably resolved issue such as withdrawal of life-sustaining treatment, still evoke public controversy, as was witnessed in Terri Schiavo's death in 2005.[2]

The previously mentioned definition of *euthanasia* provided by the *Merriam-Webster* dictionary leaves out these degrees of voluntariness and focuses primarily on the act itself (*"killing* or *permitting the death* . . . in a *relatively painless* way"). In doing so, the lexical entry almost implicitly characterizes *euthanasia* as an external act, or a deed performed by an actor other than the patient himself/herself.

Such an interpretation, of course, neglects the question of *rational* suicide— often interchangeable with *euthanasia* in today's public imagination. *Rational* suicides are cases in which mentally competent persons with incurable diseases or with advanced illness hasten their deaths with or without assistance from others. Often referred to as *assisted suicide* (when aid is provided by a layperson) or *physician-assisted suicide*, these situations are less opaque in terms of voluntariness as the decision to bring about death is, of course, primarily controlled by the individual who is dying.

As the reader can surmise, *good deaths* go by many names and their conceptual distinctions often reflect socially constructed differences dictated by moral values *en vogue* in one era or another. Here, I deliberately chose to avoid the terms *euthanasia* and *suicide* in characterizing the selected object of study. Instead, I opted for more neutral, overarching terms—such as *assisted death* and *aid in dying*—as an attempt to circumvent a metonymic simplification of efforts that have been far more nuanced than the immediate moral charge that terms such as *euthanasia* and *suicide* would evoke.

My choice was also designed to reflect the path taken by legalization advocates in most of the world. Since shortly after World War II, activists have consistently distanced themselves from the term *euthanasia*, given its association with the Nazi *Aktion T4* program.[3] For instance, in German-speaking countries, including Switzerland, the word *euthanasie* is avoided and one speaks instead of *sterbehilfe* (literally, "help in dying") or *freitod* ("free death"). In the United States, proponents of aid in dying decriminalization as well as medical groups (e.g., the American College of Legal Medicine) and public organs (e.g., the Oregon Department of Health) have also refrained from using the terms *suicide* and *assisted suicide* in reference to terminally ill patients' hastening their deaths (see Meisel & Cerminara, 2009, p. xxxvii, for a discussion).

Terminology changes such as these have contributed to significant strategic developments within the pro-legalization movement. For example, claims-making of assisted death as a *right*, which emerged shortly after the Nazi atrocities, gave the movement a momentum it had until then lacked. Equally important has been the recent repudiation of the term *(assisted) suicide*, in the hope it might help increase target constituency and secure more popular support in direct democracy processes. Hence, more than a mere lexical option, the choice of an all-encompassing term reflects my attempt to analyze the common thread of legalization efforts proposed by a movement that has strategically worn many hats throughout its long history. Interestingly, however, in the Benelux countries, *euthanasia* and *suicide* remain very much part of the legal lexicon.

## *GOOD DEATH*: MEDICALIZED DEATH?

The inevitability of death is a hackneyed theme. Less predictable, however, are the circumstances surrounding the dying process: its timing, manner, and place. From a diachronic perspective, these circumstances have changed radically, particularly in the past century and especially in the Western societies.

In brief, nowadays, those living in more developed countries die older, of more prolonged deaths, and more publically than ever, due in part to the many technological and medical advances that have emerged since 1900.[4]

The United States is an example. Americans born in 2000 are expected to live on average nearly 30 years longer than those born a century earlier (from 47 years in 1900 to 77 in 2000; Centers for Disease Control and Prevention, 2012). Life expectancy at age 65 has increased by roughly 30 percent since 1950 (from 12.8 years in 1950 to over 16 years in 2000; Centers for Disease Control and Prevention, 2012). Additionally, the leading causes of death since 1900 have changed from infectious diseases (e.g., pneumonia, influenza, tuberculosis, and diarrhea) to chronic illnesses (e.g., heart disease, cancer, and stroke).

Besides living longer and often experiencing chronic diseases later in life, beginning in the 1880s American families also started to depend increasingly on strangers for care at times of sickness and approaching death. Between that time and the 1920s, two crucial changes occurred that would later come to affect the debates and decisions surrounding end-of-life care: namely, the professionalization of nursing and the emergence of hospitals as we know them today. For example, in 1800 there were two hospitals in the United States (one in Philadelphia and another in New York); by 1909 the number surpassed 4,300 (Rosenberg, 1995). Rates of hospital beds per person then doubled between 1909 (4.578 per 1,000 population) and 1940 (9.313 per 1,000 population) (Thomasson & Treber, 2008).

With this rapid growth and the institutionalization of care by strangers, Americans slowly moved from dying almost exclusively at home to doing so increasingly in hospitals and other medical institutions. In 1980, according to Field (2009, p. 70), 74 percent of deaths occurred in healthcare-related settings: 60.5 percent in hospitals and the remaining 13.5 percent in nursing homes and other institutions.

It was around that time that the term *medicalization* emerged through the work of highly influential scholars, such as Michel Foucault (1973), Thomas Szasz (1970), Irving Zola (1972), and Ivan Illich (1975).[5] *Medicalization* is a *process* by which a redefinition of social problems into medical ones takes place. As a theoretical framework, it seeks to describe and analyze the underpinnings of the expansion of medical jurisdiction that accompanies such redefinitions and the social implications that follow from them. In the words of one of its scholars, medicalization can be seen as "defining behavior as a medical problem or illness and mandating or licensing the medical profession to provide some type of treatment for it" (Conrad, 1975, p. 12). The key, then, to understanding medicalization is *definition*; "once a problem becomes defined in medical terms, described using medical language, understood through the adoption of a medical framework, or 'treated' with a medical intervention," it has become "medicalized" (Conrad, 2007, p. 5).

The framework's emphasis on *definition* and on the attendant shift in social control to the medical dominion is suggestive of medicalization's intellectual roots in two equally influential, yet quite different, sociological theoretical streams: the societal reaction perspective and the Parsonian notion of medicine as an institution of social control (Conrad, 1975). Earlier studies on medicalization and its consequences (Freidson, 1988; Zola, 1972) were based in large part on the social constructivist notions underlying "labeling theory" and on Parsons's (1951) influential concept of the "sick role," which helped legitimize the medical conception of deviance as illness.[6]

This social-constructivist bent of the framework highlights how medicalization is in fact a *process* and as such is influenced by several dynamic social factors that have set the context for its occurrence by either facilitating its emergence or deterring its development over time. Among commonly listed social factors fostering medicalization are "the diminution of religion; an abiding faith in science, rationality and progress; the increased prestige of the medical profession; the American penchant for individual and technological solutions to problems; and general humanitarian trends in Western societies" (Conrad, 2007, p. 8).

Because it is dynamic, medicalization, as its proponents argue, is bidirectional. Once medical treatment is no longer deemed an appropriate intervention, demedicalization occurs. Such was the case for phenomena such as masturbation, long ago a target of medical intervention (Engelhardt, 1974), and for physical and cognitive disabilities, in recent times demedicalized and reframed in terms of access and civil rights (Conrad, 2007; see also Oliver, 1996).

Though when literally interpreted, medicalization's definition is free of any value judgment—"to make medical"—the framework's analytical tendency has become tainted, because much of the writing on the topic has been built on criticism of *over-medicalization* and its consequences. In this sense, it is crucial to clarify that no such assumption is a given in the framework, and one can describe a range of problems that have become historically demedicalized and that vary in the degree of consensus regarding whether they *legitimately* belong to the medical realm or not (e.g., from studies on the medicalization of baldness and epilepsy [Schneider & Conrad, 1985], to those applied to alcoholism and homosexuality).

Over the past century, the number of *social ills* that came to be defined as "medical problems" has increased enormously. One example is the status transformation of disruptive childhood behavior "from badness to sickness," beginning with the discovery of hyperkinesis in the 1950s and followed two decades later by the attention-deficit hyperactivity disorder (ADHD) diagnosis (Conrad & Schneider, 1992). Another commonly cited example of medicalization is alcoholism. The perspective is thus used mostly to examine how behaviors once defined as immoral, sinful, or delinquent/criminal have been given medical status—a shift often accompanied by legal change of one kind or another.

Not surprisingly, medicalization studies have traditionally focused on the medicalization of deviance, especially in the 1960s and 1970s (see, for instance, Pitts, 1968; Conrad, 1975). Since its initial coinage, however, medicalization has become applicable beyond *behavioral* issues and is currently used to explain a wide range of common life *processes* and *events* that have entered medical jurisdiction. Childbirth is among these common life events/processes frequently discussed within the demedicalization framework, as it has swung from one end of the medicalization scale to the other—and is now returning whence it came.

To explain, giving birth in the United States has changed dramatically since colonial times—from an all-female-centered activity taking place in the home's kitchen or bedroom to the highly medicalized birth procedures dominating in the 1950s, which involved complete sedation of the mother and episiotomies and were followed by strong recommendation of feeding the newborn exclusively with artificial formula. In recent years, however, with the growth of the alternative birth and midwifery movements, deliveries have experienced a dramatic reduction of medical intervention if compared to post–World War II practices (Wertz & Wertz, 1989; see also Simonds, Rothman, & Norman, 2007).

Along the same lines, I examine the decriminalization of assisted death from a medicalization perspective by looking mainly at two interrelated aspects. First, death, just like birth, has indisputably become a medicalized event since the 1900s (Illich, 1975). This echoes in part the explanatory authority of medical advances—in terms of technological development and expertise—commonly cited by many euthanasia scholars. But it also takes it a step beyond by grounding the claim in a systematic analysis of some of the aspects that proponents of the medicalization approach have suggested, namely its advocacy aspect.

"Far from medical imperialism," which can be measured in terms of the conquest of new diseases and like progresses, medicalization is in fact conceived of as "a form of collective action" (Conrad, 2007, p. 9). Even though physicians and other medical professionals can be central to the process, especially for successful claims-making, patients and other laypeople time and again actively collaborate in the medicalization of their problems by promoting and shaping their diagnoses.

Since medicalization can exploit the avowal of the medical profession but does not necessarily depend on it, its usage often serves the purpose of conferring the authority and legitimacy of medical parlance to problems and procedures that are not *ipso facto* medical, but that if so perceived are more likely to yield support or empathy of some kind. This was the case of the medical model of alcoholism, primarily proposed and promoted by Alcoholics Anonymous and only hesitantly (and years later) embraced by the medical field (Haines, 1989).

Another example is the prevalent use of lethal injections in capital executions. As scholars have pointed out, "death penalty advocates sought medicalization and physician involvement to increase the public acceptability of the practice" (Emanuel & Bienen, 2001, p. 923). The medicalization of social control in such instances, carried out in clinical-like settings inside prisons, is said to have rendered the executions "more palatable to many who find other methods unacceptable" (Haines, 1989, p. 442).

It has, however, provoked an intense refutation by organized medicine, fundamentally on ethical grounds derived from the *primum non nocere* maxim.

The repudiation by the medical community of any involvement of physicians in capital punishment practices is clear in the American Medical Association's ethical guidelines, which state: "An individual's opinion on capital punishment is the personal moral decision of the individual. A physician, as a member of a profession dedicated to preserving life when there is hope of doing so, should not be a participant in a legally authorized execution" (*AMA*, 2000).[7] Until recently, organized medicine expressed the same sentiment toward assisted suicide. Ten years into the Oregon experience, the public position of many such institutions is changing (as of 2012, four major national medical professional and health policy organizations had adopted the policy of "studied neutrality" or in support of aid in dying; for a discussion, see Tucker, 2008).

As mentioned earlier, my assessment of the decriminalization of assisted death implies a second issue beyond—but interrelated with—the medicalization of death as an *event*. To explain, another aspect of interest is the notion that the medicalization of the dying process has brought about an expansion of medical jurisdiction—and thus of social control—over human behavior at its most consequential stage. I suggest, therefore, that the medicalization of death, practically absent until the beginning of the twentieth century, has accompanied the gradual redefinition of (assisted) suicide from sin/crime to a decriminalized, secular solution to pain and suffering.

To echo Conrad's definition of medicalization presented earlier, death today is not only defined as a medical problem but, as a medicalized event, it also mandates or licenses the medical profession to provide some treatment for it. Ultimately, for advocates of assisted death, terminal illnesses are now paradoxically seen as conditions for which death is a prescribed treatment. In an *amicus brief* by the American College of Legal Medicine to *Quill,* for instance, the organization rejects the term "physician-assisted suicide" as a "misnomer that unfairly colors the issue and . . . evokes feelings of repugnance and immorality" and instead refers to the practice as "treatment intended to end life" (Zaremski, 2008, p. 1).

This shift—moral, philosophical, cultural, social, but above all *legal*—can be examined in terms of how the law governing matters related to assisted death has progressively conceded to medical judgment (e.g., in terminal sedation, in passive euthanasia, and in some places physician-assisted suicide). The subsequent chapters of this book illustrate that displacement. In the *Epilogue*, I return to the issue of medicalization to assess the role of physicians in modern aid in dying models from different countries.

## NOTES

1. The American Veterinary Medical Association first published guidelines for *animal euthanasia* in 1963. However, heightened public concern surrounding a *gentle death* for animals can be traced to a few years earlier. In a piece discussing the passage of the

1958 *Humane Methods of Livestock Slaughter Act*, the first American legislation of this kind, the *New York Times* attributes the following statement to President Eisenhower: "If I depended on my mail, I would think humane slaughter is the only thing anyone is interested in" (Blair, 1958).

2. Terri Schiavo was a brain-injured Florida woman who spent 15 years with a diagnosis of persistent vegetative state. During that time, she was kept alive with the assistance of a feeding tube. In 1998, two years after the injury, Terri's husband requested the withdrawal of the feeding tube, alleging that Terri would not have wished to continue life-prolonging measures. After a lengthy legal battle, intense public protest, and direct interference of political figures—including members of the Florida Legislature, the U.S. Congress, and President George W. Bush—the feeding tube was removed in 2005 and Terri Schiavo died 13 days later.

3. *Aktion T4*, also known as the *Euthanasia Program*, was officially in effect in Nazi Germany from 1939 until 1941. During that period, physicians killed roughly 70,000 suffering patients judged incurably sick, as well as long-term inmates of mental asylums. Later, the Nuremberg Trials found evidence that German physicians continued the extermination of patients after 1941 and that the number of people killed under *T4* exceeded 275,000.

4. Between 1900 and 1920, the major breakthroughs in medical history included the discovery of the four blood types, hormones, and vitamins. It wasn't until 1921 that insulin was used to treat diabetes—ranked as the 10th most common cause of death in the following year (Centers for Disease Control and Prevention, n.d.). Seven years later, penicillin was discovered, and its widespread use in World War II, followed by its commercialization in 1944, revolutionized the way people died. In addition, during the years preceding World War II, several lifesaving medical advances were made, especially the first open-chest heart operation ever performed and the discovery of a cure for tuberculosis. This move from an era of humoral pathology, which laid the foundation to Western medicine well into the 1800s, to a modern medical faith in computer-guided scanners, radiation, genetic engineering, and so on, has allowed for the diagnosis of many new diseases to emerge as well as keener prognoses by healthcare professionals.

5. The concept of *medicalization* as a theoretical framework has evolved since its early articulation in the 1960s. Robert Nye (2003) offers a thorough history of the concept, tracing its theoretical developments and applications in interdisciplinary scholarship. This body of work, as Nye suggests, is diverse, and one should speak of "theories" and not of a single "theory of medicalization." Here, at risk of oversimplifying more than 50 years of intellectual development of a concept first articulated by none other than Michel Foucault (who, himself, revised his understanding of the phenomenon throughout his work published in life and posthumously), I focus only on the "second wave" of scholarship on this topic.

6. Parsons's "sick role" concept is central in sociological thought about health and illness. In *The Social System* (1951), Parsons posed that in addition to the physiological dysfunction brought about by disease (its "status"), being sick is also a "role" that is governed by social expectations. He named four rights/obligations of the sick: exemption from normal social role responsibilities, usually legitimated by some authority (frequently a medical one); exemption from responsibility of being sick, which entails responsibility by others to look after those who are ill; given the undesirability of illness, those who are sick are obliged to *desire* to get better; finally, those who are sick are expected to seek professional help and cooperate in getting better. Parsons's contribution in systematizing

the "sick role" is highlighting these many aspects of the social regulation of illness—from the mechanisms that assure compliance among sick persons, their restoration to a healthy status, and insurance that exemption from normal responsibilities is granted exclusively to those who are genuinely sick. His attention to such components results in characterizing sickness as a "sanctioned deviance" and institutes the need to provide for authoritative regulation—which is usually performed by the medical profession.

7. To elaborate, the ethical controversies regarding the role of medical personnel in chemical execution transpired in *Baze v. Rees*, a recent case in which the Supreme Court decided that Kentucky's three-drug lethal recipe does not violate the Eighth Amendment's ban on "cruel and unusual punishment." To be clear, the protocol is used by the federal government and in most states where the death penalty is permitted. It first releases a dosage of barbiturates through an intravenous drip intended to render the inmate unconscious and immune to pain. The third drug injected, potassium chloride, is designed to stop the heart. The second drug, and the one at issue in *Baze*, is pancuronium bromide, an anesthetic agent that paralyzes the nerves and thus prevents spasms that accompany death—which the state argued could discomfort witnesses to the execution.

The principal contention by opponents of the method is that a potential miscalculation of the barbiturates dosage may cause inmates to lie paralyzed, while suffering excruciating pain brought about by the potassium chloride. In an *amicus curiae* filed on behalf of neither party in *Baze*, the American Society of Anesthesiologists stresses the skepticism of its members in relation to the medicalized practice of chemical executions by describing "how executions by lethal injection, as currently performed in the United States, can never conform to the science, art and practice of anesthesiology" (Brief No. 07-5439).

Incidentally, the same three-drug concoction discussed within the death penalty debate was also the means through which Jack Kevorkian assisted in the death of most of his *patients*. The parallels with euthanasia, though not centered on Kevorkian's *modus operandi*, were not ignored in *Baze*. References to the use of a paralytic agent (such as pancuronium bromide) as a protocol in cases of euthanasia in the Netherlands, where the practice is legal, highlight the paradoxes of lethal injection as a *humane* means to bring about death in the two legal contexts. As Justice Breyer writes, "Why, one might ask, if the use of pancuronium bromide is undesirable, would those in the Netherlands, interested in practices designed to bring about a humane death, recommend the use of that, or similar, drugs?" (*Baze v. Rees,* 2008, pp. 5–6, Justice Breyer's concurring opinion).

# PART 1

## The American Experience

# In the Chambers: The Origins
# of the 1906 "Chloroform Bills"

THE MODERN LEGAL DEBATE over whether or not the state should permit assisted death first flourished in the United States at the turn of the twentieth century. In 1906, two legislative bills entertained by the Ohio and Iowa legislatures proposed exactly that—physicians should be able to "painlessly part incurables from this world" by administering to them a lethal dose of chloroform (*The Spokane Press*, Mar. 17, 1906).

Soon dubbed by the media the "chloroform bills," the issue was divisive enough to capture the interest of journalists writing in places as diverse as rural Kansas and Washington states and the emerging metropolises of Los Angeles, San Francisco, Philadelphia, and New York. Defined as a "new topic of freak journalism" (*The New York Times*, Jul. 15, 1897), the discussion of assisted death in the media was prolific. The debate focused mainly on the arguments put forth by "euthanasiasts" and their rivals (*NYT*, Feb. 3, 1906). Disapproval was grounded on a few main points: one, legal precautions that would safely guard against potentially harmful abuse; two, the inviolability of human life; three, the uncertainty of drawing a clear line between inevitable death and possible recovery; and, finally, the "barbaric" aspect of euthanasia, which opponents characterized as "the common practice of savages in all parts of the world, [whose] gradual abandonment has always been a mark of advancing civilization" (*NYT*, Feb. 3, 1906).

On the defensive, prestigious physicians, clergymen, and prominent literary authors[1] were ready to point out that they were not a "bloodthirsty lot, standing about the bedsides of [the] sick with bludgeons in our hands, ready to annihilate at the first adverse word of the physician" (Sheldon, 1906a). On the contrary, they argued, there was nothing new about euthanasia, "as it has been discussed and practiced, in some degree, in all ages, and its moral effects have not been deleterious" (Sheldon, 1906b). In addition, proponents reasoned that critics' belief in the sacredness of human life questionably excluded "cases of war, governmental assassination, capital punishment, slow starvation of the submerged sixth,[2] or other form of patriotic, national, judicial, or industrial manslaughter" (Royce, 1906). These forms of state-sanctioned death, they added, by which society "puts to death an able-bodied, useful, non-suffering man because he has offended a social fiat" (Sheldon, 1906b) were no less a tendency toward savagery than euthanasia.

Although the legal controversy surrounding the issue of assisted death did, in fact, only crystallize with the introduction of these proposals, its modern sociolegal roots date back to mid to late 1800s, when dynamics surrounding the deathbed were profoundly transformed. To understand the emergence and failure of the "chloroform bills," this section will focus on explaining how, in the 50 or so years prior to their introduction in Ohio and Iowa, death moved from a supernatural experience to a natural and medicalized one. In this sense, the catalyst role played by the modern understanding and alleviation of *pain* is discussed. Additionally, the attendant shifting dynamics surrounding the deathbed, cradled by the consolidation of medical authority and concomitant weakening of the clergy, are analyzed vis-à-vis the legislative bills. Finally, contemporaneous issues of law and agency are considered in relation to the proposed legal change. For now, however, I turn my attention to the bills themselves.

## THE "BILLS TO KILL"[3]

*H. B. 145* and *H. F. 367* were introduced in Ohio and Iowa at the behest of Ms. Anna S. Hall. Hall, daughter of Arctic explorer Charles F. Hall, had recently lost her mother to a harrowing, long struggle with liver cancer (*NYT*, Dec. 24, 1924). "An attractive and cultured lady" (Appel, 2004, p. 619) and by all measures "conscientious" (Appel, 2004, p. 619) in 1906, Anna Hall was a sociology student[4] who had just inherited a small fortune—some $25,000 previously awarded to her mother by the government upon her father's disappearance during a government-sponsored expedition (*NYT*, Dec. 24, 1924). An active member of the Audubon and Humane societies, Hall's motivation to draft, sponsor, and gather support for the bills was grounded on her belief that "only intolerance, bigotry and superstition stood in the way of a humane ending of life where death was certain and its slow approach meant hours of terrible agony to the sufferer" (Appel, 2004, p. 615).

In her efforts to settle this matter legally, Anna Hall's humanitarian appeal first echoed with Democratic representative Henry T. Hunt[5] from Cincinnati, who took to the Ohio legislature a bill proposing the involvement of physicians in hastening patients' death. The bill (Ohio H.B. 145, 1906) read:

[A]ny person of lawful age, of sound mind, who is fatally injured or is so ill of disease that recovery is impossible, or who is suffering great physical pain or torture, may be treated by a physician, not a relative or interested in his or her estate, and in the presence of three witnesses he may ask the patient if he or she cared to be put to death according to law. Should the patient's answer be in the affirmative then three reputable physicians are to be called in, and if they concur—that is, if they decide there is no chance for a recovery—then an anesthetic is administered until death ensues. (*Kentucky Irish American*, Jan. 27, 1906, p. 2)

Despite the safeguards in place (multiple witnesses and doctors' unanimous agreement on the poor prognosis), the bill had fatal flaws, critics argued, particularly that it did not provide the suffering person with an *exit strategy*, in case he or she changed his or her mind about the inducement of death. A *New York Times* reader, in a sarcastic letter to the paper that assumes the passage of the law, exploits this omission. Working with a hypothetical scenario under which a certain "Mr. Smithers" is run over by an automobile, the author of the letter explains how the accident victim fulfilled the bill's requirements: Smithers was of sound mind, of legal age, and fatally hurt. Found by a physician soon after the incident, Smithers is asked by the doctor, again in compliance with the bill, whether he wanted to be killed. The answer is in the affirmative and witnesses are summoned, as well as two other medical men (an osteopath and a veterinarian), again to fill the bill's mandate. The man is deemed incurable, an anesthetic is furnished, and Smithers is rendered unconscious. While he lies there, the medics cannot agree on how the fees for their services will be paid—the bill is silent on this matter as well—and enough time lapses so that Smithers, not fully overdosed, awakes and is ordered home by the doctors until they sort out the pecuniary obstacle. Three days pass, the letter's author tells us, and, "would you believe it?," Smithers is still alive and, having changed his mind, carries around a six-shooter, determined to stop the three doctors who, presumably looking to comply with the law, would come after him to put an end to Smithers's now "unrighteous and illegal existence" (Tomlinson, 1906).

Not surprisingly, due to its controversy and practical shortcomings such as the ones parodied by the *New York Times's* reader, *H. B. 145* was met with instant opposition. Soon after Hunt presented the bill, a representative moved to have it rejected on the basis that it amounted to "an insult to the intelligence of every member of the House" (Appel, 2004). The motion to reject failed (79 nays and 19 yeas), the bill was read for the first time, and the legislation was referred to the Committee on Medical Jurisprudence (Ohio General Assembly, House of Representatives, 1907, pp. 99–100).[6] This favorable outcome, however, was short lived and the bill eventually died in committee.

Soon after the defeat, Hall's arguments in favor of legalizing assisted death crossed state and party lines. Republican assemblymen Ross H. Gregory and F. N. Buckingham, both eminent physicians, introduced in Iowa a bill patterned after the one from Ohio, but which contained a significant difference— *H. F. 367* built in a compulsory "duty to kill":

> When any person more than ten years of age, of sound mind, suffering from extreme physical pain and believing ultimate death to be an inevitable consequence, shall summon a reputable physician and express a desire that his or her life be terminated by artificial means, it shall be the duty of such physician to call two other reputable physicians and the county coroner into consultation for the purpose of determining if it is possible to avert the patient's death and, if not, how long it may be deferred and to what extent the patient's agony may be alleviated. If they unanimously agree

that the illness, disease or wound of said patient must necessarily prove fatal and that extreme physical pain must characterize the remainder of said patient's natural life, it shall be their duty to so advise the two next of kin of said patient who may be within the jurisdiction of said coroner, and in event of no kin being found therein, then to so advise the patient's guardian or next friend. If the said kin, guardian or next friend shall then express in writing, duly verified, a desire that the said patient's request for artificial termination of life be complied with, *it shall be the duty of said physician and coroner to administer an anaesthetic to said patient until death shall have ensued.* (Appel, 2004, p. 620; my emphasis)

The requirement built into the Iowan legislative piece also carried a hefty penalty:

Any physician or coroner who, having been summoned to perform the duties set forth in the foregoing sections of this act, fails or refuses to perform them, shall, upon conviction thereof, be adjudged guilty of a misdemeanor and imprisoned in the county jail not less than six months or more than one year, and be fined not less than two hundred ($200.00) dollars or more than one thousand dollars ($1,000.00). (Iowa House File no. 367, in Appel, 2004, p. 620)[7]

Justifying his position to fellow medics, Dr. Ross Gregory defended:

You'd do as much for an old horse which had lost its teeth or broken a leg. Humanity to human animals is what I propose.... All surgeons do as much even now but they're taking long chances when they do it. I would make such murder not only legal but compulsory. (Appel, 2004, p. 621)

Parenthetically, the comparison of assisted dying to animal euthanasia was prevalent. For instance, the *American Humane Association*, whose primary goal at the time was to secure humane treatment for working animals and livestock in transit, lent its support to the cause early on.[8] Additionally, leaders of other charitable organizations also echoed the disparate acceptance of treatment dispensed to insufferable animals and human beings: "Especially harrowing," argued Maude Ballington Booth, one of the leaders of the *Salvation Army* and cofounder of *Volunteers of America*, "is the thought of the brave engineer, held beneath the iron wreckage of his locomotive, scalded by steam and yet awfully alive to every torture of slow-coming death. If a dumb animal were seen in similar circumstances we would instantly end its misery with a swift blow or merciful shot" (*Los Angeles Herald*, Jan. 14, 1906).[9,10]

The fate of Iowa's bill was no different than that of the one entertained in Ohio. Although the bills' ultimate failure may have reflected the negative sentiment of many Americans toward the proposed laws, several others saw the "chloroform bills" as rational, utilitarian, humane solutions to pain in dying. Encapsulated by the then pervasive humanitarian movement and its emphasis on the dignity of the individual and institutionalization of compassion, modern debates on assisted death at the turn of the twentieth century revolved primarily on the cruelty of suffering. Indeed, contemporaneous entries of the word *euthanasia* in reference books, such as the one offered here earlier, and others,[11] often allude to *painlessness* as its definitional character. Although pain and suffering were obviously not novel sensations in modern times, the sociocultural sensibilities regarding affliction, especially as experienced in the deathbed, were profoundly transformed over the course of the nineteenth century. I discuss that change next.

## THE EVOLVING VALUE OF PAIN AND SUFFERING IN THE NINETEENTH CENTURY

### Necessity, Absurdity, and Medicalization

In the early 1800s, the utility of pain was defended at once by both religious and medical men. For the former, the mystification of pain as redeeming, rooted in Christ's Passion, meant that only through suffering, men could overcome their sins. In the preface to *Our Work for Christ among His Suffering People*, a book "written for hospital nurses," a vicar reminded his audience to "look at the various trials and difficulties surrounding them in the exercise of their profession from a religious point of view" and not from a "sense of duty." With regard to the moribund patient, he taught about the necessity of suffering:

> If we are to be able really to help our patients in their times of sickness, it is essential that we should regard suffering rightly. At first sight, and until we have learnt to know better, we are inclined to look upon pain and disease as unmitigated evils; and it is only when we have been taught by experience and observation that his estimate is a false one that we learn to understand the *healing power of pain*. We have seen that our Lord Jesus Christ learnt obedience by the things that He suffered, and it must be with his people even as it was with Him. Gold must be tried by fire; and a man's soul in the furnace of affliction, otherwise the gold will not be purified and the dross of earthly passions and earthly afflictions will mar the soul of man. It is only after suffering that we may hope for freedom from pain, and for the attainment of such perfection as is possible to us in this world. (Morrell, 1877, p. 65; emphasis in the original)

Likewise, nineteenth-century American patients saw the surgeon as God's enforcer and regarded the doctor as part of their "deserved punishment for sin" (Pernick, 1994, p. 57). For their part, early 1800s medics also considered pain an essential part of the curative process[12] and, indeed, a sign of vitality. "Physical sensations," a notable French physician explained, "all require sound and healthy organs" and thus medicine's axiom should be "that the greater the pain, the greater must be our confidence in the power and energy of life" (Pascalis, 1826, p. 80).

Paradoxically, it was in such a climate that the medical world witnessed one of its most influential developments: a revolution in the use of anesthetics and the attendant medicalization of human suffering (Pernick, 1994). If, for many nineteenth-century physicians, religious men, and patients,[13] pain was useful, therapeutic, pedagogical, and thus necessary, increasingly for a few others the senselessness of pain, justified on humanitarian basis, invited its mastery.[14] For the latter, pain control was a "subject which should interest every philanthropic heart ... those devoted hearts that beat in sorrowing sympathy for the afflicted" (Thomas, 1855, p. 2).[15]

Additionally, at this point, attitudes regarding the value of pain were also being affected by the rising power of surgeons (Winter, 2000, p. 167). The advances made with the advent of the germ theory of disease slowly increased positive outcomes for surgical procedures, particularly childbirth, thereby conferring novel authority to medical surgeons. For the most part, however, surgery in the early nineteenth century remained a gruesome, violent, and painful task. For the patient undergoing an amputation, "to recall and confess the anguish and humiliation of such a personal experience" was nearly unbearable:

> [S]uffering was so great that it could not be expressed in words, and thus fortunately [could] not be recalled. The particular pangs are now forgotten; but the blank whirlwind of emotion, the horror of great darkness, and the sense of desertion by God and man, bordering close upon despair, which swept through my mind and overwhelmed my heart, I can never forget, however gladly I would do so. (Ashhurst, 1896, p. 379)

For these surgeons, alleviating pain also had practical implications; the sounds of patients thrashing and screaming filled operating rooms and made it difficult for doctors to concentrate (Gawande, 2012; for an excellent reconstruction of the surgical room and the medical experiences therein, see Thorwald, 1957). For instance, following a mastectomy for which English writer Fanny Burney had received a mere wine cordial to numb her senses, she reported: "I began a scream that lasted un-intermittently during the whole time of the incision—& I almost marveled that it rings not in my ears still! So excruciating was the agony" (Fanny Burney, 1811, in Papper, 1995, p. 12).

## Killing Pain

The surgical need to overcome pain was at first unmatched by science. Painkillers derived from willow bark, coal tar, and opium had been around for millennia. However, their effectiveness in countering profound pain was limited. Of these three pharmaceuticals, opioids, such as paregoric, laudanum, and "black drop,"[16] were the most powerful and frequently used in mitigating pain, but they were inefficient when employed in surgery.

It was not until the discovery of morphine in 1804 that physicians truly had a powerful tool to master pain and suffering. By mid-century, *morphia* had become a panacea for a long list of maladies, ranging from alcoholism to menstrual and menopausal disorders (Seppala & Rose, 2010). Its isolation from opium made possible the transition from analgesia (αν, "without" and άλγος, "pain") to what Oliver Wendel Holmes came to term "anesthesia" later on (αν, "without" and αἴσθησις, "sensation").[17]

Morphine's analgesic power is only matched by its equally powerful habit-forming capacity. A physician of the time, explained one of them, "finding pain, 'nervousness' and hysteria constantly claiming his attention, and that nothing relieves them so well as opium, or its alkaloid *morphia*, which is six times the parent strength, . . . resorts to their use more and more freely" (Kane, 1881, p. 18). As a result, "the patient, having once experienced relief, insists upon the further use of the drug, sometimes feigning illness, in order to procure it."[18]

The ever-growing addiction to morphine in the first half of the 1800s prompted doctors to search for a safer, but equally efficient method of pain mitigation. Of particular interest to them was the pursuit of an agent that would last long enough to allow for surgical procedures to be executed. The answer, at first, was not medical; "mesmeric anesthesia"[19] was widely practiced, and long lists of amputations and surgeries conducted on mesmerized patients were published (see, e.g., Elliotson, 1843). In a letter to her surgeon, a woman who had been mesmerized to undergo the removal of a tumor related her experience:

> Sir,—I am happy to say that the tumor from my wrist is quite dispersed, and perfectly free from pain; and should I at any time have to undergo an operation, it should be under the influence of mesmerism, as I am positive I never felt the slightest pain while you performed the operation. Having therefore derived benefit, I can speak with confidence upon the science.
>
> I remain your's [*sic*] respectfully,
> A Friend to Mesmerism
> (*The Zoist*, 1851, p. 326)

The phenomenology of mesmerism quickly found a competitive rival among dentists. Interested in minimizing the pain of their patients during tooth extractions, dentists first experimented with nitrous oxide (*laughing gas*) and then ether.[20] Following their success with the latter, in 1846, the first recorded surgical operation using ether as an anesthetic was executed. At Massachusetts General Hospital, Dr. John C. Warren "carried out an amputation painlessly in the presence of a crowd of medical students" (*NYT*, Oct. 16, 1946, p. 26). The medical press was quick to stress the medical character of ether by juxtaposing it to mesmerism. Ether was "scientific" and "restricted to respectable practitioners"; it was no trickery or farce, its composition was no secret, and a patent had been secured. As the surgeon proclaimed at the end of the successful demonstration at Massachusetts General Hospital, ether, unlike the mesmeric practice, was "no humbug!" (Winter, 2000, p. 177).

## Painless Dying

Recognition of the utility of ether in mitigating the pains that preceded death was a rational consequence of its success as a surgical anesthetic—even where such drugs were used in dosages that were themselves fatal. If pain, up until the discovery of anesthesia, was rationalized religiously or medically as a necessity, now physicians were able to subject it to medical discipline. Pain, especially on the deathbed where its symptomatic effect did little for the moribund patient, thus became frivolous and was now corrigible.

Therefore, a year after the demonstration at Massachusetts General Hospital, it was also Warren who suggested the use of ether "in mitigating the agonies of death" (Warren, 1848, p. 70). Since the "establishment of ethereal practice in surgical operations," the physician described employing the substance in a "more free and decided manner" with the purpose of enhancing the value of the recently discovered anesthetic powers of ether (Warren, 1848, p. 70).[21] Warren justified the terminal palliative use of ether on the basis that the "number of those who are called on to suffer in the struggle between life and death is greater than that of those who are compelled to submit to pain of surgical operations." He argued that if "the means of preventing or relieving these pains" could be found, "the great change [i.e., "death" might] be viewed without horror, and even with tranquility."

With Warren's proposal, the distinction between relief of suffering and hastening of death had become fuzzy. By 1885, "effective stimulation," or the palliative treatment of terminal illness using narcotics, was commonplace. In an interview published in *The Iola Register*, a progressive newspaper based in Kansas, a "physician of large general experience said that sixty percent of the patients who die while under the treatment of able modern physicians are under the direct influence of narcotics" (*The Iola Register*, Oct. 9, 1885). The practice was also acknowledged on the occasion of President Grant's passing, in 1885:

> The fact that narcotics were freely used throughout the illness of General Grant to secure sleep, ease and freedom from pain, and were asked for by the patient and promised to him openly by his physician, in the event of their being needed, to procure a quiet and painless death, seems to have been accepted quite as a matter of course by people in general. (*The Sun*, Aug. 23, 1885)

Although a few doctors expressed concern about the widespread employment of "effective stimulation," the practice was for the most part accepted because the intent of the physician was consistent with one of his principal duties: to alleviate human suffering. Terminal sedation in these cases was—and is, still—on a par with the age-old theologian doctrine of "double-effect."[22] Framed as "excusable homicide," its acceptance was inscribed in the authoritative *Medical Ethics*,[23] written by English physician Thomas Percival: "When medicines administered to a sick patient, with an honest design, to produce the alleviation of his pain or cure of his disease, occasion death, this is misadventure, in the view of the law;

and the physician or Surgeon who directed them is not liable to punishment criminally" (Percival, 1849, p. 90).

In other words, the permissibility of killing, as laid out in Warren's *Etherization* (and openly practiced by President Grant's physicians), hinged on doctors' intention.[24] Clearly, the employment of anesthetic substances in terminal palliation rendered the line between life and death blurred. However, finding refuge in the ethical principle of *double effect*, physicians of the time—and of today—argued that they did not cross it. It would take an English layman's essay to inflame the medical debate by proposing the administration of chloroform by physicians with the intent to bring about death. His proposal is reviewed in the next subsection.

### Chloroform: Oblivion at the Extremes

As progress in the field of pain management developed, chloroform quickly became the drug of preference among surgeons, its popularity attributed to its easier administration, a favorable smell, non-inflammability, and a lower incidence of vomiting and excitability when compared to ether (Simpson, 1848; Urman, Gross, & Phillip, 2011). Its discovery as an anesthetic agent by an obstetrician, James Young Simpson, in 1847, translated into its immediate application in diminishing childbirth pains.

Of all possible physical anguishes, the pains of labor were the quintessential example of excruciating suffering at the time that chloroform was introduced. From a Christian point of view, the "curse of Eve" stood as a metaphor for all pain, christening one's entrance into the world, setting the stage for a lifetime of suffering that would be released only at death. Medically, the pains of childbirth in early nineteenth-century America, often equated with the agonies of martyrs tortured during the Middle Ages, were largely attributed to women's inherent weakness and underdeveloped reproductive systems caused by educational demands placed upon them (Wolf, 2009).[25]

The use of chloroform in labor was at first fiercely opposed by the majority of obstetricians, who subscribed to one or both of the views presented earlier. In an 1848 article, Dr. Simpson responded to his colleagues' antagonistic view of the practice by claiming that "[t]he ladies themselves insist on not being doomed to the suffer, when suffering is so totally unnecessary," remarking that the obstetric employment of chloroform "gains converts every day" and predicting that "those who most bitterly oppose[d] it" would in 20 years or so be "amazed at their own cruelty," in allowing their "medical prejudices to smother and over-rule the common dictates of their profession and of humanity" (p. 673). As late as the end of World War II, chloroform remained common practice in hospital nursery wards (Wertz & Wertz, 1989).[26]

This unprecedented treatment of such prototypical pain did not stop at birth; it soon diffused to the deathbed. To elaborate, at least one historian traces the origins, or as he puts it, "the spark of the modern euthanasia debate," to an essay published in 1870 under the auspices of the *Birmingham Speculative Club* (Kemp, 2002, p. 11; see also Emanuel, 1994). The *Club* itself was not well known, and its members were mainly amateurs who met periodically to discuss social and philosophical issues. The essay on euthanasia—which soon captured scholarly and media's attention, thus fueling public debate—was written by a school teacher, Samuel D. Williams.

The essay advocated that "in all cases of hopeless and painful illness," chloroform should be used "to destroy consciousness at once and to put the sufferer to a quick and painless death" (Williams, 2008 [1870], p. 212). Anticipating the controversy that would follow, Williams pointed out how earlier applications of chloroform, initially met with skepticism, had by then become commonplace on the basis of compassion. Specifically, he commented on the use of the substance to relieve labor pains during childbirth: "[I]t is difficult to understand why chloroform should rightly be recurred to, to render less painful the naturally painful passage into life; and yet, that it should be almost an offence to so much as suggest a like recurrence to it, in the still more painful passage out of life" (p. 211).

On the one hand, most religious writers were quick to dismiss the parallelism proposed by Williams: "[T]he bringing a child into the world is a mere surgical operation" whereas the "passing out of this world is a *moral act*" (Tresidder, 1871, p. 317; my emphasis). On the other hand, among a few doctors Williams's proposal was received more sympathetically. At a meeting of the South Carolina Medical Association held nine years after the essay's publication, Dr. T. T. Robertson, urged that

> [t]he time had come when scientific men should discuss this and similar questions, regardless of theologians. Euthanasia was as sure to be accepted as the doctrine of evolution, and that would be as surely as the Copernican system in astronomy. Society was not prepared for it as yet, but the time had come to discuss the question as whether physicians are ever justified in shortening life. He believed they were, and was sure the scientific world would sooner or later come to it. He himself had practiced it. He knew it would shock some and antagonize the theologians. He had heard remarks made on his practice, and had heard of people saying that he might just as well have driven a rifle ball through the patients' heads. He was prepared, however, to resort to the same practice again under certain circumstances. (*The Keowee Courier*, Apr. 17, 1879)

T. T. Robertson's remarks were echoed by others during the meeting, such as prominent physicist John Tyndall,[27] who affirmed that he "did not fear to give chloroform when the patient was dying from some loathsome and torturing disease such as cancer" (*The Keowee Courier*, 1879).

The differing attitudes toward dying with assistance, captured in the two excerpts cited earlier, were cradled by a marked, ongoing conflict between opposing worldviews—science and religion—that characterized most of the nineteenth century. A few years into the 1900s, William H. O'Connell, Archbishop of Boston, characterized the situation thus:

> [C]uriously enough, in accordance with the atmosphere of the age, which tends to remove God and religion altogether, physical scientists have usurped the place belonging to others, assuming to themselves an infallibility which no religion has ever dared to claim.... If physical science were to treat only of minerals, lightning rods, railroads, automobiles, and such things, it might indeed be interesting and instructive to follow its theories, and they would not concern us morally to any very great extent, but if the physical scientist leaves that field and begins to invade a higher field; if, for instance, he comes into medicine and acts as if there were no immortal soul, if he rejects a moral responsibility, if he arrogates to himself the right which is God's alone when he decides whether he shall prolong or put an end to life, or even prevent life, then it is too much. No longer is it a matter of automobiles or lightning rods. It concerns the true dignity of humanity—the general and spiritual nature. (*NYT*, May 15, 1910)

With scientific progress increasingly driving a wedge between theologians and medical men,[28] the issue of pain and suffering at the end of life prompted doctors to claim a permanent spot alongside the deathbed. In the following section, I discuss this changing of the guard.

## DEATHBED'S SHIFTING DYNAMICS

### Doctors and Clergy: Claiming a Spot Alongside the Deathbed

While from a social perspective the discovery of surgical anesthesia and the attendant use of chloroform in birthing procedures were happening amidst a larger context of humanitarianism in medicine (see notes 14 and 15), concomitantly the scientific understanding of suffering and disease was changing in such a way that the secularization of pain was inevitable. As Caton (1985) argues, a sudden change in the connections between disease and religion happened in the early nineteenth century.[29]

For instance, the understanding of mental illness had transformed from a manifestation of the devil to its conception as a disease that could be treated by therapeutic means (Watt, 2004). More importantly, by the time the modern debates on assisted death emerged, humoral pathology,[30] which implied an inextricable link between body and soul, was in frank decay. It was exactly this bond that had until then provided the basis for clerical involvement in the care of the sick (Caton, 1985). In tandem, developments in fundamental concepts of neuroscience—such as the discovery of neurons *ca.* 1830s—redefined pain in physiological terms (Clark & Jacyna, 1992). Increasingly, thus, pain began to fall outside the realm of the occult and under the authority of the physician. Supernatural aspects of suffering—for example, pain as a result of sin—were becoming naturalized, could be located anatomically, and controlled therapeutically. This naturalization of the process reduced pain to a purely biological fact, entrusted to the competent management of medicine and devoid of existential meaning.

The secularization of pain also opened the doors to the naturalization or desecration of death. Up until the late 1880s, there was a paucity of medical writings on management of dying. The subject was not taught in medical schools and was therefore learned by physicians in practice (Munk, 1887). As medics acquired mastery over the pains that typically accompanied death, their stay alongside the deathbed was justified until the very end. As Wood & Williamson (2003, p. 20) put it, "the place of the confessor at the bedside was increasingly filled by that of the medical practitioner."

The turf war between clerics and doctors around the moribund patient's bed took place in the context of an even larger battle. Many nineteenth-century physicians had grown increasingly uncomfortable with the presumption of clergymen who ministered to bodies, as well as souls (Pernick, 1999). The large role played by clergy in American medicine was owed, in part, to a shortage of doctors in the colonial period (Shryock, 1960). In the early days of American medicine, for example, it was common for the sick to be treated by family members, and if their skills proved useless, they often called on the healing expertise of religious ministers (Christianson, 1997). Even after medical training was somewhat established in the United States, a much larger number of students still acquired degrees in "Divinity" than in medicine. Between 1778 and 1792, for instance, about 10 percent of those graduating from Yale were medical students, whereas roughly 28 percent chose religion (Christianson, 1976).

By the mid-1800s, however, doctors' dissatisfaction with the clerical doctoring reached a boiling point. Reverends, priests, and other religious men often— and publicly—advocated patent medicines developed by quacks. In a climate of blatant competition between the latter and the *learned* medical man, clerics' cooperation with *charlatans* was seen as insulting. In a meeting held by the South Carolina Medical Association, for instance, it was resolved that

> [w]hereas, it has been the custom of physicians to extend to clergymen the courtesy of their services gratuitously, in consideration of the respect justly due their sacred office, but, in consequence of the deplorable fact that numerous clergymen have become the advocates of quackery and imposture, by recommending secret medicines and preparations publicly in the newspapers, and more frequently privately to their parishioners, thus using their extensive influence against the true interests of science and the advancement of the medical sciences more particularly, it becomes the duty of physicians to discriminate between those who are or are not the friends of quackery. (Buchanan and Morrow, 1849, p. 425)[31]

The clergy, for its part, recognized the estrangement between the professions. The tension is clear in a commencement speech delivered at Albany Medical College in 1858 by Rev. Duncan Kennedy. In the address, he "allude[s] to a complaint not unfrequently [*sic*] made against [his] profession, of evincing a disposition to endorse, by certificates and otherwise, the claimed efficacy of quack medicine" (Kennedy, 1858, p. 17). But he then quickly moves on to yet another matter "which has occasioned some irritation" between the two professions. "You," says the reverend to the medics, "have sometimes found fault with us for seeming interference at the couch of sickness; and we have sometimes found fault with you, for a seeming disregard of our prerogatives at the same place" (p. 20). The reverend admits: "There doubtless are clergymen who . . . suppose themselves to be practicing the virtue of faithfulness in their calling, when it is only rudeness and insolence" (p. 20). As for physicians, he adds, there are a few "who from a disregard to the salutary influence of religious sympathy [and] a conceit of professional superiority . . . treat the pastor with less respect than they accord to the most menial in attendance" (p. 21). Rev. Duncan continued, hoping to persuade the medics that they should "comprehend [their] mutual rights in the premises," that while the duties of their profession "lead [them] to their patient," the duties of his lead him to visit his parishioner. The point, he concludes, is that "[i]t is not for us to quarrel over a dying bed" (p. 22).

By the mid-1800s, when the reverend delivered this address, the medical profession was bolstered by an increasing acceptance of a worldview that challenged the assumptions of faith and was committed to scientific progress. Indeed there was no need to "quarrel over a dying bed." In the same way that religion had slowly relinquished its control over other major institutions, such as education, health management was equally no longer part of a superstitious system of belief and was instead under the dominion of medical science. And so was death and dying. In sum, medicalization came to replace the "religionization"[32] of health matters.[33]

## Physicians' Increased Authority

By the end of the nineteenth century, science had all but replaced religion in the hierarchy of beliefs. Christianity in the United States was becoming more and more sectarian. The emergence of Christian Science, Seventh-Day Adventists, Jehovah's Witnesses, Mormons, and others illustrates the fragmentation of religion from within (Wacker, 2000). This path, as we will see later, was inverse to that of conventional medicine, which, following the template put in place by the rise of labor unions, trade associations, and so on, was becoming tightly organized (Starr, 1984, p. 110).

Although most Christian denominations feverishly defended against assisting in hastening death,[34] one antitraditionalist sect organized during that time viewed the practice more sympathetically. In a letter to the *New York Journal*, reprinted in two medical journals (*Medical Review* and *American Practitioner and News*), a Unitarian reverend, Charles W. Wendte,[35] openly argued for the institution of hastened death for terminally ill individuals: "I . . . believe that the time is rapidly approaching when the painless destruction of incurables will be considered eminently wise, humane, and Christian" (Yandell & Cottell, 1896, p. 430). Aware of religious opposition to the idea, the reverend argued:

> [M]y theory meets with the greatest opposition in clerical circles. In the first place, I am told that He who gives life should take it. Now, I hold that in that case all capital punishment, all forcible resistance to personal violence which may cause death, and war, either offensive or defensive, is wicked and cannot be justified. The murderer should go free, the assassin should go unhanged, and the greatest generals, in place of being lauded as patriots, should be condemned as malefactors. It is plain therefore that this doctrine is untenable, and is constantly and rightly ignored by society.... 
>
> Another thing which my clerical critics assert is that God sends pain to discipline and purify us, and we ought not to resist his will. In that case the discoverers of ether and chloroform were guilty of great impiety.... Now I argue, as a general thing, that pain—excessive pain, I mean—does not purify the spirit of man. On the contrary, it blunts, hardens, and brutalizes it.... By our present methods we drive men to suicide by our inhumanity toward them. (Yandell & Cottell, 1896, p. 431)

Curiously, when discussing the matter of agency, however, Rev. Wendte was not prepared to exclusively entrust "the medical man" with "so grave a responsibility" (p. 431). Instead, he proposed:

> Shall we, then, continue as now, powerless to relieve the fearful suffering of so many unfortunates, turning a deaf ear to their entreaties and leaving them but one resource—suicide? In the name of humanity, I say, No! ...
>
> I suggest that there should be formed a properly constituted tribunal, acting only when duly called upon by suffering humanity, and then under every necessary safeguard and restraint. Let this jury consist of a number of medical men, representatives of the Government, and any others who might advantageously serve. To this tribunal have submitted any petition for examination and release which might be made by the incurably diseased and indorsed [sic] by their families. Then, if they were found incapable of recovery and sure to endure needless and great agony, the tribunal shall be empowered to gently, painlessly, and humanely put them out of suffering and give them a release into the better world. This, then, is my plan. The surgeon must give pain to effect a cure. So humankind, which, under God gives life, may, in the divine spirit of justice and mercy, take it back again. (Yandell & Cottell, 1896, p. 432)

Beyond the then-typical quarrel between clergy and medics, briefly discussed earlier, the reverend's plan to assemble a multidisciplinary tribunal to preside over euthanasia cases speaks to the issue of the escalating omnipotence of physicians, particularly *regulars* or allopathic doctors. By the late 1890s, the regulars had grown more cohesive, advances in science and technology strengthened their authority in furnishing diagnoses, and they had produced two associations, the *American Medical Association* and the *Association of American Physicians*.[36] This was a striking contrast to their status a decade prior, when allopathic physicians were engaged in bitter feuds with different sects of medical practice.[37]

Concurrently, as the country became more urban, Americans came to rely on the care of strangers, especially at hospitals. Hospitals had morphed from social welfare institutions into places of medical science and were increasing in number at an unprecedented rate. For example, in 1800 there were two hospitals in the United States (one in Philadelphia and another in New York), whereas by 1909 the number surpassed 4,300 (Rosenberg, 1995). Rates of hospital beds per person doubled between 1909 (4.578 per 1,000) and 1940 (9.313 per 1,000 population) (Thomasson & Treber, 2008). The care of the sick by strangers was also affected by the concomitant professionalization of nursing in the United States, inspired by Florence Nightingale's work across the Atlantic.[38]

The introduction of the "chloroform bills" happened precisely when orthodox medics had finally achieved dramatic growth and credibility. The negative connotations brought about by an eventual legalization of *euthanasia* were perceived by many as a threat to that conquered authority. As one doctor put it: "At this stage of our civilization I believe it would be of doubtful benefit to the community to delegate to physicians generally the legal power to hasten the death of hopeless cases, for in the end I believe it would bring the profession into discredit" (Tracy, 1906). Therefore, in spite of the support offered by respected scientists, the *American Medical Association* was not ready to lend its imprimatur to the practice. "[No] physician should declare his willingness to be a scientific assassin," sums up an editorial published in the *JAMA* in 1885 (American Medical Association, 1885, p. 383). Euthanasia, in the piece, was equated to "professional murder," as the physician was being asked to "don the robes of an executioner" (p. 382).

## LAW AND AGENCY: SUICIDE, ASSISTANCE, AND "MEDICAL MURDER"

It is remarkable that cries for legalization of assisted death, like the legal attempts described in this chapter, increasingly relied on their execution by physicians. As physicians' efficiency in healing and in prolonging life grew, and as more Americans trusted their care, perhaps it was only natural to expect that medics would become omnipresent ministers, extending themselves into the arena of death beyond the mere palliation of pain. As argued earlier, pain after all was no longer a supernatural experience and could be physiologically located and medically controlled. But if a gravely infirm man or woman wanted to hasten his or her death back then, was there really a need to involve the white robe in the process? Could they not simply do it themselves? The question may seem naive, but the answer is a bit more sophisticated.

Although during the first 15 years of the twentieth century, *regular* physicians wrested control over pharmaceuticals—a key component of assisted death as conceived in the United States since the "chloroform bills"—poisonous substances, unlike today, were widely accessible. Opioids such as morphine and laudanum did not come under strict regulation until 1914, with the passage of the *Harrison Tax Act*.[39]

Indeed, self-murder, reportedly on the rise during the late 1800s, was often committed by ingesting poisonous substances such as strychnine (Kiernan, 1892, p. 64).[40] Along with "incendiarism, infanticide, [and] kleptomania," suicide was treated as an epidemic and was amply debated at the turn of the nineteenth century (Winslow, 1895, p. 472). Durkheim's (2006 [1897]) influential work exemplifies just how salient the issue was then. According to one contemporary observer who had reviewed official records on the subject, the top causes of suicide in London toward the end of the nineteenth century were "poverty, domestic grief, reverse of fortune, drunkenness and misconduct, gambling, dishonor and calumny, grief from love," among others (Winslow, 1895, p. 472).

The ranking goes on, but terminal illness as a reason for self-murder did not make the list. It did, however, make the headlines. In 1908, burdened by disease, Albert Billings, a San Francisco janitor, "cried long and loudly" after ingesting ammonia, turpentine, and chloroform liniment (Associated Press, Jan. 1, 1908). Several others also chose that fate. Billings did not die immediately, instead enduring a slow and painful death at the central emergency hospital. The entrustment to physicians with the duty to carry out the killing themselves, instead of leaving it to the patient, was perhaps an attempt to bypass the likelihood of botched (and painful) suicides.

Medical involvement, besides being reassuring, also had legal and economic tentacles. *Suicide*, once considered a crime in six of the American colonies,[41] had become legal by the nineteenth century. *Attempted suicide*, on the other hand, was still punishable in some jurisdictions (Rapalje & Lawrence, 1883).[42] Perhaps the competence of doctors was procured not only to ensure a painless death but also to make law evasion a certainty, thereby avoiding fines and other punishments in the case of failed suicides.

Gradually, it was also at that time that cultural understanding of suicide moved from a satanic phenomenon to its conception as a serotonin imbalance (Kushner, 1991; Brown, 2001; see also Szazs, 1977; 1984). No longer sinful, suicides were now primarily depicted as lunatics.[43] It is possible that the stigma associated with the act could be mitigated, cleansed, by the involvement of doctors in the act.

In that sense, a few defended the legitimacy of "rational suicide." Among these was Gustav Boehm, a New York attorney who argued before the Medico-Legal Society's annual congress that although self-murder was frequently "a consequence of melancholia," in certain cases the decision to end life was not the product of a "diseased mind" and was instead a calculated act, "the result of deep thinking and ripe judgment [and thus not] the doings of an imbecile" (Boehm, 1898, p. 80). In those cases, he argued, suicide should be seen as a "right," which "ought not to be withheld from the sufferer by any law of God or man" (Boehm, 1895, p. 464). Primarily, Boehm defended the suicide of bankrupts[44] and other suffering individuals, including those burdened with physical illnesses (*NYT*, Sept. 6, 1895).

Although ideologically defensible, Boehm's view, echoed by others,[45] went against a practical implication of conceiving suicide as the result of mental illness. In order for the deceased's family to be allowed to recover life insurance benefits, the suicide had to be determined an act of insanity (see, e.g., *The Chronicle: A Weekly Journal Devoted to the Interests of Insurance*, 1875). Additionally, many life insurance companies excluded from its beneficiaries those deaths deemed caused by the use of opiates.[46]

The issue of insuring life during nineteenth-century United States goes hand in hand with the desecration of death that was brought about by the increased presence of physicians at the moribund patient's bed. The care of the dying by professionals, the move of death to the hospitals in lieu of the family home, the emergence of the funeral industry, the business of official estate planning, and the institution of insurance benefits in the case of death were all part of a "general movement to rationalize and formalize the management of death" that began in the nineteenth century (Zelizer, 1978, p. 595). By the 1890s, death had become a commodity. New professions relied on it, as did new businesses. This economic management of death was accompanied by an interest to manage death from a legal standpoint as well—hence the "chloroform bills," clearly conceived under the influence of the rising legal positivism of the time.

Vis-à-vis the illegality of the practice, it is important to note that the bills discussed here did not propose that the patient would himself or herself ingest a poisonous substance. They also did not propose physicians' *assistance* in one's suicide. Apropos assisted suicide, throughout the nineteenth century, was largely proscribed. Even though suicide itself, as argued earlier, was by then legalized, its previous conception as a crime had significant, persistent ramifications. First, since completing a suicide was once a criminal act, as pointed out previously, one who *attempted* to kill himself or herself was subject to the misdemeanor sanctions that were imposed to anyone who attempted to commit a felony (The American Law Institute, 1980, §210.5).

Additionally, the common law-based doctrine of complicity was thought to be fully applicable to the act of suicide, with the result that one who *aided* (or encouraged) suicide became liable as an accomplice to that crime. In part as a result of that rationale, the offense of aiding in a suicide was transferred to statutes throughout the United States. Accordingly, the first American statute to outlaw assisting suicide explicitly was enacted in New York in 1828 (Marzen, 1985). Between 1857 and 1865, a New York commission led by Dudley Field drafted a criminal code—a forerunner to the "Model Penal Code"—that prohibited "aiding" a suicide and, specifically, "furnish[ing] another person with any deadly weapon or poisonous drug, knowing that such person intends to use such weapon or drug in taking his own life" (Marzen, 1985, pp. 76–77). By 1868, at least 9 of 37 states had adopted laws making the assisting of suicide a crime; others relied on the common law proscription.

Quite differently, however, death, according to the Iowa and Ohio bills, would be precipitated by an action performed by the doctor, in this case the administration of an anesthetic. As such, it was the legalization of homicide, or "medical murder" as a few put it (*New-York Daily Tribune*, Jan. 21, 1906), that proponents of the "chloroform bills" were asking to be condoned. The issue of agency may indeed have been the primary reason why the "bills to kill" did not pass. Although *euthanasia* was sympathetically received among many lay-men, influential intellectuals, prestigious physicians, and even a few nontradi-tional clergymen, "the greatest difficulty it encountered," as declared by a Medico-Legal committee that entertained the subject a few years prior to 1906, lied in its legalities: "According to all codes of civilized men, the law was dis-tinct and clear: 'thou shall not kill' " (Brinton, 1879, p. 479). Unlike "effective stimulation," where the intent of the physician met the maxim of *primum non nocere* through the "double effect" reasoning, the Ohio and Iowa bills clearly stated their design to expedite death at the patient's request. Legally, those who defended the proposals grounded their argument on the idea that the relief of the sufferer by death would amount to "justifiable homicide," because the killing would be requested by the patient in accordance with the precepts of the bills (see *Law Notes*, 1912, p. 121). However, the consent, or supplication, of the deceased made for bad defense in homicide case law up to that point in time.[47]

If passed, the bills would have accomplished something more than just decriminalization of assisted death; the proposals would have *regulated* a prac-tice that, proponents argued, was widespread.[48] As Lavi (2003) argued, bringing assisted death under the dominion of the law was a necessity, as medicine was unable to govern the practice of euthanasia on its own. With no clear ethical guidelines to inform physicians' choice between the newly discovered tech-niques of prolonging life and hastening death, the practice, subjected to physi-cians' discretion, was frankly open to abuse.

All of this helps to illustrate several points in regard to the modern debate on assisted death, with an emphasis on three of them. First, the ascension of medical authority over pain and death issues, brought about by the discovery of anes-thetics, validated the naturalization and medicalization of dying. This was accompanied by a second phenomenon, namely the decline of the clergy's influ-ential power alongside the deathbed and its replacement by the medical man. Finally, I explored issues of law and agency as they relate to the "chloroform bills' " intent to authorize physicians to offer death as a medical treatment in cases of terminal illness. The bills' failure did not discourage their proponents. Dr. Ross Gregory, one of the sponsors of the bill introduced in Iowa, admonished the incredulous: "Laugh if you will, but you'll see the day when such a law is in force. It may be a step in advance of our time, but it's bound to come" (*New-York Daily Tribune*, Mar. 11, 1906). It did, almost 100 years later, when voters in Oregon approved physicians' aid in dying—a law that has contours very similar to the ones drawn in 1906. How the issue evolved between the "chloroform bills" and the Oregonian initiative is the focus of the next two chapters.

## NOTES

1. Among the illustrious figures that supported Anne Hall's bill were Lurana W. Sheldon, George Bernard Shaw, Edith Wharton, John Kendrick Bangs, and others.

2. The "submerged sixth" was a term used in the nineteenth century to refer to the working class. Charles Dickens employs it in his 1854 classic, *Hard Times* (for contextualization, see Sutherland, 1989).

3. The title of this section is borrowed from a sardonic piece, *A Bill to Kill*, in which political author and humorist R. K. Munkittrick captured the essence of *H. F. 367* while mocking its sponsors. The poem was published in *Harper's Weekly* in 1906.

4. In reaction to one of Ms. Hall's publicized ideas, a journalist argued: "To the euthanasia of the idiotic and insane and hopelessly diseased is now added another form of the same idea. A lady, who is also a sociologist, proposes to chloroform the children of the poor, to relieve them of squalor and starvation. This is indeed radical. It also passes the limit. It raises a different issue entirely. Let us hope that the suggestion is made in order to call attention to the need of relief. What such children need is not chloroform but food! Charity can afford a present supply, and the draining off of congested city population will abolish the cause of much abject poverty. The miseries of want are greatly due to a defective distribution of population. If the people of this country were placed properly, it is probable that starvation would be as rare as cannibalism among us. If immigration were limited so that every year would not add a million to the congested population of our cities, the situation would improve. Chloroform is not a remedy that should be considered for a moment, and if sociology have no better remedy to offer it must retire to a seat among the pseudo-sciences" (*The San Francisco Call*, Jan. 14, 1906).

5. Henry T. Hunt, a Yale law graduate, later became mayor of Cincinnati. During his reelection campaign, the *New York Times* (Sep. 24, 1913) praised Hunt's "service in behalf of the defenseless and unfortunate."

6. That same session, the Ohio legislature also considered four other medicine-related bills, including one regarding the regulation of magnetic healing by physicians in the state (*H. B. 582*).

7. When corrected for inflation, the penalty values would be around $5,100.00 and $25,500.00 in 2013.

8. Prior to approaching legislators on the matter of introducing her bill, Ms. Hall obtained the endorsement of a few influential organizations. Among them was the *American Humane Association*, which resolved in a conference held in 1905 that it would "approve the practice of those physicians who, in cases of hopeless suffering, make painless the last hours of life by the use of anaesthetics, and we protest against the practice of prolonging, by artificial means, the agonies in incurable diseases" (*Los Angeles Herald,* Jan. 14, 1906).

9. As discussed later, the debate over assisted death seems to peak around fatalities over which individuals have little control. Just as with AIDS in the 1980s, in the early twentieth century, *euthanasia* often was offered as a solution to the victims of railroad accidents. As trains became faster, especially after the 1870s, railroad wrecks became more common and were treated as sensational news by the media (Stover, 1997).

10. Ambrose Bierce, best known for his *Devil's Dictionary* (2012), also weighed in. In an essay published in the *Cosmopolitan* magazine, "On the Uses of Euthanasia," Bierce adheres to the sympathetic discourse: "Pain is cruel, death is merciful. Prolongation of a mortal agony is hardly less barbarous than its infliction. To the suffering animal we grant the *coup de grâce*—to 'put it out of its misery.' Is our own race unworthy of that compassionate rite?" (1911, p. 196). Incidentally, although Bierce's *Dictionary* does not define "suicide" or "euthanasia," the entry for "Longevity" reads thus: "n. Uncommon extension of the fear of death."

11. See, for example, from *Green's Encyclopedia and Dictionary of Medicine and Surgery*: "Euthanasia. — A painless death, or, more particularly, the result of the measures which can be adopted to prevent the suffering (mental and bodily) which often precedes death" (Ballantyne, 1907).

12. See, for instance, *On the Physiology, Pathology and Therapeutics of Pain* (1848), a treatise on the subject by John P. Harrison, then vice-president of the recently formed *American Medical Association*.

13. According to Pernick (1994, p. 56), occasionally physicians recorded cases in which patients refused surgical or dental anesthesia for reasons of religious beliefs.

14. Besides the humanitarian ethic, historians of medicine, such as Pernick (1994), locate this new level of medical concern for suffering during the latter half of the 1800s on the increased influence of Thomas Percival's *Medical Ethics*, on the growth of "anti-heroic medicine" sentiments advanced by nonorthodox physicians (e.g., Homeopaths), as well as mid-century sentimentalism/romanticism clearly captured in literary works produced at the time (e.g., *Uncle Tom's Cabin*).

15. The influence of "Humanitarianism" as a powerful ethic in pain control became solidified later in the century; the discovery of anesthesia and its employment in surgery was compared then to reformist causes such as feminism, antislavery, capital punishment, abolitionism, etc., all of which had a preoccupation with pain (see, e.g., Simpson, 1847; also see Caton, 1985). Additionally, the growth of conservative medicine as a new moral norm in the field (a middle course between heroic medicine and absolute neglect) justified a certain degree of risk-taking brought about by anesthetics proportional to the degree of pain relief. In sum, as long as the application of anesthesia maximized patient benefit and minimized pain, its use was seen as morally legitimate (for a discussion of this proportional calculus and ethical ramifications, see Sharpe & Faden, 1998).

16. *Laudanum*, or tincture of opium, was first developed by the alchemist Paracelsus in sixteenth-century Salzburg, where he discovered that opium alkaloids dissolve more readily in alcohol than in water. The resulting tincture was highly potent as an analgesic and was named to suggest the "praise" due to God for its discovery. It also had uses as a cough suppressant and an antidiarrheal, which, in combination with its property of pain suppression, made it an excellent treatment for the symptoms of cholera and dysentery. *Paregoric*, or camphorated tincture of opium, was invented in the 1700s by Jacob le Mort in Leiden and has similar uses. Significantly less potent than laudanum, it was a household remedy in the United States throughout the eighteenth and nineteenth centuries for coughs and diarrhea, though its opium content was sufficient both to give it analgesic properties and to result in the addiction of some patients. *Black drop* was the name given to a concoction in which opium was mixed with vinegar and spices. Closely associated with the poet Samuel Taylor Coleridge, whose lifelong addiction to opium began with an introduction to black drop, the exact origins of the name remain obscure with several competing concoctions of the same name available across the nineteenth century.

17. The text of the letter in which Holmes coined the term can be read here: www.general-anaesthesia.com/misc/index.html. Dated November 1846, it was sent to William Thomas Green Morton, the American dentist who first succeeded in demonstrating the use of ether as an inhalation anesthetic.

18. Addiction to morphine among soldiers was rampant during the Civil War and the issue was dubbed "soldier's disease." During the Civil War, opium and its

variants were used widely both as an analgesic and to treat chronic pain from injuries and amputations.

19. "Animal magnetism" or "mesmerism" was a practice in which one person claimed to influence another through the movement of his or her hands near the surface of the other person's body. Mesmerism was developed in the late eighteenth century by an Austrian physician, Franz Anton Mesmer, who claimed to have discovered a means of manipulating physical forces, or "magnetic fluids" for health benefits. In order to prove its capacity as an anesthetic procedure, the mesmerist accompanying the surgeon would fire pistols near the patient's ears, prick his or her skin with needles, and wave smelling salts beneath his or her nostrils (for a detailed account of the development and demise of mesmerism, see Winter, 1998; 2000).

20. The recreational consumption of ether had been popular during the nineteenth century, in what became known as "ether frolics": public gatherings in which members of the audience were encouraged to inhale diethyl ether to demonstrate the mind-altering properties of these agents while providing much entertainment to onlookers. Curiously, during the early half of the 1840s, ether was attacked as an obstacle to medical reform. Medical students' fondness for consuming the inebriating vapor in "ether frolics" was undermining their education and encouraging habits of dissipation (Winter, 1998). It was in one of these gatherings that a Bostonian dentist, William T. G. Morton, realized the potential utility of the vapor in rendering patients unconscious for surgical procedures. For an interesting account of his accidental discovery, along with testimonials of its use, see "Circular. Morton's Letheon," published in 1847.

21. In *Etherization: with surgical remarks*, Warren (1848) describes in great detail how he etherized a 90-year-old dysenteric patient with a goal of treating her "pain of mortification" (p. 71).

22. The term "double effect" was first used by St. Thomas Aquinas in the context of self-defense: One who uses lethal force for defense against attack may not intend the assailant's death but that occurrence, although knowingly and voluntarily induced, would be an "acceptable side-effect." The analogy applies in the cases of assisted death thus: The intent of the physician in administering morphine, for instance, is to control pain, not shorten life. Hence, the action is not euthanasia but palliative care. The ethical rationale continues to be invoked in medicine today and, as it will be discussed in later chapters, has been sanctioned by the U.S. Supreme Court in the 1990s.

23. *Medical Ethics* was influential in shaping the *American Medical Association*'s (AMA) first code of professional conduct and is deemed as the most important codification of medical duties since the *Hippocratic Oath*. For a deeper, insightful analysis of the history of the AMA's codes, see Baker et al. (1999).

24. The *American Medical Association* defends that doctors' intent can be ascertained, for instance, in reviewing the patients' charts for the recorded dosages of analgesics and opioids (Boyle, 2004). As Margaret Battin (2008b, p. 29) further explains, " 'one large dose' or 'rapidly accelerating doses' of morphine may signify a bad intention—seeking to cause death—whereas 'repeated doses or continuous infusions' are benign." Battin argues that this rationale is "naive in the extreme" as it is "the slyest courtier who poisons the emperor gradually; what could equally well be inferred from repeated doses and continuous infusions is a clever attempt to cover one's tracks." Her view is shared by proponents of "euthanasia" who see the doctrine of double effect as an implausible,

hypocritical effort to draw a completely bright line between terminal sedation and physician-assisted death (see Billings & Block, 1996).

25. The solution, it followed, was to decrease women's exposure to education in order not to "overtax" their brains because they monopolized the energy their bodies needed for maturation (see Wolf, 2009, for a discussion).

26. In the United Kingdom, for instance, 17 percent of births recorded in 1946 still employed chloroform—this is nearly 100 years after the development of this technique (Findley & Chamberlain, 1999, p. 927). The properties of chloroform rendered the employment of the drug practical in other arenas; chloroform was widely used in the commission of crimes, such as rape and burglaries. Several of these incidents appear on the newspaper articles of the period, which covered them in a sensationalist manner.

27. Coincidentally, Prof. Tyndall died from an overdose of chloral hydrate, when, in his seventies, he found himself "in delicate health [and] for about three years, wrestling with death." The overdose was ruled accidental (NYT, Dec. 25, 1893).

28. For a discussion, see Frank Turner's (1978) informative and nuanced perspective on the conflict between science and religion in Victorian England. For an American perspective, see Andrew Dickson White's The Warfare of Science, written in 1876 when he was president of Cornell University and prefaced by Prof. Tyndall.

29. Koenig (2000) offers an insightful review of the separation of medicine from religion as a result of the scientific discoveries that took place during the Enlightenment.

30. According to humorism, disease was a result of an imbalance of the four elements—air, water, fire and earth—as manifested in the body.

31. The estrangement between the two professions occupied pages and pages of medical bulletins. See, for instance, discussions published by the Medical Times and Gazette, 1876, the Philadelphia Medical Register, 1882, and the illustrious British Medical Journal, 1860. Oliver Wendell Holmes also depicted the cultural tension between the declining authority of the church and the rising power of the medical profession in what he called his first "medicated novel," Elsie Venner: A Romance of Destiny (the novel was published in the Atlantic Monthly as a series, in 1858–1859).

32. The term is Imber's (2008, p. 235).

33. Ironically, the basis of medicine's increasing cultural authority throughout the nineteenth century derived precisely from the proximity of the established, yet declining, public influence of the clergyman. As Imber argues, the insistence by the church (Catholic and Protestant) that the "physician must first be a believing Christian," and thus a righteous person, gave added public credibility to a physician's position of authority in society (2008, p. 18).

34. Most of the writings by clergymen vis-à-vis euthanasia reflect to a great extent the opinion of Rev. Dr. S. Parkes Cadman, of the Central Congregational Church in Brooklyn: "I am of the opinion that the power of ending life under all conditions should be left in the hands of God, except in those cases where the law of the land inflicts capital punishment for murder" (New-York Daily Tribune, Jan. 21, 1906).

35. Wendte was a graduate from Harvard and was brought up in an environment that valued liberal Christian ideals. In his autobiography, he states: "[M]y religious nature was never tampered with in childhood or youth. No cloud of morbid fear, or self-torturing doubt, ever was drawn over my conscience; through no agonizing struggles did I attain to inward light and peace. From the very first I was encouraged to think with entire freedom on religious and moral subjects, and to cherish a serene faith in the Eternal Goodness

that lies at the heart of things. I was taught to accept no authority, however imposing, and no tradition, however venerable, against the dictates of my reason and the better promptings of my moral nature, the voice of God within the soul. This normal religious development, this spiritual freedom and faith, have been to me as the breath of life, the central loyalty of my nature, the source of my deepest trust, most unalloyed happiness, and most worthy performance" (Wendte, 1927, p. xxvi). Although one would be tempted to attribute Wendte's defense of *euthanasia* to his peculiar worldview, the truth is that Unitarians became central figures in the search for legalization of assisted death. Dowbiggin (2003) discusses this in detail and the topic is revisited later in this book.

36. Sir William Osler, one of the founders of Johns Hopkins Hospital, was among them. In 1905, in a light-hearted farewell speech at that hospital, Dr. Osler discussed the relative uselessness of men over the age of 60. He facetiously referred to a novel in which men above this age retired for a year of contemplation, after which they were peacefully "chloroformed." American newspapers were quick to take his words out of context and argue that Dr. Osler was advocating the use of chloroform to euthanize all men over the age of 60 (for a thorough analysis of the coverage, see van Gijn & Nieuwkamp, 2002).

37. Until the mid-1870s orthodox medics were competing fiercely against "irregular" practitioners, or the ostheopaths, hydropaths, Christian scientists, and so on. Additionally, of the three "learned professions," that is, the ones that required a collegiate education, namely divinity, law, and medicine, embracing a career in the latter hardly held the prestige it does today and often did not lead to wealth (Starr, 1984, pp. 82–84).

38. Nightingale herself recalled that when she told her "extremely well-to-do" family of her desire to become a nurse, they reacted "as if I had wanted to be a kitchen-maid" (Strachey, 1948, p. 131). According to her biographer Lytton Strachey, "[a] 'nurse' meant then a coarse old woman, always ignorant, usually dirty, often brutal . . . sobriety was almost unknown among them and they could hardly be trusted to carry out the simplest medical duties" (Strachey, 1948, pp. 131–132). In old age, Nightingale contemplated suicide while a patient at St. Thomas Hospital, in London, but was dissuaded by a personal friend, Oxford theologian Benjamin Jowett (Strachey, 1948, p. 187).

39. Concomitantly to the introduction of the "bills to kill" in Ohio and Iowa, the first piece of legislation ever directed at regulating the manufacture of drugs, the *Pure Food and Drug Act*, was passed—but it did not regulate the dispensation of drugs by competent professionals. The Act was a result of a concerted effort by muckraking journalists and allopathic physicians. The former were interested in exposing the dangers of patent medicines, while the latter wished to eliminate the competition posed by nostrum makers. Among the most vocal journalists, Samuel Hopkins Adams successfully helped stir public opinion and support for drug reform (Cassedy, 1964; see also Holbrook, 1959). In *The Great American Fraud*, a series of exposé articles published in the popular *Collier's Weekly* magazine in 1905–1906, Adams ably attacked the religious endorsement of nostrums, and particularly ads ran by the religious press, while helping confirm the rising authority of orthodox medics. The *Journal of the American Medical Association* reprinted Adams's articles and distributed them to physicians throughout the country who in turn lobbied for regulation (Anderson, Jr. & Wiley, 1958).The following is an excerpt of Adams's article appearing on *Collier's Weekly* (February 17, 1906): "Whether, because church-going people are more trusting, and therefore more easily befooled than others, or from some obscure reason, many of the religious papers fairly reek with patent-medicine fakes. Take for instance the *Christian Endeavor World*, which is the

undenominational organ of a large, powerful and useful organization, unselfishly working toward the betterment of society.... Running through half a dozen recent issues of the *Christian Endeavor World*, I find nineteen medical advertisements of, at best, dubious nature. Assuming that the business management of the *Christian Endeavor World* represents normal intelligence, I would like to ask whether it accepts the statement that a pair of 'magic foot drafts' applied to the bottom of the feet will cure any and every kind of rheumatism in any part of the body? Further, ... I would call attention to the ridiculous claims of Dr. Shoop's medicines, which 'cure' almost every disease; to two hair removers, one an 'Indian Secret,' the other an 'accidental discovery,' both either fakes or dangerous; to the lying claims of Hall's Catarrh Cure, that it is a 'positive cure for catarrh' in all its stages, to Dr. Kilmer's Swamp Root, of which the principal medicinal constituent is alcohol; and finally to Dr. Bye's Oil Cure for cancer, a particularly cruel swindle on unfortunates suffering from an incurable malady. All of these ... appear in recent issues of the *Christian Endeavor World*."

Later, the Propaganda Department of the American Medical Association (1922) published a thorough analysis of the cure for cancer developed by Dr. Bye. It was revealed that the "oil cure" was basically cotton seed oil combined with a few ordinary tonics. In 1907, Dr. Bye's medical license was revoked by the Board of Health of the State of Missouri.

40. On that note, a Chicago physician, Dr. Jas G. Kiernan, reflected on why "Rough on rats" and strychnine were so "astonishingly popular considering the painful death produced by them and the ease with which morphine and laudanum could be procured" (Kiernan, 1892, p. 64).

41. According to Burgess-Jackson (1982), in colonial America the legal status of suicide varied widely, depending in large measure to how closely each colony followed the English Common Law, if at all. Virginia, North and South Carolinas, Georgia, New York, and New Hampshire considered suicide a crime per Common Law. In these places, suicide was punished with forfeiture of deceased's property, denial of a Christian burial, and bodily mutilation. Rhode Island and Massachusetts enacted specific legislations criminalizing suicide and prescribing similar punishments. Pennsylvania, Delaware, Massachusetts, and New Jersey did not consider it a crime. Connecticut's legal status at the time is unclear.English jurist William Blackstone characterized suicide as "self-murder" and thus a form of felonious homicide. He described it as the "highest crime of against the law of nature that man is capable of committing" (Blackstone & Aird, 1873, p. 306). Three separate rationales justified the view of suicide as a crime and were cited on one occasion or another by those concerned with its proscription. First, as advanced by St. Thomas Aquinas, suicide was seen as a violation of nature's most fundamental laws, that of self-preservation. Second, suicide infringed upon the King's peace, therefore depriving him of one of his subjects. And third, suicide prevented its actor from realizing his or her potential as a contributing member of society.Interestingly, however, exceptions of culpability were those suicides committed in an abnormal emotional state, induced, for example, by old age, a physical infirmity or disability, or severe and prolonged pain (Brandt, 1975). Blackstone also commented on the exception: "If anyone, sinking under the pressure of grief, or weariness of life, disease, madness, or shame, shall prefer death, his conduct shall not be considered to the prejudice of his character" (1916, p. 189). Another English jurist, Henry de Bracton, echoed: "[I]f a man slays himself in weariness of life or because he is unwilling to endure further bodily pain, he may have a successor"; that is, his property would not be forfeited (in *Compassion in Dying v. State of*

*Washington*, 1996). The definitional difference in these cases was due to the actor's intention, which meant no harm to anyone, but rather was designed "to escape a condition of physical debilitation" and thus fell outside the "customary animus" with which the legal system treated suicide (Burgess-Jackson, 1982, p. 75).Toward the end of the 1800s, as suicide became gradually conceived, state by state, as a result of "melancholia," its previous criminalization and punishment came under attack: "To punish suicide as a crime is to commit a solecism in legislation. The unfortunate individual by the very act of suicide places himself beyond the vengeance of the law. He has anticipated its operation. He has rendered himself amenable to the highest tribunal, namely, that of his Creator. No penal enactment, however stringent, can affect him. What is the operation of the law under these circumstances? A verdict of *felo-de-se* is returned, and the innocent relatives of the suicide are disgraced and branded with infamy, and that, too, on evidence of an *ex parte* nature. It is unjust, inhuman, unnatural and unchristian that the law should punish the innocent family of the man who in a moment of frenzy terminates his own miserable existence. It was clearly established before the alteration of the law respecting suicide, the fear of being buried in a crossroad and having a stake driven through the body had no beneficial effect in decreasing the number of suicides.... [N]o penal law can act beneficially in preventing self-destruction—first, because it would punish the innocent for the crimes of the guilty, and, secondly, that, owing to insanity being present in every instance, the person determined on suicide is indifferent as to the consequences of his action" (Winslow, 1895, p. 475).

42. According to Livingston, the 1881 Penal Code of New York State changed the legal status of unsuccessful attempt at suicide from a misdemeanor to a felony (Livingston, 1895, p. 91). Additionally, at the time the "Model Penal Code" was drafted, as late as the 1960s, several states treated attempted suicide as a crime by statute (The American Law Institute, 1980).

43. Incidentally, in 1860 the rate of "insane" per 1,000,000 population was 765 in the United States. Two decades later, that number was up to 1,883 per 1,000,000. Suicide rates for the United States in 1890 were 10.31 per 100,000 (MacDonald, 1903, p. 12). In 2010, according to the Centers for Disease Control, that rate was 12.4 per 100,000.

44. The preoccupation with bankruptcy in Boehm's argument could be because that in 1895, when his essay was presented, the American economy was still deeply affected by what became known as the Panic of 1893, a serious economic depression resulting from the overbuilding—and overfinancing—of railroads. Although unemployment figures were not directly measured until 1929 in the United States, estimates of the period indicate that the unemployment rate exceeded 10 percent for five or six consecutive years since 1893. The only other time this occurred in the history of the U.S. economy was during the Great Depression (Romer, 1986).

45. The wife of a physician (Dr. Louis Schlesinger), apparently partaking in the same opinion as Boehme's, defended its justifiability in a letter to the *San Francisco Call*. The letter, which was included among a full-page discussion about the insane nature of suicides, stated: "There are circumstances ... that to my mind would render suicide justifiable. If one were stricken with a loathsome disease that meant a loathsome death— I believe that were the end hastened, the person would be justified in so doing" (*San Francisco* Call, Aug. 2, 1896).

46. For an in-depth discussion, see Hudnut's *Semi-Centennial History of the New York Life Insurance Company 1845–1895*.

47.  See, for example, a 1908 case from Tennessee, *Turner v. State*, where the defendant claimed to have shot his lover four times at her request: "He stated that he first shot her through the mouth, and that she said, 'Shoot me again, here' (holding her hand to her abdomen), whereupon he shot her again, when she said, 'Shoot me again, here' (placing her hand on her breast), when he shot her a third time, and she sank down on the ground" (*Turner v. State*, 1908). The accused paramour was sentenced to death for murder.

48.  "Physicians use them [anesthetics in hastening death] now but always at a risk, as they are legally committing murder when they help some agonized sufferer to a quick and peaceful end," argued Anna Hall (*Philadelphia Press*, Oct. 12, 1905).

# 4

## At the Bedside: 1911–1950s, the "Mercy Killing" Era

BETWEEN 1906, WHEN Anna Hall's pro-legalization attempts failed in Ohio and Iowa, and World War II, much of the debate surrounding hastened death centered on two distinct, yet interrelated, rationales: the idea of humanely killing misfits and the notion of mercifully ending a moribund's life. Taken together, though, trends such as eugenics, positivism, social Darwinism, and scientific naturalism, in conjunction with the ideals of the Progressive movement, helped create a climate in which the notion of humanely hastening the death of hopelessly ill persons was acceptable policy.

In the first three decades of the twentieth century, as the eugenics movement peaked in the United States, *euthanasia* was proposed, along with forced mass sterilization, as a means to eliminate the *defective*. Society's *feeble-minded*, such as criminals, the poor, *morons*, epileptics, *imbeciles*, and others were deemed good candidates for the lethal chamber.[1] Although eugenic *euthanasia* was advanced as the *painless killing* of unwanted segments of the population, thus conceived, the use of the term is merely a euphemism, if not a misnomer. In this context, the goal of bringing about a *humane* death—primarily by gas poisoning—was intrinsically motivated by the ideal of achieving a *better* human race.[2]

This is intellectually different from *euthanasia* seen as a *merciful killing* of those craving death due to physical agony. Throughout the first half of the 1900s, a series of highly publicized *mercy killings* captured national attention and tested the congruency between the law on the books and the law in action, and measured the legal tolerance for compassion as a motive for killing. The first such instance involved pineapple-growing Shakers from Florida, who confessed to hastening the death of one of their sisters, doomed by tuberculosis. As a *New York Times* reporter put it, "[T]he Shaker tragedy offer[ed] the first practical demonstration of the theory of Miss Anne [*sic*] Hall of Cincinnati" (*The New York Times*, Sept. 14, 1911).

As the century unfolded and the world grappled with two wars and unprecedented economic depression,[3] many more of these cases were disclosed, frequently drawing sympathy from those involved in the decision-making surrounding the mercy killers' legal fates. As one study showed, among the more than 70 mercy killing cases documented between the 1920s and the 1960s, nearly

half did not arrive at the courts; in those that did, over 60 percent of the defendants were acquitted, and those who were sentenced, typically received very short
prison terms or were fully exempted from punishment (Lavi, 2005, p. 145).[4]

Carol Ann Paight was among those who escaped punishment. In the fall of
1949, the young woman from Connecticut stood trial for killing her father, a
cancer-stricken policeman. Paight's case, furthermore, set the stage in New
England for what would become a news event worthy of international attention:
the unprecedented prosecution of a physician in what appeared to be a merciful
act.[5] Just as Carol Paight's trial came to a close in the early months of 1950,
Hermann Sander, a New Hampshire doctor, was accused of murdering one of
his patients by injecting air into her arm.

Although mercy killing cases, such as Paight's, frequently did not involve "the
white-robed physician" or "the black-robed lawyer" (Lavi, 2005, p. 144), it was precisely the prosecution of Hermann Sander that renewed pro-*euthanasia* advocates'
hope that legalization would soon occur: "This is absolutely the best case yet for
our cause ... because of the doctor's integrity and because he didn't hide what he
had done" (*NYT*, Jan. 3, 1950). Sander's case, for the proponent, illustrated a need
to "amend the law to avoid other tragic cases like [it] where a physician renders
himself to a charge of murder for shortening the suffering of an incurable patient."[6]

The Shakers', Paight's, and Sander's cases are described later. Together,
they allow for a discussion of the legal, medical, and social contexts in which
*assisted death* for incurables was advanced between the "chloroform bills" and
mid-century. In presenting the cases, the related issues of judicial nullification,
the establishment of organized activism, the golden age of American medicine,
the diversification of religious views on euthanasia, and some conclusions about
why mercy killing *cases* did not live up to reformers' aspirations are debated.

## THE SHAKERS, 1911

In 1905, 28-eight-year-old Sadie Marchant arrived in the *Sunshine Home*, a
tuberculosis sanitarium in Narcoossee, Florida. Doctors in Providence, Rhode
Island, where she came from, had given her a prognosis of four months. Shortly
after her arrival at the sanitarium, the institution announced that it would close.
Lacking financial means to return to the Northeast, at the advice of Dr. John
Ennis, the sanitarium's owner, Ms. Marchant joined the *Olive Branch*, a small
Shaker colony established nearby (Cole, 1993; see also Stein, 1994).[7]

Under their care, Sadie Marchant lived six more years, with only one functioning lung, until a Sunday in the late summer of 1911, when she was "taken
with the last stage of consumption" (*Kissimmee Valley Gazette*, Sep. 4, 1911)
and, suffering intensely, begged the Shakers to help her "pass out of the body"
(*NYT*, Sep. 16,1911). Her caregivers, Brother Egbert Gillette and Sister Elizabeth
Sears, "prayed over the matter for hours, and the answer came it would be right

for [them] to end the agony of Sister Marchant" (*NYT*, Sep. 14, 1911). Mr. Gillette described their act thus:

> Sister Sears and I loved Sister Marchant dearly.... She was afflicted with consumption, and her death was only a matter of time. We cared for her tenderly and did all we could to alleviate her sufferings, which became frightful, and she begged us to give her something that would put an end to them. She said she could not live long and that it would be a mercy to end her agony.... So we obtained some chloroform and administered it to our dear sister and ended her sufferings. She blessed us as we did so, and we feel that we did no wrong. We simply ended the agony of a dearly loved sister. We feel that we were doing God's work. (*NYT*, Sep. 14, 1911)

Although there was no secrecy about the administration of the chloroform—the other four members of the colony knew and approved of the act after praying together for 12 hours "for divine guidance"—only Brother Gillette and Sister Sears were arrested (*NYT*, Sep. 17, 1911). At that point, they "frankly told their part with simple directness," reflecting the Shakers ideals of obedience and truthfulness (*The Citizen*, Sep. 22, 1911).

The Shaker case "excited intense interest" and "public opinion [was] greatly divided, many holding that the accused committed no crime" (*NYT*, Sep. 14, 1911). Albert Gilchrist, then Florida's governor, stated that "even if the two Shakers should by any chance be convicted he would not allow them to be hanged" (*NYT*, Sep. 17, 1911).[8] Fervent support emanated from the community as well, who had "universal respect of the people" and regarded the Shakers as "simple honest type[s]," "the personification of quiet, peaceful righteousness" (*NYT*, Sep. 21, 1911; *Washington Times*, Sep. 13, 1911).

Gillette and Sears were soon released on bail, their bonds "signed by wealthy citizens of Kissimmee, who think it was a merciful act to administer the chloroform to the woman" (*NYT*, Sep. 17, 1911). Two lawyers volunteered to defend Gillette and Sears. A coroner's inquest determined that Gilbert should be charged with *willful murder*, and the case was sent to a grand jury for further deliberation. Judge Parker, presiding over the case, "made it plain he did not believe the couple were [*sic*] actuated by criminal intent" (*The Mathews Journal*, Sep. 21, 1911). The grand jury failed to find a "True Bill" (indictment) and the charges against the Shakers were dismissed in January 1912.[9]

*The Washington Times* opined that "euthanasia was upheld" and explained that the sympathy demonstrated by the grand jury toward the "old Shakers" played a role in their decision to adjourn without indicting Gillette and Sears: "The simplicity and calmness of the defendants ... and the meek manner in which they related all the incidents connected with the case developed widespread sorrow for their plight" (*The Washington Times*, Dec. 2, 1911).

Sister Sears, in a letter to the Heads of the Whitewater Shaker colony in Ohio, indicated that their mistake was giving Sister Marchant the "quieting medicine" themselves, "instead of getting a physician to do so" (*NYT*, Sep. 16, 1911).

"Since the occurrence," she explained, "we have been told doctors and nurses are doing these same things constantly, but they have the authority, which we have not" (*NYT*, Sep. 16, 1911). Sister Marchant was right; there seemed to be some acceptance of *euthanasia* as practiced by physicians, perhaps reflecting increasing ascension of the medical profession's authority.[10] Just as the Shakers' case unfolded, Chicago doctors were praised for giving a seven-year-old boy a "painless death to end agony of rabies" (*The Evening World*, Sep. 23, 1911).[11]

## SUBSEQUENT LEGISLATIVE ATTEMPTS, ORGANIZED ACTIVISM, AND CATHOLIC RESISTANCE

Between the Shakers' case in 1911 and the 1930s, *euthanasia* discussions were primarily drawn from the eugenics discourse, but mercy-motivated killings were habitually the subject of press coverage.[12] In 1925, for example, four *mercy-killing* cases that happened within the space of a month enlivened the debate on the topic, drawing varied support from medics, lawyers, and laymen worldwide.[13]

The (potentially dangerous) clandestine aspect of these *mercy killings* prompted other legalization attempts in Illinois and Nebraska,[14] in 1931 and 1937, respectively. Bills were introduced in each of the states, but failed to garner further support. When calling for the regulation of what opponents and proponents agreed was a widely tolerated and frequent practice (Appel, 2004, p. 614), one advocate stressed the urgency of the issue:

> [This] act of mercy should not be performed by private citizens as it is increasingly done today. Nor should it be done secretly by physicians. The law itself should speedily be brought into accord with public opinion. Euthanasia should be legalized and supervised. (Potter, in Lavi, 2005, p. 145)

Concomitantly, organized actions to regulate euthanasia were taking shape in Britain. In 1935, the Voluntary Euthanasia Legalisation Society (VELS), led by several of that country's most prominent physicians, was formed (Emanuel, 1994b, p. 797). The example of the British society prompted Americans to organize, and in 1938 the Euthanasia Society of America (ESA) was incorporated.

Unlike VELS, the American organization was led mainly by social activists and intellectuals who also identified with—and took part in—other reform causes such as women's suffrage and birth control (Dowbiggin, 2003; Garrett, 1998; Russell, 1977). However, although law-breaking tactics were then commonly used to push the latter two issues, pro-euthanasia activists focused instead on change via legal reform. In sum, the society's mission was to make it "unnecessary for people to attempt euthanasia unlawfully" (ESA, 1939), and its members were confident that a legal victory was forthcoming. As Dowbiggin (2005, p. xv) discusses, the society was "convinced that with the vote for women won, the decriminalization of birth control imminent, and the enactment of eugenic sterilization laws in the

1920s, the next victory would be the legalization of active euthanasia." Accordingly, in its first year the ESA drafted a model bill and directed legislative lobbying at "a few progressive" New York senators who had previously shown interest in the issue (Garrett, 1998, p. 37). The efforts, however, failed to generate legislative sponsorship, and the bill was never introduced.

By the 1940s, it was clear that the society had few reasons to be optimistic. The movement's legislative attempts produced nothing, the ESA failed to expand its constituency, and key interest groups—such as physicians—were both ethically divided and at best unsure about the prospects of legalization. In 1943, the ESA had only 249 members, funds were meager, and media coverage of euthanasia had dwindled substantially (Garrett, 1998, pp. 39–42). Public attention had, of course, shifted to the war, and *euthanasia* quickly became associated with the Nazi atrocities against mental patients and the disabled.

Opposing groups—especially the Catholic Church—capitalized on the opportunity to publicly denounce euthanasia and used the Nazi program to bolster their counterarguments. In 1943, for example, Pope Pius XII condemned euthanasia of the "the deformed, the insane, and those suffering from hereditary disease," which, he claimed, was "hailed by some as a manifestation of human progress, and as something that is entirely in accordance with the common good" (Pope Pius XII, 1943).

Though Catholic opposition was not new, the Roman Catholic Church, increasingly robust during the McCarthy era, successfully connected the legalization of euthanasia to a philosophy of materialism and state absolutism, most evident in totalitarian regimes (see, e.g., Dowbiggin, 2003, p. 93; Russell, 1977, p. 88). Reflecting the era's overall sentiment, church leaders characterized the bill drafted in New York, for example, as "un-American and a menace" (Monsignor McCormick, quoted in Russell, 1977, p. 92). In this view, both materialism and absolutism led to a cheapened regard for the sanctity of human life and a belief that some lives are not worth living.

This mindset, the church argued, would inevitably lead to abuses, should euthanasia be decriminalized. As contended by a legal scholar at the time, "the legal machinery initially designed to kill those who are a nuisance to themselves may someday engulf those who are a nuisance to others" (Kamisar, 1958, p. 976). Thus, terminally ill patients might be coerced by self-interested relatives and friends into hastening their deaths, or the state, for monetary reasons, might decide on terminating the lives of individuals deemed unfit.

Activists affiliated with the ESA pursued two avenues to garner influential support that would counter the Catholic Church's opposition. First, the society announced in 1946 the formation of a committee of 1,776 physicians in favor of legalizing voluntary euthanasia, led by Dr. Robert Latou Dickenson—one of American Medical Association's former chairmen and then vice-president of Planned Parenthood. Secondly, in 1949 the ESA brought forth organized support from churchmen, which culminated in a petition signed by roughly 400 Jewish and Protestant clergymen urging New York's legislature to proclaim that "the ending of the physical existence of an individual at his request, when afflicted with an incurable disease which causes extreme suffering is, under proper safeguards, not only medically indicated, but also in accord with the most civilized and humane ethics and the highest concepts and practices of religion" (*The Brookshire Times*, Jan. 28, 1949). Though these efforts created some attention and controversy, the New York bill, as mentioned earlier, was never introduced.

Although these futile legislative attempts helped focus public attention and organized advocacy on the issue of assisted death, the most highly publicized and controversial episodes related to *assisted death* in this period stemmed from the mercy killing cases—like the one involving the Shakers—that unfolded during the first half of the twentieth century. Though sensational, none of these cases pushed the issue as far as the trial of Dr. Hermann Sander. Sander's trial took place one week after the acquittal of another New England *mercy killer*, this one a young woman from Connecticut. We turn to her case next.

## CAROL ANN PAIGHT, 1949–1950

On September 23, 1949, just as President Truman announced that the United States had evidence of USSR's first nuclear device detonation, Carol Ann Paight, a tall, blonde, "quiet, well balanced, [and] mature" girl from New Hampshire, shot her father in the head (*NYT*, Sep. 26, 1949). Ms. Paight and her father, Police Sergeant Carl Paight, were by all accounts deeply attached. Before she left to New England College to study zoology, the two often went "swimming, hunting and sailing together" (*NYT*, Sep. 26, 1949). As her mother, a school teacher, summarized, "Carol adored her father with every fiber in her being" (*NYT*, Feb. 1, 1950). "They were practically inseparable," the mother added (*NYT*, Feb. 1, 1950).

Ms. Paight, then 21 years old, was summoned home that fall to accompany her family to Stamford Hospital in Connecticut, where her father was scheduled to undergo an "exploratory operation" (*NYT*, Sep. 26, 1949). Her 52-year-old father had been hospitalized for a week, with abdominal pains. During the procedure, she and her mother, who were both Roman Catholic,[15] went to St. Mary's Church, "where they lighted candles and prayed" (*NYT*, Feb. 1, 1950). They returned to the hospital and Dr. William Smith, who conducted the operation, informed them that Sgt. Paight was "ridden with cancer," which was inoperable (*NYT*, Jan. 27, 1950). The doctor suggested that the policeman "had about six weeks or two months to live" (*NYT*, Jan. 27, 1950).

Upon receiving the news, Ms. Paight "became hysterical ... sobbing and pleading that her daddy must never know he had cancer," explained Dr. Smith (*NYT*, Jan. 27, 1950). Ms. Paight had lost an aunt and a great-aunt to cancer during her childhood and had "showed a great deal of emotion then and long after" whenever the subject was discussed (*NYT*, Feb. 12, 1950). Physicians described her as being affected by "cancer-phobia" (*NYT*, Feb. 12, 1950).[16]

While Sgt. Paight was still under the effect of anesthesia, in an attempt to calm Ms. Paight down, her mother took her home. On their way there, Mrs. Paight had to pull over to make the girl "stop shrieking" (*NYT*, Feb. 1, 1950). Carol Paight then suddenly turned "wooden," her eyes "glassy," and all "the color . . . left her face." Once home, the two went inside and, shortly after, Ms. Paight drove away in the family car. Her mother assumed she had gone to visit a friend.

Instead, Carol Paight had retrieved her father's .38 caliber service revolver from a closet and proceeded to a secluded wooded area where she fired a practice shot. Next, "with the gun wrapped up in a jacket," she drove to the hospital where a nurse heard what she thought "was a tray falling" (*Time Magazine*, Feb. 6, 1950). The nurse walked into Sgt. Paight's room, where she found him dying, shot through the left temple.

She also found Carol Paight there, "looking like a moron" and "walk[ing] like a machine," her face pale, her hands folded, her head against the wall (*NYT*, Jan. 27, 1950; Feb. 4, 1950). Ms. Paight told the nurse, quietly: "I shot him" (*NYT*, Jan. 27, 1950; Feb. 4, 1950). The girl was then taken to the nurse's lounge, where she became frenzied and was given a large dose of *sodium amytal*—a sedative then also commonly used as a *truth serum*.[17] Later that evening, Carol Paight explained to Captain William Lynch, one of her father's colleagues who had arrived to investigate the incident, that she "didn't care what people thought or what they would do to her; that she couldn't see him suffer anymore" (*NYT*, Jan. 27, 1950). The next day, she claimed that she did not remember shooting her father.

Carol Paight was arrested on a second-degree murder charge, which carried a mandatory life sentence if convicted, and was held without bail. "Community leaders and other residents [of Stamford, CT] expressed deep sympathy" for Ms. Paight (*NYT*, Sep. 26, 1949). George Barrett, then mayor of Stamford, struck a compassionate note when he argued:

> We are just beginning to understand . . . the mental lapses which permit the body to perform acts which have no connection with a normal intent or inclination of the person who commits the act. In such cases . . . where great sentimental strains are in force, we are in duty bound to ask ourselves just how well we would have stood the pressures of these tremendous and unusual forces. . . . In the present case, practically every condition which appeals to our sense of mercy and leniency is present. It is my honest belief and firm conviction that the case of Carol Paight deserves extreme sympathy and leniency. (*NYT*, September 26, 1949)

Echoing the mayor, Rev. Dr. Lloyd Worley, who officiated Sgt. Paight's funeral, called for "divine compassion for the girl" (*NYT*, Sep. 27, 1949).[18] Paight's father's doctor advised that cases like this did not belong in prisons, which were "already overcrowded" and a former judge opined that Ms. Paight should be "treated very gently" (*NYT*, Sep. 26, 1949). In addition, "a group of leading citizens" requested the Stamford Police Association "to sponsor a widespread appeal" for a defense fund for Ms. Paight. Although the association declined to help, indicating it would be "incompatible to its members' duties to sponsor" such a defense fund, several of the police officers expressed their support during court procedures, by shaking hands with Ms. Paight or kissing her cheek (*NYT*, Oct. 2, 1949; Oct. 12, 1949).

It was in this sympathetic climate that trial proceedings began. In examining the prospective jurors, Carol Paight's chief defense attorney, David Goldstein,[19] conceded that she had shot her father but made it explicit that the defense would argue that she was "temporarily insane" (*NYT*, Jan. 25, 1950). "The intent of the defense," he declared, was "to show that at the time of the shooting of her father [Ms. Paight] did not have the mental capacity to distinguish between right and wrong, sufficient mental capacity to know the nature and quality of the act" (*NYT*, Jan. 25, 1950).

By resorting to the *sanity* issue, Mr. Goldstein intended to minimize any discussions of *mercy* as a motive for the killing. But the topic of *euthanasia* was raised a few times during jury selection by state attorney Lorin Willis, who at one point asked a juror: "Do you believe it is proper or justified to take a human life simply to put a person out of his suffering?" (*NYT*, Jan. 26, 1950). The woman, a 40-year-old mother of two, responded that she did not know. "Assume this," the prosecutor went on, "that it does appear in the evidence what actually motivated this girl in killing her father was the idea of putting him out of his suffering—would you consider that in reaching your verdict?" (*NYT*, Jan. 26, 1950). She answered affirmatively. The woman was accepted as a juror and was ultimately joined by eight other women and three men, all parents, to decide Ms. Paight's fate.[20] At one point, the judge presiding over the trial commended the jury for bringing to his attention pamphlets on the benefits of euthanasia that had been sent to some of them. Rev. Charles Potter, one of the ESA founders who were attending the trial as an observer, denied that the letters had been sent by his society (*NYT*, Jan. 28, 1950). No apparent action was taken by the judge to purge the jury of any possible bias that might have resulted, however.

Nearly 50 witnesses were called at trial. Thirty of them testified to Ms. Paight's good character, while the remainder were nurses, police officers, and physicians who had come into contact with her in the hours surrounding the event. To make a case that Carol Paight was not sane when she shot her father, the defense produced two expert witnesses: the same physician who was treating Sgt. Paight and a psychiatrist, Dr. Clifford Moore, director of an institution for "mental and nervous disorders" and former president of the local medical association (*NYT*, Feb. 2, 1950). Doctor Moore testified that when Carol Paight was told about the cancer, "she went insane instantly" and that she was still insane when she shot her father (*NYT*, Feb. 2, 1950). Testifying on her daughter's behalf, Mrs. Paight added that insanity ran in the family.

In turn, the prosecution's expert, neuro-psychiatrist Joseph Lesko, characterized Ms. Paight "as sane the day of the shooting, the day after, and at present" (*NYT*, Feb. 4, 1950). Carol Paight's mental problem, the doctor testified, was "a genuine amnesia" produced by "repression," in a true attempt to "forget the painful, unpleasant, and shameful experience" of shooting her father. During his testimony, Dr. Lesko's remarks provoked "a few scattered 'boos' from the spectators."

The two tactics employed by the attorneys in Paight's case constituted a "curious reversal of position of 'mercy killing,' " as the defense maintained that the shooting was not an act of mercy, while the prosecution argued that it was (*NYT*, Feb. 8, 1950). Mr. Goldstein maintained that "[t]his is no mercy killing case . . . because the law does not sanction 'mercy killing.' " The state's attorney, in his turn, argued that "mercy was the only logical motive for a girl who loved her father and wanted to put him out of his suffering," and it was precisely the logical nature of such a motive that proved her sane. Testimony in the trial, as mentioned earlier, had suggested an admission of "mercy killing" by Ms. Paight to two witnesses, a nurse and a police officer. In his instructions to the jury, Judge Cornell advised the jurors that "no matter how pure or kindly the motive, . . . the law does not justify one person's taking the life of another to save that one from suffering, actual or anticipated, or any disease or malady with which he may be afflicted." He then added that the "first basic fact" to be determined was whether or not Ms. Paight was sane. "If not," the judge explained, "[you] must acquit."

And they did. Carol Paight was found not guilty and *temporarily insane*, and she left the court that day—with no prescription for formal treatment. Harold Faber, the *New York Times* journalist assigned to cover the case, described Carol Paight's reaction to the verdict thus: "With the words that set her free, [she] dropped her face to her hands and cried and was led from the courtroom" (*NYT*, Feb. 8, 1950). At that point, "no one paid attention to the judge, the clerk or the jury," as scores of photographers surrounded Carol Paight and her family. Ms. Paight returned to New England College to finish her studies[21] and married a fellow student shortly after.[22]

## Judicial Nullification

The case of Carol Ann Paight exemplifies a point made by theologian and ethicist Daniel Maguire in the early 1970s. According to him, resorting to an insanity defense is a common tactic in mercy killings, which illustrates "a flight to psychiatry when there is no help from the law" (Maguire, 1974; see also Collester, Jr., 1977). These cases were not rare, and in May of 1950, just three months after the Paight verdict, Michigan bass violist Eugene Braunsdorf was also acquitted in the mercy death of his 29-year-old paralyzed daughter. His insanity defense prevailed, despite a determination by a sanity board that the musician was of sound mind. Mr. Braunsdorf, like Carol Paight, admitted to the killing and explained in court that he had shot his "hopelessly crippled" daughter five times "because [he] was afraid he would die before she did, and she wouldn't have anyone to take care of her" (United Press, 1950).

Table 4.1 presents other mercy killing cases that took place in the years surrounding Carol Paight's trial. A contemporaneous editorial by the *New York*

**Table 4.1 Sympathy in *Mercy Killing* Cases, 1938–1958**

| Year | Defendant | Summary |
| --- | --- | --- |
| 1938 | Harry Johnson | Johnson was charged with murder after asphyxiating his cancer-doomed wife. Two years prior, the wife had been told by doctors that she had but two years to live. "Go to sleep, darling.... You'll be all right," Johnson said, before piping gas into the wife's room (United Press, Oct. 3, 1938). The grand jury did not indict after some evidence of *temporary insanity* was presented. Johnson himself was physically unwell. |
| 1939 | Louis Greenfield | Greenfield chloroformed his 17-year-old imbecile son, whose mental age corresponded to that of a two-year-old. He stood trial for manslaughter. A grand jury "refused to indict him for murder ... and the prosecution [was] as deferent as the law will permit" at trial (United Press, May 10, 1939). He was later acquitted after testifying he had acted out of love. His defense team was led by Samuel Leibowitz, defense attorney for the *Scottsboro Boys.* |
| 1947 | Louis Repouille | Using an overdose of chloroform, Repouille killed his teenage son, who had suffered from birth from a brain injury "destining him to be an idiot, blind, mute, deformed, and a 'physical monstrosity' " (*Repouille v. United States*, 165 F. (2d) 152). He was indicted on manslaughter and was found guilty of manslaughter in the second degree with a recommendation of clemency. He was then given a suspended sentence. Five years later, Repouille applied for citizenship, which was declined on the basis that he had not been of "good moral character." |
| 1950 | Eugene Braunsdorf | Braunsdorf, a musician, shot his disabled daughter and then tried to kill himself. He was indicted but found not guilty by reason of temporary insanity. |
| 1953 | Herman Nagle | Nagle, a former police officer, shot his daughter suffering from cerebral palsy when he learned that he had cancer. During an interview by police, he explained that he did not want her "to be left alone" and that "the thought of putting his daughter out of her misery had haunted him for years" (United Press, Sep. 7, 1953). He was charged with first-degree murder and acquitted on the grounds of temporary insanity after 20 minutes of jury deliberations. |
| 1958 | Otto Werner | Otto Werner was 69 years old when he was charged with manslaughter after he admitted to killing his arthritic wife by stuffing rags in her mouth. The chief justice of Chicago's criminal court, Abraham Marowitz, instructed |

**Table 4.1 (Continued)**

| Year | Defendant | Summary |
|------|-----------|---------|
|      |           | Werner to withdraw a guilty plea he had previously entered, and acquitted him. When asked about his action, the judge explained that Werner was "in the twilight of his years," was unlikely going to recidivate, and "a jury would have acquitted the man anyway" (UPI, Dec. 31, 1958; Associated Press, Dec. 31, 1958). |

*Times* reflected on this issue: "Under the law, euthanasia—'mercy killing'—is the same as murder. Nevertheless, legal history reveals many cases in which juries have refused to convict persons responsible for 'mercy deaths' " (*NYT*, Feb. 12, 1950). The outcomes of each case, as described in Table 4.1, demonstrate how the judicial system routinely showed compassion toward defendants involved in such cases.[23]

Simply put, in mercy killings, prosecutorial discretion often is exercised in favor of non-prosecution, grand and petit juries engage in nullification, and lenient sentences imposed by judges "belie the written law equating euthanasia with premeditated murder" (Collester, Jr., 1977, p. 310). A contemporaneous legal commentator defended the functional use of judicial nullification in mercy-killing cases by arguing that it provides a safety valve of mercy while at the same time maintaining the deterrent of criminal law, thereby limiting the instances of euthanasia (Kamisar, 1958). In effect, he argued that nullification in euthanasia cases is a justification for nonaction by the legislature in the area.

Although largely tolerated during the first half of the twentieth century, a few judicial minds expressed outrage at the practice of nullification. In the case of Louis Repouille (see Table 4.1), for example, who had received a suspended sentence for chloroforming his mute, deformed, blind, and brain-damaged teenage son, a Second Circuit Judge wrote:

> The jury which tried Repouille did not feel any moral repulsion at his crime. Although it was inescapably murder in the first degree, not only did they bring in a verdict that was flatly in the face of the facts and utterly absurd—for manslaughter in the second degree presupposes that the killing has not been deliberate—but they coupled even that with a recommendation which showed that in substance they wished to exculpate the offender. Moreover, it is also plain, from the sentence which he imposed, that the Judge could not have seriously disagreed with their recommendation. (*Repouille v. U.S.*, 1947)[24]

The seeming discrepancy between the law on the books and the law in action would be ultimately put to test on the first case involving the prosecution of a physician. The case of Dr. Hermann Sander is described in the next section.

## HERMANN SANDER, 1949–1950

One week after Carol Paight's acquittal, the stage was set for yet another *mercy-killing* case—this one involving a physician, Dr. Hermann N. Sander. More than 100 reporters, radio broadcasters, and photographers from all over the world arrived in Manchester, New Hampshire, to cover the doctor's trial. The city, located "an hour and a quarter by rail from Boston," was then the state's largest and represented a "bustling industrial center of 85,000 population" (Porter, 1950). According to *Time Magazine*, 1,600,000 words were written about the case, and in one day alone *The Boston Post*, then the largest newspaper by circulation in Massachusetts and fourth largest nationally, "devoted 22 columns to the trial" (*Time Magazine*, Mar. 13, 1950). "The ferment [was] building up in New England," a euthanasia advocate rallied, "like that in the Scopes trial" (*NYT*, Jan. 18, 1950). And like the Scopes case, this one, advocates and media hoped, would pit scientific rationality against religion.

Hermann N. Sander, the son of a public utility executive father and a home-maker mother, was born in Schenectady, New York, in 1909. His family moved to New Hampshire when he was still a young boy. Sander studied medicine in Munich, Germany,[25] for two years before transferring to Dartmouth Medical College, where he became captain of their ski team while pursuing his medical studies. He received his medical degree from New York University, in 1938. Dr. Sander spent three years as a resident at a New Jersey hospital where he met and married Alice Dewitt, a "slightly built" nursing supervisor (*NYT*, Mar. 7, 1950). The couple had three children. Hermann Sander established his medical practice in Manchester, New Hampshire, in 1941.

On December 4, 1949, Abbie C. Borrotto, a patient of Hermann Sander's, died. Mrs. Borrotto was 59 years old and had been battling intestinal cancer for 15 months.[26] Dr. Sander had been her attending physician for several years when Mrs. Borotto's cancer metastasized and she was admitted to Hillsborough County hospital for terminal care. As a result of her condition, she had "wasted away from 140 to eighty or ninety pounds [and] had been bedridden for weeks" (*NYT*, Mar. 2, 1950). In her last few days, Abbie Borrotto had "deteriorated steadily": Her pulse was slower, her respiration more labored, she had to be fed intravenously, and, having developed some resistance to pain relievers, she was given increasingly higher doses of demerol and pentapon—both narcotic drugs (*NYT*, Feb. 25, 1950; Mar. 7, 1950).

Eight days after Mrs. Borrotto's death, following protocol, Dr. Sander dictated notations for the patient's chart to Ms. Josephine Connor, record librarian at the hospital: "Patient was given 10 cc. of air intravenously repeated four times. Expired within ten minutes after this was started" (*Time Magazine*, March 6, 1950). He also recorded the cause of death as a combination of cancer, inanition, and bronchial pneumonia on her death certificate.

About two weeks later, when Ms. Connor was assembling records for a monthly review by a medical board, she reported the notation to hospital authorities.[27] Soon after, Dr. Robert Biron, the hospital's pathologist and the county's coroner, examined Mrs. Borrotto's chart in Ms. Connor's office and asked her to summon Sheriff Thomas O'Brien.

Before the sheriff's arrival, Dr. Sander walked into Ms. Connor's office, and at that point—according to Ms. Connor's and Dr. Biron's testimonies offered at trial—he and the coroner discussed the events surrounding Mrs. Borrotto's death. Dr. Biron, "a little excited," pressed Hermann Sander about the "nature of [Mrs. Borotto's] death," inquiring also whether he "realized the seriousness of what he had done" and whether he realized "he had broken the law" (*NYT*, Feb. 25, 1950). Dr. Sander "didn't seem to be ruffled" and in his typically "quiet and reserved" demeanor explained that he did not feel he "had done anything morally wrong" and that "the law should be changed." Sander added that he "assumed the medical profession would probably reprimand him and tell him not to do it again." Still according to the librarian and the coroner, Sander explained he had been concerned about the effect of Mrs. Borrotto's agony on her husband, who suffered from a "bad heart."

Sheriff Thomas O'Brien eventually spoke with Dr. Sander and later, at the trial, corroborated *ipsis litteris* the version offered by the record librarian and the coroner. He added that the doctor had explained that Mrs. Borrotto's husband had asked him to "end his wife's life to end her suffering" and had "promised . . . he would never tell anyone about it" (*NYT*, Feb. 25, 1950).[28] Dr. Sander had also admitted having killed Mrs. Borrotto with air injections "in a weak moment" (*NYT*, Feb. 24, 1950) and, when questioned about the notation regarding the injections on the patient's chart, the physician, according to the sheriff, said he had chosen to do so because "he had nothing to hide" (*NYT*, Feb. 24, 1950). Later, Alice Sander, the doctor's wife, would remark to a journalist: "That was one time honesty didn't pay" (*NYT*, Mar. 2, 1950).

Hermann Sander was arrested, following his interview with Sheriff O'Brien. Subsequently, a grand jury returned an indictment that stated that the doctor had injected the air into Mrs. Borrotto's veins "with force of arms, feloniously, willfully and of his malice aforethought" (*NYT*, Jan. 4, 1950).[29] "In a voice that resounded through the packed courtroom," Dr. Sander pled "not guilty" (*NYT*, Jan. 6, 1950).[30] In what the prosecutor in the case would later characterize as a "somewhat unusual" procedure,[31] the doctor was granted bail, and three of his friends furnished the $25,000 bond required to keep him free (*NYT*, Feb. 19, 1950; Jan. 4, 1950).

Following his arraignment, Dr. Sander admitted injecting the air and "contended he did it as 'an act of mercy' to end her suffering" (*NYT*, Jan. 5, 1950; Jan. 12, 1950). Addressing reporters outside the courthouse, the doctor said: "All that I can say is that I am not guilty of any legal or moral wrong and ultimately my position will be vindicated" (*NYT*, Jan. 1, 1950). The doctor did not hesitate to resume his practice, and within hours of posting bail, he delivered a baby girl.[32]

Sander's self-assurance was met with great support from his community: "[H]undreds of his fellow-townspeople, his patients, and his colleagues offered to testify on his behalf and signed petitions urging the courts to dismiss the case" (*NYT*, Jan. 8, 1950). In Candia, a New Hampshire suburb where the doctor lived with his family, 605 of the town's 650 registered voters signed a petition "expressing confidence and faith in the doctor" (*NYT*, Jan. 2, 1950). The petition read:

> We the undersigned wish at this time to express our confidence and unshakeable faith in the integrity and character of our friend and fellow townsman, Dr. Herman [*sic.*] Sander. We have known him and respect him as a man of Christian virtue who has been devoted to the highest interests of human welfare at all times. With sobriety of mind, clarity of thought and consecration of heart, he has pursued his tasks and assumed his responsibility with singleness of purpose and unselfish devotion. (*NYT*, Jan. 2, 1950)

A second petition, this one circulated by a war veterans' organization, was signed by more than 200 people from Goffstown, where Mrs. Borrotto died (*NYT*, Jan. 2, 1950; Jan. 4, 1950).[33] Other petitions endorsing Dr. Sander circulated in Deerfield and Manchester (*NYT*, Jan. 3, 1950), and public demonstrations of support for the doctor were not rare.[34]

Rev. Leslie Curtis, a Congregationalist, was involved in obtaining signatures for one of the petitions, and during a New Year's service at his church, he stated, "apropos to the case: . . . Let us have the courage to act if it benefits humanity" (*NYT*, Jan. 2, 1950).[35] "Members of the congregation nodded encouragement to the Sander family." Another clergyman, Rev. Mark Strickland, also referred to the case in his Sunday radio sermon: "If this man is guilty then I am guilty, for I have prayed for those who have suffered hopelessly—prayed that they be eased into the experience of death. . . . If this man is felonious then so am I, for I have desired the time of suffering to be short and I have wanted natural and unaided courses to bring relief in death."

The case was continually a "topic for sermons" and, at one point, a Unitarian Church minister, Rev. William Peck, disclosed that clergymen had received telephone calls requesting them not to discuss the case (*NYT*, Jan. 9, 1950). Rev. Peck explained his support for mercy killings thus: "This highly charged atmosphere is due to the persistence of ancient beliefs of the early church fathers whose authority supersedes today the authority of *even* doctors. I think the . . . current discussion is a beneficial one, as quickening the intellectual interests in searching for that which is true and right" (*NYT*, Jan. 9, 1950; my emphasis). A few weeks before trial began, 22 Unitarian ministers publicly endorsed Dr. Sander's "humanitarian action" (*NYT*, Jan. 25, 1950). Methodists seem to have taken a more neutral stance.[36] Dr. Franklin Frye, a reverend in that denomination, without condoning *mercy killings*, hoped that the physician could ultimately return to practicing medicine. Rev. Lloyd Worley, pastor of the First Methodist Church in Stamford, Connecticut, said that he prayed for the *merciful release* of incurably ill patients. Rev. Worley had officiated at the funeral of Carol Paight's father, it may be recalled.

But if Congregationalists and Unitarians[37] were sympathetic to Dr. Sander's plight, the Catholic Church was not. When Sander was indicted, the Most Rev. Richard J. Gushing, archbishop of Boston, reiterated the "uncompromising position" of the Catholic Church on the matter and extrapolated to the possibility of it becoming common practice: "Human life is sacred because it comes from God . . . and the State itself does not have a right to take the life of a sick person" (*Time Magazine*, Jan. 16, 1950; see also *NYT*, Jan. 6, 1950). A Roman Catholic pastor, the Very Rev. Napoleon Gilbert, attacked *euthanasia* on the basis that "suffering on earth [is] useful in the sight of God" (*NYT*, Jan. 9, 1950). The Vatican's *semi-official* newspaper, *L'Osservatore Romano*, commented that "pity would lead to madness" and construed the injection of air into Mrs. Borrotto's arm as "inject[ing] the poison of atheism into the veins of society to free it from chronic pains" (*NYT*, Jan. 2, 1950).[38]

Religious beliefs slowly acquired increased importance during the pretrial procedures. "According to locally accepted estimates," two-thirds of Manchester's residents were Roman Catholics when Sander's trial took place (*NYT*, Feb. 19, 1950). Hillsborough County, where Manchester is located, was "about half Catholic" with much of its population being of French-Canadian or Irish descent (*NYT*, Feb. 21, 1950). Thus, when the selection of jurors began, although there was a concerted effort by the judge and legal counsels to keep "the religious issue in the background," at one point a prospective juror "blurted out that he was a Catholic and against euthanasia" (*NYT*, Feb. 21, 1950).

Others volunteered comparable remarks. For example, Louis Gagne, a local machinist, shared with the court that he "believed in a 'higher law' than the law in this case" and that "God, alone, decides when a person is to die" (*The Berkshire Evening Eagle*, Feb. 23, 1950). He was excused. And so was Mrs. Corrine English, a housewife, who volunteered that she could not sit in the jury to give a verdict: "I don't think I believe in mercy killing," she explained (*Time Magazine*, Mar. 6, 1950). "[U]nusual steps" had been taken to avoid "hampering selection of an impartial jury or causing a mistrial" (*NYT*, Feb. 21, 1950). The presiding judge, "a smooth-faced, middle-aged man with black hair" and a Congregationalist, ordered "pretrial secrecy for the names of veniremen from whom the jury [was] selected" (*NYT*, Feb. 19, 1950; Feb. 21, 1950).

An "extraordinary array of [people] was called" as prospective jurors (*NYT*, Feb. 21, 1950). Many of them were dismissed for cause, "presumably for prejudice one way or another," a newspaperman speculated. A few others were excused because they could not speak English well (these were of French-Canadian descent). Most of the peremptory challenges used by the defense team, they claimed, aimed at excluding "not all Roman Catholics, but those it seemed to think, despite denials of bias, might be bound by the traditional opposition of their church to euthanasia."

At the end of two and a half days, an all-male, middle-aged to elderly jury was chosen (*NYT*, Feb. 23, 1950; Mar. 9, 1950).[39] Except for two of the jurors, all others were married and, according to a survey commissioned by local newspapers, nine of the men were Catholic. Louis C. Cutter, a Methodist whose wife had died of cancer in the previous year, was designated as jury foreman.

Led by New Hampshire Attorney General Mr. William Phinney, the state proceeded to present its case against Dr. Sander. Mr. Phinney, "a heavy-set former agent of the Federal Bureau of Investigations" (*NYT*, Feb. 21, 1950), was also "an old friend and college mate of Dr. Sander" (*NYT*, Feb. 19, 1950). The prosecutor retold the events of December 4, when the doctor, "bending over the wasted figure of Abbie Borrotto ... told a nurse to bring a sterile syringe," inserted the needle into her arm, then "handed [it] back to the nurse and indicated that Mrs. Borrotto was dead" (*Time Magazine*, Mar. 6, 1950). The sheriff then took the stand, followed by the record librarian, one of the nurses who were caring for Mrs. Borrotto on the day she died, and the coroner who first inquired of Dr. Sander about the injections. In their testimonies, all of them recounted the facts as presented by the prosecutor.

In his opening statement, Sander's attorney, Mr. Louis Wyman,[40] made it clear that this would not be a *mercy* defense. Instead, he contended that Abbie Borrotto was already dead when the doctor injected her with air; without producing a "corpus delicti" (i.e., proof of death by a criminal act), he explained, the jurors would soon agree that the prosecution had no case (*Time Magazine*, Mar. 6, 1950).

This argument by Sander's attorneys "virtually eliminated the great moral issue that had stirred up the original excitement" about the case (*Time Magazine*, Mar. 13, 1950). Early on, Sander's case was acclaimed by pro-euthanasia advocates as a true test of the issue. The case, proponents argued, illustrated a need to "amend the law to avoid other tragic cases like [it] where a physician renders himself to a charge of murder for shortening the suffering of an incurable patient" (*NYT*, Jan. 3, 1950).[41] Another ESA leader, Rev. Charles Francis Potter, argued that Sander's case illustrated how "the law is far behind public opinion" (*NYT*, Jan. 9, 1950). "Overwhelmingly the people of New Hampshire who know him and who know the facts of the case say that Dr. Sander was morally right, but legally wrong" (*NYT*, Jan. 9, 1950). Stressing the prevalence of the practice and the timeliness of the case, Rev. Potter also insisted that "euthanasia was being practiced 'bunglingly' by desperate relatives at the request of suffering, loved ones, and more skillfully by family physicians" (*NYT*, Jan. 9, 1950). The media complained: "Our biggest problem [now]," said one reporter to *Time Magazine*, "is to give managing editors the kind of story they want—a story that was no longer really there" (*Time Magazine*, Mar. 13, 1950).

The defense strategy gained momentum during the cross-examination of Elizabeth Rose, the nurse who had fetched the syringe at Dr. Sander's request. She admitted that she had signed a statement prepared by one of the defense attorneys in which she claimed to be "certain" that Mrs. Borrotto was dead before the injections were given to her. In the statement, the nurse said that the patient was not breathing, was "motionless" and "lifeless," and had "death pallor" even before Dr. Sander entered the room (*NYT*, Feb. 25, 1950; *Time Magazine*, Mar. 6, 1950).

This version of events was echoed by Dr. Albert Snay, a colleague of Sander's who had been making his morning rounds when Nurse Rose called him to see if he could get a pulse on Mrs. Borrotto. The nurse explained that "she and others had failed to find one" (*NYT*, Mar. 4, 1950). Dr. Snay entered the patient's room to find what he described to be "a very emaciated, pallid woman . . . her lips very blue, eyes staring open and no sign of respiration." The physician examined Mrs. Borrotto further, touching her eyeball with his index finger in search of a corneal reflex and looking for a heartbeat with a stethoscope. Finding no response from Mrs. Borrotto other than "muscular twitching about the face and arm," he informed the nurse that the woman "was gone." Just then, the doctor continued, Dr. Sander entered the room and he left, informing the colleague that his patient was dead.

What ensued was a refined medical discussion by experts on both sides who attempted to ascertain whether the cause of Mrs. Borrotto's death had been pulmonary embolism from the injections or whether the woman had expired as a result of her cancer and attendant conditions.[42] The defense contended that the "muscular twitching" witnessed by Dr. Snay was the result of "somatic death," whereby certain bodily movements continue after actual death, similar to a "chicken 'flopping around' after its head has been chopped off" (*NYT*, Mar. 2, 1950).

At the crux of Sander's case was the very definition of death, which in 1950 still relied on the cessation of breathing and the absence of a heartbeat as sufficient end-of-life indicators. It was only in the late 1960s that medico-political sanction for *brain death* diagnosis was granted with the publication of a report by the Ad Hoc Committee of the Harvard Medical School. Though the brain death diagnosis had been conceptually developed in the late 1950s (by German, Belgian, and French physicians; for a history, see Machado, 2007), the committee's avowal helped sediment a change in medical acceptance of death from the cessation of heartbeat and breathing to a neurocentric diagnosis.

Besides hospital staff, the sheriff, and medical experts, numerous other witnesses took the stand during Sander's trial. Abbie Borrotto's husband and her daughter, 19-year-old Elise Borrotto, also testified. In a "faint and trembling voice," Ms. Borrotto recounted her mother's decline and how Dr. Sander had "done everything he could" to alleviate her mother's agony, even teaching the daughter how to use a hypodermic needle to administer pain relievers (*NYT*, Mar. 3, 1950). While denying any request to expedite his wife's death, Mr. Borrotto testified: "[I] could not feel more kindly toward Dr. Sander if he was my brother" (*NYT*, Mar. 1, 1950). At trial, other "twenty-three doctors, nurses, patients and friends" of the doctor testified about his character, including a judge, Hon. Peter Woodbury of the U.S. Circuit Court of Appeals, all of whom showed "an obviously deep and sincere feeling of love and admiration for the accused" (*NYT*, Mar. 4, 1950). One of Sander's patients attributed her being alive to the doctor's diligent efforts.

She explained that, when she told this to the physician, Dr. Sander replied: "But don't forget God" (*NYT*, Mar. 5, 1950). The defendant's wife also took the stand and told the court that her husband was so devoted to his patients that he frequently missed dinner with his family, answered calls at any time of day or night, often refused payment from poor patients, and "put his heart and soul into every case" (*NYT*, Mar. 5, 1950).

One of the last one to testify was the doctor himself. "In a calm voice," he recounted how he had become interested in medicine after reading a bestselling novel, *Magnificent Obsession*.[43] He insisted that his patient was already dead when he administered the air injections; denied ever intending to kill her or assenting to anyone's request to do so; denied ever admitting he had killed her out of mercy; and charged the three county officials, the nurse, and the record librarian who testified otherwise with twisting his pretrial statements. The doctor then explained that his "whole behavior [at the time of the injections] was irrational" and that the notation about the injections had been made "because it was the duty of every doctor to put down on the chart whatever he has done in connection with the patient, whether it has any effect or not" (*NYT*, Mar. 7, 1950a). During cross-examination, when pressed by his longtime friend turned prosecutor as to why he would inject air into the veins of a dead woman, Dr. Hermann Sander said: "I was obsessed to do this, and why I kept on and why I stopped, I don't know ... I was impelled to do something I can't explain" (*NYT*, Mar. 7, 1950b). "In a matter of seconds," he continued, "this thing came over me and made me do this." Mr. Phinney persisted: "You had an obsession to inject air into the veins of this poor, dead soul?" (*Time Magazine*, Mar. 13, 1950). The doctor responded affirmatively and then justified his bizarre behavior on the basis that he felt "sure that with [his] regard for a patient's life ... the very fact that she was dead gave [him] the assurance that [he] couldn't do her any harm" (*NYT*, Mar. 7, 1950). "It was just the appearance of her face and remembrance of her long suffering that might have touched me off," he added (*Time Magazine*, Mar. 13, 1950).

Prior to resting its case, the prosecution called four rebuttal witnesses to refute Dr. Snay's testimony; they contended that Sander's colleague had engaged in separate conversations with each of them in which Dr. Snay had told them that "he didn't know why [Sander] did it ... she was *practically* gone" (*NYT*, Mar. 9, 1950; my emphasis). Mr. Phinney then explained to the jurors that he too knew and liked the doctor, which made his task as a prosecutor difficult in this case (*Time Magazine*, Mar. 20, 1950). "But," he urged, "if we are to live in a society of laws, the people within that society must abide by those laws" as they apply even to "a reputable physician" (*NYT*, Mar. 9, 1950). He closed his case demanding the conviction of the 41-year-old physician.

In his summation, the lead defense attorney, with "tears ... in his eyes ... said there had been no murder, [and] euthanasia therefore was not an issue" (*NYT*, Mar. 9, 1950). "Euthanasia is not the defense," he explained, "we haven't raised it." Rather, before the jury was an overworked, compassionate physician who, for reasons he could not explain, had by his own admission "snapped" momentarily (*NYT*, Mar. 7, 1950).

The trial was on its fourteenth day when Sander's fate was handed to the all-male jury. After 70 minutes of deliberation, as they filed back to the jury box, "one of [the jurors] caught Mrs. Sander's anxious eye, grinned broadly, and tipped her a reassuring wink" (*Time Magazine*, Mar. 20, 1950). The foreman pronounced the "not guilty" verdict and a "little shriek of delight from the women spectators" broke the silence in the courtroom (*Time Magazine*, Mar. 20, 1950). "On the surface," a newsman remarked, "the verdict meant only this: that the jurors believed the doctor's story, or at least they felt there was reasonable doubt" (*NYT*, Mar. 12, 1950).

The Sanders were surrounded by supporters as they left the courtroom. A crowd outside cheered, church bells tolled, auto horns tooted. Neighbors and friends gathered at the doctor's farm later that evening for a torchlight demonstration of support. Dr. Sander told reporters he was "very pleased" and had "never doubted the result" (*NYT*, Mar. 10, 1950). He added that he expected to resume his practice in a few weeks, following a short vacation with his wife.

Soon after his acquittal, Dr. Sander's medical license was revoked by the State Medical Board. At the meeting to consider his case, the society charged the physician with "morally reprehensible action in deliberately injecting air into his patient"; no doctor should be allowed "to perform a 'senseless act' " (*NYT*, Apr. 20 and 21, 1950). Hours before the board met, the Roman Catholic Bishop of Manchester vigorously criticized *mercy killing* during a sermon. Two Catholic hospitals in the region permanently banned the doctor from practicing on their premises, and Dr. Adolphe Provost, chief of staff at one of them, claimed that "[Sander] is on trial with us now" (*NYT*, Mar. 21, 1950). When asked for a reaction to the board's decision, Mrs. Borroto's husband said: "It is damnable and hypocritical" (*NYT*, Apr. 20, 1950). "How much more blood does the board want? I think it stinks to high heaven," he added.

The board, however, allowed Sander to reapply for the license two months later. He did so, and the license was reinstated in June. The news that Dr. Sander's license had been restored was broadcast over a number of radio stations statewide, and within minutes, the doctor received a call from a man asking for help with his bursitis. Between the end of the trial, when the revocation went into effect, and the end of spring, Hermann Sander occupied himself "helping neighbors with their . . . plowing" (*NYT*, Apr. 26, 1950). Prosecutor William Phinney resigned after the acquittal and returned to private practice. Two of the nurses who testified at trial were demoted to floor duty.

From the perspective of those who hoped Dr. Sander would be a martyr for the case of *euthanasia*, the case turned out to be a dud. Nevertheless, proponents of legalization maintained that the Sander case had "focused attention on the fact that the law is far behind public sentiment" (*The Berkshire Evening Eagle*, Jan. 9, 1950).

In truth, however, by the end of the 1950s, public support for euthanasia was at its lowest, with only 36 percent favoring legalization—at least 10 percent less than in the mid-1930s (Carroll, 2006). Mercy killings, though spectacular as media events, had not fulfilled their promise as a route to legalization. No legislative body had taken up the gauntlet of defining a special category of justifiable murder on the basis of compassion. In the meantime, the putative martyrs for the cause found themselves defendants in trials where the stakes were extremely high and for the most part with no viable defense strategy than to find refuge in claiming *insanity*. Perhaps because of the persistent failure to convict mercy killers (and therefore the failure to produce the *martyrs* proponents needed), legalization did not follow. In effect, as each successive mercy killer was exonerated, they became the exception that proved the rule.

As interest in euthanasia waned, the ESA made an attempt to fuel discussion by drafting a petition later presented to the Human Rights Commission of the United Nations to amend the Declaration of Human Rights as to include the "right of incurable sufferers to euthanasia or merciful death" (United Press, 1952). The petition was not granted and the legislative efforts implemented by the society in New York, New Jersey, and Connecticut, between 1952 and 1959 were equally unfruitful.

## AMERICAN MEDICINE'S GOLDEN AGE

Just as public support for the issue dwindled, physicians' patronage was also growing scarce. It is important to note that in the decade immediately following the end of World War II, American medicine "was at a historically unprecedented peak of prestige, prosperity and political and cultural influence—perhaps as autonomous as it is possible for a profession to be" (Freidson, 1988, p. 384). Just as Hermann Sander's townspeople showed their "deep and sincere feeling of love and admiration" for the doctor as they testified on his behalf, Americans in general held physicians in a comparable degree of adulation. If by 1906 doctors had earned a place alongside patients' beds, by mid-century they were pretty much in charge of it.

The revolution in medical education, discussed in the previous chapter, as well as victory of orthodox medics over quacks and physicians' authority over drug regulation[44] helped consolidate their professional power. Enjoying institutional support from patients, from the now well-established American Medical Association,[45] from private philanthropists, and increasingly from the government,[46] by 1950 the profession of medicine had become the pinnacle of the healthcare field, in terms of both prestige and trust (Timmermans & Oh, 2010). The profession's growth in respectability and autonomy was also due to important scientific developments that happened in the first half of the twentieth century, such as the invention of diverse vaccines (including for tuberculosis) and antibiotic treatments, the discovery of penicillin, and the development of a heart-lung machine that allowed for open chest surgery. By the mid-1950s,

DNA had been discovered, the first kidney transplant had been executed, and the first successful artificial heart had been implanted in a dog. In their new (sacerdotal) role, physicians could now oppose hastening death not only on the basis of their capacity to prolong life but also on the idea that suffering was key to the development of science: "[T]here would have been no incentive to discover remedies if the human race accepted with fatalism the theory that rabies was incurable and that euthanasia was a merciful and inevitable solution" (Tinckon-Fernandez, 1950).

Public opinion polls from the 1930s to the 1950s consistently placed physicians among the most highly admired individuals (Burnham, 1997). At the bedside, physicians' authority and adulation translated into an unbalanced relationship with patients. During the first half of the twentieth century, dubbed the "golden age of doctoring" (McKinlay & Marceau, 2002), very little was shared with patients regarding their illness diagnosis or prognosis, and patients' wishes, opinions, and input were vastly disregarded.[47,48] Commenting on the decision-making that surrounded hastened death processes, Dr. Morris Fishbein, at the time editor of the *Journal of the American Medical Association*, asserted: "[T]he average doctor frequently faces the problem, [and] when it is a matter between him and his patient he may generally decide it in his own way, without interference" (*Time Magazine*, Nov. 18, 1935). Another doctor, a decade and a half later, said that he customarily prescribed his incurable patients with a week's supply of morphine and explained to the moribund that "one tablet will ease the pain but warn[ed] him to be careful because if he takes the whole bottle he may not wake up" (*NYT*, Jan. 18, 1950). "If that be murder," he challenged, "make the most of it."[49]

Concomitantly, after a decade of economic depression and war, American hospitals had begun receiving increased financial support. An attendant concentration of medical work in hospitals followed; for instance, in 1950, only 1 in 10 contacts with physicians occurred in patients' homes (Starr, 1984). Happening increasingly in the public sphere, death—and its manner—was gradually more difficult to hide.

Medics also scarcely offered public support for hastening patients' death. Although, as mentioned earlier, in the mid-1940s the ESA was able to mobilize nearly 2,000 physicians to sign a petition in favor of assisted death, that number amounted to fewer than ten percent of the physicians in practice in the United States at the time (United States Bureau of the Census, 1975). Additionally, although a few doctors were forthcoming about their participation in or favorable position about *mercy killing*, the issue did not enjoy organizational backing, with the *American Medical Association* time and again repudiating the practice. As one opponent-doctor put it, if legalized, medically hastened death would "soon [cause] the medical profession [to] lose the healthy bloom associated with the bringing forth and maintaining of life and it would acquire some of the unsocial, morbid air surrounding the hangman's trade" (*Time Magazine*, Mar. 13, 1950; for a summary of the developments between 1911 and the 1950s, see Table 4.2).

**Table 4.2 Timeline: 1911–1950s (Selected Developments)**

| | |
|---|---|
| 1911 | Shakers' case |
| 1914 | The *Harrison Act* is passed |
| 1928 | 24% of medical schools administered the *Hippocratic Oath*, in contrast to nearly 100% today |
| 1935 | British *Voluntary Euthanasia Legalization Society* is incorporated |
| 1937 | A euthanasia bill is introduced in Nebraska |
| 1938 | The *Euthanasia Society of America* is incorporated<br>A euthanasia bill is drafted in New York (but never introduced)<br>*Food, Drug and Cosmetic Act* is passed |
| 1946 | 1,776 physicians' petition to legalize euthanasia |
| 1947 | *American Medical Association's* centennial |
| 1949 | Clergymen's petition organized by the *Euthanasia Society of America* |
| 1950 | Carol Paight's case<br>Dr. Hermann Sander's case |
| 1952 | Petition to the United Nations<br>Between 1952 and 1959, legislative attempts are conducted in New York, New Jersey, and Connecticut |
| 1954 | Joseph Fletcher's *Medicine and Morals* is published |

## *SWINGING SIXTIES,* SWINGING ATTITUDES

Concern about the implications of the emerging technological advances to death and dying was not confined to moral debates, and legal scholars' attention was soon captivated. In 1957, for instance, law professor Glanville Williams published *The Sanctity of Life and the Criminal Law*, proposing that voluntary euthanasia be allowed for competent, terminally ill patients. Also in 1957, Pope Pius XII addressed the issue of passive euthanasia in a sympathetic manner and suggested that life-support respirators be kept only for as long as needed to give the infirm his or her "Extreme Unction" (Pope Pius XII, 1957). Still that year, *Time Magazine* reporter Lael Wertenbaker published *Death of a Man*, the first memoir of the kind, describing how she helped her cancer-ridden husband kill himself.

Along with such burgeoning legal interest, the 1960s ushered in a unique era of renewed attitudes toward death and dying. For example, in 1969 psychiatrist Elisabeth Kubler-Ross's path-breaking book *On Death and Dying* was published "at a time when the topic was rarely discussed in public and studiously avoided at the bedside" (Nuland, 2004). By 1968, *suicide* was no longer considered a *grave public wrong* in the New York Penal and Criminal Law. Other developments were taking place in the medical realm as well, which contributed to a change in the public's perception of the dying process. Specifically, as discussed earlier, the most colloquial criterion of determining death as we know today, namely the notion of brain death, finds its origins then.

Accompanying this shift were other significant technological advances in the field of medicine that helped transform the role of physicians and the limits of death and dying. With the invention of mechanical respirators in the 1950s, it became possible for a previously lethal extent of brain damage to coexist with continued cardiopulmonary functioning, sustaining the functioning of other organs. Was such a patient alive or dead? In the words of one Supreme Court justice, in those cases, "[m]edical technology has effectively created a twilight zone of suspended animation where death commences while life, in some form, continues."[50] Legal answers to that question began to be drafted in state courts and legislatures in the following two decades. We turn to those issues next.

## NOTES

1. For a review of early nineteenth-century policies dealing with the all-inclusive category of *feeble-minded* individuals, see Davies (1925). The piece, written by then executive secretary for the New York Committee on Mental Hygiene, discusses how segregation and sterilization were found to be ineffective and how training—habit, character, and manual training—was a better solution to "combat mental deficiency" (op. cit.).

2. For an in-depth account of the intersection between *euthanasia* and the eugenics movement, see Dowbiggin (2002).

3. There is some evidence that suicide rates spike at times of economic downturn. In 1933, when unemployment rates reached 25 percent, suicide rates were at an all-time high—causing life insurance companies, for example, to revise their clauses in order to include a two-year moratorium period for suicide claims (McDougall & Gorman, 2008). Similarly, a recent study found that suicide rates between 2008 and 2010 increased four times faster than in the eight years before the recession (Reeves et al., 2012). There may be a logical connection between financial hardship as a trigger for suicide and financial hardship as precipitating increased tolerance for assisted death. A similar argument was advanced during the incipient discussions about the *Obamacare Act* and the so-called death panels, for instance. In the 1930s, historian Ian Dowbiggin (2003) points out, the economic downturn allowed for an increased discussion about suicide and the control of the circumstances of death. By 1937, 45 percent of Americans approved of *euthanasia*; by 1947, as the postwar economic boom began, approval had dropped to 37 percent (Carroll, 2007).

4. One exception was the case of Katie Roberts, which unfolded in Michigan in 1920. Bedridden and terminally ill, the 33-year-old woman convinced her husband to prepare a poisoned drink and place it by her bed. Shortly after her death, Frank Roberts, who confessed to mixing the poison Paris Green with water and placing the concoction "within reach of his wife to enable her to end her suffering by ending her life," was found guilty of first-degree murder and sentenced to life imprisonment and hard labor (*People v. Roberts*, p. 689). The harsh sentence received by Roberts in the assistance of his wife's suicide was unusual, especially when compared to contemporaneous accounts of *mercy killings* whereby the agent directly causing death was typically ingratiated with lenient sentences or escaped judicial processing altogether.

5. Although at least three doctors had been publicly forthcoming in their involvement in *mercy kills*, for various reasons none of them had been legally processed for their acts. In 1935, Myron A. Warriner, a 79-year-old physician, confessed to killing a Massachusetts man some 50 years before. The doctor, then three years out of Harvard Medical School, had "put to death with an overdose of morphine" a man who had been mangled by an accidental shotgun charge (*The Racine Journal-Times*, Nov. 20, 1935). His story was challenged by the "victim's" daughters, who claimed their father had died as a result of the wound. "Irritated by the doubts of his confession," Dr. Warriner explained that all of the individuals who could corroborate his account were dead. He added that he had acted mercifully and "would do the same thing today." The doctor further added that "he was convinced many doctors felt likewise and were hypocritical in public statements condemning 'mercy killings.' "

Following Dr. Warriner's confession, another physician, Monroe F. Clauser, "admitted putting six sufferers to death" during an interview he gave to the Associated Press and the United Press (*Time Magazine*, Dec. 2, 1935). Dr. Clauser later recanted his statement. In 1937, Dr. Guy Peterkin shot his 22-year-old son who had been recovering from a "nervous breakdown" (United Press, July 24, 1937). He then shot himself. In a note written by Dr. Peterkin, the Seattle physician stated his belief that his son "will never be entirely well" and killing him would "save him from a life of hopeless suffering" (United Press, July 24, 1937). Another case involving a physician emerged in Miami in 1938. Dr. Frances Tuttle, a "prominent osteopath," had poisoned her nine-year-old daughter who had been suffering from a long illness (*The Syracuse Journal*, Jan. 18, 1938). The osteopath then tried to kill herself unsuccessfully and was later sent to the Miami Retreat Hospital for the insane.

6. The statements were by Eleanor Dwight Jones, executive vice-president of then recently formed *Euthanasia Society of America*. Mrs. Jones had been one of the leaders of the birth control movement and, according to one scholar, she "brought years of activist experience ... to the euthanasia movement" (Dowbiggin, 2002, p. 235). A *Who Is Who of America* published in 1914–1915 describes her as "favor[ing] woman suffrage and [a] Unitarian."

7. Having arrived in the United States in the late 1700s, by the mid-1800s followers of the *United Society of Believers in Christ's Second Appearance*—commonly known as *Shakers* for their movements while singing and praying—had reached over 6,000 (Robison, 1993). In the opening decades of the twentieth century, however, a steady closing of Shaker villages was in place. Olive branch was established in the late 1890s. "It is stated that nothing in the teachings of the sect," one newspaper clarified, "gives any basis for aiding a person to quit his life" (*The Times Dispatch*, Sep. 21, 1911).

8. Opinion among governors about the fate of the Shakers varied widely. While several politicians echoed the position of Gov. Gilchrist, others did not share his views. For instance, Governor Hadley, from Missouri, thought the killing was "against the laws of God and men" and warned that "half our murder cases might be defended on the ground of ending suffering" (*The Marion Daily Mirror*, Sep. 14, 1911).

9. Egbert Gillette eventually left the Shakers' community and married (Stein, 1994). The *Olive Branch* colony dissolved two or three years after Sister Marchant's death (Anderson, 1959). It is not clear what happened to Sister Sears.

10. Washington State Governor Marion Hay buttressed the Shakers' perception: "It is up to the doctors to decide such a question. I understand many of them are putting their patients out of their suffering when a case is agonizing and hopeless. Maybe they

could be held for it, legally, but no case has arisen in my state" (*The Marion Daily Mirror*, Sep. 14, 1911).

11. The boy had been bitten by a rabid dog three weeks prior to receiving lethal doses of chloroform at the County Hospital in Chicago. The ethical question of physician involvement was resolved by invoking the "double effect doctrine," according to which the intent was not to kill the child, but ease the spasms of hydrophobia.

12. There are also anecdotal accounts of battlefield euthanasia during World War I, such as the following:

> [O]ne man was brought in with his face covered with a bandage and when the Major came in to look at him and see what was the matter he went out and was violently sick. When he took the bandages off we saw the man had no eyes, no nose, no chin, no mouth—and he was alive! The Sergeant called me and said, "The doctor says I've got to give him four times the usual dose of morphia." And I said, "You know what that will do, don't you?" And he said, "Yes. And I can't do it. I'm ordering you to do it." So I had to go in and give him four times the dose of morphia. I laid a clean bandage on his face and stayed with him until he died. (MacDonald, 2000, pp. 309–310)
>
> Similar instances were reported during World War II. For instance, an American officer trapped in a burning compartment of an airplane was shot by a fellow officer who wanted to spare him from burning to death (*NYT*, Jan. 8, 1950). He was acquitted and his name was never released by the Air Force to protect him.

13. In Paris, a Polish actress, Mlle. Yuminska, shot her fiancé once she learned he was suffering from cancer. She was acquitted after explaining the harrowing conditions her mate was suffering (*NYT*, Mar. 22, 1925). Also in Paris, Anna Levasseur confessed to killing her sister, Anais, "because she was dying by inches from a terrible disease" (*The Singapore Free Press*, Mar. 25, 1925). An Australian newspaper covering the case queried several physicians on the matter—all of whom seemed to agree that "there was definite use" for incurables in the world (*The Advertiser*, Feb. 25, 1925). The doctors noted how R. L. Stevenson, John Keats, and Chopin "were all incurables."

In England, another case emerged that same February, this time involving a vicar, shot by his sister. The vicar had accidentally shot himself in the face and when his sister found him in that condition she asked if he thought he was going to live and if he was in pain. The vicar did not have time to answer; his sister later explained that she saw "he was dying and in agony" and so she spared him from suffering any longer (*NYT*, Mar. 22, 1925). Subsequently, she was found "temporarily insane" and sent to an asylum.

A fourth case involved an American, 40-year-old William Dunn, from Iowa. A week after the Polish actress case became sensational news, Dunn fatally shot both his father and mother. His "early octogenarians" parents were ill; the mother had cancer whereas the father had asthma. Dunn killed himself and left a note in which he explained he had done it "for their good" and that he "was willing to sacrifice [his] life for them." The *New York Times* anticipated that euthanasia advocates would argue Dunn's suicide was futile and could have been prevented if "humanitarian and legal means of providing euthanasia for those suffering incurable diseases" had been in place.

Four years after this string of *mercy killings*, another Frenchman, Richard Corbett, stood before a judge for shooting his mother. He turned to the jury and explained what he had done: "My mother was suffering torture. The doctors agreed that she could not recover. I felt that even though I broke the law, I did right. I'm willing to pay any penalty you think just. My action would not have been necessary if the State would pass a law enabling doctors to end the suffering of incurables" (*Time Magazine*, Nov. 18, 1929). At that point he was interrupted by the judge: "It was for God to consider when your mother should have died, not you. God might have prolonged your mother's life." "God," the defendant replied, "is only a religious belief." The reaction in the courtroom was intense, as "women wept hysterically" and one juror, paled, "called for brandy" and collapsed. A "not guilty" verdict was delivered soon after by the jury, all male farmers. Outside the court, reaction was equally intense; Professor Albert Einstein said he "approved unqualifiedly the action of Richard Corbett" and was "happy . . . that the spirit of justice triumphed over the dead letter of the law." A Freudian psychiatrist, Dr. Abraham Arden Brill, expressed discontent; "Society is based on repression, and the most important repression is the command 'Thou shall not kill.' " Finally, American naturalist William Beebe thought the Frenchman was "absolutely justified in what he did" and confessed to engaging in the killing of two "Indians in the British Guianas" who had had their legs crushed. Regarding himself as the exception, the naturalist explained that he did not "hold human life in as much esteem as many people." "I've been out among the savages too much," he added.

14. The Nebraska bill (titled *Voluntary Euthanasia Act*) was sponsored by physician Inez Philbrick and introduced by State Senator John H. Stock. The Act never went to vote. If it had passed, the bill would have provided for "[d]istrict Judges to act as referees to whom any adult suffering an incurable and painful disease might apply for permission for a 'merciful death' " (Associated Press, 1937). The judge would then appoint a commission of two physicians and one attorney who would confer on the case and recommend action. The Illinois effort was urged by the *Homeopathic Medical Association* and, like the Nebraska bill, it did not go far.

15. Unlike his wife and children, "Sergeant Paight was a Methodist" (*Time Magazine*, Feb. 6, 1950). Throughout her trial, Carol Paight held "a cross and a white handkerchief" in her hands (*NYT*, Feb. 3, 1950).

16. The allusion to *cancer phobia* by Paight's defenders was not innocuous. If at the time of the Shakers' mercy killing case, tuberculosis was the second most deadly disease in the United States, by the late 1930s that ranking had been replaced by cancer. As Patterson (1989) explains, throughout the nineteenth century, cancer was not feared because most deaths resulted from pneumonia, *the old man's friend*, and the real frightening killer disease was tuberculosis, dubbed the *great destroyer*. During most of that century, the epidemiology of cancer was beyond the capacity of physicians, who presumed cancer to be random and contagious and its causes to be old age, germs, or even sorrow. As the twentieth century unfolded, most of the main infectious diseases became better controlled and as a result demands that cancer be conquered next grew. An optimist, in 1925, hailed: "We live day to day on the verge of the discovery of a remedy for the greatest and most inscrutable scourge of human race—cancer" (*NYT*, Mar. 22, 1925). "Yet," he added, "euthanasia today finds well-known supporters." As medical claims mounted (in January 1950, for instance, fungi were found to grow on cancerous tumors and once more the cure was proclaimed to be near), so did death rates, and popular attention to the disease soon intensified. By the late 1930s the federal government had passed a series of measures to promote cancer research and cancer control. Part of the program included cancer education programs, which a medical commentator, in 1949, dubbed "cancer propaganda," claiming it "added to the fear of cancer" that was widespread in psychosomatic medicine

(Weiss, 1949; see also *Medical Times*, 1954). As discussed in Chapter 6 of this book, cancer remains the most diagnosed terminal illness among those choosing aid in dying in Oregon and Washington states.

17. World War II inaugurated a series of narcotic torture practices designed to *extract* truthful statements from diverse subjects. In the United States, several *truth serum* cases captured public imagination. In early 1950, for instance, at the same time Carol Paight's *mercy killing* populated newspapers' pages everywhere, another trial received equal national attention. In what became known as the "tuxedo murder case," college student Robert "Benny" Bednasek was accused of strangling his sweetheart, socialite Margaret "Gee Gee" Jackson. *Truth serum* was given to Bednasek to help him recollect the events. Peaking in the 1940s and 1950s, by the 1960s professional judgment was that *truth drugs* simply produced a relaxed state of mind, similar to inebriation from alcohol, whereby individuals spoke more but did not necessarily speak the truth (for a detailed history of the use of sodium amytal and other substances in the period, see Rejali, 2007).

18. The police sergeant was buried with military honors at the First Methodist Church in Stamford, CT. His wife and son, Carl Paight, Jr. attended the ceremony, but Carol Paight, then in custody, was not told about the funeral because "physicians said that [she] was still hysterical" (*NYT*, Sep. 26, 1949).

19. Goldstein practiced law in Connecticut for 71 years. He died in 1992 and the obituary produced by the *New York Times* on the occasion of his death mentioned his "successful defense . . . in the state's first mercy killing case" (*NYT*, Feb. 29, 1992).

20. In addition, one man and one woman were excused when they said they approved of *euthanasia* in certain circumstances (*NYT*, Jan. 26, 1950). Most of the jurors were in their fifties, and other details about them, including names, occupation, and place of residence, were published by newspapers covering the trial (see, e.g., *NYT*, Jan. 26, 1950).

21. The college issued the following statement following Paight's acquittal: "It is good news to all of us that Ms. Paight has been acquitted. Should she wish to return to New England College we shall be pleased to have her resume her studies [as] her status as a student has been maintained throughout her unfortunate ordeal" (United Press, Feb. 8, 1950).

22. According to newspaper coverage, and as quoted throughout this section, Carol Paight's reaction to her father's diagnosis is described as *hysterical* by several of those who came in contact with her around the time of the shooting, including two physicians. Interestingly,*hysteria* was one of the most commonly diagnosed *diseases* in Western medical history until 1952, when the American Psychiatric Association officially dropped the term (O'Brien, 2009). Often, the remedy prescribed to *hysterical* single women at the time was to marry and have frequent intercourse with their husbands. Carol Paight was married roughly six months after her acquittal to another New England College student, Mr. Robert Anderson (*NYT*, Sep. 18, 1950). News of their romance broke during the trial and a "special delivery letter" from Anderson to Paight arrived on the day of her acquittal, prompting the Associated Press to report their engagement (Associated Press, Feb. 8, 1950).

23. In an analysis of 112 *mercy killing* cases documented in the United States between 1960 and 1993, Canetto and Hollenshead (2000) found that, unlike in Paight's case, older women in poor health are typically the *victims* of hastened death and that men, usually the husbands, are the ones who commit the crime. A firearm, they also found, is the preferred method employed. To my knowledge, there are no systematic analyses that assess whether certain characteristics of offenders and victims in *mercy killings* are more or less likely to result in a conviction. In my survey of cases and newspapers, during the

time span shown in Table 4.1, only two cases resulted in conviction. One was John F. Noxon, Jr., who was sentenced to death for the "electrocution slaying of his 6 months old mentally deficient son" (*NYT*, July 7, 1944). His death sentence was commuted two years after the conviction. The reason for granting clemency, explained the Massachusetts governor, were "extenuating circumstances" surrounding the murder. The nature of the "extenuating circumstances" were not further clarified, but the governor did explain that "mercy killing ... was not a factor in his decision" (*NYT*, Aug. 8, 1946). A second case, which took place a few months after Carol Ann Paight's acquittal, involved 36-year-old Harold Mohr. Mohr was convicted of voluntary manslaughter in the "slaying of his blind brother" who was also suffering from cancer (*NYT*, Apr. 8, 1950). Harold Mohr's unsuccessful defense was that he had been temporarily insane.

24. Per Table 4.1, Louis Repouille applied for American citizenship five years after his mercy killing trial. He was naturalized and the government appealed the decision. The appellate court agreed that his conduct reflected a lack of the *good moral character* required of a U.S. citizen, and Repouille's naturalization was denied and his petition dismissed. It is unclear if Repouille reapplied subsequently. For the correspondence between the appellate court judges, as well as lower court transcripts, see Burt (2004).

25. While in Germany, the doctor developed an interest in "socialized medicine," and months prior to his trial, he and his wife went back to Europe to study the topic (*NYT*, Mar. 8, 1950).

26. After the diagnosis, the doctor often tried to encourage Mrs. Borrotto; on one occasion, according to the woman's husband, Dr. Sander gave her a canary and he often brought his children to visit her believing it cheered her up (*NYT*, Mar. 1, 1950).

27. When asked later why it had taken her this long to bring the matter to authorities, the librarian explained: "[I]t kind of slipped my mind" (*Time Magazine*, Mar. 6, 1950).

28. Mr. Borrotto denied in a "signed, sworn statement" having had anything to do "with this thing of Dr. Sander's" (*NYT*, Feb. 25, 1950).

29. "Murder is with malice aforethought and euthanasia is with mercy aforethought," later reacted Rev. Charles Francis Potter, one of the leaders of the *ESA*.

30. At the time of Sander's trial, a charge of first-degree murder could carry a sentence of death by hanging or life imprisonment, in the event of a conviction. The last hanging in New Hampshire occurred in 1939, 11 years prior to Sander's prosecution. Although New Hampshire has one man on death row at present, no one has been executed since that time. The state did not pursue the death penalty in Sander's case (*NYT*, Feb. 22, 1950).

31. Indeed, up to then, the physician was the "first person in New Hampshire court history to receive freedom while facing trial on a first-degree murder charge" (*NYT*, Jan. 6, 1950).

32. Mrs. Louise Crocker, the baby's mother, and Mrs. Mildred Carom, whose infant daughter had also been delivered by Dr. Sander, prayed "for his acquittal," in hopes that he would "attend the birth of their next babies" (United Press, Feb. 24, 1950). The two mothers "didn't give a second thought to the fact the doctor ... was an accused murderer." Subsequently, Hermann Sander voluntarily agreed to stop practicing medicine until the trial ended. The county and state medical societies refrained from considering his case, also pending the trial's outcome.

33. Reportedly, Dr. Sander "suffered great disappointment when old skiing injuries barred him from active wartime service in the Medical Corps" (*NYT*, Mar. 4, 1950). It is unclear whether the doctor had any other ties to military organizations.

34. For instance, as Dr. Sander and his wife were leaving the courthouse following his arraignment, "a middle-aged woman broke from the throng of spectators, grasped him by the hand, and said: 'I hope everything will come out all right for you' " (*NYT*, Jan. 2, 1950). He smiled and thanked her. Additionally, many letters were written to local newspapers and, due to their "emotional" nature, the press in Manchester and surrounding areas, while continuing to cover the trial, decided to refrain from publishing editorials and readers' mailed comments (*NYT*, Feb. 19, 1950). Curiously, weeks after his acquittal, Dr. Sander was described by reporters as having a "discolored eye" (*NYT*, Apr. 20, 1950). He declined to comment on it, when questioned by the press.

35. The reverend, Sander's own pastor, had lost his mother to cancer. On one occasion, "he declared from his pulpit: 'Our reverence for the inviolable dignity of human personality demands that we permit people to die an honorable and dignified death under conditions that would be deemed proper' " (*Time Magazine*, March 6, 1950).

36. Shai Lavi (2005) attributes the beginnings of the modern notion of euthanasia to the Methodists.

37. For a concise explanation about the support of Unitarians and Congregationalists (later unified denominations) for *euthanasia*, see Dowbiggin (2005).

38. While opposition and support for the doctor was discussed from the "pulpit to bar-rooms" (Davis, Feb. 7, 1950), a few cynics observed that the only error was to make "a notation of the air injections on the medical record" (*NYT*, Jan. 8, 1950). During trial, Dr. Sander testified that he had received letters from doctors who said: "[M]any of us have done the same thing from time to time but just haven't recorded it" (*NYT*, Mar. 7, 1950).

39. The name, age, hometown, occupation, marital status, and religious affiliation of each of the jurors were published by several of the newspapers covering the case (*NYT*, Feb. 23, 1950).

40. Hermann Sander's defense team was composed of seven lawyers and headed by 71-year-old Louis E. Wyman. Mr. Wyman was "one of the state's leading trial lawyers," but Sander's was his first criminal case (*NYT*, Feb. 21, 1950). The prosecution had three attorneys on the case. Rev. Leslie Curtice urged his churchmen and women to send contributions to a defense fund created for Dr. Hermann Sander (*NYT*, Mar. 6, 1950). His defense costs had been estimated to range between $20,000.00 and $50,000.00 (*NYT*, Mar. 5, 1950). The fund, organized by a college classmate and fraternity brother of the doctor, received donations big and small, which came "in on all kinds of stationary, 'from embossed to five-in-ten-cent-store paper.' " Many of the contributions were accompanied by testimonies about the loss of relatives and dear ones, while others praised the physician for his "courage, honesty, and self-sacrifice." Supporters raised $21,000 for the fund, from over 2,000 donors (*NYT*, Apr. 21, 1950).

41. In 1950, the *ESA* announced it would "seek the nation's first 'mercy-death' law in New Hampshire as a result of the ... case against Dr. Hermann N. Sander" (*NYT*, Jan. 3, 1950). A carefully drafted legislation, advocates explained, would prevent illegal killings "by legalizing voluntary euthanasia under control of the courts on recommendation by medical commissions with proper safeguards against abuses" (*NYT*, Jan. 18, 1950). Lacking sponsors, the bill was never drafted.

Proponents of *euthanasia* considered organizing a mass meeting in New Hampshire after the trial to push for legal change: "If it is morally right, it should be legally right," they argued (*NYT*, Jan. 3, 1950). The ESA initially had proposed a meeting to be held when the trial was in effect, but leaders were dissuaded by "three ministers, two physicians, and three women civic leaders who 'felt [it] would prejudice the case.' "

42. Another important discussion between the medical experts testifying on both sides regarded the determination of how much air is necessary to cause pulmonary embolism in a human being and specifically in patient as debilitated as Mrs. Borrotto. The *Brooklyn Daily Eagle* remarked that Sander's case "may be setting for important scientific revelations" in that "from the evidence [presented at trial] medical science may learn just what is a lethal dose of air into the veins of a human being" (United Press, Feb. 23, 1950). Up to that point, scientists had used air injections to kill animals, "but the 'experiments' never before have been performed with humans." In 2006, an 82-year-old French patient was administered, in error, 90 cc of air instead of contrast solution, while undergoing a follow-up cancer-related procedure. That is more than twice as much air as Dr. Sander admitted injecting into Abbie Borrotto's arm. The French patient was placed on his left side and supine position and recovered with no sequelae (Cuvelier & Muir, 2006).

43. *Magnificent Obsession* was published in 1929 and tells the story of two men—a playboy and a surgeon—who came near death at the same time at opposite sides of a lake. The carefree young man was involved in a boat accident, while the doctor had a heart attack. The physician, known for his devotion to patients, died. The other man is saved and, upon reading the medic's journals, decides to become a doctor himself, to make up for the surgeon's death. The book, a story of self-sacrifice and redemption, was written by Lloyd Douglas. The author was a clergyman who changed his denominations several times before retiring to become a writer—from Lutheran pastor he moved on to becoming a Congregationalist and later a Methodist minister. Atheism and the relationship between religion and science are well-developed themes in the story. Douglas's book was a best seller and was adapted to the cinema in 1935 and 1954. A spin-off, *Dr. Hudson's Secret Journal*, became a television show that aired in the mid-1950s.

44. According to Temin (1979), it was in 1938, with the passage of the *Federal Food, Drug and Cosmetic Act of 1938*, that a stunning change in the way prescription medicine would be sold was effected, thereby consolidating physicians' role as the direct gatekeepers of lethal drugs and the "natural" oversight agents of what would develop into medically hastened death. Before the 1938 *Act*, the only drugs for which prescriptions were needed were certain narcotics specified in the *Harrison Narcotics Act of 1914*. Any other drug could be obtained directly from the pharmacist, free of prescriptions.

45. In 1936, the *American Medical Association* had achieved 100,000 members (AMA, n.d.). The organization was also a powerful lobbying group; when the *Social Security Act* was passed in 1935, the AMA prevented the inclusion of compulsory health insurance. In a historical account of the evolution of Medicare, the U.S. Social Security Administration (USSSA) recounts how the AMA fiercely defended self-regulation. According to the USSSA, the debate between those who favored the notion of insurance as a way to finance health care and the medical body "became acrimonious" with the latter arguing that "[t]here are great dangers and evils in insurance practice which must be set over against the advantages of distributing the costs of medical care by this method." They added: "[A]ny plan for the distribution of medical costs ... must be under the control of the medical profession" (U.S. Social Security Administration, n.d.). In 1948, then 100 years old, the AMA launched a campaign against President Truman's plan for national health insurance (AMA, n.d.). This opposition was a sharp contrast to the AMA's actions in 1916 when debates on compulsory, state-run health insurance had warranted a favorable report by the association. Propelled by the Progressive era, this earlier endorsement was in line with what was taking place elsewhere—Germany had instituted a centralized health insurance system as early as 1883 and Britain did so in 1911.

46. Between 1900 and the early 1940s, medical research was primarily funded by private institutions and benefactors. After the 1920s, pharmaceutical companies also began sponsoring medical research. The injection of money and institutional support not only propelled scientific development but also helped consolidate the status of medicine as a scientific profession. As PaulStarr (1984) explains, World War II marked the beginning of an increased expansion of support for medicine by the federal government. Though willing to take the funding made available for the government, American medical researchers wanted to preserve functional control over where their work would be done. If earlier in the twentieth century the United States had looked to Germany as a model for medical education (Dr. Hermann Sander, for instance, had studied in Munich), by the end of the 1940s the lesson learned from the Germans was that the centralization of research under governmental auspices had in effect slowed scientific progress while advancing the agenda of the Nazi party.

47. To illustrate, in 1883 Oliver Wendell Holmes gave this advice to novice practitioners: "Your patient has no more right to all the truth you know than to all the medicine in your saddlebags.... He should just get only just so much as it is good for him.... Some shrewd old physicians have a few phrases always on hand for patients who insist on knowing the pathology of their complaints without the slightest capacity of understanding the scientific explanation. I have known the term 'spinal irritation' to serve well on such occasions." (Holmes, 1911, p. 338). Though today this paternalistic tone would likely be seen as unacceptable by the majority of patients, not too long ago a subtler version of this physician-centered approach was made clear in doctors' avoidance of using "cancer" or "malignant tumor" for such diagnoses and preferring instead to use the term "lump." In 1961, a study published in the *JAMA* revealed that roughly 90 percent of physicians surveyed chose not to tell cancer patients their diagnoses (Oken, 1961).

48. It was not until the 1960s, as the patients' rights movement gained momentum, that a shift toward a patient-centered medical approach began to take place and with it physicians' attitudes regarding patients' participation and control of the process were transformed dramatically (Laine & Davidoff, 1996). Paving the way to such transformation was the work of Joseph Fletcher, specifically his book *Morals and Medicine*. Fletcher, a moral theologian whose scholarship is often credited as "a harbinger of future bioethics" (Jonsen, 2003, p. 44), became the president of the ESA in the 1970s. In *Morals and Medicine*, he discusses the central role patients—via a "right to know"—should play in decision-making processes of various natures, including euthanasia: "[W]e shall attempt, as reasonably as may be, to plead the ethical case for our human rights ... to use contraceptives, to seek insemination anonymously from a donor, to be sterilized and to receive a merciful death from a medically competent euthanasiast" (Fletcher, 1954, p. 25). He grounded his arguments on issues of choice and responsibility—later the foundation of "situation ethics"—and tied them to the unprecedented technical advances of those times: "Choice and responsibility are at the heart of ethics and the *sine qua non* of a man's moral status.... The dimensions of our moral responsibility expand, of necessity, with the advances made in medical science and medical technology" (Fletcher, 1954, pp. 10–11).

49. This "wink" policy reemerged in Vermont in 2013, as explained in Chapter 6 of this book.

50. In *Cruzan v. Director, Missouri Department of Health*, 497 U.S. 261 (1990) (Brennan, J., dissenting) (quoting *Rasmussen v. Fleming*, 741 P. 2d 674, 678 (Ariz. 1987) (en banc)).

# In the Courts: 1960s–1990s, the *Quill* and *Glucksberg* Cases

IN THE NEARLY TWO-AND-A-HALF decades that followed the trial and acquittal of Dr. Hermann Sander, no other physician was prosecuted in the United States for involvement in a hastened death. The second such prosecution came in 1974, in Long Island, where Dr. Vincent Montemarano was accused of killing a terminal cancer patient.[1] He was acquitted, as were the other seven doctors who, between the mid-1970s and 1990, faced similar legal charges (for details of each case, see Humphry, 2005).

These *mercy killings* executed by doctors, as well as by relatives and loved ones of irremediably ill individuals, maintained a certain media appeal and continued coverage through the last three decades of the twentieth century.[2] However, between the 1970s and early 1990s, the debate surrounding aid in dying shifted from a focus on *actively* hastening death to *passively* inviting it by removing life-sustaining technology. During the period, the line between life and death and the medical circumstances blurring it increasingly became the topic of legal action in the courts. Often, these cases involved a need to reclaim a *right to die* naturally, as if death had been hijacked by a growing appetite for medicalizing discomfort and an attendant hyper-interventionist system of medical care.

From the early 1990s onward, yet another shift took place. If, until then, medics had been primarily interested in conquering death itself—the ultimate "medical nemesis"[3]—the humbling impossibility of infinite extension of life invited a changing balance between humane care and technological control within the profession. As a result, a number of physicians began asserting their desire to *enable* hastened death when their patients requested assistance in securing lethal medication.

One of them would take on the issue with unprecedented vigor. The highly controversial Jack Kevorkian admitted to aiding over 130 persons to die, many of whom were not terminally ill, most of whom were women, and several of whom were clinically depressed (Roscoe, Malphurs, Dragovic & Cohen, 2000).[4] "Dr. Death," as the retired pathologist was dubbed, was willing to serve as the martyr that Hermann Sander was not.[5] Time and again he was prosecuted for lending his "mercy machines" to dying patients, his trials resulting in acquittal or mistrial. Conviction came only after Kevorkian appeared on the TV show

*60 Minutes*, actually injecting a Lou Gehrig's patient's arm with potassium chloride. At that point, an exasperated judge, Jessica Cooper of Oakland County Circuit Court, addressed the defendant: "You had the audacity to go on national television, show the world what you did and dare the legal system to stop you. Well, sir, consider yourself stopped" (*The New York Times*, Apr. 14, 1999).

If Dr. Death's quixotic strategies attracted wide public attention and dominated the media stage, among conventional medical practitioners the debate on death assistance was led primarily by a group of well-respected physicians who would go on to become central figures in the "medically-assisted suicide" debate. Thus, in 1994, Dr. Timothy Quill, two other prominent medics, and three dying patients brought an action challenging the constitutionality of a New York State statute that proscribed suicide assistance. A few months before, similar efforts had been put in place on the West Coast, where five physicians, three terminally ill patients, and an aid in dying organization had challenged a similar ban in Washington State.[6] These two legal efforts culminated in companion cases argued before the U.S. Supreme Court in 1996—*Vacco v. Quill* and *Washington v. Glucksberg*.

Their (ultimately unsuccessful) quest for a constitutional *right to die* with medical assistance is discussed later. First, however, a discussion of the significant legal, medical, and social turning points in the death and dying arena that preceded the two cases is presented. Of particular importance was an incremental loss of confidence in physicians; the rise in medicine's authority at the moribund's bedside, traced between the discovery of anesthesia in 1847 and its culmination in the hundred years that followed, was slowly eroded from the late 1960s onward. This downswing is addressed next.

## FROM MEDICAL *BENEFICENCE*[7] TO PATIENT SELF-DETERMINATION

The radical transformation in the doctor–patient relationship that took place between the mid-nineteenth century and 1990 can be easily shown by juxtaposing two excerpts:

> Excerpt 1—The obedience of a patient to the prescriptions of his physician should be prompt and implicit. He should never permit his own crude opinions as to their fitness, to influence his attention to them. A failure in one particular may render an otherwise judicious treatment dangerous, and even fatal.
>
> Excerpt 2—The patient has the right to make decisions regarding the health care that is recommended by his or her physician. Accordingly, patients may accept or refuse any recommended medical treatment.

The first, titled "Obligations of Patients to Their Physicians," is from the American Medical Association's *Ethical Code* published in 1847. The second, "Fundamental Elements of the Patient–Physician Relationship," was extracted from the association's revised code of ethics, published in 1990. During the time that elapsed between the writing of these two codes, doctor–patient relationships evolved from a "domineering parent (physician)-submissive child (patient) model" toward an "interaction between two adults" (Quill, 1983, p. 229).

But this change in the model of patient–doctor interactions did not happen abruptly. Instead, the shift reached a *crisis* point in the 1970s, when physicians became technocratic decision-makers, and death, increasingly de-personified. It was then that, gradually, the "submissive child" rebelled. Several explanations have been given for the heightened patient discontent at the time. Hefty health care costs, bureaucratization of the profession, and specialization of physicians are among the most often cited (Betz & O'Connell, 2003). With regard to the dying patient, such discontent stemmed from an unlimited medical mandate to control symptoms, enabled by the application of technical solutions to death. The benevolent physician, who, in the early 1900s, avidly attempted to master pain, was now replaced by a *beneficent* doctor whose purpose was to master death itself.[8]

From the end of World War II onward, modern medicine, and its emphasis on technology, had produced a way of dying that involved segregation of the terminally ill in intensive-care units and a prolonged death process, maintained by respiratory and nourishing tubes and state-of-the-art electronic monitoring. Tethered to machines, by the 1970s most Americans died in hospitals (Centers for Disease Control and Prevention, n.d.), of prolonged deaths resulting from chronic diseases. In the same period, the standard of practice was to attempt resuscitation for virtually every person who died, in contrast to today's standards, whereby resuscitation is attempted for only 10 percent of the seriously ill patients who die in hospitals (*Brief of the American Geriatrics Society as Amicus Curiae Urging Reversal of the Judgments Below [Washington v. Glucksberg*, 1997; *Vacco v. Quill*, 1997]).

Concomitantly, a decline in the moral authority of physicians began to take shape. As doctor–patient relationships became increasingly more specialized, impersonal, and short lived, from 1960 to the 1970s, the sense of trust by patients in their doctors was negatively affected. To illustrate, in 1966, 72 percent of Americans expressed confidence in doctors; by 1975, only 43 percent did so (Betz & O'Connell, 2003). A more nuanced question posed by Gallup revealed that, in 1976, just 39 percent of those surveyed rated the honesty and ethical standards of medical doctors as *high*—seventeen percentage points lower than the most recent poll, conducted in 2012, amidst the *Obamacare* debate (Gallup, Inc., 2012).

New risks associated with the practice of medicine in the 1980s and 1990s also reduced the prestige of the profession. Nationwide, fewer students enrolled in medical schools, preferring instead a career in business (Wlach, 2002). The AIDS epidemic affected the decision of those who were deciding their professional paths and those who had already chosen to become doctors. For example, one contemporaneous survey found that over one third of the medical students and two thirds of the dental students indicated that they did not wish to train in a specialty or hospital with a high percentage of AIDS patients (Bernstein, Rabkin & Wolland, 1990; see also Feldmann, Bell, Stephenson, & Purifoy, 1990). Furthermore, the medical industry's movement toward increased managed care generated a feeling of loss of autonomy for those who were already practicing medicine (Cohen & Hanft, 2004) and a perception of diminished financial gains for those who were considering medicine as a career (Wlach, 2002).

Slowly, terminally ill patients began to object to the highly medicalized context where death was incrementally taking place. That loss of trust in their medical caregivers was coupled with distaste for deferring control over their lives to those who might unduly prolong it. For instance, in 1975, philosopher and theologian Ivan Illich charged the medical system with "[bringing] the epoch of natural death to an end ... as technical death has won its victory over dying" (Illich, 1975, pp. 207–208). A few years later, another trenchant philosophical critique surrounding issues of life and death emerged, this time uncovering the tension between "sanctity of life" and the increasingly accepted notion of "quality of life" (see Singer, 1983).[9]

Besides these intellectual criticisms, which were largely confined to academic realms, the latter half of the 1970s also saw an increasing number of challenges to medical authority through the actions of health-related social movements. In *The Social Transformation of American Medicine*, Paul Starr (1984) reasons that during the 1970s activists were championing the interests of many constituencies vis-à-vis medicine (women, the handicapped, mental patients, medical research subjects, and so on) thereby pressing for rights for and within health care, which ultimately contributed to the decline of medicine's uncontested legitimacy.

Benefitting from the momentum generated by the civil rights struggle a few years prior, the catalogue of rights and groups entitled to such rights expanded in both variety and detail in the 1970s. "Medical care," Starr argues, "figured prominently in this generalization of rights, particularly in the ... new movements specifically for patients' rights" (Starr, 1984, p. 388). If the civil rights movement made history by marching through the streets, assisted-death activists of that time marched to the courts and legislatures in an attempt to hammer out policy that granted Americans a "right to die" naturally. The next section addresses the legislative enactments and judicial decisions that came to light between the 1970s and 1980s.

## LETTING DIE: THE 1970s–1980s

The cultural unrest of the 1960s and the increased decay of the "golden age" of doctoring set the stage for a series of legal victories the proponents of legalization chalked up during the 1970s. By 1970, 60,000 living wills had been distributed by the Euthanasia Society of America.[10] By 1973, as the country ascertained the limits of a "right to life," activists had successfully framed the assisted death issue in terms of a self-determination issue, or a "right to die" (particularly in the context of what is commonly referred to as "passive euthanasia"). That same year, the American Hospital Association adopted a *Patients' Bill of Rights* for the first time, which included informed consent and the right to refuse treatment. The number of circulated living wills had by then quadrupled (Ekland-Olson, 2013).

Assisted death proponents benefitted tremendously from the milestones carved by the women's movement in the 1960s. Landmark cases such as *Roe v. Wade* and *Griswold v. Connecticut*—similarly fueled by "feminist calls for the end of medical paternalism" (Dowbiggin, 2003, p. 115)—at once asserted women's reproductive rights via a privacy rationale and provided the foundation that would later give basis to one of the most significant achievements of the assisted-death movement—the *Quinlan* decision.[11]

In 1976, the case of Karen Ann Quinlan—a 21-year-old woman reduced to a persistent vegetative state with no hope of recovering consciousness—imposed on the New Jersey Supreme Court the task of determining the parameters of when life-sustaining treatment can be withdrawn from incurable patients and by whom the terminal decision can be made. That court was the first to find that the constitutional right to privacy (as asserted in the *Griswold* decision and reaffirmed in *Roe*) was broad enough to encompass a person's decision to decline life-sustaining treatment in certain circumstances and that such a decision could be made by a surrogate when the patient is incompetent. In the years that followed, many other courts mirrored the New Jersey decision in finding a patient's *right to die* by declining life-sustaining treatment.[12]

While New Jersey looked to the courts for guidance in determining patients' rights and the role of surrogates in end-of-life decision-making, other states were exploring the legislative path to accomplish something similar. Concomitantly to *Quinlan*, California passed the first American living will statute, the *Natural Death Act*, which gave adults residing in that state the "fundamental right to control the decisions relating to the rendering of their own medical care, including the decision to have life-sustaining procedures withheld or withdrawn in instances of a terminal condition" (*Natural Death Act*, 1976).

The rationale informing the *Act* was not much different from the *Quinlan* decision in that the legislature recognized that patients have a right to expect dignity and privacy in end-of-life treatment. The *Act's* impact was also just as pervasive. In two years, 40 states had proposed similar legislation, and 10 years after its passage in California, 39 of those states and the federal district had enacted living will statutes.

The contours of two other significant developments in the death and dying emerged between the 1970s and 1980s and testify to a change in attitudes and to the establishment of assisted death as a cause for activism. For one, the origins of the Hospice movement date back to those times. The first American hospice opened in Connecticut in 1974 as a result of pioneering efforts by Cicely

Saunders—a prominent British nurse and physician—and psychiatrist Elisabeth Kübler-Ross. As new institutions of palliative care, these early hospices "arose as sanctuaries from traditional hospitals" (Hallenbeck, 2003, p. 4).

Secondly, proponents of assisted death decidedly distanced themselves from the *euthanasia* cause and expanded their constituency to a global level. In this sense, also in 1974, the *Euthanasia Society* renamed itself as *Society for the Right to Die*. Six years later, an effort to consolidate activism globally resulted in the foundation of the *World Federation of Right to Die Societies* (WFRDS), which at the time included a Japanese chapter, as well as societies in Australia, the Netherlands,[13] the United Kingdom, and the United States.

Alongside its international growth, activist organizations were also diversifying domestically. If until the late 1960s the *Euthanasia Society of America* was the only pro-legalization organization in the United States, by 1980 at least one other nonprofit had been formed to promote the cause from the ground up. The *Hemlock Society*, founded in California by Derek Humphry,[14] quickly became a pragmatic vanguard organization as it circumvented legislatures and took the issue directly to voters.

The first state targeted by the Hemlock Society was California. In 1986, the society unveiled its first legalization proposal, the *Humane and Dignified Death Act*—a ballot initiative that would amend the state's constitution to allow for "aid in dying," defined as "any medical procedure that will terminate the life of a qualified patient swiftly, painlessly, and humanely" (International Task Force, 1996–2009). The campaign came to an end in 1988 as advocates failed to gather the necessary voter signatures and the proposition was not introduced.

The key difference between these efforts and the legal victories granted in *Quinlan*, other like cases, and living will statutes is the fact that the Hemlock Society's activities heralded a new era in which activists were ready to move beyond the demand of a "right to die" through withdrawal of medical intervention and onto a claims-making era of affirmative hastened death within a medical context. Two factors might have contributed to such readiness. Public support for the issue was at its peak. According to Roper Polls commissioned in 1986 and 1988, 62 percent and 58 percent of Americans (respectively) answered affirmatively when asked the following question: "When a person has a painful and distressing terminal disease do you think doctors should or should not be allowed by law to end the patient's life if there is no hope of recovery and the patient requests it?" (*Hemlock Quarterly 24*, July 1986; *Hemlock Quarterly 32*, July 1988).

Moreover, the debate in the academic medical realm was becoming increasingly publicized. Though one can suspect that physicians' assistance in hastening patients' death is far from a novel practice—the mere existence of an ancient code proscribing it suggests its existence—rarely did doctors come forth confessing their involvement in such instances. When they did, as discussed in the previous chapter, the debate about the appropriateness of assisted death tended to take place in the media, and not necessarily in medical bulletins.

This changed in the late 1980s when the reputable *Journal of the American Medical Association* published "It's Over, Debbie"—an account written by an anonymous gynecologist who had administered a lethal dose of morphine to a terminal cancer patient. Defending the essay's publication, which was met with profuse criticism by other physicians and by the *American Medical Association* itself (Garrett, 1998), the *Journal's* editor, Dr. George Lundberg, explained the pedagogical effect of the piece by pointing out that "[s]uch discussions should not be confined to whispers in doctors' dressing rooms and hallways" (Garrett, 1988, pp. 2142–2143).[15]

Three years later, another doctor presented a case-based argument supporting physician-assisted death for terminally ill patients. Dr. Timothy Quill's article, published in the *New England Journal of Medicine*, openly discussed his role in assisting in one of his terminally ill patients' death. Quill's efforts to legalize physicians' assistance in hastening death culminated in one of the movement's central legal battles. Before we get to Quill's eventual journey to the Supreme Court, in part prompted by his confession in the *Journal*, we turn to the larger context of legal attempts—and victories—in which proponents of hastened death engaged in the 1990s.

## DYING WITH DIGNITY: THE 1990s AND BEYOND

Though medically assisted death has been legally permitted in five states since the 1990s (Oregon, Washington, Montana, New Mexico, and Vermont), these were equally turbulent times for proponents. For one, as discussed later, the milestone achieved with the passage of the *Oregon Death with Dignity Act* was not without struggle, and effective legal diffusion to other states took as long as a decade.

Secondly, in the past 20 years or so, proponents' legal efforts were hindered from within and from without. Radical actions by figures from within the pro-legalization realm—such as those of Jack Kevorkian—were as troublesome for activists as was the moral link successfully drawn by Right-to-Life activists between assisted death and abortion.[16] At the same time, hospice and palliative care grew in popularity as a more temperate end-of-life choice, especially since its inclusion as a Medicare benefit in the mid-1980s, thereby increasing skepticism toward the need to have assisted death as a legal option.[17]

Roughly a decade and a half after the New Jersey decision in *Quinlan*, the U.S. Supreme Court confronted a similar question in *Cruzan v. Director, Missouri Department of Health*.[18] Nancy Cruzan was 25 years old when she was injured in an automobile accident and left in a persistent vegetative state. Four years later, her parents requested physicians to remove the feeding tube that kept her alive. Citing a Missouri law that required "clear and convincing" evidence that a person in such condition would have wanted to forgo life-sustaining therapy, the doctors refused to remove the tube and the family sued the hospital and the state's Department of Health.

As evidence of their daughter's desire, the parents offered a statement Nancy had made to a friend, according to which "she would not wish to continue her life unless she could live at least halfway normally" (Irons, 2006, p. 503). Though the trial court ruled in Cruzan's favor, the decision was later reversed in the state's high court, which held that the friend's statement did not meet Missouri's "clear and convincing" standard. The U.S. Supreme Court ultimately ruled that while a competent person has a constitutionally protected right to refuse lifesaving hydration and nutrition, such a right is balanced by the state's interest in preserving life. In that case, the court decided that Missouri's evidentiary rule was not an undue burden on the right to refuse life-sustaining therapy. The case was remanded, and only after three other of Nancy's acquaintances came forth with similar statements about her wishes did a judge allow removal of the feeding tube. She died a few days later.

If court decisions such as this were celebrated by activists as a "significant triumph for the 'right to die' movement," it was equally acknowledged as "a disaster for the Cruzan family" (Concern for Dying, 1990, p. 1). During the 1990s, this distinction between end-of-life decision-making as a private act versus its potential status as public policy finally went beyond "passive euthanasia," Do-Not-Resuscitate Orders, and health proxy procedural regulations, to fully include a candid discussion of "assisted suicide" and "active euthanasia" by key policymakers.

One such example is the New York Task Force on Life and the Law, convened in 1984 by Governor Mario Cuomo to recommend public policy on issues raised by medical advances. Though the Task Force's original mandate did not include euthanasia and assisted suicide, in one author's words, "the level of societal agitation about [these topics]" justified such extension (Stephens, 1995, p. 320) and in 1994 a final report was published.

In their *When Death Is Sought: Assisted Suicide and Euthanasia in the Medical Context*, the Task Force on Life and the Law (1994) recommended that New York laws prohibiting assisted suicide and euthanasia should not be changed and that focus should be placed instead on palliative care and pain relief for terminal patients. Though the well-balanced composition of the Task Force's membership included diverse views on whether assisted suicide is inherently immoral or incompatible with medical practice, the report was unanimous in concluding that even "ethical, compassionate actions by thoughtful individuals in some cases cannot be translated into good public policy." "Assisted suicide and euthanasia," members argued, "would carry us into new terrain" (1994, p. 2).

That same year Oregon seemed ready to tread into that "new terrain" and become the first American state to allow physicians to prescribe lethal doses of medication to end a terminally ill patient's life. *Ballot Measure 16*, which brought into effect the *Oregon Death with Dignity Act*, was approved by 51.3 percent of voters in the general elections of 1994. The *Act* established that adult Oregon residents whose life expectancy had been estimated to be six (or fewer) months by at least two physicians would be able to voluntarily request a prescription for lethal drugs. The *Act* granted health care providers the right to refuse to participate and allowed patients to choose whether to notify their friends and family. Safeguards built into the *Act* included a 15-day waiting period, two oral and one written request by the patient, and counseling for those with impaired judgment from depression.

However, the provisions of the *Act* were soon halted by a legal battle that dragged out for years, thereby keeping aid in dying illegal in Oregon until 1997. Attempts to repeal the measure began in the courts shortly after the elections. A decision in *Lee v. Oregon*, a lawsuit filed by the National Right to Life Committee days after the passage of *Measure 16*, granted plaintiffs an injunction on grounds that the *Act* violated the Constitution's Equal Protection Clause. The District Court found in *Lee* that the *Oregon Death with Dignity Act* "provided insufficient safeguards to prevent an incompetent (i.e., depressed), terminally-ill adult from committing suicide, thereby irrationally depriving terminally-ill adults of safeguards against suicide provided to adults who are not terminally ill" (*Lee v. Oregon*, 1995). The injunction was not lifted until 1997, when the Ninth Circuit of Appeals dismissed the lawsuit and the U.S. Supreme Court denied the plaintiff's request for review. The first death under the *Act* happened in March 1998.

Concomitantly to court efforts, other attempts to repeal the *Oregon Death with Dignity Act* were put in place by opponents to legalization, particularly the Oregonian Right to Life chapter and the Oregon's Catholic Conference. These two organizations lobbied the Oregon State Legislature to introduce *Measure 51* in the ballot of the 1997 statewide special elections. If successful, *Measure 51* would have supplanted *Measure 16*; it was unequivocally defeated, with 60 percent of voters against the abrogation of the previously approved measure.

The *Act* would come under attack again in 2000, when the Bush administration "mounted an effort to block Oregon's doctors from prescribing lethal medications that were 'controlled substances' under federal law" (Irons, 2006, p. 507). Attorney General John Ashcroft[19] sued the state seeking to revoke the licenses of physicians who used these drugs to assist their patients in hastening their deaths. The case was argued before the U.S. Supreme Court and, in 2006, the court upheld Oregon's law (*Gonzales v. Oregon*, 2006). In 2008, ten years after the *Act's* enactment, 88 prescriptions were written for lethal doses of medication, compared to 24 prescriptions in the first year the law was in place; overall, a total of 401 patients had died under the terms of the *Act* (Department of Human Services, 2008).

## A CONSTITUTIONAL RIGHT TO DIE? *QUILL* AND *GLUCKSBERG*

During the years in which Oregon's *Death with Dignity Act* was enjoined, pro-legalization campaigners actively supported and sponsored legal efforts in Washington and New York. A few months before *Measure 16* was introduced in Oregon, *Compassion in Dying*, then one of the principal social movement organizations promoting aid in dying, joined Dr. Harold Glucksberg, four other physicians, and three terminally ill patients in a lawsuit challenging a Washington statute proscribing assisted suicide (*Compassion in Dying v. State of Washington,* 1994).[20] A related challenge began that same year in New York, where Dr. Timothy Quill, joined by two other physicians and three patients *in extremis,* disputed a similar ban (*Quill v. Koppell,* 1994).

Largely funded by *Compassion in Dying,*[21] a pro-aid in dying organization and plaintiff in one of the cases, these physicians and their irremediably ill patients went to court. Suffering the harrowing symptoms associated with their terminal conditions, these patients were deemed mentally competent and wished to "commit suicide by taking physician-prescribed drugs" (*Compassion in Dying v. State of Washington,* 1994, p. 1457). The doctors in the suit regularly treated terminally ill patients, had been asked more than once for help in hastened deaths, and believed that medically assisted suicide was consistent with their professional standards.

## Patients and Doctors

Washington patient-plaintiffs were identified by pseudonyms—Jane Roe, John Doe, and James Poe. Roe, a 69-year-old retired pediatrician, had been fighting breast cancer since 1988. The tumors had now metastasized to her bones and she had been referred to hospice care. Bedridden for months at that point, Roe suffered from bedsores, incontinence, lack of appetite, and acute nausea, and the pain resulting from her cancer was not adequately alleviated by medication.[22]

Doe was a 44-year-old artist dying of AIDS. Nearly blind, he had lost the ability to paint due to a degenerative disease associated with his terminal condition. Doe had been the primary caregiver to his long-term partner, who died of AIDS two years before. Since his diagnosis in 1991, he had experienced two bouts of pneumonia; chronic, severe skin and sinus infections; seizures; and extreme fatigue.

Poe, a 69-year-old retired salesman, experienced a constant sensation of suffocation due to emphysema. Connected to an oxygen tank at all times, Poe needed regular intake of morphine to ameliorate the sensation of panic associated with his feeling of suffocation. He also suffered from heart failure; as a result of the poor circulation caused by that condition, Poe's legs were in constant, severe pain. Roe, Poe, and Doe had sought advice from *Compassion in Dying* regarding their end-of-life options.

Doe, Roe, and Poe were joined by five physicians, all of whom had been asked by dying patients for lethal medication to hasten death and were deterred—not by the Hippocratic Oath, but by the Washington statute. "It's deterred me," commented Dr. Thomas Preston, a cardiologist who routinely treated terminally ill individuals and one of the plaintiffs (Ostrom, 1994a). "I've had patients plead with me, and I've not done it. And I feel cowardly about it," he added. Preston was joined by Dr. Abigail Halperin, a family practitioner who occasionally treated AIDS and cancer patients. Dr. Halperin had declined a request made by a breast cancer patient for assistance in hastening her death. Shortly after, the patient had used a plastic bag to suffocate herself.

Other physicians in the suit had seen similar violent outcomes following their rejection of patients' requests for aid in dying. Dr. Harold Glucksberg, an oncologist and Professor of Medicine at the University of Washington, denied repeated requests by one of his dying patients suffering from AIDS-related lymphoma. The patient had refused aggressive pain management because "he did not wish to die in a hospital in a drug-induced stupor" and as a result had been "enduring four excruciatingly painful months" because of his illness (*Compassion in Dying v. Washington*, 1996, p. 834). His solution was to jump from the West Seattle Bridge. "Fortunately," his doctor explained, "he did not survive the plunge and [thus did not] require permanent hospitalization in an even more exacerbated state of pain." Another physician-plaintiff, Dr. John Geyman,[23] Professor Emeritus of Family Medicine at the University of Washington, echoed the concerns about extended, humiliating death processes that result in violent suicide attempts—often botched.

Besides the gruesome suicide alternatives to which dying patients resort in the absence of legal medically assisted death, one doctor explained that the prolonged, harrowing death process experienced by terminally ill patients also had alienating effects on the families. In his declaration to the courts, Dr. Peter Shalit, an internal medicine specialist who treats individuals with AIDS, recounted how one of his patients' "oozing Kaposi's lesions," "gangrenous fingers," and inability to urinate created a scene of such horror that family members refused to visit because they could not tolerate observing their loved one's "torture" (*Compassion in Dying v. Washington*, 1996).

New York patient-plaintiffs shared the same underlying illnesses as those killing the ones in Washington—cancer and AIDS. They were also mentally competent and wished to hasten their deaths with legally prescribed drugs, "if and when . . . suffering becomes intolerable" (*Quill v. Vacco*, 1996, p. 720).

Jane Doe, a 76-year-old retired physical education instructor, was dying of thyroid cancer. The tumor, she explained in her declaration to the courts, was "collapsing [her] esophagus and invading [her] voice box" thereby diminishing her ability to swallow. Since the cancer's metastasis to her pleural cavity, it had become painful to yawn or cough and the medication to ameliorate the pain rendered her lethargic (*Quill v. Vacco*, 1996, p. 720).

The other two patients in the claim against the New York assisted suicide ban were dying of AIDS. George Kingsley, then 48 years old, was a publishing executive.[24] Like Washington's John Doe, Kingsley was nearly blind from an AIDS-related virus. Due to a permanent Hickman tube connected to his artery to deliver medication, Kingsley could not take showers and simple daily routines had become burdensome. Other required, daily injections of medicine designed to increase his white cell counts were described by Kingsley as very painful.

Finally, William Barth, a 28-year-old former fashion editor, shared with the courts the variety of medical treatments he had undergone to improve the symptoms of diseases he had acquired due to his frail immune system. Kaposi's sarcoma (a type of opportunistic cancer affecting the skin), cytomegalovirus (an opportunistic herpes virus), microsporidiosis (a parasitic infection), cryptosporidiosis (another parasitic infection), pneumonia, and other conditions had affected Barth since his infection with the HIV virus and he was "unwilling to accept this for an extended period of time" (*Quill v. Vacco*, 1996, p. 721).

To his physician, Dr. Howard Grossman, William Barth was known simply as "Willy" (France, 1997). Like many other AIDS patients,[25] when the pain became intractable, Willy sought Grossman's assistance in securing a "certain" and "humane" death by lethal prescriptions (*Quill v. Vacco*, 1996, p. 720). Grossman was a general internist who specialized in HIV/AIDS. Remarking on the harrowing dying process that accompanied his AIDS patients, he told a reporter: "AIDS docs are a different breed.... We have dealt with a lot more death in a lot more intense way, over a concentrated period of time.... I'm [42 years old]; I'm not supposed to have twenty boxes full of dead-patient charts" (France, 1997, p. 26).

Deterred by the assisted-suicide statute, Dr. Grossman joined his patient in the legal complaint.[26] Jane Doe's similar requests to her physician, Dr. Samuel Klagsbrun, also prompted him to join the suit. Dr. Klagsbrun was a psychiatrist with specialization in cancer as well as a professor of clinical psychology at Albert Einstein College of Medicine.[27]

Klagsbrun and Grossman's involvement in the legal action in New York is owed in part to *Pulitzer Prize* finalist, Larry Kramer. Widely known for his many novels and plays, Kramer is also a vigorous AIDS activist. HIV positive himself, Kramer had been helping *Compassion in Dying* in their search for allies in New York State to file a suit in the East Coast similar to the one they had begun in Washington (France, 1997). He enlisted Dr. Grossman, "an old friend," who discussed the case with many patients and Willie expressed his wish to be involved (Grossman, 1997). Kramer also enrolled his own therapist, Dr. Klagsbrun.[28]

By the time Grossman and Klagsbrun were recruited, George Kingsley's primary-care doctor, Dr. Timothy Quill, had been approached by *Compassion in Dying* to serve as the lead plaintiff in the New York suit. Quill's advocacy for hastened death had begun years earlier, when he published in the prestigious *New England Journal of Medicine* a sensitive account about his assistance in the suicide of 45-year-old "Diane," one of his longtime patients who was suffering from leukemia. It was the attention garnered by that article that motivated *Compassion's* leaders to seek Quill's help in the New York suit (Gross, 1997). In the essay, the doctor disclosed his agony over what to do when "Diane" expressed her wish to die, how he had suggested that she seek help from a right-to-die organization, and the extent of his involvement:

> [Diane] phoned me with a request for barbiturates for sleep. Since I knew that this was an essential ingredient in a Hemlock Society suicide, I asked her to come to

the office to talk things over. She was more than willing to protect me by participating in a superficial conversation about her insomnia, but it was important to me to know how she planned to use the drugs and to be sure that she was not in despair or overwhelmed in a way that might color her judgment. In our discussion, it was apparent that she was having trouble sleeping, but it was also evident that the security of having enough barbiturates available to commit suicide when and if the time came would leave her secure enough to live fully and concentrate on the present. It was clear that she was not despondent and that in fact she was making deep, personal connections with her family and close friends. I made sure that she knew how to use the barbiturates for sleep, and also that she knew the amount needed to commit suicide. (Quill, 1991, p. 691)

Following the publication of the essay, criminal justice officials traced the patient's name and an autopsy was performed, confirming death by overdose of barbiturates—and not acute leukemia, as her death certificate asserted.[29] A grand jury was convened to decide whether Quill should be prosecuted for aiding in Diane's suicide—a crime punishable by up to four years in prison in New York State. The grand jury declined to indict him. The district attorney did not seem surprised: "[T]hese are very difficult cases because the law is in conflict with people's perception of the right to die" (*NYT*, Mar. 7, 1991).

Three years after Quill's failed prosecution for his involvement in Diane's death, the two cases orchestrated by *Compassion in Dying* in Washington and New York were filed. Their claims are as follows.

## Plaintiffs' Claims, Initial Legal Decisions, and Appeals

The claims made by the plaintiffs were similar in both cases.[30] Drawing heavily on the U.S. Supreme Court decisions in *Cruzan*, summarized earlier, and *Planned Parenthood of Southeastern Pennsylvania v. Casey*, they asserted that the state criminal laws in Washington and New York that prohibited physicians from providing assistance in dying violated the equality and liberty rights guaranteed by the Fourteenth Amendment, via its Equal Protection and Due Process clauses.

Simply put, the patients argued that it was unreasonable to allow terminally ill individuals to hasten their deaths by withdrawing life-sustaining treatment, as sealed by the decision in *Cruzan*, while prohibiting a hastened death by ingestion of medication. They contended that this distinction was "irrational" and ultimately inequitable: If a few terminally ill patients could decide to die by having a respirator or feeding tube removed, while others, who were terminally ill but not dependent on life support could not, such a distinction amounted to discrimination against the latter group of dying patients (*Quill v. Koppell*, 1994; *Compassion in Dying v. State of Washington, 1994*).

Furthermore, the patients argued that the decision they were facing—whether to succumb to the harrowing symptoms of their terminal diagnoses or choose to control the time and manner of their deaths—was deeply personal. New York and Washington States' absolute ban on *assisted suicide* therefore amounted to undue governmental interference in their ability to make that choice freely, with the help of a physician. They asserted that personal decisions relating, for instance, to marriage, procreation, family relationships, contraception, and education had a longstanding constitutional protection. *Planned Parenthood of Southern Pennsylvania v. Casey*, where the Supreme Court revisited the abortion issue and upheld *Roe v. Wade*, was instructive—plaintiffs claimed. As explained in *Casey*,

> these matters, involving the most intimate and personal choices a person may make in a lifetime, choices central to personal dignity and autonomy, are central to the liberty protected by the Fourteenth Amendment. At the heart of liberty is the right to define one's own existence, of meaning, of the universe, and of the mystery of human life. Beliefs about these matters could not define the attributes of personhood were they formed under compulsion of the State. (*Planned Parenthood of Southeastern PA v. Casey*, 1992, p. 851)

Patient-plaintiffs hoped to persuade the court that like the decision to terminate a pregnancy, the decision by a hopelessly ill patient to terminate his or her life is among "the most intimate and personal choices a person may make in a lifetime," and "central to personal dignity and autonomy."[31]

Meanwhile, the New York doctors argued that the state statute banning "assisted suicide"—under which Quill could have been fully prosecuted if the grand jury had so determined—hindered their ability to practice medicine according to their best professional judgment, which included prescribing lethal medication for terminally ill patients. They argued that because their patients presumably had a constitutionally protected right to terminate their lives, they also had a corresponding constitutional right to be free from prosecution for rendering assistance on those occasions. Washington physicians made an identical claim (*Compassion in Dying v. Washington,* 1994).

The states, in both cases, defended that laws criminalizing assisted suicide served several purposes. Primarily, the statutes advanced the government's general interest in preserving life, a specific interest in suicide prevention and protection of those at risk of suicide from undue influence and abuse, and an interest in protecting the integrity of the medical profession. Washington and New York also asserted the distinction between *natural* and *artificial* death, in order to distinguish between life-support-dependent terminally ill individuals and those who were dying but did not depend on respirators and such.[32]

Although the cases emerging in Washington and New York were virtually identical, the lower courts' decisions in each were contradictory. In the West Coast, the U.S. District Court for the Western District of Washington held that the state law at issue was unconstitutional. In her opinion, Chief Judge Barbara Rothstein reasoned:

> This court is well aware of the ... divisive controversy about the appropriateness of suicide by the terminally ill. But the underlying constitutional issue is whether the State of Washington can resolve the profound spiritual and moral questions surrounding the end of life in so conclusive a fashion as to deny categorically any option for a terminally ill, mentally competent person to commit physician-assisted suicide. This court concludes that the suffering of a terminally ill person cannot be deemed any less intimate or personal, or any less deserving of protection from unwarranted governmental interference than that of a pregnant woman. (*Compassion in Dying v. State of Washington,* 1994, p. 1460)

The court also could not find a differentiation between the refusal of life-sustaining treatment and the request for assisted suicide by patients who were mentally competent adults, doing so voluntarily. By creating an exception for terminal patients on life support to hasten their deaths while denying "the equivalent option" to all dying patients, Washington's law infringed the fundamental rights of those who, albeit dying, did not need life-sustaining technology (*Compassion in Dying v. State of Washington.* 1994, p. 1467).

In the East Coast, however, the U.S. District Court for the Southern District of New York upheld the legality of the statutes, holding thus that patients do not have a fundamental right to physician-assisted suicide. Unlike the case emerging from Washington, in New York the court validated the state's distinction between "allowing nature to take its course" and the intentional use "of an artificial death-producing device" by reasoning that suicide evokes a different legal significance than refusing medical treatment. Furthermore, while the court recognized constitutional protections for many personal decisions as central to the liberty enshrined by the Fourteenth Amendment, it determined that precedent failed to establish such a right under the constitution. Particularly, the court reasoned that Quill et al. had "pointed to nothing in the historical record to indicate that [physician-assisted suicide] has been given any kind of sanction in our legal history which would help establish it as a constitutional right" (*Quill v. Koppell,* 1994, p. 84).

The state appealed in Washington, whereas Dr. Quill et al. appealed the federal court decision in New York. In 1996, the two cases were decided by the (*en banc*) Ninth and Second Courts of Appeals, favoring the physicians and other plaintiffs, and thus asserting, in essence, a constitutional right to physician-assisted suicide.[33]

The Court of Appeals for the Ninth Circuit, commenting on how the case in hand "raise[d] an extraordinarily important and difficult issue," one that compelled the court to "address questions to which there are no easy or simple answers, at law or otherwise," found that "a liberty interest in controlling the time and manner of one's death is protected by the Due Process Clause of the Fourteenth Amendment" (*Compassion in Dying v. Washington,* 1996, p. 816). The court emphasized one final point:

> Some argue strongly that decisions regarding matters affecting life or death should not be made by the courts. Essentially, we agree with that proposition. In this case,

by permitting the individual to exercise the right to choose we are following the constitutional mandate to take such decisions out of the hands of the government, both state and federal, and to put them where they rightly belong, in the hands of the people.

We are allowing individuals to make the decisions that so profoundly affect their very existence—and precluding the state from intruding excessively into that critical realm. The Constitution and the courts stand as a bulwark between individual freedom and arbitrary and intrusive governmental power. Under our constitutional system, neither the state nor the majority of the people in a state can impose its will upon the individual in a matter so highly "central to personal dignity and autonomy."

Those who believe strongly that death must come without physician assistance are free to follow that creed, be they doctors or patients. They are not free, however, to force their views, their religious convictions, or their philosophies on all the other members of a democratic society, and to compel those whose values differ with theirs to die painful, protracted, and agonizing deaths. (*Compassion in Dying v. Washington,* 1996, p. 839)

The Court of Appeals for the Second Circuit by contrast focused its legal analysis on the Equal Protection clause. It found that the distinction between life-supported dying patients and those who, albeit terminal, were not tethered to machines, was invalid. The court reasoned that the discontinuance of life-sustaining processes or their refusal allows patients to hasten deaths "by means that are not natural in any sense" (*Quill v. Vacco,* 1996, p. 729). There is "nothing 'natural' [about] causing death by means other than the original illness and its complications," and as the court noted "the withdrawal of nutrition brings on death by starvation, the withdrawal of hydration brings on death by dehydration, and the withdrawal of ventilation brings about respiratory failure" (*Quill v. Vacco,* 1996, p. 729). Furthermore, the court added, writing a lethal prescription to be taken by the patient involves a far less active role for doctors than it is required of them when excising equipment designed to maintain vital nourishment and/or respiration. "Physicians do not fulfill the role of 'killer' by prescribing drugs to hasten death any more than they do by disconnecting life-support systems" (*Quill v. Vacco,* 1996, p. 730). In weighing the state's general interest in preserving life, the court charged: "What interest can the State possibly have in requiring the prolongation of a life that is all but ended? . . . What business is it of the State to require the continuation of agony when the result is imminent and inevitable?" (*Quill v. Vacco,* 1996, p. 730).

Although the legal vantage points of the two appellate courts differed, they each unequivocally agreed that states could not outlaw the practice of assisted suicide entirely. Arguing that hastened death "is a watershed issue of public policy that requires the review and analysis of our nation's highest court," Washington's Attorney General Christine Gregoire[34] announced her state would appeal (*The Seattle Times,* Mar. 25, 1996). Likewise, New York State's Attorney General Dennis Vacco issued a statement denouncing the Second Circuit Court decision as a chilling precedent. In allowing medically assisted suicide, the court was giving "those who swear an oath to preserve life a license to kill" (Bruni, 1996).

## The Supreme Court Decisions

Soon after, the U.S. Supreme Court granted certiorari. On June 26, 1997—curiously only a couple of weeks following Oregon Legislature's decision to refer *Measure 51* to the special election's ballot—the high court handed down its judgment in the companion cases *Washington v. Glucksberg* and *Vacco v. Quill*. In a pair of 9-0 decisions,[35] the Supreme Court reversed the appellate courts' judgments and ruled that neither the Washington nor the New York ban infringed upon a fundamental right.

### Deep roots, autonomy, and the state's interests

In *Washington v. Glucksberg*, the court began by examining a history of suicide law in that state and throughout the country, noting that assisting in a suicide was a crime in 44 states, the District of Columbia, and two territories. As discussed in Chapter 4, those assisted-suicide bans, mostly dating from the nineteenth century, had remained on the books even after suicide itself and attempted suicide had been decriminalized. After reviewing the historical legal record, the court concluded that such a right to physician-assisted suicide was not "deeply rooted in this Nation's history and tradition" (521 U.S. 728, quoting *Moore v. City of East Cleveland, Ohio*, 431 U.S. 494, 503 [1977]).

The court also acknowledged that several proposals to decriminalize medical aid in dying, via legislative and direct democracy processes, had been introduced in numerous states in recent years. However, the opinion pointed out that these pro-legalization attempts were continually rejected—including in the state of Washington, in 1991.[36] Although the court recognized that attitudes toward suicide had changed in the past century, it was unconvinced that it should depart from centuries of well-settled tradition.[37]

The court then focused on the Due Process claim. It refuted the logical analogy between *Casey* and *Cruzan* proposed by Dr. Glucksberg and the other physicians. The liberty interest inferred from *Cruzan*, the court instructed, was rooted in the nation's longstanding legal doctrine that equated coerced treatment to battery. In regards to *Casey*, the court explained that not all "important, intimate, and personal decisions" are sheltered by the Due Process Clause just by virtue of the fact that most liberties and rights have their roots in personal autonomy (521 U.S. 727). Thus, it concluded, the "right to assistance in committing suicide" is not constitutionally protected. Finally, the court found that the assisted suicide ban in Washington implicated a number of legitimate government interests, such as preserving life and preventing suicide, preserving the integrity of the medical profession, protecting the vulnerable, and preventing a "slippery slope" toward involuntary hastened death.

*All dying patients are equal, but some . . .*

In *Vacco v. Quill*, the Supreme Court maintained that all competent persons have a right to refuse lifesaving treatments, but that this right is not the same as suicide—a distinction long recognized by both medical and legal professions. Relying on the legal principle of causation, the court reasoned that there is a difference between *letting* a patient die, that is, allowing nature to take its course, and *making* a patient die. This distinction, said the court, is "important, logical, and well-established" (117 SCt 2293). An analysis from the legal perspective of "intent" also proved particularly relevant to the court. The physician who excises life-support machinery from a patient's body per his or her request is merely honoring the patient's right to bodily integrity. The doctor's intent, in these cases, is "only to respect his patient's wishes and to cease doing useless and futile or degrading things to the patient when [the patient] no longer stands to benefit from them" (521 U.S. 801, 802). Furthermore, the court equaled the intent involved in withdrawal of support to the "double effect" doctrine (see Chapter 3 for a discussion). When a physician engages in aggressive palliative care, the drugs employed may produce patient's death, but physician's intent is only to ease pain. By contrast, a "doctor who assists a suicide must, necessarily and indubitably, intend primarily that the patient be made dead." Finding grounds on these two principles of *causation* and *intent*, the court contended that New York's statute criminalizing assisted suicide was defensible.

*Glucksberg* and *Quill* were considered by the Supreme Court in a context of heightened public concern and democratic action regarding hastened death. Contemporaneous opinion polls, for instance, both among the general public and medics, by and large showed significant support for the practice (Blendon & Szalay, 1992; Bachman et al., 1996). A growing number of physicians were admitting involvement in suicide assistance or represented their willingness in engaging in it (Back et al., 1996). Though still under injunction, Oregon had passed its *Death with Dignity Act* via democratic process, while referenda in Washington State and California had been narrowly defeated. Even Jack Kevorkian's unusual tactics had, at that point in time, yet to garner him unfavorable legal outcomes, with juries refusing to convict him for his "medicides" (see Rodick, 2007). The intensity of public interest in the case can be verified by the number of *amici curiae* briefs submitted to the court.[38] In the federal cases, 60 *amici curiae* briefs were filed by diverse interest groups, governmental agencies, physical and mental health providers, religious organizations, academics, philosophers, individual practitioners, and such. Forty-one of them sided with New York and Washington States, whereas the remaining 19 supported decriminalization.[39]

The reaction to the rulings was just as vocal. For example, in an official statement released on the day the decisions were published, President Bill Clinton[40] reasserted his long opposition to the practice:

I believe [assisted suicide] is wrong and I have always believed it to be wrong. The issue is unavoidably heart-rendering, and we must never ignore the agony of the terminally ill patients, but the Supreme Court made the right decision today. The risks and consequences of physician-assisted suicide are simply too great. (National Archives and Records Administration, 1999, p. 830)

## Table 5.1  Timeline: 1970–1990s (Selected Developments)

| | |
|---|---|
| 1970 | The *Euthanasia Society of America* distributes 60,000 "Living Wills." |
| 1973 | *Patient Bill of Rights* is created. |
| 1976 | New Jersey: *Quinlan* is decided.<br>California: *Natural Death Act* is enacted. |
| 1980 | Pope John Paul II issues the Church's *Declaration on Euthanasia.* |
| 1986 | California: Ballot measure drafted but not introduced due to failure to gather enough signatures (*Humane and Dignified Act*). |
| 1988 | *It's Over, Debbie*, an anonymous confession by a resident doctor describing a lethal injection given to a patient is published in the *Journal of the American Medical Association.* |
| 1990 | Timothy Quill's account of assisting a patient to die is published in the *New England Journal of Medicine.*<br>Jack Kevorkian's first assisted death takes place.<br>*Cruzan* is decided.<br>*Patient Self-Determination Act* is enacted. |
| 1991 | Washington State: Ballot Initiative (I-119); defeated. |
| 1992 | California: Ballot measure (Proposition 161); defeated. |
| 1994 | Oregon: Ballot Initiative "Death with Dignity Act" (Measure 16); passed.<br>Washington State: *Compassion in Dying et al.* is filed; decision favors legalization of medically assisted death.<br>New York: *Quill et al. v. Koppell* is filed; decision does not favor legalization of medically assisted death. |
| 1995 | Washington State: *Compassion* is argued before Court of Appeals for the Ninth Circuit.<br>New York: *Quill* is argued before the Court of Appeals for the Second Circuit. |
| 1996 | Washington State: *Compassion* decision by *en banc* Court of Appeals for the Ninth Circuit favors legalization of medically assisted death. The state appeals.<br>New York: *Quill* decision by the Court of Appeals for the Second Circuit favors legalization of medically assisted death. The state appeals.<br>U.S. Supreme Court announces that it will review *Quill* and *Glucksberg*. |
| 1997 | *Quill* and *Glucksberg* are argued (January 8) and decided (June 26).<br>Oregon: Ballot measure (Measure 51) to repeal the "Death with Dignity Act" is introduced and defeated. |
| 1998 | Michigan: Ballot initiative (Proposal B); defeated. |
| 1999 | Jack Kevorkian is convicted for second-degree murder of a "patient." |

Among legalization proponents, however, the Supreme Court rulings did not come as a surprise. Dr. Klagsbrun, the psychiatrist who joined Timothy Quill and Howard Grossman in the New York legal challenge, admitted that their case had been brought as a "test" and that they "never expected it would go this far" (France, 1997). *Compassion in Dying*, one of the plaintiffs in Washington and the financier of the two cases, stated that despite the court's unanimity, they were "far from discouraged" (*Connections, Issue 8*, 1997).

Their optimism was not unfounded. The rulings in *Glucksberg* and *Quill* did not mean a permanent closure of the issues, as the court noted that the discussion should be held in a different forum, that is, "the arena of public debate and legislative action" (*Washington v. Glucksberg*, 1997, p. 720). The decision then handed the dilemma back to the states. As Chief Justice William Rehnquist noticed in the principal opinion, "Throughout the nation, Americans are engaged in an earnest and profound debate about the morality, legality, and practicality of physician-assisted suicide. Our holding permits this debate to continue as it should in a democratic society" (*Washington v. Glucksberg*, 1997, p. 735).[41]

And so it did. After two failed referenda processes in Michigan (1998) and Maine (2000), and following the (ultimately unsuccessful) introduction of bills patterning the *Oregon Death with Dignity Act* in several states, activists' efforts finally came to fruition elsewhere. In 2008, Washington became the second American state to legalize aid in dying. Like in Oregon, the law resulted from a direct democracy process; *Washington Initiative 1000* (I-1000) was approved by nearly 58 percent of the voters. The long path to legalization in that state is detailed next (see Table 5.1 for a summary of the developments discussed in this chapter).

## NOTES

1. Montemarano's case was strikingly similar to Sander's. The death in question involved a terminal cancer patient, a syringe, a well-liked doctor, and a confession by Montemarano. Like in Sander's trial, the doctor asserted "he did not think he had done anything wrong" (Silver, 1974). Mercy dominated out-of-court discussions, whereas in court the issue hinged on whether it could be proved that the patient died as a result of the injection. Montemarano's trial attracted worldwide attention; hundreds of spectators and journalists from near and far gathered inside and outside a little courtroom. When the "Not guilty" verdict was reached, following less than one hour of deliberation, "people in the courtroom broke into loud and prolonged applause" (Silver, 1974).

2. In 1985, for instance, Roswell Gilbert shot his wife to death, ending her suffering from Alzheimer's disease. Gilbert was in his seventies when he was sentenced to 20 years in prison for murdering his wife. His case was as publicized as Dr. Hermann Sanders'—"20 months of news stories, interviews, courtroom sketches, minicam graphics, sermons and editorials" were devoted to his trial (Hilton, 1987).

3. The term is Illich's (1975).

4. Jack Kevorkian's first patient, Janet Adkins, suffered from early stages of Alzheimer's disease. She died in a van, parked in a National Park in Michigan, on May 19, 1990. Murder charges were brought against Kevorkian but dropped soon after. For a review of Kevorkian's cases, see Rodick (2007).

5. Kevorkian's defense team at one of his trials actually likened him to the great martyrs of intellectual and medical history persecuted for advocating ideas ahead of their time. Curiously, Kevorkian himself compared his ordeal to the famous Scopes trial of the twenties. Dr. Death's chief defense attorney, flamboyant Geoffrey Fieger, added: "This is more than the Scopes trial. This is the trial of Socrates" (Rosenbaum, 1991).

6. The New York suit began after a favorable decision was rendered by a lower court in Washington. According to Ralph Mero, the executive director of *Compassion in Dying*, which funded the two cases, finding support in other states with laws similar to Washington's was part of a strategy developed by the nonprofit (Ostrom, 1994b). As he explained, if the organization could "get two or three cases in review at the appeals-court level, it's more likely that the U.S. Supreme Court will take the case."

7. *Beneficence* is used here in the sense proposed by Pellegrino and Thomasma's (1988) influential work, "For the patient's good: the restoration of beneficence in health care." For the authors, the duty of beneficence forms the primary ethical foundation for the patient–doctor relationship. The goal of medicine, they argue, is to be beneficent; physician's respect for patients' autonomy should be superseded by the concern for what can most help the patient.

8. Arguably, the most controversial case emerging in the 1980s that involved technological innovation in conquering death was that of *Baby Fae*. Born with a serious congenital heart defect, Fae was a doomed infant, who received the heart of a baboon in a transplant operation. She died 20 days later.

9. Though the term "quality of life" has become widely used, it is a relatively recent phrase in the academic literature—it wasn't until the mid-1970s that it appeared in the *Index Medicus*, for example (Bond & Corner, 2004, p. 2).

10. The first "living will" was drafted in 1967 by attorney Louis Kutner, a member of the Euthanasia Education Fund (a tax-exempt division of the Euthanasia Society of America). Addressed to "My family, my physician, my clergyman, my lawyer," the first living will requested that in case of "reasonable expectation of . . . no recovery from physical or mental or spiritual disability," one be "allowed to die and not be kept alive by artificial means or heroic measures" (Euthanasia Educational Fund, 1970). Notably, that same year a right-to-die bill was proposed in Florida, followed two years later by another bill introduced in Idaho's legislature. Both bills failed.

11. The paths of women's rights activism and assisted death had crossed before, particularly at the dawn of the *euthanasia* debate in modern times. For one, women's traditional role as caregivers, as well as their likelihood to outlive men (and thus witness the agony of partners' death), have contributed to their *natural* alliance to end-of-life causes. Additionally, and more specifically, the history of obstetrics anesthesia, as well as the mobilization surrounding birthing issues (e.g., the natural birth movement), often intersects with the social history of dying. In Chapter 3 I explored that nexus in the context of chloroform sedation in childbirth.

12. See, for example, the following 1980s decisions: *McConnell, Longeway, Drabick, Bouvia, Barbet, Bartling, O'Connor, Conroy,* and *Jobes.* Appellate decisions from the same decade include, for example, *In re Gardner* and *Brophy v. Mount Sinai Hospital.*

13. In 1973 Dr. Gertruida Postma, who gave her dying mother a lethal injection, received a light sentence in the Netherlands. The development was a seminal event for euthanasia advocacy in that country. In 2002, the *Termination of Life on Request and Assisted Suicide (Review Procedures) Act* was enacted. The *Act* allows for physician-assisted as well as physician-performed hastened death for terminally-ill adults.

14. Derek Humphry is a British journalist and one of the original organizers of the World Federation of Right to Die Societies. Humphry is the author of *Jean's Way* (with Ann Wickett), a best-seller memoir in which he describes his assistance in the death of his cancer-stricken wife, and *Final Exit: the Practicalities of Self-Deliverance and Assisted Suicide for the Dying*, a controversial manual on hastening death. In 1991, the *USA Today* elected *Final Exit* among the 25 most memorable books of the past 25 years (*USA Today*'s list is headed by J. K. Rowling's *Harry Potter and the Sorcerer's Stone*; for the complete list, see http://www.usatoday.com/life/top25-books.htm).

15. A grand jury issued a subpoena of the *JAMA*'s files, including the cover letter submitted with the manuscript that would identify the doctor who wrote it. The *American Medical Association*, which is based in Chicago and under whose auspices the *JAMA* is published, invoked the "Illinois Reporters Protection Act" and the First Amendment, thus refusing to comply with the subpoena (*Los Angeles Times*, Feb. 17, 1988). Because no one—except the editor for the *JAMA*—knew where the crime allegedly took place, prosecutors in Illinois were unable to prove jurisdiction and the subpoena was eventually quashed.

16. In the interest of conciseness, I will not focus here on Jack Kevorkian's feats; instead, the aim of this section is to document the actual legal advances (and resistance efforts) that took place since the 1990s. Much has been written about "Dr. Death." I point the interested reader to Nicol and Wylie (2006), an account by Jack Kevorkian's assistant that covers much of the doctor's early life and involvement in assisted dying; Kevorkian's own book, *Prescription Medicide* (1991), where he discusses among other things the use of death row inmates' organs in transplants subsequent to their deaths, and Gailey's (2003) analysis of media coverage of Kevorkian's trials. For a briefer account, see Rodick (2007).

17. However, in 2007, the *American Academy of Hospice and Palliative Medicine* adopted a position of "studied neutrality" on whether assisted death should be regulated or legalized (see http://www.aahpm.org/positions/suicide.html, accessed on December 13, 2008). This differs sharply from that association's previous position, which in the 1990s was explicitly contrary to legalization of assisted death (for the AAHPM's previous position statement, see their "Comprehensive End-of-Life Care and Physician-Assisted Suicide," published in 1997).

18. It is valid to note that even though *Cruzan* was effectively the first case heard by the high court on whether there exists a federal constitutional "right to die," other cert petitions on the topic had been filed with the Supreme Court throughout the previous decades, including *Quinlan* (Colby, 2002, p. 287).

19. John Ashcroft was Missouri's governor at the time *Cruzan* was litigated. According to William Colby, attorney for the Cruzans, Ashcroft was actively involved in the case. See Colby (2002) for an in-depth discussion of the case's politics.

20. Although Washington State did not (and does not) have a law against suicide itself, assisting in a suicide is a crime that can result in five years of imprisonment and a $10,000 fine (Washington Revised Code § 9A.20.021(1)(c), 1994, section 9A.36.060). In 1994, death and dying, and the involvement of physicians therein, were also regulated in Washington State by another law, the *Natural Death Act*, which immunized a physician

from liability for carrying out a directive from a competent, terminally ill patient to withdraw life-sustaining treatment (Washington Revised Code § 70.122.010, 1994).

21. Established in 1993, *Compassion in Dying* was among the first organizations to offer information, consultation, and emotional support to terminally ill patients regarding a wide range of end-of-life options (intensive management of pain, hospice, comfort care, as well as consultation about obtaining the means for a hastened death should all other options fail).

Besides providing information, the organization orchestrated—legally and financially— the two litigation processes emerging in New York and Washington. In the early stages of the cases, Kirk Robinson, chair of the Fundraising Committee for *Compassion*, appealed for donations through the nonprofit's newsletter: "[E]ven grassroots, volunteer-led organizations have inescapable expenses, and these are magnified by the costs of advocacy litigation. Our attorneys have donated countless hours of pro bono or uncompensated time, but still the costs of our cases will be well over $200,000. A few pioneering foundations have helped subsidize this work, but the vast majority of our income is in the form of small checks from about 3,000 dedicated contributors" (*Connections, Issue 5*). Unfortunately, I could not locate final cost figures for the litigation.

22. Roe died shortly before the case was favorably decided by the appellate court. After her death, her husband, also a physician, told the press that she "was bound and determined to exert her independence and be self-sufficient" in death as she had been in life (*The Seattle Times*, May 4, 1994). Roe was never in private practice; instead she used her medical training in volunteer work, at Planned Parenthood, youth centers, and a women's clinic she helped to found.

23. John Geyman and Harold Glucksberg undoubtedly lent credibility to the case in Washington, given their standing in the medical community. Besides his 25 years of practice, Geyman has served as editor for two influential journals in the field of family medicine and has written several books and numerous journal articles on health care reform. He is currently a blogger for*The Huffington Post*. Glucksberg, also an academic physician, had several articles published on prominent journals in his area of expertise, that is, oncology.

24. In an interview by *The New York Times*, Kingsley explained that he thought it was important to use his real name when discussing the issue because it "lent credibility and a certain humaneness to his story" (*NYT*, June 14, 1994). He also stated that during the many years since his HIV-positive diagnosis, he had "managed simply to live with it," until one day he "got very, very sick." When his doctors could not identify what was causing his symptoms, he turned to friends for help in committing suicide. Eventually, hospital tests revealed that Kingsley had parasitic infections, which were treated with antibiotics. Since the infection diagnosis, Kingsley hoarded enough drugs to kill himself, if he wished to do so. Having the means to commit suicide, he told *The New York Times*, "has diminished my horror, as though I was facing an enemy on a battlefield stark naked and now I have armor."

25. Suicide among AIDS-affected men is notably high. For instance, research conducted a couple of years before Barth and Kingsley joined the suit found that the relative risk of suicide in men with AIDS aged 20 to 59 years was over 36 times that of men aged 20 to 59 years without this diagnosis, and over 66 times that of the general population (Marzuk et al., 1988).

26. Among doctors treating HIV/AIDS patients, like Dr. Howard Grossman, a majority favor aid in dying. In surveys conducted with such doctors in 1990 (before suit was filed in Washington and New York) and again in 1995 (after legal action

had commenced), one study found a significant increase in physicians' willingness to assist in the death of an AIDS patient (from 28 percent to 48 percent of doctors; Slome et al., 1997).

27. Interestingly, among physicians, psychiatrists tend to score high in their support for assisted death (Cohen, Fihn, & Boyko, 2000). By contrast, the majority of medical professionals who specialize in oncology do not support the practice. Surveys of oncology nurses and practicing oncology physicians, for instance, have found that roughly 75 percent of respondents opposed assisted death (see, e.g., Emanuel et al. [2000]; see also Cohen et al. [1994]).

28. In 1991, Klagsbrun published an essay in the *Journal of Pain and Symptom Management* in which he describes the criteria that he understood as prerequisite for assisted suicide: (1) the desire to die must not stem from depression; (2) the request must not stem from pain and discomfort that can be alleviated; and (3) the patient and physician involved must have a deep, intimate and long relationship.

29. An anonymous tip led Monroe County district attorney to Diane's identity. Patricia Diane Trumbull had been Quill's patient for eight years when she died. Her body was at Monroe Community College, where it been donated for medical research (*Associated Press*, June 17, 1991).

30. In the case originating in Washington, as pointed out earlier, *Compassion in Dying* was also a plaintiff. *Compassion* contended that terminally ill patients had a right to receive assistance from aid in dying organizations, including "counseling and delivering or mixing the drugs that are to be used" in a hastened death (*Compassion in Dying v. State of Washington*, 1994, p. 1459). As discussed in Chapter 6, the implementation of the Death with Dignity Acts in Oregon and Washington allows for staff from similar nonprofits to provide counsel and mix the lethal drug for the patient.

31. All of the patients who were plaintiffs in these cases died before their legal plight arrived at the Supreme Court. Their claims were then sustained by the physicians.

32. Interestingly, in New York, the state also argued that there was no justiciability (actual controversy) between the parties and thus the case should be dismissed. In other words, the state argued that the doctors were "not under actual threat of prosecution" (*Quill v. Koppell*, 1994, p. 81). In his opinion, however, Chief Judge Thomas Griesa pointed out that the grand jury proceeding against Timothy Quill indicated the state's clear "intention of acting against physicians" on these matters (*Quill v. Koppell*, 1994, p. 82). He added that "since the issue of assisted suicide is being pressed by segments of the medical community and has sparked sharp public debate . . . it . . . is unlikely that the conduct at issue in this case would be ignored by the law enforcement authorities."

33. On appeal, a three-judge panel for the Ninth Circuit initially reversed the lower court's decision and held the Washington statute to be constitutional (*Compassion in Dying v. State of Washington*, 1995, p. 588). In the court's opinion, Judge Noonan invoked Dostoyevsky's *The Idiot* to drive the point that compassion, albeit a "necessary component of judicial character" is not the most important trait in judicial decision-making:

> Compassion, according to the reflections of Prince Myshkin, is "the most important, perhaps the sole law of human existence" . . . [Dostoevsky, *The Idiot*, 292 (Alan Myers, trans.) (1991)]. In the vernacular, compassion is trumps. No one can read the accounts of the sufferings of the deceased plaintiffs supplied by declarations, or the accounts of the sufferings of their patients supplied by the physicians, without being

moved by them. No one would inflict such sufferings on another or want them inflicted on himself; and since the horrors recounted are those that could attend the end of life anyone who reads of them must be aware that they could be attendant on his own death. The desire to have a good and kind way of forestalling them is understandably evident in the declarations of the plaintiffs and in the decision of the district court. . . . Unrestrained by other virtues, as *The Idiot* illustrates, it leads to catastrophe. Justice, prudence, and fortitude are necessary too. Compassion cannot be the compass of a federal judge. That compass is the Constitution of the United States. Where, as here in the case of Washington, the statute of a state comports with that compass, the validity of the statute must be upheld. (*Compassion in Dying v. State of Washington*, 1995, p. 588)

Then, after rehearing the case *en banc*, the Ninth Circuit reversed the earlier panel and affirmed the lower court's decision (*Compassion in Dying v. State of Washington*, 1996, p. 839). For a procedural history and detailed analyses of each of these decisions, see Testa (1998).

34. Gregoire became governor of Washington, holding that office at the time aid in dying became legal in that state via direct democracy process. That topic is fully discussed in Chapter 6.

35. In an issue of *Compassion in Dying's* newsletter, "Connections" (n.d.), published before the Supreme Court decision, advocates hazarded a vote count: "Careful consideration of the Court's current composition, including analysis of voting in both *Cruzan* and *Casey*, and consideration of the changes in the Court since those cases were decided, enables us to reasonably hope to garner votes from six of the nine justices."

36. That ballot process is recounted in detail in Chapter 6. In addition to these prolegalization attempts, which the court perceived as a serious engagement by the states in considering the issue, the justices also referred to the New York State Task Force on Life and the Law as evidence of states' thoughtful examination of end-of-life policy. The report produced by the Task Force and its recommendation has been mentioned earlier.

37. Interestingly, by framing the issue in their original legal challenge as an *assisted suicide* matter, proponents of decriminalization had to deal with this longstanding legal history proscribing suicide, attempted suicide, and suicide assistance, as they form the background against which their constitutional claims were assessed.

Although the Supreme Court framed the issue in the same manner, the *en banc* Second District Court's opinion chose to call the issue a "right to die with dignity" (Supreme Court Justice Breyer offered the same approach in his concurring opinion). More than semantics, framing the issue thus allowed the Appellate Court to take a broader approach to the historical record, by examining the history of "rational suicide," reviewing the attitudes toward the practice since Greek and Roman times, and demonstrating that the historical record is "far more checkered" than a narrower approach would suggest. Curiously, in none of the opinions are the 1906 "chloroform bills" mentioned.

38. The arguments put forth by the friends of the court on both sides played a valuable role in informing the courts about the societal, physiological, psychological, and policy aspects of death and dying. The U.S. Supreme Court justices directly referenced certain briefs more than 20 times in their opinions. According to Samuels (2004), this extensive use of direct citations is unusual. The briefs also illuminate the legal rationales in each of the cases, especially regarding whether the statutes in Washington and New York conflicted with the Due Process and Equal Protection clauses. Because a

constitutional analysis of the issue falls beyond my interests here, I point the interested reader to Behuniak and Svenson's (2002) book *Physician-Assisted Suicide: The Anatomy of a Constitutional Law Issue* (see also Samuels, 2004).

39. Briefs of *amici curiae* supporting the Appellate Courts' ruling that found the WA and NY statutes unconstitutional were filed by: the American Civil Liberties Union; Americans for Death with Dignity, a pro-assisted-death organization that sponsored the unsuccessful ballot initiative introduced in California in 1992; Choice in Dying, another pro-legalization organization; the American Medical Student Association; the American College of Legal Medicine; the Washington State Psychological Association; the Coalition of Hospice Professionals; the Center for Reproductive Law & Policy; the National Women's Health Network; the Council for Secular Humanism; 36 Religious Organizations, Leaders, and Scholars; Gay Men's Health Crisis, an organization founded by Larry Kramer, who, as discussed previously, recruited two of the physicians who became plaintiffs in *Quill*; a group of Bioethicists; a group of Law Professors; a group of State Legislators; Dr. Julian M. Whitaker, a physician and practitioner of alternative medicine; Surviving Family Members in Support of Physician-Assisted Dying; Philosopher Ronald Dworkin and others; and a *John Doe* from Washington. Most of these briefs were submitted in both the *Quill* and *Glucksberg* cases.

Briefs seeking to persuade the court against finding a fundamental "right to die" were filed jointly by the states of California, Alabama, Colorado, Florida, Georgia, Illinois, Iowa, Louisiana, Maryland, Michigan, Mississippi, Montana, Nebraska, New Hampshire, Oklahoma, South Carolina, South Dakota, Tennessee, Virginia, Washington, and New York, as well as the territory of Puerto Rico. The state of Oregon filed its own brief. Richard Thompson, Oakland County (Michigan) prosecuting attorney, filed a brief relating his difficulties in convicting Jack Kevorkian. Michael McCann, a district attorney in Milwaukee, also filed a brief. A number of organizations opposed the Appellate Courts' decisions and filed briefs; they are: the Agudath Israel of America; the American Association of Homes and Services for the Aging; the American Center for Law and Justice; the American Geriatrics Society; the American Hospital Association; the American Suicidology Foundation; the Catholic Health Association of the United States; the Catholic Medical Association; the Christian Legal Society; the Evangelical Lutheran Church in America; the Family Research Council; the Institute for Public Affairs of the Union of Orthodox Jewish Congregation of America; the Legal Center for Defense of Life, Inc; the National Association of Prolife Nurses; the National Catholic Office for Persons with Disabilities; the National Hospice Organization; the National Legal Center for the Medically Dependent and Disabled; the National Right to Life Committee; the National Spinal Cord Injury Association; the Project on Death in America, sponsored by George Soros; the Rutherford Institute; the Schiller Institute; the United States Catholic Conference; Senator Orrin Hatch; several members of the New York and State Legislatures; a group of bioethics professors; Dr. Gary Lee, an oncologist and lead-plaintiff in action seeking injunction of the measure that legalized death with dignity in Oregon (*Lee v. Oregon*); the International Anti-Euthanasia Task Force, since renamed to Patients' Rights Council, is one of the first opposing nonprofit organizations and is led in part by lawyer and radical bioethicist Wesley J. Smith; the Southern Center for Law and Ethics; the Medical Society of New Jersey; the American Life League; Dr. Jerome J. DeCosse, a prominent oncologist; Not Dead Yet, a disability advocacy organization, joined by other such groups; and the United States Justice Department. Most of these briefs were submitted in both *Quill* and *Glucksberg* cases.

40. The Clinton administration had a reliable record of opposing medically assisted suicide, evidenced in part by his signing into law the "Assisted Suicide Funding Restriction Act of 1997" (H.R. 1003), which, in the president's words "reaffirms current Federal policy banning the use of Federal funds to pay for assisted suicide, euthanasia, or mercy killing" (Clinton, 1997-). Curiously, when administration officials contemplated asking Congress to make assisted suicide a federal crime, Elena Kagan, then serving as an adviser in the White House domestic policy office, suggested to the president in a handwritten note that this was "a fairly terrible idea." Her note was released along with other documents related to Kagan's tenure at the White House, all of which were disclosed by the Clinton presidential library as part of the filings in advance of confirmation hearings on her nomination to the Supreme Court (her files are digitized and the collection can be found here: http://www.clintonlibrary.gov/kagan.html).

41. Additionally, in his concurring opinion, Justice Stevens specified that the court's holding did not "foreclose the possibility that an individual plaintiff seeking to hasten her death, or a doctor whose assistance was sought, could prevail in a more particularized challenge. Future cases will determine whether such a challenge may succeed" (*Washington v. Glucksberg*, 1997, p. 750). The chief justice agreed in a footnote that the court's "opinion does not absolutely foreclose such a claim" (*Washington v. Glucksberg*, 1997, p. 735, fn. 24).

# 6

# On the Ballot: 1990s Onward, the Washington I-1000 Ballot Initiative Process

ON A TUESDAY MORNING in 1998, just as the winter was coming to a close in the Pacific Northwest, a woman who had been battling breast cancer for some 20 years washed down a lethal dosage of "Seconal."[1] Then in her eighties, she was the first patient to die under the provisions of Oregon's *Death with Dignity Act* (ODDA). In a tape recorded for the press, the woman, whose identity was never publicly disclosed, stated her intentions: "I'm looking forward to it because, being I was always active, I cannot possibly see myself living out two more months like this" (*The Seattle Times*, Mar. 30, 1998).[2]

A decade after that death, Washington State residents entertained a ballot initiative that mirrored their neighbor's law. Like the ODDA's provisions, Washington's *Initiative 1000* (*I-1000*) called for allowing terminally ill adults seeking to end their life to request lethal doses of medication from physicians. *I-1000* passed with strong approval: 58 percent of voters were in favor of decriminalizing medically assisted death.

The trajectory of the legalization of medical aid in dying in Washington is at once tortuous and fascinating. It involves a West Coast governor and a *West Wing* president. It includes an *Oscar* nomination and a *Pollie*[3] award. And it was long in the making. Besides Dr. Glucksberg et al.'s (ultimately unfruitful) two-year journey to the U.S. Supreme Court, as discussed previously in this book, efforts to legalize assisted death in Washington were diverse and relentless.

After failing at the ballot box in 1991, proponents lobbied politicians to give it a try in the legislature. Three times—in 1995, 1997, and 2006—bills shepherding the legalization of medically assisted death were introduced in the state Senate merely to fail after referral to appropriate committees. Legalization came only after the issue had been tested for 10 years in Oregon, after it had survived many legal challenges, including a federal one in *Gonzales v. Oregon*;[4] and at a time when supporters found the right champion for their cause and, in an unprecedented manner, out-raised the opposition. Finally, legalization happened when *gen-Xers*, *boomers*, and the *lucky few*, as a constituency, found they had one thing in common—the desire to *die with dignity*.

Later, I will present a history of prior failed attempts to legalize hastened death in Washington, a description of the campaign, opposition efforts, the resulting law, and its use. Finally, I will explore subsequent pro-legalization efforts, particularly those in Montana, New Mexico, and Vermont.

## DEATH WITH DIGNITY IN THE MAKING: 15 YEARS OF BALLOT, LEGISLATIVE, AND COURT ATTEMPTS

The first time death with physicians' assistance was put to popular vote in the United States happened in the state of Washington—but not in 2008.[5] The state had been previously targeted by legalization activists in 1991, when a broader ballot initiative (*I-119*), which would have allowed not only for physician-*assisted* but also for physician-*performed* death, was promoted and ultimately defeated.[6]

The introduction of *I-119* in Washington was part of a concerted, national effort by legalization activists to push the envelope like never before. Between 1991 and 2000, voters in California (1992), Michigan (1998), and Maine (2000)—besides, of course, Oregonians (1994)—also entertained the legalization of medical aid in dying via direct democracy processes. In addition, legislative bills were equally on advocates' agenda. Between the decriminalization in Oregon and 2000, 54 bills were introduced in 21 states. None passed.[7]

During that period, two of these bills were presented in Washington. In 1995, Democrat State Senator Cal Anderson—the first openly gay member of that state's legislature—championed *SB 5596*, an "act relating to recognizing and regulating the right of mentally competent terminally ill adults voluntarily to request and receive physician aid in dying." The bill, pushed by the American Civil Liberties Union of Washington,[8] was prompted in part by Oregon's passage of the *Death with Dignity Act* in the previous year, as well as by an initial legal victory that had, at that point, just been achieved by advocates in Federal Court[9] (*The Seattle Times*, Jan. 25, 1995). *SB 5596* was read on January 27, 1995, and was referred to the legislature's *Health and Long-Term Care Committee*, but the committee failed to act on it during that session.[10] Senator Anderson died, roughly six months later, of AIDS-related lymphoma (*The New York Times*, Aug. 6, 1995). In the following year, another Democrat, Pat Thibaudeau, a social worker by education and a longstanding pro-choice legislator, won the race for the late Cal Anderson's seat.[11] Senator Thibaudeau reintroduced Anderson's bill in 1997 (*SB 5654*). The timing once more seemed appropriate as *SB 5654* was first read in February, just a few months after the U.S. Supreme Court had granted certiorari in *Glucksberg* and just as attempts to repeal the Oregonian law had failed.[12] However, like the previous bill, *SB 5654* also died in committee.[13]

Nearly a decade later, in yet another attempt to seize on the momentum created by the U.S. Supreme Court decision in *Gonzales* to uphold Oregon's *Death with Dignity Act*, an additional bill (*SB 6843*) seeking legalization of physician-assisted death was introduced in the Washington State Senate. Once again championed by Senator Pat Thibaudeau, the bill was presented with little expectation of getting a hearing (*The Seattle Times*, Jan. 27, 2006).[14] Instead, the legislator hoped to "begin the discussion about [assisted death, as] this will increasingly become an issue." Her prediction was correct and, that same year, pro-death-with-dignity advocates began organizing actions that would ultimately turn Washington into the second American state where residents can die with the help of physicians. Their path to the ballot and repercussions are discussed in the following sections.

## LUCKY NUMBER 1,000

The defeat of *Initiative 119* in 1991 discouraged a few of its key proponents. Ralph Mero, a Unitarian minister who had led the legalization efforts at that time, bitterly remarked afterward:

> Initiatives are very uncertain and unlikely of success regardless of the issue.... Almost all are defeated, except those promising relief to the taxpayer. If you had an initiative today on the Ten Commandments, I doubt it would pass. If Americans were asked to vote tomorrow on the Bill of Rights, some ad agency would launch a campaign against it. (*NYT*, Nov. 14, 1993)

The minister was not all that accurate about the odds involved. For instance, between 1914 (when the process began in Washington State) and 2001, voters weighed in on 136 initiatives (Ballotpedia.org, 2013). Sixty-eight passed, 68 failed.[15] Overall, Washington voters have entertained a number of different issues via direct democracy: alcohol regulation, drug control, gun control, nuclear waste, salmon fishing and timber harvesting, animal rights, civil rights, abortion, the death penalty, and assisted suicide, among others.[16] Indeed, up to 1991, when the first aid in dying initiative was defeated, taxes had been the top-ranked legislative issue proposed by citizens via ballot (a total of 19 initiatives, in contrast, e.g., to only two health-related measures). But contrary to Mero's statement, roughly 40 percent of the tax measures failed, including one on the ballot that same year.[17]

Odds aside, Mero makes a good point when he raises the decisive role played by ad agencies in citizen-led initiatives. In the journey that gets a ballot measure from individual outrage or social grievance to actual law on the books, how strategies are deployed—the contests over meaning, the targeting of constituencies, besides, of course, the political, cultural, and social opportunities—matters. Political sociologists have devoted decades conceptualizing and dissecting these processes (e.g., Robert Benford, Doug McAdam, David Meyer, and Sidney Tarrow are but a few scholars whose life-long research agendas are prolific on this topic). Fully applying their theories to explain the efforts behind the passage of *I-1000* is beyond the scope of this work. However, to the extent certain insights derived from such scholarship are advantageous in understanding how medically assisted death became legal in Washington, dabbling in them becomes relevant. Of particular importance are the *instrumental* aspects of getting the measure on the ballot (e.g., resources, patronage, etc.). Accordingly, later I discuss funding, advertising, public opinion mobilization, voters' demographics, and other means that propelled the passage of assisted death in Washington State in 2008.

## The Path to the Ballot

In 1991, when *I-119* failed, Booth Gardner, a Democrat, was finishing his second term as governor of Washington State. At the time, he expressed certain ambivalence about that particular initiative—while Gardner endorsed personal choice and was "inclined to support the measure," he also was concerned about potential abuse, such as pressure by caregivers on their terminally ill relatives to hasten the dying process (*The Seattle Times*, Jan. 23, 1991). Gardner's tenure in public office ended a year later, and he left with "sky high" approval ratings (*The Spokane Chronicle*, Jan. 14, 1987).[18] In 1994, while working in Switzerland as the appointed U.S. ambassador to the General Agreement on Tariffs and Trade (GATT),[19] he was diagnosed with Parkinson's disease. Gardner retired from public life only to reemerge over a decade later as a powerful champion for the legalization of "death with dignity" in the Evergreen State.

In 2006, during a ceremony in which Governor Booth Gardner was honored for his public service,[20] he announced three goals he wished to attain in the following five years (Hughes, 2010, p. 162). One, he would like to propose alternatives to the Washington Assessment of Student Learning (WASL), a high school graduation requirement that in his view was prejudiced against children with learning disabilities and those with cultural challenges. Two, he wanted to write a textbook, filled with case studies and examples taken from his public life. Goal number three, he warned, would offend a few of those attending the event. In his 70 years, Gardner explained, he had made all of the "tough decisions" himself— how hard to study, what sports to play, which college to attend, whom to marry, and how many kids he would have; now, he felt he "ought to have the right to make the last decision, when it's time for me to go and how I go." He had decided: "So I'm going to head up an initiative and we're going to get that assisted-death law approved in our state. When this one is over, I'm through. This is my last campaign."[21,22]

Booth Gardner quickly put his money where his mouth was. He contributed $455,000 to the "Yes on *I-1000*" campaign, which he chaired. Four family members of Booth Gardner's (Stephen G. Clapp, James N. Clapp, Margaret Clapp, and Linda Henry) donated another $302,000.00 combined.[23] Other large, individual donors were: Andrew Ross, an inventor and retired lawyer from Ohio who had lost his mother and a client to prolonged deaths, donated $400,000.00 (*The Olympian*, Nov. 3, 2008). Medical businessman Loren Parks, said to be "the top donor to political causes in Oregon history," donated $275,000.00 (Ballotpedia.org, 2012c).

Parks also had made a sizeable contribution to the measure to uphold Oregon's *Death with Dignity Act* in 1997. Professor Judy Sebba, now "Director of the Rees Centre for Research in Fostering and Education" at Oxford University, donated $253,555.00.[24] Institutional donations came mostly from national and international death with dignity organizations,[25] as well as the American Civil Liberties Union, which gave $61,562.00 to campaigners. In total, four days prior to the election, financial support for *I-1000* amounted to nearly $5.5 million, in contrast to $1.5 million reported by opponents, the "Coalition against Assisted Suicide." This was the first (and only) time that proponents' fundraising ultimately exceeded that of the opponents in a ballot initiative or legislative battle anywhere in the country (Death with Dignity National Center, n.d.).[26]

Simultaneously to Governor Gardner's patronage, the board of directors of the Death with Dignity National Center (DDNC), the lead national aid in dying nonprofit organization, identified Washington as a target state for a ballot initiative. Their rationale was grounded on three facts, primarily. One, Washington's previous legalization attempts, via ballots and bills, maintained the issue's salience in the media and assured that the citizens of the state were educated on the topic. Two, activists hoped that Washingtonians' proximity to Oregon would have promoted their familiarity with the evidence-based success of Death with Dignity in the neighboring state.[27] And three, Washington's tradition of using the ballot,[28] as well as its electorate demographics, made it a prime candidate for a new campaign.

"Washington State's electorate is different," stated Christian Sinderman, spokesman for *I-1000*, "We're a state that values people's privacy and civil liberties" (*The Spokesman-Review*, Apr. 30, 2008). The state also has an especially high proportion of nonreligious residents (16 percent, surpassed only by Oregon with 18 percent and Idaho with 17 percent; Jones, 2004). Research has found that support for assisted death decreases as religious involvement increases (Caddell & Newton, 1995). Additionally, according to Gallup, only eight of the continental American states have fewer than 80 percent of their residents identifying themselves as Christians—Washingtonians are among them. Of the Judeo-Christian denominations, support for assisted death is least likely found among Roman Catholics. Roman Catholics in Washington make up just 17.6 percent of the population, about six percentage points lower than the national profile (Jones, 2004; Newport, 2004). More importantly, in the two years prior to the 2008 election, Washingtonians' confidence in the Catholic Church leadership was at an all-time low, when a series of clergy sexual abuse scandals emerging from *Spokane* dominated the media.[29] Finally, Washington, like Oregon and other states west of the Rocky Mountains, has higher-than-average suicide rates; in 2009, the U.S. suicide rate was 12 per 100,000, whereas Washington's rate in the same year was 14 per 100,000 (McIntosh, 2012). Between 2008 and 2010, Washingtonian men over the age of 75 accounted for the highest suicide rates in the state (Washington State Department of Health, 2013). Suicidal thoughts are also higher than average in the state. A study conducted by the Centers for Disease Control and Prevention, which looked at the years 2008 and 2009, found that roughly 1 in 20 Washington residents reported suicidal thoughts, conferring the state the seventh position nationally (Utah ranked highest, Georgia ranked lowest; Crosby, Han, Ortega, Parks, & Gfroerer [2011]). Taken together, these numbers may signal a higher *desensitization* to the issue among residents of Washington, when compared to other states.[30]

Booth Gardner's popularity was an asset in helping galvanize grassroots efforts and mobilize the electorate. Over 3,600 volunteers participated in collecting the required signatures to qualify the initiative for the ballot. They gathered 320,000 signatures—nearly 100,000 in excess of procedural requirements (Death with Dignity National Center, n.d.).[31]

But getting the measure to the ballot was, of course, no guarantee of its final success; it simply inaugurated the need to persuade voters to cast favorable ballots. With proponents arguing for *the right to choose a death with dignity* and those against the initiative vehemently opposing *physician-assisted suicide*, media consultants had a prominent role in shaping how the issue was presented to voters.

Although research on the relationship between levels of expenditure on advertisement and actual outcomes in direct democracy yields unclear results (Richards, Allender, & Fang, 2013), political ads are widely used and strategically employed.[32] Advertising agencies increasingly stand to profit from the oft-polarizing issues that go onto state-level ballots (Gerber, 1999) and in this case it was not different. During the campaign, opponents of assisted death hired actor Martin Sheen as their spokesperson. Sheen, best known for his role as a U.S. president with multiple sclerosis on the popular television series *The West Wing*, lent his celebrity status to the TV ads ran by the *No on Initiative 1000* committee.[33,34] In the commercial, Sheen appears in suit and tie, strikingly resembling the presidential character he played, and warns voters about potential slippery slope issues related to the legalization of death with assistance, urging them to side with him and vote *No* on the proposal.

In an *Oscar*-nominated documentary about Booth Gardner's involvement in the campaign pro-assisted dying (Junge, 2009), the governor's reaction to the commercial in which Sheen stars is depicted. Fairly impressed, the governor and his committee resorted to hiring Nashville-based agency Fletcher, Rowley, Chao, Riddle, Inc. (FRCR) to coordinate and produce all paid media efforts (Death with Dignity National Center, n.d.). FRCR produced and aired two TV spots and one radio ad in late October, aimed at undecided voters; despite their lead in the polls at the time the ads aired, proponents feared "a last minute media blitz" by opponents (Kirtley, 2011, p. 100). One of the commercials featured Dr. Christina Nicolaidis, a general internist whose mother died under Oregon's DWDA.[35] In the 30-second ad, the doctor tells viewers about how her mother wanted to die as she had lived, "with her dignity." After explaining how similar the Oregonian law is to *I-1000*, Dr. Nicolaidis emotionally concludes, as the camera zooms in, "as a doctor and a daughter, I can tell you the . . . law is safe . . . it works." The ad, titled "Doctor-Daughter," won a silver Pollie award (see note 3) to FRCR.[36]

The other commercial, titled "Getting the Facts Straight," featured Barbara Roberts, Oregon's sitting governor when the *Death with Dignity Act* passed in that state, defending the law's use against what the *Yes on I-1000* committee deemed to be *lies* spun by the opposition.[37] Besides Roberts, other prominent politicians also publicly supported the measure. Former Washington governor Dan Evans and former secretary of state Ralph Munro, both Republicans, along with former governor Gary Locke, a Democrat, also backed the *death with dignity* proposal, among many other representatives from the state legislature (Turner, 2008). Christine Gregoire, at the time governor of Washington, remained neutral throughout the campaign, justifying her position in that "this is a deeply personal issue and [she is not] going to tell people how to vote" (*Los Angeles Times,* June 22, 2008). Gregoire, who was running for reelection in 2008, was no stranger to the topic; roughly a decade prior, she was the attorney general for the state in what became the Supreme Court case *Washington v. Glucksberg*. Additional support from religious leaders of the Methodist, Unitarian, Episcopal, and Jewish faiths were published on the *Yes on 1000* Web site (http://www.yeson1000.org). Finally, most newspapers in circulation in the state endorsed the measure (per campaign materials made available to me by Christian Sinderman, campaign manager for Washington's *I-1000*).

Resistance to *I-1000* was founded on religious and secular social justice arguments. On the one hand, Christian organizations, particularly the Catholic Church and its members, defended a theological and moral understanding of dying and suicide that placed emphasis on the value of human life as a sacred gift and on God's exclusive power over the manner and timing of one's death.[38] Led by Dominican Sister Sharon Park, executive director of Washington's Catholic Conference, the Church mobilized

> because *I-1000* runs contrary to a basic church teaching and because its fundraising is far behind the measure's proponents. It's a vital issue for our society and it certainly is an issue of paramount importance to us in terms of protecting life. What does this do to a society, for a group of people namely, physicians to take the lives of their patients? The message [if I-1000 passes] would be that some lives are not as valuable as others . . . and that which is legal [then] becomes that which is moral. (*The News Tribune*, Sep. 2, 2008)

Echoing Sister Park's concerns regarding the *value of human life*, sympathizers of *Not Dead Yet*, a national grassroots disabilities rights group, articulated their opposition mainly on the basis that legalizing assisted death for terminally ill patients would likely be expanded to apply to those with *diminished* quality of life (i.e., disabled) as well as the poor.[39] Finally, although a few medically related organizations supported *I-1000*—including the American Medical Student Association and the Medical Women's Association, in addition to the Washington State Public Health Association—the *Coalition against Assisted Suicide* had its share of doctors and nurses opposing the measure. Among the most influential was the Washington State Medical Association,[40] whose president, Brian Wicks, stated firm opposition to the practice during a press conference on the eve of the election:

> We believe physician-assisted suicide is fundamentally incompatible with the role of physicians as healers.... Patients put their trust in physicians and that bond of trust would be irrevocably harmed by the provisions of this dangerous initiative.... Initiative-1000 gives doctors power which we do not want and which we believe is contrary to good medical practice. The initiative is a dangerous distraction from symptom-directed end-of-life care that provides comfort for dying patients and their families. Our focus should remain on caring for terminally ill patients and should never shift toward helping them kill themselves. (Frankham, 2008)

A substantial percentage of the cash donation gathered by opponents of *I-1000* (44 percent) originated from Catholic institutions, such as the Knights of Columbus, numerous archdioceses, parishes and churches, as well as religious health care providers, such as the Catholic Health Association of the United States (followthemoney.org, n.d.).[41] Among individuals who donated large sums to the *Coalition against Assisted Suicide* were: Richard Alvord, a private investor who had been ranked the #9 political financier in the state and was considered a patron of conservative politics (*The Seattle Times*, Aug. 30, 1998); Dr. Shane Macauley, a radiologist and spokesman for the Coalition; and Betty S. Wheeler, a retired woman from *Spokane* with a consistent record of donating funds to the Republican National Committee (fundrace.huffingtonpost.com). Ms. Wheeler is also among the major benefactors of Gonzaga University, a private Roman Catholic institution; cumulatively, she had donated between $1 million and $2 million to the university by 2011 (Gonzaga University, 2011).[42]

The fate of *I-1000* was highly contested. Polls conducted two months prior to the elections showed an advantage to supporters of *I-1000*: 51 percent of those surveyed indicated they would vote *Yes*, 26 percent opposed the measure, and 23 percent were undecided (Ertelt, 2008b). Just a few weeks prior, another state-wide poll had shown many more undecided (39 percent) and neither side had a majority.[43] By late September, those in favor were up to 54 percent (American Medical Association, 2008). On Election Day, *I-1000* was approved by 58 percent of the voters (Washington Secretary of State, 2008).

The majority of votes for the measure emerged from regions west of the Cascades, where the traditionally more liberal counties are. Votes against the measure were concentrated in nine counties, mostly eastern, all of which have either a conservative stronghold,[44] family income below state averages, or a peculiarly large percent of Hispanics and strong ties to the Catholic Church[45] when compared to the rest of the state. An exit poll conducted by CNN (2008) revealed that the majority of supporters were male (60 percent), liberal (81 percent), and did not identify themselves with any religion (79 percent). Ideologically, votes for *I-1000* are straightforward; that is, one would expect greater support among nonreligious, liberal voters. In terms of gender, the voting pattern is consistent with Oregon, for example, where males were also found to favor assisted death more than female voters (Crutchfield, 2008).

Another demographic aspect among voters that is especially relevant to aid in dying is age. Of particular interest is the voting behavior of the older population, since this group is disproportionately more likely to fit the criteria of the proposed law, that is, to be affected by a terminal illness accompanied by acute suffering (Strate, Kiska, & Zalman, 2001). In turn, younger adults have been found to report higher levels of anxiety toward death, and tend to fear bodily decomposition, pain, and helplessness at a higher rate than older adults (Thorson & Powell, 1994). Accordingly, they may be more likely to support assisted death than older individuals as a result of these concerns (Strate, Kiska, & Zalman, 2001). Additionally, younger adults may vote altruistically; that is, they may support assisted death to prevent the suffering of their (grand)parents. In line with this argument, the *poster child* for the *Yes on I-1000* committee was Kim Porter, a middle-aged woman from Renton whose mother had died of pancreatic cancer. Porter's message on the brochures widely distributed by supporters read: "In the last months of her life she struggled with constant, unmanageable pain, dependent on others to assist with every basic function. I support I-1000 so that others will have the option to die with dignity that my mother did not."

According to exit polls, *I-1000* found roughly equal support among *baby boomer* and *generation X* cohorts. Sixty percent of baby boomers (those aged 50–64 in 2008) were in favor, as were 59 percent of generation X voters (30–49 years). Support was weaker, though still overall in favor, among the *lucky few* (65 and older), of whom 52 percent voted for the measure (CNN, 2008). This pattern of weaker support among the oldest voters is replicated across time and place in similar polls on assisted death legislation (Crutchfield, 2008; Public Policy Polling, 2012). Explanations for this relationship vary, with attributions frequently made to the greater religiosity and political conservatism of older individuals (e.g., Strate, Kiska, & Zalman, 2001). While valid, these hypotheses have been scantily tested and the potential mediating effects of attitudes toward death on patterns of support for aid in dying across age groups remain unexplored.

Among all the age groups, the voting behavior of baby boomers is particularly salient. As the *pig in the python* moves closer to old age, end-of-life questions are likely to grow in relevance. Indeed, as baby boomers grow old, opportunities are increasingly ripe for various legal issues raised by—and related to—the elderly population.[46] No literature has examined systematically the distinct question of what importance, if any, the emergence of the baby boom cohort itself will have on opinion and policy in the area of aid in dying as these individuals reach an age when end-of-life issues become personally relevant for the first time.

Compounding the issue is the fact that voting turnout tends to increase with age. For instance, in the 1972 presidential election (when young voters would have been disproportionately attracted to the ballot due to the Vietnam War draft and the adoption of 18 as the minimum voting age), 54 percent of those in the boomer cohort, then under 30 years of age, voted. In 2008, when boomers were approaching retirement age, 69 percent of them cast ballots (The Center for Information & Research on Civic Learning and Engagement, 2010). Moreover, for the first time, in 2012 more than half of the nation's voting age population was over 45 years (Gurwitt, 2012). Due to sheer force of numbers and potential attachment to the issue, in direct democracy processes such as the one that legalized assisted death in Washington, boomers potentially could be a decisive constituency.[47]

Boomers, however, are not a homogenous bloc. In a recent report about generational voting behavior, the Pew Research Center (2011) found that older baby boomers, those who came of age during Richard Nixon's presidency, are more Democratic in their voting. Younger boomers, though, have been significantly more Republican than average in their party affiliation and voting preferences. The *Pew* report attributes this difference to the fact that the younger half of the *boomer* generation came of age during a period of disillusionment with Democrat Jimmy Carter and during the beginning of the popular presidency of Republican Ronald Reagan. In this regard, younger *boomers* have more in common with the older portion of *generation X*, whose formative political experiences occurred during the later Reagan presidency and the early years of George H. W. Bush, than with older *boomers* (p. 18). The picture is thus complex and I will return to the possible nuances and implications of the association between age and support for assisted death in the context of the *silver tsunami* in my discussion.

## THE AFTERMATH OF *I-1000*: LEGAL CONTOURS

The law (RCW 70.245) resulting from the passage of *I-1000* in Washington went into effect in March 2009. Eli Stutsman, a Portland-based attorney and lead drafter of the *Oregon Death with Dignity Act*, also authored the Washington legislative piece. In line with the neighboring state's law, the *Washington Death with Dignity Act* (WDDA) stipulates eligibility and requirement criteria as described below.

*Residency*: The patient must be a Washington resident, that is, must possess a state-issued driver's license, be registered to vote in Washington, or have evidence of property ownership or lease in the state (RCW 70.245.130). The residency requirement was built originally into the law in Oregon, to prevent "suicide tourism" to that state. When the law passed in Oregon and in Washington, a few officials worried that flocks of people would migrate to both states for the drugs, in the manner that foreigners seek to die in Switzerland, where there is no residency requirement for assisted death. As a professor Barbara Glidewell put it, "There was a lot of fear that the elderly would be lined up in their R.V.'s at the Oregon border" (Hafner, 2012).

*Age and State of Mind*: The patient must be a competent adult (18 or older) who, in the opinion of either a court or the patient's physicians, psychiatrist, or psychologist, has the ability to make and communicate an informed and voluntary decision to health care providers (§70.245.010).[48] The age requirement is more stringent in the United States than elsewhere. In the Netherlands, for instance, requests from minors (12- to 17-year-olds) can be granted (Regionale Toetsingscommissies Euthanasie, 2011). Belgium is currently considering an amendment to its euthanasia law that, if passed, would also allow children the option to seek death with assistance (Roberts, 2013).

Once a request for lethal medication is made, physicians must recommend that the patient notify the next of kin of his or her decision (§70.245.0080). If a patient declines or is unable to notify family members, that does not disqualify his/her request for the medication.[49] The fact that notification of relatives is a recommendation—and not a requirement—has come under attack by opponents. A similar assisted death measure, introduced in Massachusetts in 2012, mirrored the notification provision described earlier. The opposition seized on the absence of a requirement and ran an ad that asked: "How would you feel if you came home and your mother had decided to take her life?" (NYT, Dec. 6, 2012). Joe Baerlein, whose public relations and lobbying firm marshaled the opposition in Massachusetts, believed that the lack of a requirement contributed to the defeat of the initiative: "Voters couldn't get their arms around that," he said.

In addition, if the physicians involved in the request process believe that the patient is suffering from a psychiatric or psychological disorder or depression causing impaired judgment, the patient must be referred for counseling (§70.245.060). In such cases, the process is halted until counseling has taken place and a determination has been made that the patient's judgment is not impaired. Again, opponents often criticize the law for not mandating that a psychiatrist be one of the two physicians a patient has to consult.

*Diagnosis and Prognosis*: The patient must be terminally ill; that is, he or she must have an incurable and irreversible disease that has been medically confirmed by two physicians and will, within reasonable medical judgment, produce death within six months (§70.245.010). The terminal illness criterion limits eligibility to a very small group of people and excludes patients who, like Governor Booth Gardner, are suffering from severe chronic illnesses such as Parkinson's. Unlike the American death with dignity laws, the Netherlands allows assisted-dying in nonterminal cases where "suffering is unbearable, with no prospect of improving," and Belgium allows it for nonterminal patients when their suffering is "constant" and "cannot be alleviated" (*Termination of Life on Request and Assisted Suicide Review Procedures Act*, 2002; *Act of Belgian Parliament on Euthanasia*, 2002).

Those who dispute assisted death often attack the reliability of medical prognosis by providing anecdotal evidence of patients who were deemed terminally ill and lived much longer than the six-month projection. For example, in 2012, those opposing an aid in dying ballot measure introduced in Massachusetts ran an ad showing a young widow whose husband lived a year and a half longer than expected.[50] The unreliability of diagnostic precision is a theme that first emerged in 1906, when medical science was far more immature than today. Accordingly, the *Times-Dispatch* (the newspaper of record of Richmond, VA) asked:

> Who is to determine when a malady is incurable? Our doctors? But even the most infallible doctor makes mistakes—has made plenty of them. If euthanasia sent one man to his death who might have gotten well and lived, would not the whole practice stand condemned? Save in the case of criminals, the termination of human life has hitherto been left wholly to superhuman will. Where is the physician so sure of his diagnosis that he is willing to wrest this responsibility from Providence? (*Times-Dispatch*, Jan. 9, 1906)

*Self-Administration*: The law does not authorize a physician or any other person to end a patient's life by lethal injection, mercy killing, or active euthanasia (§70.245.180). Patients, therefore, must be able to take the medication without help. As stated in note 1, the lethal dosage may involve up to 100 pills, depending on the substance chosen to terminate life. When that is the case, a patient's relative or friend or a counselor from one of the assisted-death national advocacy organizations may empty each medication capsule and mix its contents with water or apple sauce for easier consumption. To be free from legal liability, they may not aid the patient in any way with the actual ingestion of the mixture. Therefore, to be eligible, patients themselves need to be able to hold a container, feed themselves, swallow the drugs, and digest them. Critics of this model of assisted death charge that it carries risk of complications (i.e., regurgitation) since many terminally ill patients are unable to swallow, hold down, and/or absorb the lethal drugs (The World Federation of Right to Die Societies, n.d.). They propose instead that active euthanasia, that is, the administration of the drugs by a physician, minimizes such complications and should thus be adopted.[51] Opponents of assisted death, in turn, charge that the mere possibility of botched procedures warrants striking down the practice altogether. Although rare, as Table 6.1 shows, incomplete ingestion and/or medication tolerance, followed by patients regaining consciousness, has occurred in Oregon.

*Requests, Rescissions, and Waiting Periods*: A patient must first make an oral request to his or her attending physician, which is followed by a written one. Subsequently, patients' requests must be reiterated orally to their doctor at least 15 days after the initial oral request was made. At that time, the attending physician must offer the patient an opportunity to rescind the request (§70.245.090). Additionally, patients may rescind their request for lethal medication at any time and in any manner without regard to their mental state (§70.245.100). At least 48 hours must elapse between the date when the patient signs the written request and the writing of a prescription by his/her doctor (§70.245.110). A patient's written request must be signed and dated by himself or herself in the presence of at least two witnesses (§70.245.030). At least one of the witnesses must not be related to the patient by blood, marriage, or adoption; must not be legally entitled to patient's estate; and must not be professionally related to the health care facility where the patient is

**Table 6.1 Use of *Death with Dignity Act* in Oregon State, Selected Characteristics**

| Oregon State | 1998 | 1999 | 2000 | 2001 | 2002 | 2003 | 2004 | 2005 | 2006 | 2007 | 2008 | 2009 | 2010 | 2011 |
|---|---|---|---|---|---|---|---|---|---|---|---|---|---|---|
| Number of patients for whom medication was dispensed | 21 | 33 | 39 | 44 | 58 | 67 | 60 | 64 | 65 | 85 | 88 | 95 | 96 | 114 |
| Number of patients who died after ingesting the medication | 15 | 27 | 26 | 19 | 36 | 39 | 35 | 32 | 35 | 46 | 54 | 53 | 59 | 63 |
| Demographic characteristics of patients who died as a result of lethal medication | | | | | | | | | | | | | | |
| Male | 53% | 59% | 44% | 38% | 71% | 45% | 49% | 61% | 57% | 53% | 50% | 53% | 59% | 37% |
| Age: median (in years) | 69 | 71 | 69 | 68 | 69 | 73 | 64 | 70 | 74 | 65 | 72 | 78 | 72 | 70 |
| White, non-Hispanic | 100% | 96% | 96% | 95% | 97% | 98% | 100% | 95% | 98% | 98% | 98% | 98% | 100% | 96% |
| Married | 13% | 44% | 67% | 38% | 53% | 36% | 41% | 53% | 50% | 43% | 52% | 46% | 51% | 38% |
| College graduate (or higher) | 27% | 48% | 19% | 33% | 26% | 48% | 51% | 37% | 41% | 39% | 60% | 48% | 42% | 49% |
| No health insurance | 7% | 0 | 0 | 0 | 3% | 3% | 0 | 0 | 2% | 0 | 3% | 1% | 3% | 3% |
| Underlying illness: cancer | 87% | 63% | 78% | 86% | 84% | 83% | 78% | 84% | 87% | 86% | 80% | 78% | 79% | 82% |
| End-of-life concerns[1] | | | | | | | | | | | | | | |
| Loss of autonomy | 80% | 81% | 93% | 94% | 84% | 93% | 87% | 79% | 96% | 100% | 95% | 97% | 94% | 89% |
| Less able to engage in activities making life enjoyable | 67% | 81% | 78% | 76% | 84% | 93% | 92% | 89% | 96% | 86% | 92% | 86% | 94% | 90% |
| Inadequate pain control or concern about it | 7% | 26% | 30% | 6% | 26% | 21% | 22% | 24% | 48% | 33% | 5% | 10% | 15% | 32% |
| Number of patients who died without ingesting the medication[2] | 6 | 5 | 8 | 14 | 16 | 18 | 13 | 15 | 19 | 26 | 22 | 30 | 20 | 25 |
| Number of physicians who wrote prescriptions | 14 | 14 | 22 | 33 | 33 | 42 | 40 | 39 | 40 | 45 | 59 | 55 | 59 | 62 |

Notes:
[1] Data on end-of-life concerns shown here were obtained from follow-up interviews with prescribing physicians conducted by the Oregon Health Department. In a few of the reports, data on end-of-life concern obtained from interviews with family members of the deceased are also shown. Most questions on the family interview were

**Table 6.1 (continued)**

analogous to those asked of participating physicians, including questions probing specific concerns that may have contributed to the patients request for lethal medication. Additional questions were asked regarding physical suffering, finances, and hospice care. Some family members had difficulty separating pain from other aspects of physical suffering (for example, difficulty breathing, difficulty swallowing, and medication side effects); so, the reports do not distinguish pain from physical suffering in assessing family responses. Consequently, physician responses about pain are not directly comparable to family responses about physical suffering. However, it should be noted that relatives' responses on this category are consistently higher than physicians'.

[2]The totals depicted in this table refer to the number of deaths under the *Death with Dignity Act* (DWDA) of patients who obtained a prescription and died during that year. In some cases, patients obtain their lethal medication in one year and take it on the following year. In those cases, the total of deaths under the *DWDA* exceed the numbers above. Those are noted as follows. Because the percentages provided by the Oregon *DWDA* reports were calculated on the total of deaths presented above (and do not count the deaths of patients who obtained prescriptions in previous years), I chose to present those numbers in the table. Also noted are the few circumstances when the medicine was partially ingested, regurgitated, or tolerated resulting inpatients regaining consciousness and ultimately dying of the underlying illness. Two patients were still alive in 1999; an additional patient who obtained a lethal prescription in 1998 died in 1999 under the *Act* and for that reason the total deaths on the table exceeds 27. Five patients were still alive in 2000; an additional patient who obtained a lethal prescription in 1999 died in 2000 under the *Act* and for that reason the total deaths on the table exceeds 26. Eleven patients were still alive in 2001; two additional patients who obtained lethal prescriptions in 2000 died in 2001 under the *Act* and for that reason the total deaths on the table exceeds 19. Six patients were still alive in 2002; two additional patients who obtained lethal prescriptions in 2001 died in 2002 under the *Act* and for that reason the total deaths on the table exceeds 36. Ten patients were still alive in 2003; two additional patients who obtained lethal prescriptions in 2002 and another who obtained a prescription in 2001 died in 2003 under the *Act* and for that reason the total deaths on the table exceeds 39. Twelve patients were still alive in 2004; two additional patients who obtained lethal prescriptions in 2003 died in 2004 under the *Act* and for that reason the total deaths on the table exceeds 35. Seventeen patients were still alive in 2005; six additional patients who obtained lethal prescriptions in 2004 died in 2005 under the *Act* and for that reason the total deaths on the table exceeds 32. Furthermore, one 2004 prescription recipient, who ingested the prescribed medication in 2005, became unconscious 25 minutes after ingestion, then regained consciousness 65 hours later. This person did not obtain a subsequent prescription and died 14 days later of the underlying illness (17 days after ingesting the medication). Eleven patients were still alive in 2006; eleven additional patients who obtained lethal prescriptions in 2005 died in 2006 under the *Act* and for that reason the total deaths on the table exceeds 35. Thirteen patients were still alive in 2007; three additional patients who obtained lethal prescriptions in 2006 died in 2007 under the *Act* and for that reason the total deaths on the table exceeds 46. Twelve patients were still alive in 2008; six additional patients who obtained lethal prescriptions in 2007 died in 2008 under the *Act* and for that reason the total deaths on the table exceeds 54. Twelve patients were still alive in 2009; six additional patients who obtained lethal prescriptions in 2008 died in 2009 under the *Act* and for that reason the total deaths on the table exceeds 53. In 2010, two of the patients who took the medications did not die after ingestion, but died later from their underlying illness. At the time of this writing, status was pending for 15 patients according to the *DWDA* 2010 report. Additionally, six patients who obtained lethal prescriptions in 2009 died in 2010 under the *Act* and for that reason the total deaths on the table exceeds 59. In 2011, ingestion status is unknown for 25 patients for whom *DWDA* prescriptions were written. Three of these patients died and follow-up questionnaires were received, but ingestion status could not be determined. For the remaining 22 patients, both death and ingestion status are pending. Of the 114 patients for whom *DWDA* prescriptions were written during 2011, 64 ingested the medication; 63 died from ingesting the medication, and one patient ingested the medication but regained consciousness before dying of underlying illness and is therefore not counted as a *DWDA* death. The patient regained consciousness approximately 14 hours following ingestion and died about 38 hours later. Incomplete ingestion was reported for the patient. Additionally, nine patients with prescriptions written in previous years ingested the medication during 2011; eight of these patients died from ingesting the medication, and one ingested the medication but regained consciousness before dying of underlying illness and is therefore not counted as a *DWDA* death. The patient briefly regained consciousness following ingestion and died approximately 30 hours later. Possible medication tolerance was reported for the patient. Thus, two patients ingesting lethal medication in 2011 awoke and ultimately died of their underlying illness. One patient received their prescription in 2011 and the other received their prescription in 2010. (The information presented here was compiled from all of the annual *Death with Dignity Act* reports produced by the Oregon Health Authority incompliance with the *Act* (public.health.Oregon.gov/providerpartnerres ources/evaluationres earch/de athwithdignityact/page s/ar-index.aspx).

being treated or resides (§70.245.030). The patient's physicians (attending and consulting) also may not serve as witnesses (§70.245.030). Finally, if a patient's request for lethal medication is altered or forged, or if a rescission is concealed or destroyed, those responsible are liable for civil and criminal sanctions (§70.245.200). Coercion and/or undue influence on patients are also punishable (§70.245.200).

In addition to the criteria stated earlier, to comply with the WDDA, physicians must counsel patients about the importance of having another person present when the medication is ingested and of not taking the lethal prescription in a public place (§70.245.190).[52] Upon writing the prescription and with patient's written consent, the physician must first contact the pharmacist who will dispense the drug and then forward the prescription to be filled (§70.245.040). Physicians and pharmacists are not obligated to accept patients' requests to hasten death (§70.245.190). In such cases, they may or may not refer the patient to another health care provider who would be willing to participate. Over the 15 years that the law has been in effect in Oregon, the number of physicians who wrote prescriptions under the *Act* has increased from 14 in 1998 to 62 in 2011 (see Tables 6.1 and 6.2). In Washington, 53 physicians wrote lethal prescriptions in 2009, whereas in 2011, 80 doctors did so.[53] Research on physicians' attitudes toward aid in dying indicates support for the practice among medics. In a survey conducted prior to the legalization in Oregon, Emanuel, Fairclough, Daniels, and Clarridge (1996) found that nearly half of surveyed oncologists from six American states supported some form of physician-assisted death. Accordingly, another study drew on a national sample of physicians and found that 45 percent of them favored the practice (Meier et al., 1998). More recently, another prospective survey found that 86 percent of medical residents would be willing to aid patients die (Bold & Schneider, 2001).[54] Besides physicians, participation by pharmacists also shows increase. Unlike Oregon, Washington also reports data on the number of pharmacists dispensing the medication. When the law first went into effect, 29 pharmacists filled prescriptions to hasten death, versus 46 two years later (see Table 6.2).

The right to refuse participation is extended to hospitals under the WDDA (§70.245.190). Additionally, if a hospital chooses to participate, it may not require individual physicians to take part in the practice. Hospitals can, however, prohibit their health care employees from participating in aid in dying on the premises controlled by said hospitals. Although hospitals must inform the public when they choose not to participate in assisted death as stated by the WDDA (§70.245.190), currently there are no comprehensive lists of which institutions are participants in the practice. Among the largest secular hospitals in the state (those with over 400 beds), the University of Washington Medical Center allows its doctors to take part in aid in dying.[55] A few other hospitals affiliated with the university also participate in the WDDA. For instance, the University of Washington Northwest Hospital and Medical Center (with 281 beds) is among them. However, although Northwest "has decided that a patient's or provider's

**Table 6.2 Use of *Death with Dignity Act* in Washington State, Selected Characteristics**

| Washington State | 2009 | 2010 | 2011 |
|---|---|---|---|
| Number of patients for whom medication was dispensed | 63 | 87 | 103 |
| Number of patients who have died[1] | 47 | 72 | 94 |
| Demographic characteristics, as a percentage of deceased patients | | | |
| Male | 55% | 50% | 52% |
| Age: 55 and older | 87% | 95% | 87% |
| White, non-Hispanic | 98% | 95% | 94% |
| Married | 46% | 51% | 46% |
| Some college education | 61% | 62% | 75% |
| Private, Medicare, Medicaid, or combination of health insurance | 89% | 88% | 87% |
| Underlying illness: cancer | 79% | 78% | 78% |
| End-of-life concerns[2] | | | |
| Loss of autonomy | 100% | 90% | 87% |
| Less able to engage in activities making life enjoyable | 87% | 87% | 89% |
| Inadequate pain control or concern about it | 25% | 36% | 38% |
| Number of patients who died after ingesting the medication | 36 | 51 | 70 |
| Number of patients who died without ingesting the medication[3] | 7 | 15 | 19 |
| Number of physicians who wrote prescriptions | 53 | 68 | 80 |
| Number of pharmacists who dispensed medication | 29 | 40 | 46 |

Notes:
[1]For the remaining 4 people, no documentation was received indicating that death had occurred in 2009. The same is true for 15 individuals in 2010 and 9 individuals in 2011 (*Washington State Department of Health 2011 Death with Dignity Act Reports*, 2009–11).
[2]Other concerns listed include "loss of dignity," "loss of control over bodily functions," "being a burden," "concern over costs of treatment." Totals are greater than 100% because patients may have selected more than one option.
[3]For the remaining 4 people, ingestion status is unknown in 2009. The same is true for 6 individuals in 2010 and 5 individuals in 2011 (*Washington State Department of Health Death with Dignity Act Reports*, 2009–11).

participation . . . is his or her own choice [and thus] will not interfere with the patient-provider relationship, nor with any treatment plans the patient and provider have mutually agreed to pursue," the hospital "will not manage, prescribe, dispense or administer, or allow patients to self-administer, life-ending medication during their stay" (UW Medicine, n.d.). Cassie Sauer, vice-president of Communications for the Washington State Hospital Association, which adopted a position of neutrality with respect to the WDDA, summed up the complexity of hospital usage shortly after the passage of *I-1000*:

About a third of the hospitals are allowing their doctors and staff to participate if they want to. Another third are saying that they will allow some things but not others. They might say that you can't be the prescribing doctor but can give the second opinion. You can do it in our office buildings but not in the hospital. You can do it in the hospital, but our pharmacy won't fill the prescriptions. Reporters are pretty frustrated with this part. They want us to have a list that's a yes-no list. They want hospitals to be in, or be out. But it's not that easy. (Heisel, 2009)

Such complexity is aggravated by the fact that Washington not only has the lowest number of hospital beds per capita in the United States (Washington State Hospital Association, 2011) but many of those beds are under the control of a religious health care entity—mostly Catholic. The Catholic health care system is the largest private nonprofit provider in the United States. In Washington, between 2007 and 2009, 15 hospitals belonged to Catholic health care systems (Hapenney, 2011). This represented roughly 3,000 beds in Catholic-run hospitals then and that number is growing, as Catholic-sponsored medical centers are increasingly merging with smaller secular hospitals (*NYT*, Feb. 20, 2012). Apparently prompted by the passage of the *Obamacare*, the expansion of the religious dominion over health care comes with ideological strings attached. For instance, hospitals that traditionally offered elective abortions have agreed to stop those services once the merge with Catholic system *Providence Health and Services* goes through. If reproductive rights have been negatively affected, it is plausible that availability of aid in dying will too.[56]

Records of patient requests, prescriptions, and medication dispensation are required and annually reviewed by Washington's Department of Health (§70.245.150). To ensure transparency, statistical reports containing data as shown in Tables 6.1 and 6.2 are published every year. Language surrounding the practice, in turn, is euphemistic. The law, as adopted in Washington, frames the practice as a medical treatment and prohibits the use of "suicide" or "assisted suicide" in state-issued reports; instead, such reports must refer to the practice as "obtaining and self-administering life-ending medication" (§70.245.180).

To comply with the WDDA, doctors and other medical certifiers also are prohibited from using any of the following words/terms: "suicide, assisted suicide, physician-assisted suicide, Death with Dignity, I-1000, mercy killing, euthanasia, Secobarbital or Seconal, Pentobarbital or Nembutal" (Washington State Department of Health, 2009). As a result, death certificates of those under the WDDA record the individual's underlying illness as his/her natural cause of death (§70.245.040). This requirement has prompted critics of the practice to charge the law as requiring "physicians to falsify death certificates" (Patients Rights Council, 2013).

Finally, the provisions set forth by the WDDA provide safeguards to patients and their families in the context of life insurance, in that they prescribe that "[a] . . . patient's act of ingesting medication to end his or her life in a humane and dignified manner shall not have an effect upon a life, health, or accident insurance or annuity policy" (§70.245.170). Customarily, life insurance policies contain suicide clauses, whereby the policy becomes null and void if the insured kills himself or herself within a specified time—usually two years after the purchase date, although some states provide a statutory one-year suicide clause (Garman & Forgue, 2007). By this legislation, however, such exclusions should not be involved in deaths under the WDDA.

## WHO *DIES WITH DIGNITY?* AND HOW, WHEN, WHERE, AND WHY THEY DO IT

The following was published on *The Seattle Times*'s obituary section in the fall of 2011:

> Meg HOLMES—Meg died on October 1st, at age 57, after a two-year journey with brain cancer. She was a scientist by profession, a musician by avocation and loved the outdoors. (*The Seattle Times*, 2011)

Five days after she died, Meg Holmes's husband, Andrew Taylor, blogged about the circumstances of her death:

> Suffering from a disease that robs one of intellect and dignity, she had the option, as a Washington resident, to choose the time of her death. She used the provisions of Washington's "Death with Dignity Act" to hasten her death, while she was still able to converse with and understand her family members. . . .
> Her family gathered on Friday and spent the day with her. She was much more alert and animated than of late and visited with each of us. Despite knowing that her death was the next day, we all slept well that night (I slept much better than for many weeks), showing us that we were prepared for her passing. Social workers (she met privately with one from hospice and one from Swedish Hospital[57] to affirm her decision) and the volunteer from "Compassion and Choices Washington" all remarked on her readiness (and that she had not been ready the previous week). . . . [58]
> Meg died peacefully and quickly, with no signs of discomfort. It was a remarkable end to a long struggle, and released Meg from what we all knew could be a long, distressing, undignified and inevitable end. Our preparations, the company of relatives, Meg's peaceful passing and the knowledge of her command of the situation all served to make her passing much easier for us all.

In many ways Meg Holmes epitomizes the other 252 Washingtonians for whom lethal medications had been prescribed by the end of 2011—she was white, married, educated, over 55 years old; had health insurance; and suffered from cancer.[59,60]

Deaths under the *Act* are relatively rare; between 2009 and 2011, of the 253 individuals for whom death-hastening medication was prescribed, 213 took the lethal drugs. To put it in context, 49,386 Washingtonians died in 2011—roughly one quarter of those deaths (12,198), like Holmes's, were due to cancer, 2 percent

(992) resulted from suicide (not performed under the WDDA), and 0.2 percent (94) were due to lethal medications prescribed under the *Act* (Washington State Department of Health, 2012).

Patients who choose to hasten death infrequently are accompanied by their doctors when they take the prescribed drugs. In 2009, when the law went into effect, prescribing physicians were present at 8 percent of recorded deaths under the Act (Washington State Department of Health, 2011). In subsequent years, that proportion dropped to 4 percent and 3 percent (in 2010 and 2011, respectively). In roughly half of the deaths, however, a health care provider—other than the patient's physician—was present (47 percent, 53 percent, and 51 percent, in 2009 through 2011; Washington State Department of Health, 2012). The absence of physicians at the bedside at the time of death may be attributed, in part, to the typically short duration of their relationship with the patient. Even though these relationships range from 3 weeks to 27 years, most physicians report knowing the patients for whom they prescribe the lethal drugs for less than 24 weeks.

In the majority of cases (93 percent), patients take their medication between three weeks and six months after they first request it. Once the drug is ingested, most patients are rendered unconscious in less than 10 minutes and most die within 90 minutes of consumption (a range of 57 percent to 71 percent between 2009 and 2011). In addition, before dying, at least two patients briefly recuperated consciousness after ingesting the lethal drugs.

Overwhelmingly, WDDA deaths take place in private residences (patients', family members', or friends' homes): Between 90 percent and 94 percent of deaths happened at home in the three years for which data are available, whereas in the same period only six deaths took place in "long-term care, assisted living, or foster care facilities." No one died in hospitals. In Oregon, where the ODDA has been in effect for 15 years, only one patient has ever used their law in a hospital (Oregon Public Health Division, 2013). Advocates argue that the ability to die at home is "[o]ne of the great benefits of having [the] law" (Compassion and Choices of Washington, 2009).

This is consistent with research in palliative medicine, which often finds *home* to be exactly where most individuals would prefer to die (Gomes, Calanzani, Gysels, Hall, & Higginson, 2013). It is also reflective of certain structural constraints built into the law itself. First, patients are advised not to take the medication in public places (see note 52). Secondly, as explained by Tom Preston (Medical Director of the Washington chapter of *Compassion and Choices*), although a few hospitals do not disallow their physicians from participating in the law, "very few want it done on the premises [and] consequently, cases of patients dying in the hospital are exceedingly rare—they die at home" (personal communication, February 28, 2013).[61]

At the crux of the argument in favor of aid in dying are the twin goals of maximizing individual autonomy and minimizing human suffering. Those who support assisted death believe that patients should be able to control the decision of when to end their own lives and that they should be able to avoid unwanted suffering (Appel, 2007). According to data collected by the Washington Department of Health and provided by physicians in compliance with the WDDA, patients' top end-of-life concerns are a "loss of autonomy," "diminished quality of life," and "loss of dignity."[62] "Inadequate pain control," however, tends to rank low in physicians' perception of patients' motivations for requesting the lethal prescription.[63]

Although one must consider that these are physician-reported data, similar results have been found in surveys with family members of those who died under the "Death with Dignity" acts (Ganzini, Goy, & Dobscha, 2008; Pearlman et al., 2005; but see notes, Table 6.1). The fact that pain, apparently, is not central to patients' decision-making in hastening death is interesting in many ways and its implications will be raised in the next chapter.

Contradicting the assessment by physicians and by patients' loved ones of the centrality of pain as a motive in WDDA, the use of *suffering* and other pain synonyms and correlates is still very much dominant in the discourse of those who propose the legalization of assisted death. For instance, in his outreach letter, Governor Booth Gardner's appeal begins as follows:

"Dear Friend,
In the midst of agony, there is potential for peace.
When we or a loved one are experiencing unbearable suffering . . . there is a grace inside our humanity that is capable of saying,
'It's time.' " (Gardner, 2008)

Echoing Gardner's tone, family members of Linda Fleming, the first person known to die under the *Death with Dignity* Act in Washington State, released a statement she had prepared whereby Fleming explained her choice to hasten her death: "The pain became unbearable and it was only going to get worse" (*The Sequim Gazette*, May 27, 2009). Linda Fleming had pancreatic cancer. Research also suggests that an appeal to pain intractability is not a mere strategy by proponents to attract empathy; studies have shown that most terminally ill patients receive inadequate pain relief due to physicians' lack of training, fear of audit by a regulatory body, among many other reasons (Mercadante, 1999; Chang, 1999; Induru & Lagman, 2011).

Meanwhile, there is some evidence that palliative care and awareness actually has improved *after* the passage of the "Death with Dignity Act" in Oregon (see, e.g., Steinbrook, 2008; to my knowledge, none has yet emerged in Washington). Results of a survey mailed to physicians who deal with terminally ill patients revealed that 76 percent of them made efforts to improve their knowledge of the use of pain medications in the terminally ill, while 30 percent reported that they had increased referrals to hospice (Ganzini et al., 2000; see also Quill, 2007).[64]

## SUBSEQUENT ATTEMPTS TO LEGALIZE ASSISTED DEATH

In 2009, another Western state became the third American jurisdiction to permit aid in dying. Unlike Oregon and Washington, the option to choose hastened death in Montana resulted from a court ruling by that state's Supreme Court. In what amounted to a state version of *Quill* and *Glucksberg*, Kathryn Tucker, the legal director of *Compassion and Choices*,[65] filed a suit against the state and Montana's attorney general on behalf of Robert Baxter, a 75-year-old terminally ill patient, four physicians, and the aid in dying organization. Plaintiffs in *Baxter* claimed that the state statutes proscribing assisted suicide violated several sections of the Montana constitution, more specifically, the privacy and dignity clauses.

The pursuit of aid in dying legalization in that state via constitutional reform had started 40 years earlier. Montana's constitution, ratified in 1972, was drafted by a unique and professionally diverse group of Montanans elected as delegates by the voters. During the process, Mrs. Joyce M. Franks, an aid in dying activist and Montana resident, submitted a proposal to the state's Bill of Right Committee to include a "right to die" provision in the revised constitution, under the human dignity clause (*Baxter v. Montana*, 2009, p. 63; Russell, 1977, p. 272). During her testimony before the Constitutional Convention, Mrs. Franks explained: "What I am working for is that every person shall have the right to determine, barring accident, the manner of his dying. And then, I am advocating the twin right to make it legal, if he desires this type of death, for a person to receive a quick and easy medicated death somehow" (*Baxter v. Montana*, 2009, p. 64).

Though Mrs. Franks's proposal did not bear fruits then, its core argument surfaced again in 2008 when District Judge Dorothy McCarter ruled in Baxter et al.'s favor, thus justifying her decision: "The Montana constitutional rights of individual privacy and human dignity, taken together, encompass the right of a competent terminally ill person to die with dignity" (*Baxter v. Montana*, 2008, p. 64 [2008 Mont. Dist. LEXIS 482]). The lower court decision was appealed and on December 31, 2009, the Montana Supreme Court upheld the legality of medically hastened death in the state.

Avoiding the constitutional questions of a "right" to assisted suicide as privacy and dignity matters, the state's high court instead ruled that state law protects physicians in Montana from prosecution for prescribing lethal doses of medication to terminally ill patients. Such circumvention of the larger question posed by plaintiffs impoverished the importance of this legal battle for aid-in-dying proponents; a ruling to uphold the lower court's decision would have enshrined *Baxter* as the case that, for the first time, guaranteed the citizens of a state the right to aid in dying. As bioethicist and medical historian Jacob Appel explains, "a Montana ruling favoring aid in dying would require a constitutional amendment to overturn," an unlikely prospect and thus a more definitive victory when compared to Oregon's and Washington's statutes, "which could be revoked by legislatures at any time" (*The Huffington Post*, Sep. 2, 2009). The ruling in *Baxter* has proven to be potentially just as fragile. In February 2013, Montana's House of Representatives passed a bill (*H.B. 505*) designed to void the decision in *Baxter*. Authored by House Judiciary Committee Chairman Krayton Kerns (Republican), *H.B. 505* prescribed a penalty of 10 years in prison for physicians who provide aid in dying. The bill was later defeated in the Senate, on a 27–23 vote (Ertelt, 2013).

Advancing aid in dying at the ballot box, in legislatures, and state courts, advocates of assisted death claim to be well positioned to "battle the injustice of limited end-of-life choice in various states *simultaneously*" (Compassion and Choices, 2013). Indeed, as citizens went to the ballot to decide President Obama's reelection, Massachusetts voters also weighed in on the issue of aid in dying. Opponents of assisted death prevailed, by a narrow margin, with 51 percent of the votes (Associated Press, Nov. 7, 2012). The defeat in Massachusetts was promptly followed by introduction of a bill in the legislature of that state that, if approved, would legalize assisted death much in the same manner as the ODDA and the WDDA had done by ballot initiative (*House Draft 1183*). Similar bills have been introduced in Hawaii, Kansas, New Jersey, and Connecticut. Arizona, New York, and New Hampshire are also considering bills related to aid in dying.

Just recently, two other states—Vermont and New Mexico—joined Montana, Washington, and Oregon in affirmatively allowing aid in dying for terminally ill patients. In January 2014, a state court in New Mexico recognized the right of competent, terminally ill patients "to choose aid in dying" and of physicians to provide such aid (*Morris v. Brandenberg,* No. D-202-CV 2012-02909 at II, NN). Distinguishing that his judgment differed from the U.S. Supreme Court's decision on *Glucksberg*, New Mexico's Judge Nan G. Nash acknowledged that while the U.S. Constitution denies the existence of such right, the constitution of the state of New Mexico provides "greater rights to New Mexico defendants than those rights provided in the federal constitution in many instances" (*Morris,* No D-202-CV 2012-02909 at Z).

Judge Nash's decision is the culmination of a case filed by advocates in 2012, which was patterned after *Baxter*. In *Morris v. New Mexico,* two physicians and a patient contended that the state statute outlawing "assisting suicide" (NM Statute 30-2-4) never was intended to apply to physicians treating patients in the late stages of terminal illnesses. Their rationale lied on the idea that the dying process was not considered part of the statute, as opposed to assisting in suicide in which an individual would otherwise live. "In the New Mexico case," said Kathryn Tucker, legal affairs director for Compassion and Choices, "[w]e hope to clarify . . . that a vague statute that makes a crime of 'assisting suicide' does not reach the conduct of a physician providing aid in dying, because of course the choice of a dying patient for a peaceful death is not, and ought not be conflated with, 'suicide' " (Carman, 2012).

**Table 6.3 Timeline: 1991–2014 (Selected Developments)**

| | |
|---|---|
| 1991 | Washington State: Ballot initiative (I-119) defeated |
| 1992 | California: Ballot measure (Proposition 161) defeated |
| 1994 | Oregon: Ballot initiative (Measure 16) passed, making medically-assisted death legal in Oregon. Legal injunction halts the practice in the state. Washington State: In January, *Compassion in Dying*, two physicians and their patients file what would later become *Washington v. Glucksberg*. The case is argued in March and in May a decision favorable to assisted death is issued. The State appeals. New York: Three physicians and three terminally ill patients file what would later become U.S. Supreme Court case *Vacco v. Quill*. |
| 1995 | Washington State: Legislative Bill (S.B. 5596) is introduced and dies in Committee |
| 1996 | The U.S. Supreme Court grants certiorari to companion cases *Glucksberg* and *Quill*. |
| 1997 | Washington State: Legislative Bill (S.B. 5654) is introduced and dies in Committee *Washington v. Glucksberg* is argued (January 8) and decided (June 26) Oregon: Ballot measure to repeal ODDA (Measure 51) defeated. Injunction lifted and implementation of ODDA begins. |
| 1998 | Michigan: Ballot initiative (Proposal B) defeated Oregon: First death under the ODDA takes place in March |
| 2000 | Maine: Ballot initiative (Maine's "Death with Dignity Act") defeated Note: Between 1994 and 2000, 54 bills pro-legalization of aid in dying were introduced in 21 states. |
| 2006 | Washington State: Legislative bill (S.B. 6843) is introduced and dies in Committee Oregon: *Gonzales v. Oregon* is decided (originally filed in 2001) |
| 2008 | Washington State: Ballot initiative (I-1000) passed |
| 2009 | Montana: *Baxter v. Montana* decided |
| 2010 | New Mexico: *Morris v. Brandenberg* filed |
| 2012 | Massachusetts: Ballot initiative (Question 2) defeated; Legislative Bill (House Draft 1183) introduced Hawaii, Kansas, New Jersey, Connecticut: Legislative bills introduced |
| 2013 | Vermont: *Patient Choice and Control at the End of Life Act (Act 39)* passes |
| 2014 | New Mexico: *Morris v. Brandenberg* decided |

One year before the decision in *Morris,* the "Patient Choice and Control at End of Life Act (Act 39)" was passed by the Vermont General Assembly, making it the first state to legalize physician aid in dying via legislative efforts (for a summary of the developments discussed in this chapter, see Table 6.3).

*Act 39* provides eligible Vermont residents with terminal diseases the option to be prescribed a dose of medication that, if taken, will hasten the end of their life. Vermont's law patterns the Oregon and Washington models and mimics the safeguards built into the ODDA and WDDA (e.g., requests must be voluntary, a waiting period must be observed, a second physician must be consulted, the drugs must be self-administered). One salient difference, however, is that in 2016 many of the oversight provisions will drop. For instance, doctors will no longer be required to report the requests by patients nor will they be required to report the prescriptions issued in accordance with the Act; aid in dying, thus, will become largely a private matter between Vermonter doctors and their patients.

Proponents of decriminalization and regulation of assisted death argue that the U.S. Supreme Court's invitation, in *Glucksberg*, to test the issue in the "laboratory of the states" has been proven viable, with successful implementation in Oregon for 15 years and in Washington, Montana, Vermont, and New Mexico subsequently. As they engage in concerted efforts to advance assisted death throughout the country, terminally ill patients in American states where aid in dying remains legally proscribed increasingly resort to a planned death via nonmedical measures, particularly voluntary starvation and dehydration. The implications of emerging demedicalized models of hastening death, such as this, along with a discussion of the role of physicians in the future of "death with dignity," are the topic of my concluding remarks. First, however, I turn my attention to the experience of other countries, namely, the Netherlands, Belgium, Luxembourg, and Switzerland, where aid in dying is allowed.

## NOTES

1. *Seconal* is the brand name of secobarbital sodium, a barbiturate drug containing anesthetic, anticonvulsant, sedative, and hypnotic properties. About 10 g (100 capsules) of the drug are needed for overdose. Because of the large number of capsules required to induce death, patients are encouraged to open each of them, dispense the powder into a container, and mix it with 6 oz. of room-temperature water. Most of the deaths under the ODDA are accompanied by volunteers of a nonprofit organization, *Compassion and Choices*. In those cases, the volunteer may prepare the lethal liquid. In *How to Die in Oregon*, an award-winning HBO documentary about the law, Roger Sagner, the 343rd patient to choose *death with dignity* in that state, reported that the mix tastes *woody*.

*Nembutal*, or pentobarbital, has also been used in legal medically assisted deaths. Because of its cost—over $1,000.00 compared to Seconal's market price of $130.00—it is sparingly chosen by patients. Nembutal was the drug of choice of Hollywood stars as well. Marilyn Monroe and George Sanders died partly as a result of an overdose of Nembutal, and Oscar-nominee Sally Kirkland attempted suicide in the 1960s using the drug.

2. Commenting on the nondisclosure of the patient's name, Barbara Coombs Lee, head of what then was the largest pro-assisted dying advocacy group, *Compassion in Dying*, stated: "The public doesn't deserve to know anything except to know the law is available and the rules are being followed" (*The Seattle Times*, Mar. 30, 1998).

3. *Pollie* awards are the most prestigious awards in the field of political campaign and public affairs industry. It is conferred by the American Association of Political Consultants in recognition of the best professionals among hundreds of political campaign and public affairs categories.

4. As discussed in Chapter 5, *Gonzales v. Oregon* (2006) was a U.S. Supreme Court case that ruled that the U.S. attorney general could not enforce the federal *Controlled Substances Act* against physicians who prescribed drugs in compliance with the ODDA.

5. Five years prior to *I-119*'s filing in Washington, California advocates crafted the *Humane and Dignified Death Act*. The *Act* was a ballot initiative that would have amended that state's constitution to allow for "aid in dying," defined as "any medical procedure that will terminate the life of a qualified patient swiftly, painlessly, and humanely" (Patients Rights Council, 2005). The measure did not qualify for the ballot, as advocates failed to gather the necessary voter signatures, and therefore the proposition was not introduced.

6. *I-119* was devised by Ralph Mero, a Unitarian Universalist minister who cofounded *Compassion in Dying*, an organization composed of social workers, doctors, nurses, clergymen, and others, designed to provide aid in dying. *Compassion's* members offered advice on lethal doses, counseled bereaved family members, convinced wary doctors, held patients' hands at the moment of death; they did not, however, provide or administer the drugs used in the suicide (*NYT,* Nov. 14, 1993). Mero's involvement in the cause was, as it seems to be true with most advocates, personal. Mero's father's death came at the end of a long, difficult struggle with emphysema and heart disease and shortly before the minister attended a conference on euthanasia organized by the *Hemlock Society* (at the time the only assisted death organization). Concomitantly, Mero's brother-in-law was suffering from AIDS. Having spent considerable time with his brother-in-law and other AIDS patients, Mero later explained that he "was utterly horrified and outraged that lovely human beings should have to die in such a decimated state."

Proponents of *I-119* needed 150,001 signatures to file the initiative (*The Seattle Times,* Oct. 14, 1990). They gathered 218,327 (Ballotpedia.org, 2012b). A few months before the election, proponents had raised $672,583, at that point making it "the second most successful fund-raising effort supporting a state initiative since record-keeping began in 1975" (*The Seattle Times*, July 18, 1991). This was a striking contrast to opponents fundraising results: The "*I-119* No!" committee had collected less than $60,000 by July 1991. What seemed to be an auspicious sign for proponents was quickly transformed into disappointment. *I-119* was defeated; roughly 54 percent of voters were against the measure (Ballotpedia.org, 2012b). When questioned about the results, Ralph Mero partly blamed Jack Kevorkian for the failure of *I-119*. According to the minister, in a conversation with Kevorkian, "Dr. Death" had informed him that he was timing one of his assisted suicides to coincide with the election in Washington. Indeed, about 10 days prior to voters' first test of the issue, Kevorkian helped in a double suicide. According to Mero, the "deaths took place in a cabin in the woods and provided a visual image for our opponents to use suggesting that doctor-assisted suicide was reckless and macabre. It had a very negative effect" (*NYT,* Nov. 14, 1993).

7. During the same period, seven states passed laws against suicide assistance (Iowa Code § 707A.2 [1996]; La. Rev. Stat. 14:32.12 [1995]; Md. Ann. Code Art. 27, §416 [1999]; Mich. 1931 PA 328, MCL 750.329a [1998]; R.I. Gen. Stat. Tit. 11, ch. 60 [1996]; S.C. Code Ann. §16-3-1090 [1998]; Va. Code Ann., § 18.2-76.3, 18.2-76.4 [1998]).

Other than Oregon and Washington, where medical aid in dying is legal, all American states, except Nevada and Utah, prohibit assisted suicide by statute, common law, or case law. However, Utah's *Advance Health Care Directive Act* states that it "does not authorize mercy killing, assisted suicide or euthanasia" (Utah Code § 75-2a-122 [2]), whereas Nevada's law regarding withholding or withdrawing medical treatment states that it does "not condone, authorize or approve mercy killing, assisted suicide or euthanasia" (Nev. Rev. Stat. § 449.670 [2]).

8. The ACLU has a long record of support in legalizing assisted death in the shape of legal advice (e.g., multiple *amici curiae* briefs filed in pivotal cases (e.g., *Washington v. Glucksberg, Vacco v. Quill, Gonzales v. Oregon, Baxter* etc., and most recently the New Mexico case filed by two oncologists, *Morris v. Brandenberg,* seeking to determine the scope of a state statute as to include aid in dying by physicians). ACLU's support has been financial as well (e.g., approximately $61,000.00 were donated to the Washington *I-1000* committee); unfortunately, I could not locate cumulative figures.

9. This favorable decision refers to the early legal stages of *Glucksberg,* discussed in Chapter 5. To recapitulate, in late January 1994, *Compassion in Dying,* then one of the principal social movement organizations promoting aid in dying, joined Dr. Harold Glucksberg, three other physicians, and three terminally ill patients in a lawsuit challenging a Washington statute proscribing assisted suicide (*Compassion in Dying v. Washington,* 850 F. Supp. 1454, 1459). The case was argued in Federal Court on March 17 of that year and a favorable decision was issued in May. In her opinion, Judge Barbara Rothstein declared the Washington statute "unconstitutional because it places an undue burden on the exercise of a protected Fourteenth Amendment liberty interest by terminally ill, mentally competent adults acting knowingly and voluntarily, without undue influence from third parties, who wish to commit physician-assisted suicide" (850 F. Supp. 1459). Furthermore, the court also found the statute to be "unconstitutional because it violates the right to equal protection under the Fourteenth Amendment by prohibiting physician-assisted suicide while permitting the refusal or withdrawal of life support systems for terminally ill individuals" (850 F. Supp. 1459).

10. The committee was chaired by Democrat State Senator Kevin Quigley, presently Washington's secretary of the Department of Social and Health Services. It is unclear why this bill—and subsequent ones—did not get further consideration by the committee. However, given the small percentage of bills that actually are reported, this is not surprising. During the 112th Congress, for instance, 10,870 bills, or 88 percent of total bills being considered, were deemed "inactive legislation," whereas 2 percent, or 241, were "enacted laws" (GovTrack.us, n.d.). Unfortunately, similar data are not available from the Washington legislature.

11. Anderson had wanted to be succeeded by the other Democratic candidate, Ed Murray. Murray, who is openly gay as Anderson was, had made an issue carrying on the late senator's legacy in his campaign (*The Seattle Times,* Sep. 20, 1995).

12. The ODDA first passed in 1994 with voters' approval of Ballot Measure 16 by a margin of 51 percent to 49 percent. However, implementation was delayed by a legal injunction only lifted in 1997. In November of that year, a measure asking Oregon voters to repeal the ODDA was placed on the general election ballot (Measure 51). Voters rejected this measure by a margin of 60 percent to 40 percent, thus retaining the *Death with Dignity Act.* The first death under the law did not happen until March 1998, as described in the opening paragraph of this chapter.

13. Besides being championed by State Senators Anderson and Thibaudeau, respectively, both bills were co-sponsored primarily by other Democrat state senators. *SB 5596* was endorsed by Democrat Jeanne Kohl, Darlene Fairley, and Dwight Pelz (currently chair of the Democratic Party), as well as by a moderate Republican, Eugene Prince. In 1997, Senator Pelz resigned and was replaced by Adam Kline, also a Democrat. Senator Kline, then, along with Jeanne Kohl and Eugene Prince, co-sponsored *SB 5654.*

Senator Fairley was the first disabled politician in the Washington legislature since 1950. She became paraplegic following a car accident in the late 1970s. Upon her election in 1995, Tacoma newspaper *The News Tribune* (Jan. 17, 1995) remarked that "[b]ecause of Fairley's disability, even Republicans admit she brings a unique perspective to the debate on health care reform, which has begun to shape up as a focus of controversy this session." Although she did not co-sponsor the 1997 bill, Senator Fairley lent her support to the victorious *I-1000* in 2008. As chair of the "Yes on *I-1000* Disabilities Caucus," Fairley stated that "as a matter of personal control and autonomy, it makes sense to let patients themselves decide what kind of medical care they want to receive and how long they want to suffer with a terminal illness" (Ballotpedia.org, 2012a). Fairley's support in 2008 was especially significant because one of the most outspoken groups against legalizing assisted death is "Not Dead Yet," a disability rights group.

14. Co-sponsors of *S.B. 6843* included senators Farley and Kohl-Wells, who had previously co-sponsored the similar bill introduced in 1997. Two other Democrats, senators Ken Jacobsen and Craig Pridemore, were also co-sponsors of *S.B. 6843.* The 2006 bill was referred to the *Committee on Health and Long-Term Care* and did not advance further.

15. By 1991, the approval rate was not that different: 104 ballot initiatives had been introduced in Washington State, of which 43, or 41 percent, passed (Initiative and Referendum Institute, 2001).

16. Many other initiatives were filed in Washington but failed to make the ballot either because proponents did not gather a sufficient number of signatures or because they were withdrawn. Among the former was *I-337*, devised by Kevin McKeigue, an Independent politician who later ran for senator and lost. *I-337* would have asked voters: "Shall an initiative be adopted promoting the pursuit of peace through principles of mutual love and respect?" (1977). Roughly two decades later, another initiative, *I-654*, would have asked voters to answer: "Shall government be prohibited from placing children for adoption or foster care with any person who practices right-wing fundamentalist Christianity?" The list goes on.

17. *I-559* would have adjusted property values for tax purposes.

18. Such high approval had been the case throughout his public office tenure. In his biography, *Booth Who? Washington's Charismatic 19th Governor*, commissioned by the Washington State Heritage Center, author John C. Hughes comments on Gardner's popularity: "It's been 17 years since he was Washington's governor, but everyone still knows his name. In 1983, however, when he decided to challenge a sitting governor, he was little known outside Pierce County where he grew up. His brain trust put 'Booth Who?' on a button and it became the catchiest campaign slogan in state history. He was handily elected twice and could have had a third term—maybe more—or a seat in the U.S. Senate. In terms of sheer popularity, his only rival to date is the late Henry M. 'Scoop' Jackson, who served in Congress for 42 years" (Hughes, 2010, p. 1).

19. Later that year, the GATT was ratified as the *World Trade Organization.*

20. The event in question was a Gala ceremony, organized by TVW, Washington's Public Affairs Network, during which Governor Booth Gardner received a *Founder's Award*. An archived video of the event can be watched at http://www.tvw.org.

21. Gardner did not write a textbook. The WASL, on the other hand, was replaced by alternative testing in 2009.

22. It is baffling that Governor Gardner chose to champion a ballot initiative on assisted death instead of simply lobbying for *S.B. 6843*, the bill introduced by Senator Thibaudeau in January of the same year. Maybe the answer lies in his statements about the 1991 ballot measure, which was introduced during his second term as governor. In accordance with the direct democracy process in Washington, once enough signatures are gathered to qualify a measure for popular vote, the state legislature has three options: directly approve the measure, send it to the voters for a binding decision, or approve alternatives to accompany the initiative on the ballot. Governor Gardner's advice to the legislature when the 1991 initiative was filed was that the measure should go straight to citizens of Washington: "On an issue of that significance, I think the people ought to go ahead and vote on it. I also think that if they vote on it, they'll put it to rest for a long period of time" (*The Seattle Times*, Jan. 23, 1991).

23. Other relatives were not so supportive. Doug Gardner, the governor's son, was appalled by the campaign. A born-again Christian, Doug told the Associated Press that he would "join the coalition of groups and residents against the assisted suicide measure" led by his father (Ertelt, 2008a). He explained: "We don't need Booth and Dr. Kevorkian pushing death on us. Dad's lost. He's playing God, trying to usurp God's authority.... I fear the day when he meets his maker" (*The Oregonian,* Mar. 26, 2006). Governor Gardner's reaction to his son's opposition was more measured: "[Doug] believes in Democracy and he believes in fighting for what his rights are and he feels the existing system is right for him" (Jenkins, 2008).

For more on the Gardners' father–son dynamics, see Daniel Bergner's compelling piece published by *The New York Times Magazine* one year before *I-1000* was subjected to popular vote (Bergner, 2007).

24. A total of 13,201 individuals made cash donations to the "Yes on *I-1000* Committee" (followthemoney.org, n.d.).

25. Fifty-three institutions made cash donations to the "Yes on *I-1000* Committee" (followthemoney.org, n.d.). Several chapters of "Compassion and Choices," the "Death with Dignity National Center," the Australian organization "Dying with Dignity," "End-of-life Choices of Connecticut," the "Euthanasia Research and Guidance Organization," Georgia and Illinois chapters of "Final Exit," the "Hemlock Society," and the "Oregon Death with Dignity PAC," among others, donated nearly $2 million, excepting in-kind contribution (data are from *Washington State Public Disclosure Commission, Schedule B for "Yes on I 1000,"* reports dated July 8, 2008, July 11, 2008, October 28, 2008, and Ballotpedia.org, 2012a).

26. This unprecedented success in financial contributions to proponents took all by surprise, including the *Yes on I-1000* committee. In his outreach letter, Governor. Booth Gardner had stated: "Our campaign budget is roughly $1.0 million and we will need every penny. We fully expect to be outspent by the extreme elements that oppose us. And we know that we are also up against a statewide network of churches and other religious settings where the 'Death with Dignity' law will be pummeled and distorted" (Gardner, 2008).

27. Spatial diffusion scholarship provides evidence that states are indeed influenced by other states in their vicinity (see, e.g., Grattet, Jenness, & Curry, 1998, on the diffusion of hate crime laws). Geographic proximity, as these scholars argue, promotes ongoing

communication and shared knowledge, which in turn leads to greater influence with regard to social policies. For instance, since information may easily transcend state borders via shared media (newspapers, radio, and television), these avenues of communication may increase a state's exposure to and knowledge of legal changes in bordering states. As a result, policies adopted in one state may affect the likelihood of the adoption of a similar policy in neighboring states.

28. Currently, Washington is the only American state where same-sex marriage, recreational marijuana use, and medically assisted death are legal. It should come as no surprise, thus, that Washington (tied with Oregon) rank third among liberal states according to a recent Gallup poll (*Gallup, Inc.*, n.d.). All three legal milestones were achieved in Washington via direct democracy processes in the last two elections, but the state's history of ballot measures began in 1907. Since then, of the 24 states in which popular initiatives are allowed, Washington ranks sixth in use of the process, behind California, Oregon, Colorado, North Dakota, and Arizona (Initiative and Referendum Institute, 2013).

29. The Catholic Diocese of Spokane filed for bankruptcy as a result of the numerous sexual abuse suits brought against its clergy members. In 2008, the diocese, by collecting $48 million from its parishioners and insurers, along with selling property, settled with 176 people who claimed they were sexually abused by clergy (*The Seattle Times,* Nov. 13, 2008). Perhaps this explains why most of the cash donation to the "Coalition against Assisted Suicide" originating from Catholic parishes came from out of state.

30. This assertion needs to be taken with caution because the general issue of suicide is very different from its particular applications in the context of physician-aided death. For example, suicide as a result of depression, which dominates the local and national rates, is antithetic to the *Death with Dignity* dying process, where if one of the physicians involved determines that the patient's judgment is impaired, the process is halted and the patient must be referred for a psychological examination. What I call attention to is the possible increased tolerance to suicide as a consequence of its heightened prevalence. Some research into an analogous "desensitization to death" among institutionalized elderly patients (Lavigne-pley & Lévesque, 1992) as well as physicians (Coombs & Powers, 1975) and police workforce (Henry, 1995) has explored how repeated exposure to death in institutional/professional settings may engender desensitization to it.

31. The number of signatures gathered to get *I-1000* on the ballot placed it as number 24 among the top initiative petitions filed in the state (Washington Secretary of State, 2012). Number one, with nearly 700,000 signatures, was *I-282*, introduced in 1973, which limited elected officials' salaries.

32. Just as Ralph Mero warned and I quoted earlier, "If Americans were asked to vote tomorrow on the Bill of Rights, some ad agency would launch a campaign against it."

33. Martin Sheen, born Ramón Antonio Gerardo Estévez, adopted that stage name partly in honor of *The Venerable* and *Most Reverend* Fulton J. Sheen, an American archbishop. Martin Sheen has described watching the preacher on television when he was a child and being drawn to his *magnetic character* (http://www.youtube.com/watch?v=UJul03NPFGU). Son of a Spaniard and an Irish, Martin Sheen is a "devout Catholic" (*Los Angeles Times*, Aug. 25, 2010), "carries a rosary in his pocket" ("Keeps me from cursing," he says), and is an "almost daily communicant" (Kupfer, 2003). He has also been arrested over 60 times for civil disobedience in social justice protests.

34. *The West Wing's* cast has since been used in another political ad, this time by a law professor running for a seat at the state Supreme Court in Maryland. The ad can be

watched here: http://www.theblaze.com/stories/2012/09/21/the-cast-of-the-west-wing
-reunites-for-a-local-mich-campaign-ad/

35. Christina Nicolaidis completed her MD degree at Columbia University and her
MPH at the Washington University. She is currently an associate professor of Medicine
and Public Health and Preventive Medicine at the Oregon Health and Science University.
Her research interests are primarily focused on autism and depression among underserved
populations. In 2006, she published an opinion piece on the *JAMA* about her mother's
choice to die (Nicolaidis, 2006).

36. Watch it here: https://www.youtube.com/watch?v=O2JSBgRkyws

37. Watch it here: https://www.youtube.com/watch?v=Tx5K4rjsZtM. Governor
Roberts also lent her support in outreach letters soliciting donations for the campaign.

38. The "Coalition against Assisted Suicide" sponsored the production of a DVD
titled "In God's Time," which explained the Catholic doctrine on end-of-life issues. The
DVD was sent to 290 parishes of the Archdiocese of Seattle (Kirtley, 2011). Watch it here:
http://www.youtube.com/watch?v=keHn2xeBVfY (Part 1) and http://www.youtube.com/
watch?v=wDW_cZF1YOA (Part 2).

39. In line with concerns raised by "Not Dead Yet" that a disabled life may not be
worth living and therefore may be an incentive in hastening death, just recently, Belgium
allowed 45-year-old twin brothers who were born deaf and were turning blind to end their
lives with physician assistance (Hamilton, 2013). By contrast, "Autonomy, Inc.," an
American disabilities rights group, seeking to clarify that, unlike proposed by "Not Dead
Yet," assisted death found support among disabled persons as well, filed an *amicus curiae*
brief in *Baxter v. Montana.* The case, as discussed elsewhere in this chapter, indemnified
physicians who prescribed lethal medication for terminally ill patients in the state of Montana in 2009 (the final fate of that court decision is yet to be determined, as mentioned at
the end of this case study). "Autonomy's" brief argued that the notion posed by some that
"assisted suicide threatens the easily influenced and vulnerable" is "paternalistic," "an
anathema to . . . numerous members of the disability community" and "moreover, it threatens to set back decades of legislation and advocacy devoted to empowering persons with
disabilities," as it "erroneously assumes that individuals with disabilities are incapable of
making rational, voluntary and independent decisions to hasten their own imminent and
inevitable deaths" (*Amicus Curiae* Brief by Montana Residents with Disabilities and
Autonomy, Inc., 2009, p. 7).

40. The Washington State Medical Association (WSMA) represents nearly 7,000
doctors. Although the organization's official position is against assisted dying, a survey
of its members, conducted by Elway Research in 2008, revealed that 50 percent of
respondents would support a measure like *I-1000* and 42 percent would oppose it. Female
physicians were most likely to support such a law. The survey yielded 502 responses (*The
Seattle Times*, Sep. 22, 2008). Similar results were obtained in 1994 and were published in
the *New England Journal of Medicine.* In that study, questionnaires were sent to 1,355
Washington physicians—including all oncologists and hematologists and a disproportionately high numbers of internists, family physicians, psychiatrists, and general surgeons.
938, or 69 percent, of physicians responded to the survey. Fifty-three percent of respondents thought physician-assisted suicide should be legal in some circumstances (Cohen
et al., 1994).

41. In September 2008, Greg Magnoni, spokesman for the Archdiocese of Seattle,
said the Church had authorized 290 local parishes to take up a collection for the "Coalition

against Assisted Suicide." Materials were sent to the parishes and the priests or pastors were encouraged to mention the opposition to the measure during the services. Donations were voluntary, and according to Magnoni, "[t]here will be envelopes in the pews" (*The News Tribune*, Sep. 2, 2008).

42. In 2004, Ms. Wheeler co-sponsored a lecture series at Gonzaga University titled "Suffering and the God of Abraham: C. S. Lewis and the Problem of Pain."

43. According to a national poll conducted by Gallup, "doctor-assisted suicide is moral issue dividing Americans most"—with 45 percent finding it "morally acceptable" and 48 percent decrying the practice (Gallup, Inc., 2011). Other polls suggest that a majority of Americans (55 percent) favor it, while 45 percent oppose it (Hensley, 2012).

44. According to the Office of Financial Management of Washington's secretary of state (http://www.thestranger.com/seattle/welfare-state/Content?oid=6686284), Adams, Columbia, Garfield, Lincoln, Benton, Grant, and Stevens counties, all of which voted against *I-1000*, also consistently tend to be red counties (61–70 percent of votes in 2008 were Republican).

45. According to the U.S. Census Bureau, 45.8 percent of Yakima county's residents are Hispanic/Latino, versus 11.6 percent statewide. Nationally, 16.7 percent of Americans are of Hispanic/Latino origins (www.quickfacts.census.gov). Yakima's agricultural market has attracted a huge population of Mexicans who, over the years, have established residence in the area. A national amnesty in 1986 legalized 2.3 million Mexicans, including almost 1 million farm workers. Schools offer bilingual programs and masses at Catholic churches are performed in Spanish (*The Seattle Times*, June 21, 2000). Additionally, even though the state of Washington has an elderly dependency ratio relatively low (18.7) by comparison to national average (20.5), Yakima county stands out as one of the metropolitan areas with highest elderly dependent ratios—more than 10 points higher than the U.S. mean (File & Kominski, 2009).

46. For example, Honorable Patricia Wald (1997) has argued that besides end-of-life litigation, boomers may increasingly bring to court challenges to zoning laws (for instance, whether extended family members can live in the same household, or whether group homes for the elderly can locate in certain neighbor hoods), tort law (e.g., what duty of care is ascribed to an elderly person and what value is placed on an elderly person's life), and criminal law (treatment of the elderly in prison as increasing numbers of inmates serve life sentences without parole).

47. In 2000, Maine was targeted by pro-legalization advocates partly because of its high proportion of boomer residents—the assumption being that the issue would find greater support among the cohort. Thirty percent of those who live in Portland, ME, are boomers (Kurtzleben, 2011); statewide, Maine has 18 percent more baby boomers per capita than the nation (Economic Modeling Specialists International, 2010). *Question 1* allowed Maine voters to consider the issue of assisted death much like those in Oregon: "Should a terminally ill adult who is of sound mind be allowed to ask for and receive a doctor's help to die?" The measure was defeated with those against it amounting to 51 percent.

48. Between 2009 and 2011, a total of 10 of the participants had been referred for psychiatric/psychological evaluation (Washington State Department of Health, 2011).

49. In the three years for which data on the circumstances surrounding WDDA deaths are available, 89 percent, 85 percent, and 96 percent of those who hastened death informed family of their decision (Washington State Department of Health, 2011).

50. Watch it here: http://www.youtube.com/watch?feature=player_embedded&v=6voYh5x9u4c

51. In 1999, David Schuman, then Oregon deputy attorney general, was asked by State Senator Neil Bryant whether disabled individuals who could not self-administer would have to be helped to die under the Death with Dignity law. Schuman replied that in the spirit of the state constitution and in accordance with the equal treatment provisions of the Americans with Disabilities Act, Oregon would probably be required to make "reasonable accommodations [to] enable the disabled to avail themselves of the [Death with Dignity] Act's provisions" (Smith, 2004, p. 82). Faced with the challenge, a patient who had lost the use of his limbs due to *amyotrophic lateral sclerosis* (*Lou Gehrig's* disease), and for whom a lethal prescription had been written, explained that he would get around the self-administration requirement by "tipping a cup into his feeding tube" (*NYT*, Aug. 11, 2012).

52. The importance of not taking the drugs in a public place is justified on the basis that "[a]ny governmental entity that incurs costs resulting from a person terminating his or her life under this chapter in a public place has a claim against the estate of the person to recover such costs and reasonable attorneys' fees related to enforcing the claim (§70.245.210).

53. In 2010, there were 6,612 active primary care physicians in the state of Washington and 17,788 active physicians overall (Center for Workforce Studies, 2011).

54. Across the Atlantic, between 30 percent and 40 percent of British physicians are in favor of decriminalization of assisted death (Tallis, 2012).

55. The WDDA requires nonparticipating hospitals to inform the public of its decision, by releasing a statement to the media or by posting their position on the hospital's Web page. To illustrate, the Valley General Hospital (with 123 beds), located in Spokane, issued a statement indicating its belief that "hospitals exist to heal, educate, and provide comfort" and although its Ethics Committee "believes in the principle of autonomy and individuals' right to choose," the hospital and its employees would not be taking part in the WDDA (Valley General Hospital, 2009). Contrastingly, there are no comprehensive lists indicating which hospitals in Washington actually participate in aid in dying, fully or in part. The information was obtained through personal communication with staff at the hospital's medical director's office on February 26, 2013. When I asked a hospital administrator whether there was any statement by the hospital regarding their participation to which I could refer, the administrator reacted, chuckling: "I doubt there is a public statement."

56. *C&C Connection*, the newsletter of *Compassion and Choices of Washington*, documented the recent hospital alliances in the state, along with changes in policy for some of the health-care-providing institutions impacted by the mergers with Catholic-run systems. For details, see Issue 16, Winter (2012). *Compassion and Choices* is one of the nation's leading pro-assisted death advocacy organizations.

57. Based in Seattle, the Swedish Hospital is one of the once secular health care institutions that are now under the control of a Catholic-run health care system, as discussed earlier.

58. As of 2012, *Compassion and Choices*, one of the nation's leading pro-assisted death advocacy organizations, had 130 "End-of-Life Consultation" (EOLC) volunteers in 26 states. EOLCs are trained to work directly with individual clients who live within their communities and help them "effectively navigate the health care system, gain access

to effective palliative and hospice care, complete advance medical directive, and to stay in charge of their own dying" (Compassion and Choices, n.d.). Often, these individuals are present at patients' deaths and are allowed to prepare (but not to administer) the lethal mixture of drugs and water or food that will hasten death. When they do not attend the dying moment, they usually stay on the phone through the process with family members who request it. To watch EOLCs' in action, see "The Last Campaign of Gov. Booth Gardner" and *Frontline*'s "The Suicide Plan."

59. The portrait of those dying under the *Act* in Oregon is not substantially different. The total of prescriptions and the selected demographics presented here are based on three years of reporting, as depicted in Table 6.1.

60. Andrew Taylor maintained a blog (http://meg-holmes.blogspot.com) as "an easy way for [him] to update friends and relations of the progress of his wife's recovery from her brain tumor." The blog postings start in 2009, when Meg Holmes is diagnosed. Those "friends and relations" (and the occasional morbid peep like myself) are gradually presented with her surgery details, the 15 months of "almost symptom-free days," the recurrence of her illness, the ins-and-outs of hospice care, and her death. The blog narrative is powerful because it is presented in "real time." The text is interspersed with pictures of Meg and her husband and their children, Elyspeth and Dan. Because it is a blog, it is possible to read Meg's dear ones' well wishes and mourning messages. In reading it, searching for clues about her resolution to die in this manner—as opposed to letting "nature run its course"—I almost feel as if my research interests were engulfed by the intimate character of this law. Though Meg Holmes fit the mold of the typical Washingtonian who dies under the *Act*, in writing this portion, I was reminded of how consequential this law really is.

61. See also the discussion, earlier in this chapter, about the increasing number of Catholic-run hospitals that in adhering to the Church's religious directives about care may curtail their providers' participation in the law as well, of course, as patients' ability to die on their institutions' premises.

62. After a patient dies from the lethal medication, physicians are required to fill out an "After Death Reporting Form" to be mailed to the Washington State Department of Health. The form records various aspects of doctor–patient relationship (i.e., duration), health insurance details, and whether the patient was receiving hospice care during the illness. It also collects information about the prescription itself (i.e., if it was written or phoned in) and about who was present at the patient's bedside when he or she chose to take the medication; whether the medication was taken as directed and if complications resulted; if 911 was called; the amount of time that lapsed between ingestion of the medication, unconsciousness, and death; the physical mobility of the patient prior to taking the medication; the place where it was taken; and physician's specialty and years practicing medicine. Moreover, the form asks the attending physician to determine possible concerns that may have contributed to their patient's decision to request death-hastening medication. Seven possible concerns are offered, followed by check-boxes labeled "yes, no, don't know." The choices are "the financial cost of treating or prolonging his or her terminal condition; the physical or emotional burden on family, friends or caregivers; his or her terminal condition representing a steady loss of autonomy; the decreasing ability to participate in activities that make life enjoyable; the loss of control of bodily functions, such as incontinence and vomiting; inadequate pain control at the end of life; and a loss of dignity."

63. Linda Ganzini, professor of Psychiatry and Medicine at the Oregon Health and Science University, was the lead author in the first evaluative study of patients using the Oregon Death with Dignity Act. In the study, published in 2009 in the *New England Journal of Medicine*, Ganzini and others interviewed the next of kin of patients who had died under the provisions of the *Act*. Most families mentioned that the most important reason their loved ones requested the medication was the desire to control the circumstances of their deaths (Ganzini et al., 2008). Pain and suffering were deemed important only in the context of fear of experiencing it in the future. In an interview given to *The New York Times*, Ganzini expressed surprise at the results: "Everybody thought this was going to be about pain. . . . It turns out that for this group of people, dying is less about physical symptoms than personal values" (*NYT*, Aug. 11, 2012).

64. Concerns about finances were rarely reported (four percent on average for the three years of reporting; Washington State Department of Health, 2011).

65. Compassion and Choices is an aid in dying organization that resulted from the merge of *Compassion in Dying* (one of the plaintiffs in *Glucksberg*) and End-of-Life Choices (itself an evolvement from the *Hemlock Society*, active in the 1980s).

# PART 2

## Assisted Death in Europe

# 7

# Doctors and Needles: Assisted Death in the Netherlands, Belgium, and Luxembourg

AS DISCUSSED IN THE PREVIOUS CHAPTERS, the history of attempts to decriminalize aid in dying in the United States is relatively long; nearly 100 years unfolded between the 1906 "chloroform bills" and the first death under the "Oregon Death with Dignity Act" in 1998. In the Netherlands, however, meaningful debate on the issue started only much later, gaining special prominence from the late 1960s onward. Notwithstanding its relatively short record, the Dutch experience with aid in dying was quickly translated into decades of legal tolerance and eventually culminated in legislative codification of the practice. In this chapter, I recount the main legal developments in the Netherlands, as well as in its neighboring countries—Belgium and Luxembourg.

Taken together, the Benelux nations are recognized as extreme models of medically assisted dying, in that in these countries not only "physician-assisted suicide" but also "active euthanasia" by doctors are allowed. This model is not without controversy. Often, the Benelux experience has captured Americans' attention, with charges of potential abuse dominating the debate. In 2012, for instance, Republican presidential candidate Rick Santorum warned Americans that elderly citizens in the Netherlands lived in constant fear that they would be put to death against their will and hence had adopted the habit of wearing bracelets conveying their desire not to be euthanized (Posthumus, 2012).[1]

Such charges, while deeply grounded in political and moral convictions and motivations, have virtually no empirical backing.[2] Public opinion polls in each of these countries have consistently supported physicians' involvement in aid in dying (see, e.g., Schoonman, Thiel, & Delden, 2013), and empirical research for the most part dispels the notion that systematic nonconsensual killing of the elderly actually takes place (see van der Heide et al. [2007] for a discussion). However, for the sake of argument, it is worth unfolding Santorum's statement. What does it expose about the American approach to aid in dying?

At a minimum, it attempts to seize on Americans' distrust in doctors and in the health care system. Such distrust is virtually absent in Benelux countries. Secondly, it emphasizes the "autonomy" discourse; doctors in the Netherlands, the Republican argued, kill against patients' will. Interestingly, Americans' attempts to legalize aid in dying have to a large extent relied primarily on the notion of self-determination: "Has a patient the right to die?"—Americans have asked, time and again. As we will see, the issue of patients' autonomy in the Netherlands is taken for granted, and thus it is less central than that of medical beneficence: "Has a doctor the duty to kill?"—the Dutch asked instead.[3]

I refer to Santorum's remarks simply to sensitize the reader to the cultural, social, and legal differences that have affected the development of the American and foreign models of aid in dying. In that same spirit, before turning my attention to the chronological development of medically assisted dying in the Netherlands, I offer a "preamble" to the Dutch experience, designed to highlight structural and cultural differences that determined this development. Albeit short, the history of the Dutch practice is quite complex and involves a number of court cases, legislative bills, government-sponsored committees, guidelines, and national-level studies. Here, my attention is restricted solely to the main legal events, particularly as they relate to the encroachment of medicine on the deathbed.[4]

## THE NETHERLANDS

Stereotypical images of the Netherlands evoke a land of tulips, blue-and-white windmills, wooden shoes, Gouda cheese, and masterful painters, such as Vincent van Gogh and Rembrandt. Probing deeper, Dutch culture reveals a great deal of progressive thinking, typified, for instance, by pioneering policies adopted in the past 20 years in the areas of drug regulation, prostitution, and same-sex marriage. In the following, I identify four salient features of the Dutch legal, cultural, and medical systems that have affected the debate and attendant legalization of medically assisted death in the Netherlands: the notion of "legal tolerance" or "forbearance" (*gedoogbeleid*); the Dutch indisposition toward taboos, or their understanding that everything should be freely discussed (*bespreekbaarheid*); their historically unparalleled trust in physicians; and the Dutch ethos of "conflict avoidance." These characteristics should orientate the reader when reviewing the legal developments in the Netherlands described later in this chapter.

The notion of "tolerance" (*gedogen*), as applied to the Dutch context, has specific policy-related meanings: it consists of "declaring in advance that under certain specific conditions offenders against a particular norm do not need to fear punishment" (Gordijn, 2001, p. 230). This judicial policy of forbearance is an accepted legal practice in the Netherlands[5] (Weyers, 2012). Hence, as it will be discussed, although physician-performed euthanasia and physician-assisted suicide had remained criminal offenses until their legalization in 2002, beginning in the 1980s a series of requirements were established through court cases that elucidated the conditions under which doctors engaging in aid in dying did not need to fear prosecution.[6] It follows that in the two decades or so prior to decriminalization, medically assisted dying was *de facto* practiced and tolerated, if certain conditions were met.

Another characteristic of the Netherlands that should be kept in mind when assessing the country's experience with decriminalization of aid in dying is what James Kennedy (2002) termed *bespreekbaarheid* (or "discussibility")—the Dutch belief that problems are best handled by discussing them openly. Although this trait is also seen in other Western societies, for instance, with Swiss-American psychiatrist Kübler-Ross's (1969) groundbreaking work *On Death and Dying*, in the Netherlands the overt discussion about aid in dying was often led by doctors and organized medicine. There was, in the 1960s and 1970s, a prevalent belief that physicians should be able to admit their "euthanatic" deeds openly (Kennedy, 2012). For instance, reflecting this sentiment against medical hypocrisy and clandestine behavior, Gertruiida Postma, a physician who killed her mother (upon her request) and stood trial for her actions, declared after informing authorities: "It shouldn't have to happen sneakily" (cited in Kennedy, 2012, p. 16). Years later, the Royal Dutch Medical Association (KNMG) would join in, becoming the first (and to date the only) medical society to affirmatively support the involvement of physicians in aid in dying.

The issue of doctor–patient "trust" in the Dutch context also merits some commentary. As will be presented, the first prosecution of a physician in the Netherlands happened only a few years after the German forces had occupied Holland during World War II. During the occupation, Arthur Seiss-Inquart, Reich Commissar for the Occupied Netherlands Territories, had ordered Dutch physicians to accomplish the Nazi public health agenda—which, of course, included carrying out the euthanasia and eugenics program. As Himmelstein and Woolhandler (1998) explain, the Netherlands's doctors unanimously rejected this order, turned in their medical licenses, and remained adamant even after 100 doctors were sent to concentration camps. In doing so, Dutch physicians insisted that the patient–doctor relationship is private, not public, and that their duty was to their patients—and not to the State.

Their efforts were lauded worldwide. For instance, in 1949, the Chief of Counsel for War Crimes held in Nuremberg published a piece on the *New England Journal of Medicine*, where he recounted the Dutch doctors' actions as an example of successful resistance by the medical profession in relation to dictatorship regimes (Alexander, 1949). Ironically, it was precisely this sense of obligation and commitment by Dutch physicians to their patients—epitomized in their resistance to the Nazi public health program—that would later propel the profession to claim that hastening patients' deaths was their duty.

The patient–physician trust in the Netherlands has not eroded since the 1950s. Today, 97 percent of Dutch patients feel confidence in their *huisartsen* (GPs) (Kmietovicz, 2002). Such trust likely stems from the close, long rapport between patients and their GPs, facilitated by universal access to health care in the Netherlands. There, on average, GPs examine each of their patients nearly five times per year; approximately 20 percent of these contacts happen at the patient's home; and, more often than not, the GP serves as the physician for entire families (Griffiths, Bood, & Weyers, 1998, p. 37). This confidence in doctors, particularly with respect to the *huisartsen*, becomes especially salient in end-of-life discussions: the GP is the "doctor of care" (or attending physician) in about 43 percent of all deaths in the Netherlands, including those taking place - at home.

Finally, rooted deeply in Dutch history is an ethos of "conflict avoidance." This is crucial to policy-making decisions in the Netherlands, where the political system relies heavily on the need to compromise and form coalitions. To that end, when faced with an ideologically divisive matter (such as "euthanasia," but also abortion or gay marriage), the solution commonly adopted by Dutch legislators tends to be one of avoiding confrontation at all costs (Griffiths et al., 1998). Such politics of conflict avoidance is accomplished through postponement of debate and/or through the "depoliticization" of polarizing issues. As will be discussed, postponement and depoliticization are often achieved through the appointment of advisory commissions and the undertaking of empirical research studies on a national scale. These strategies have the pragmatic effect of turning potentially heated debates into seemingly objective, neutral discussions, with experts—lawyers, doctors, and social scientists—to a large degree shaping policy processes (Barak, 2000). In the context of decriminalization of medically assisted dying, these strategies have served to delay the legislative codification of the practice in that country.

The review of the legal developments of the Dutch model of aid in dying offered here extends between the first prosecution of a physician in 1952 and the enactment of the "Termination of Life on Request and Assisted Suicide (Review Procedures) Act" fifty years later. First, we will explore the "prelude" to legal change that was taking place in the Netherlands from the 1950s to the early 1980s. Besides important sociocultural transformations, this period was marked by two landmark cases—*Postma* and *Wertheim*—that unequivocally entrusted physicians with the task of providing help for suffering individuals to die.

## Prelude to Legal Change

In 1952, shortly after Americans were drawn to the trial of Dr. Hermann Sanders, a Dutch physician, Arnold Berman, stood trial "for putting his pain-racked brother out of his misery" (Reuters, 1952). In court, Dr. Berman explained that his 52-year-old brother, Jan, had been suffering from tuberculosis for eight years and often pleaded with him "to end his torture." On February 9, 1950, the physician gave Jan 20 pills of "codinovo" (a narcotic analgesic) and then injected the sibling with 60 mg of morphine. Dr. Berman "waited for the end," called the police, and explained that what he had done did not amount to killing; "I did not take his [brother's] life—his existence no longer deserved the name of life," he said. The Dutch physician received a one-year suspended sentence and, since his confession, his medical practice had "increased by 30 per cent." "Everybody here trusts him," explained one of Dr. Berman's neighbors.

Dr. Berman's trial was the first prosecution of a physician in the Netherlands for his role in hastening death.[7] It did not, however, receive much attention by the media (Weyers, 2001) nor did it serve to advance the debate over the practice in any significant way. It was only in the early 1960s that the legal contours of aid in dying began to take shape meaningfully in the Netherlands. At that point, the Dutch had already settled the permissibility of "passive euthanasia"—or the withdrawal of life support in cases of inevitable death—[8] and influential texts by a lawyer,[9] a Catholic ethicist,[10] and a prominent psychiatrist[11] made the case for limiting medical interventions at the end of life; the latter went beyond and strongly suggested the active intervention of physicians in hastening death when life is no longer "meaningful."

In the years between Dr. Berman's trial and the writings of these influential experts, the Netherlands went through a profound transformation—from a staunchly religious society with conservative moral values to "one of the most secularized countries in the Western world" (Knippenberg, 1998), with its Red Light districts rapidly becoming as well known internationally as the Dutch tulips and windmills.[12] Griffiths et al. (1998) emphasize that the sociocultural developments that took place in the Netherlands in the 1960s and 1970s were a crucial watershed for that society, transforming the country into a hotbed of cultural and social experimentation. Progressive trends resulting from that transformation were seen in different realms of Dutch life. For example, although, in 1965, 73 percent of the Dutch believed that a woman should remain a "virgin" until marriage, by 1974 only 38 percent thought so (Ketting, 1982). Around the same period, tolerance with respect to homosexuality climbed from 56 percent in 1968 to 84 percent in 1974 (Ketting, 1982). This general context of changing societal values from traditional mores to liberal ones, marked by secular and individualistic ideas, also influenced the contemporaneous debate on death and dying in the Netherlands. Discussions about different types of support in the dying process were prolific in the media and by parliamentary actors (Griffiths et al., 1998). Dutch's openness to the topic captured Americans' attention early on. For instance, a CBS Evening News broadcast in 1974 reported on the Netherlands's willingness to address end-of-life issues candidly: "The euthanasia debate in Holland is proceeding in a remarkably undogmatic, democratic fashion. The Dutch people seemed determined now to talk about the problem, to stop pushing death aside as an obscenity . . ." (Simon, 1974).

## The Postma Case

It was in that largely progressive context that, in 1971, Dr. Geertruida Ebeldina Postma helped her mother die.[13] Dr. Postma's mother, Mrs. Margina Van Boven, had endured a stroke five months earlier, and as a result, she suffered from partial paralysis, had difficulty hearing and talking, and was constantly confused. She found her situation to be so precarious that she had once thrown herself out of bed in a desperate attempt to commit suicide. Van Boven had repeatedly asked her daughter for help in ending her life. On October 19, Dr. Postma arrived at the nursing home to find Van Boven tied up on a toilet chair unconscious. Having previously discussed the situation with her husband, who was also a physician, Dr. Postma shouted in her mother's ear: "It's all right, Mother! I will take care of you." (*Time Magazine*, Mar. 5, 1973). She came back the next day and injected a lethal dosage of morphine into her mother's arm while her husband stood guard. They called in the nurse and, later, Dr. Postma recounted her actions to the director of the nursing facility. He called the police.[14] When they failed to act, the director called the public prosecutor of Leeuwardeen. The prosecutor charged Dr. Postma for "killing on request" (Article 293, Dutch Penal Code); if convicted, she could be sentenced to up to 12 years in prison.[15]

Dr. Postma's trial took place in February 1973, in the Leeuwarden District Court, and lasted seven hours. During the hearing, the district's medical inspector testified that providing morphine to alleviate the pain of dying patients even when the risk of hastening their death is present had become acceptable practice among physicians. The inspector pointed out that in such cases, provided certain conditions were met, the practice of "terminal sedation" was medically ethical. The conditions he enumerated were as follows: (1) The patient is incurably ill; (2) the patient's suffering is unbearable; (3) the patient has expressed the wish to die; (4) the patient is terminal; and (5) a doctor, preferably who is responsible for treatment, should be the one to accede to the request (Jackson, 2013). The prosecutor, "convinced that Dr. Postma [was] a woman of integrity," asked for a conviction but also for a relatively light sentence: one month (suspended) accompanied by two years on probation (*Time Magazine*, Mar. 5, 1973).

A verdict was reached two weeks later. Relying largely on the testimony offered by the local medical inspector, the Court ruled that even though Dr. Postma had complied with the conditions under which hastened death may be acceptable,[16] she had erred in using an injection that was immediately lethal.[17] She was found guilty, but the Court was lenient—Dr. Postma received a one-week suspended sentence and a year's probation. Sympathizers awaited outside the courthouse with flowers. Later, when asked whether she regretted her actions, Dr. Postma explained that she "should have done it much earlier" (*Time Magazine*, Mar. 5. 1973).

The *Postma* case is considered by many to have been instrumental in opening the discussions about aid in dying in the Netherlands (Cohen-Almagor, 2002). The investigation and subsequent trial of Dr. Postma attracted widespread media attention and support. More than 1,700 residents from Noorwolde, mostly patients of Geertruida Postma or her husband, signed a petition against her prosecution. Other physicians wrote an open letter to the Minister of Justice stating that "each had committed the same crime at least once" (*Time Magazine*, Mar. 5, 1973). Advocates of aid in dying formed the first Dutch Association of Voluntary Euthanasia (Nederlandse Vereniging voor Vrijwillige Euthanasie, hereafter NVVE) to support Dr. Postma and procure legalization of aid in dying. One week after its inception, the organization had 3,000 members (*Time Magazine*, Mar. 5 1973).[18] Today, it has more members than the largest political party in the Netherlands (Timmermans & Breeman, 2012).

## *The* Wertheim *Case*

In the spring of 1981, one of the NVVE's members, Ms. Corry Wertheim-Elink Schuurman, was arrested for assisting in the suicide of a 67-year-old woman suffering from multiple mental and physical discomforts. The woman had repeatedly asked her physician to help her die and, when he declined to assist her, she turned to Wertheim. Wertheim met with the woman a few times prior to providing her with 30 tablets of Vesparax, mixed in chocolate pudding. She fed the woman the lethal mixture followed by a dose of vermouth to enhance the effect of the pills (NVVE, 2013). Wertheim was charged with suicide assistance, a violation of Article 294 of the Dutch Penal Code.[19]

The trial took place in the fall of 1981 in Rotterdam. The Court conceded that suicide is not always unacceptable and that occasionally the assistance of others is indispensable (Griffiths et al., 1998). However, due to the proscription set forth by Article 294, the Rotterdam Court reasoned that such assistance is justifiable only when certain conditions are met. Relying largely on the criteria delineated by the Leeuwarden Court in the *Postma* case, the Rotterdam Court in the *Wertheim* case established the following conditions as requirements for permissibility of assisted suicide: (1) the individual's suffering is unbearable; (2) their suffering and desire to die were enduring; (3) the decision to die was made voluntarily; (4) the person was well informed about his or her situation and available alternatives, and was capable of weighing the relevant considerations; (5) there were no alternative means to improve the situation; and (6) the person's death did not cause others any unnecessary suffering. The Court also enumerated requirements for the assistance itself: (1) The decision to provide assistance must not be made by one person alone; (2) a doctor must be involved in the decision to give assistance and must determine the method to be used; and (3) the decision to give assistance must exhibit utmost care, which includes discussing the matter with other doctors if the patient's condition is terminal or, if the patient has not yet reached this phase, consulting other experts such as a psychiatrist, a psychologist, or a social worker (Griffiths et al., 1998). According to the Court, Wertheim had not met these criteria, and thus she was found guilty of "assisting suicide." Like Dr. Postma, Wertheim, who was then 76 years old, received a lenient sentence: a conditional sentence of six months, subject to one-year probation.

Following this decision, in 1982 the Dutch Committee of Procurators-General established that cases invoking Article 293 ("killing on request," as in *Postma*) or 294 ("assisted suicide," as in *Wertheim*) were to be referred to the

Committee for a decision on whether prosecution would be pursued. The aim of the Committee was to establish national uniformity on prosecutorial policy related to aid in dying. The series of criteria set forth in *Postma* and *Wertheim* were adopted as the "golden rule" for the decisions by the Committee. These guidelines exemplify the issue of legal tolerance or forbearance introduced earlier.

Besides this national effort by the Committee, local prosecutors had previously tried to encourage physicians to be more open about their life-shortening practices. Doctors were reluctant to report "nonnatural" deaths because the attendant investigation by the police often had "substantial emotional and practical consequences" for the physician and the family of the deceased (Weyers, 2001, p. 23). In the early 1980s, therefore, a few prosecutors began actually cooperating with doctors in designing procedures to report and investigate aid in dying cases. Particularly influential was Adelbert Josephus Jitta, the chief prosecutor of the Alkmaar district. In what became known as the *Alkmaarse Methode*, Mr. Jitta developed a protocol by which regional doctors engaging in aid in dying could bypass the police by alerting the coroner directly about the circumstances of the death and submitting a full written report of what had transpired. In the first few years after the policy was adopted, the Alkmaar district saw a sharp increase in assisted death cases reported by physicians (Griffith et al., 1998, p. 67).[20]

## A Duty to Kill: The "Necessity" Defense

Brought about by the rulings in *Postma* and *Wertheim*, the decision-making policy instituted in 1982 indeed equipped criminal justice agents with general guidelines for prosecution. However, the prosecutorial policy fell short of clarifying the legal basis that legitimized the practice of aid in dying. Practically speaking, aid in dying still constituted a violation of Article 293 ("death on request") or 294 ("assisted suicide") of the Dutch Penal Code. In theory, a number of doctrinal approaches could be invoked to legitimate behavior that violated these prohibitions. Three lines of defense were thus available for those facing prosecution in these circumstances.

First, a straightforward line of defense claimed that the prohibitions set forth in Articles 293 and 294 were plainly not applicable to doctors. According to the doctrine of "medical exception," a physician is allowed to engage in acts that are formally prohibited by the law if such acts are necessary within the scope of "normal medical practice." Thus, for instance, a physician who, in the course of a surgery, uses a knife to cut into a patient's abdomen is not committing battery or assault against that patient. Several prominent Dutch jurists[21] argued that aid in dying, just as an abortion performed to save a woman's life, should be considered part of the services commonly rendered by physicians to their patients and hence fall outside the scope of Articles 293 and 294. The defense of "medical exception" was presented to the Dutch courts in more than one instance; it was, however, always rejected.[22]

Second, defendants facing charges of infringing Article 293 or 294 have proposed that their actions did not amount to a "substantial violation of the law," that is, they posited that aid in dying violates the "letter" but not the "spirit" of the law. In this sense, proponents of this doctrine argued that the drafters of the Dutch Criminal Code had not intended for Articles 293 and 294 to apply in medically assisted dying. Instead, the criminal statutes had been designed to prevent "Romeo-and-Juliet" types of suicide with assistance or killing on request—but not cases where a patient's choice to die in the face of unsurmountable suffering had to be facilitated by a physician.[23]

A third line of defense ultimately proved successful when tested before the *Hoge Raad*—the Dutch Supreme Court. According to Article 40 of the Dutch Criminal Code, "[a] person who commits an offense as a result of a force he could not be expected to resist ['overmacht'] is not criminally liable" (Rayar et al., 1997).[24] The concept of *overmacht* in Dutch law is bifurcated; it can imply a psychological defense of "duress" or a duty-based defense of "necessity." Dr. Postma, for instance, fruitlessly invoked duress as justification for her killing of her mother. In this case, the Leeuwarden Court rejected her defense reasoning that physicians can rationally be expected to resist pressure from patients. The defense of "necessity," however, invoked by Dr. P.L. Schoonheim, a general practitioner in the early 1980s, supplied a legal rationale that allowed the Dutch courts, for the first time, to acquit a doctor who had intentionally hastened the death of a patient following her request. Unlike a plea of duress, Schoonheim's resort to necessity as a defense refers to a "conflict of duties" experienced by a physician whose patient is suffering unbearably: the duty to preserve life and the duty to relieve suffering.[25]

We turn to *Schoonheim*'s case next, but first it is worth considering that the defense of necessity as a legal mechanism of change in aid in dying is not unique to the Dutch system. In fact, as mentioned in Chapter 4, the rationale was raised in the mid-twentieth century by Glanville Williams (1958, 1961). Considered one of the leading jurists of his time, Professor Williams (1958, p. 283) proposed that, in certain circumstances, "the sanctity of life may be submerged by the overwhelming necessity of relieving unbearable suffering in the last extremity" and a doctor may find that the "value of saving the dying patient from pain is preferred to the value of postponing death" (Williams, 1961, p. 288). Although his proposal generated prolific debate, Glanville Williams's common-law formulation of the necessity defense as a choice, made by a doctor, of the lesser of two competing evils never gained legal traction in the English-speaking world.[26] More recently, necessity as a defense was tested in the United Kingdom. In this case, Tony Nicklinson, who suffered from "locked-in syndrome," and Paul Lamb, who became paralyzed in a car accident, asked the court to allow for a common law necessity exception for a doctor willing to help them die. Neither man was physically able to end his life without assistance. The British court ultimately denied their request, remarking "... it is simply not appropriate for the court to fashion a defence of necessity in such a complex and controversial field; this is a matter for Parliament" (*R (Nicklinson) v. Ministry of Justice* (2013) EWCA Civ 961, (2013) MHLO 65). As we will see in the next section, the Dutch court acted otherwise.

## The Schoonheim *Case*

Dr. P. L. Schoonheim, a family physician, had been treating Mrs. Maria Barendregt, then 95 years old, for nearly a decade prior to injecting her with a lethal combination of diazepam, thiopenthal, and curare. Barendregt, "who prided herself on her independence" (Sneiderman & Verhoef, 1995, p. 389), had, in the last years of her life, become incontinent, bed-ridden, nearly blind, and hard of hearing. She was, nonetheless, conscious and perfectly coherent. It was in that state of mind that time and again she asked Dr. Schoonheim whether he would consider giving her a lethal injection. Initially, he consistently failed to respond (Sneiderman & Verhoef, 1995).

In the week leading up to her death, Barendregt could no longer swallow and had periodic lapses of consciousness. At one point, having briefly regained the ability to speak, she urged her doctor and his assistant to end her life. A series of conversations between the patient, the two physicians, her son, and daughter-in-law ensued, culminating in Dr. Schoonheim's action to expedite Maria Barendregt's death. The doctor reported his patient's cause of death as "unnatural" and called the police.

His trial began in 1982. Dr. Schoonheim was acquitted in the lower court of Alkmaar, but, upon appeal by the prosecution, the verdict was overturned. Although the Court of Appeals of Amsterdam recognized that the doctor's actions might have been desirable, especially in terms of Barendregt's rights of self-determination (Otlowski, 2000), it found the physician criminally liable. The appellate court, however, imposed no punishment; it determined that the doctor had acted with integrity and due caution.

In 1984, with the sponsorship of the NVVE, Dr. Schoonheim appealed to the Dutch Supreme Court. In his appeal, Schoonheim invoked the necessity defense.[27] In line with this defense, his attorney contended that the doctor had faced a conflict of duties in treating Barendregt, that is, the duty to preserve her life (as codified in Articles 293 and 294 of the Dutch Penal Code) and his professional duty to relieve his patient's suffering. In weighing those duties, Schoonheim argued that he had to abide by his suffering patient's request. The Supreme Court agreed; it found that

> in accordance with norms of medical ethics, and with expertise which as a professional he must be assumed to possess—[Dr. Schoonheim] balanced the duties and interests which, in the case at hand, were in conflict, and made a choice that—objectively

considered and taking into account the specific circumstances of this case—was justifiable. (Schoonheim, Supreme Court, 27 Nov. 1984, N.J. 1985, no. 106, translated in Griffiths et al., 1998, Appendix II-1, 326-7)

Because the Supreme Court in the Netherlands does not function as a final arbiter, it referred the case to the Court of Appeals of The Hague. It directed the appellate court to weigh the conflict of duties and to consider (1) whether, according to professional medical judgment, increasing disfigurement of the patient's personality and/or increasing deterioration of her already unbearable suffering was to be expected; (2) whether it was to be expected that Barendregt would soon no longer be in a position to die with dignity; and (3) whether there had been other less drastic means to alleviate her suffering (Leenen, 1987; Otlowski, 2000; Sneiderman & Verhoef, 1995).

To consider the case from an objective medical perspective, the Court of Appeals of The Hague turned to the Royal Dutch Medical Association, the *Koninklijke Nederlandsche Maatschappij tot bevordering der Geneeskunst* (hereafter KNMG), for insight. During the two years of Schoonheim's litigation, interest in the issue of doctors' aid in dying had increased, as had organized action by the KNMG on the matter. In 1973, amid discussions raised by the *Postma* case, the KNMG had issued a statement that approved of the practice of "terminal sedation," but was ambivalent on the issue of "active euthanasia" or "physician-assisted suicide"—although it defended maintaining the legal *status quo*, the KNMG suggested that the courts may have to consider whether a doctor, whose patient is incurably ill and dying, could in certain cases, due to a conflict of duties, be justified in bringing about death (Gevers, 1987).

The medical profession's ambiguity would change dramatically in the next decade. In 1983, an influential Dutch medical journal, *Nederlands Tijdschrift voor Geneeskunde*, published an editorial defending the practice, as well as articles by physicians relating their actions and/or hesitations about possible prosecution (Halper, 2000, p. 92). In the same year, the KNMG set up a committee to examine the practice of hastened death "carefully and sincerely" (Cohen-Almagor, 2002, p. 99). In 1984, the KNMG asked the Minister of Justice to intervene and seek a change in the law to allow doctors to provide aid in dying. When this request was declined, the KNMG issued a report, "Vision on Euthanasia," where, while taking no moral stance on the practice,[28] it declared that physician's involvement in aid in dying was already a reality, and hence it should follow certain "requirements of careful practice" (translation to English from KNMG, 1996). These requirements, designed to protect both the doctor and the patient, were in line with the prosecutorial policy put forth by the Dutch Committee of Procurators-General in 1982: (1) the request by the patient must be voluntary and (2) well considered; (3) the patient's desire to die must be a lasting one; (4) the patient must consider his suffering unbearable; and (5) the doctor must consult with a colleague.[29] To date, the KNMG remains the only medical association to affirmatively support the legalization of a physician's active assistance in patients' deaths (Weyers, 2001).

The decision by the Court of Appeals of The Hague on Dr. Schoonheim's fate came three months after the KNMG published its *Vision*. In fact, the association's position statement, a few argued later, functioned as an *amicus curiae* brief for the decision in *Schoonheim* (Weyers, 2001, p. 19). Relying largely on the association's position, the Court of Appeals of The Hague acquitted the physician. The court reasoned that no norms of medical ethics forbade what Dr. Schoonheim had done; instead, the opinion states, although no consensus seemed to exist on the matter, in reality numerous physicians considered "active life-termination as medically-ethically possible" (Halper, 2000, p. 94). Reacting to the final verdict, one of Dr. Schoonheim's attorneys, Mr. Eugene Sutorius, defended: "Euthanasia is done in secret in Holland ... This doctor, for his conscience, wanted it public" (*The New York Times*, Nov. 28, 1984).

Others did so, too. In the summer following the *Schoonheim* decision, another physician, Dr. Pieter Admiraal, an anesthetist who had expedited the death of a patient suffering from multiple sclerosis, was also acquitted. The court concluded that Dr. Pieter Admiraal had found himself facing a conflict of duties and had followed the "requirements of careful practice" when he injected his patient with lethal barbiturate and curare. Shortly after his acquittal, the Dutch Minister of Justice announced that doctors who comply with the requirements of careful practice published by the KNMG would not be prosecuted (Griffiths et al., 1998). Thus, if *Schoonheim* in effect legitimized a medical exculpation to the crimes of "homicide on request" and "assisted suicide," *Admiraal* made it unequivocal that, provided certain criteria were met, doctors should not fear helping their patients die.[30]

*Schoonheim* and *Admiraal* were litigated in a climate of heightened interest in the issue, particularly by political actors. In the spring of 1984, only a few months before *Schoonheim* was decided, the first legislative bill calling for legalization of physician aid in dying had reached the parliament. Introduced by a social-liberal member of the parliament, Ms. Elida Wessel-Tuinstra, the bill had patterned the guidelines put forth by the KNMG, the 1982 Dutch Committee of Procurators-General, and the court decisions since *Postma*. It was the legislature's role, explained Wessel-Tuinstra, to close the gap between the law on the books (Articles 293 and 294 of the Dutch Criminal Code) and the law in action (prosecutorial discretion and judicial tolerance) (D66, 1984). Parliamentary action on the Wessel-Tuinstra bill was postponed; ultimately, this original bill to a great extent provided the basis for the existing "Termination of Life on Request and Assisted Suicide (Review Procedures) Act," approved and implemented in 2002 by the Dutch legislators.

Although legislative efforts by a few members of the parliament to reform the law had resulted, at that point, in a stalemate, other official gubernatorial agents were moving the debate forward. In the summer of 1985, the State Commission on Euthanasia, established three years earlier by the Minister of Health and the Minister of Justice to advise the government on future policy on aid in dying, published a report that explicitly advocated the modification of the Dutch

Penal Code to permit physicians, in certain cases and subject to certain conditions, to accede to their patients' request for help in dying (Gevers, 1987).[31]

In the majority (13 votes out of 15) opinion conveyed in the "Final Report," the Commission argued that delineating the boundaries of the practice was a task for the legislature: "[it] is essential for Parliament to make plain its position on euthanasia" (Anonymous, 1987, p. 166). A change through case law, the report defended, would take too long, such that there would "be many years before an exact definition emerges of what is and what is not an offence." Additionally, the Commission posited, the prosecutorial policy established in 1982 also had fallen short of providing the clarity and legal certainty required in these cases.

## 1990s–2001: Science, Suffering, and the Law on the Books

Thus, by the mid-1980s, it appeared that time was ripe for legal reform in the Netherlands; support for physician aid in dying had by then emanated from the prosecutors, the courts, the medical profession, advocates, legal scholars, and public opinion,[32] as well as from diverse political actors, including an official gubernatorial commission.[33] Instead of legal codification, however, what ensued was a longwinded process of conflict avoidance. This strategic process, which is entrenched in Dutch politics, resulted among other things in the commissioning of rigorous scientific studies to assess the merits of legal reform—although medically assisted dying had been overtly tolerated for several years, in reality very little was known about who was choosing to die, why, where they die, and how often doctors were offering assistance.

Accordingly, in 1990, a "Commission Appointed to Carry out Research Concerning Medical Practice in Connection with Euthanasia" was installed. Chaired by then Attorney General of the Supreme Court, Professor Jan Remmelink, the Commission retained the Institute for Social Health Care of the Erasmus University in Rotterdam to conduct a nationwide survey of Dutch physicians regarding the prevalence and circumstances of their involvement in aid in dying practices.

The results of the empirical study were published in 1991.[34] A few findings, both reassuring and unsettling, received much attention in the Netherlands and abroad. First, only one-third of requests by patients to have their deaths hastened were granted by physicians, indicating their reluctance to engage in the practice without first exhausting other options.

Second, the study revealed that physicians' involvement in aid in dying was not as prevalent as anticipated—of the nearly 130,000 deaths occurring annually in the Netherlands, approximately 2,300 individuals (1.8 percent of all deaths) had died by lethal injection administered by a physician upon request, and 400 (0.3 percent of all deaths) had died by ingesting lethal medication prescribed by a doctor. This finding was in stark contrast to speculations, particularly by international critics, about the prevalence of medically assisted dying in the Netherlands.

Third, researchers found that, although doctors were forthcoming in their answers to the study, they were less so in reporting their involvement in hastened deaths—only 486 physician-assisted deaths had been officially notified as such. More often than not, "natural" death certificates had been issued in instances where the patients' deaths had been facilitated or caused by a physician. Even though at that point the practice remained illegal and prosecution was still possible, the climate of legal tolerance surrounding physician-assisted death had created the expectation that doctors would operate with more transparency.

Fourth, and fueling opponents' fears, there were indications that the principle of patient autonomy was to a great extent undermined; the research found that in roughly 1,000 instances (0.8 percent of all deaths), physicians had actively and deliberately hastened their patients' deaths without their express consent or knowledge (Scherer & Simon, 1999, p. 58). In over half of these cases, however, the "report" suggested that patients' consent had been expressed earlier, while competent.

The political response by the legislature and the parliament to the findings of the "Remmelink Study" was one marked by a *laissez faire* attitude. Because medical assistance in hastening death was found to be a relatively rare occurrence, members of the political coalition in power at the time did not see the need for legislative change. Instead, legislative attention shifted to regulatory matters, particularly those aimed to increase the notification of cases of physician-assisted deaths.[35]

## The Nature of Suffering

From 1994 onward, further refinements of the conditions in which medically assisted death was deemed legally acceptable began to take shape in the courts. Specifically, a series of cases emerged in which the courts had to ponder on the nature of a patient's suffering as a prerequisite for the necessity defense. As the reader recalls, the legal strategy of doctors facing prosecution for help in hastening death was the notion that their duty to relieve a patient's unbearable suffering outweighs, in some circumstances, their duty to preserve life. Therefore, in cases where the patient is not terminally ill and his or her suffering is nonsomatic, that is, stemming from a nonphysical condition, does the same rationale apply? Those questions were definitively answered by the Dutch Supreme Court in *Chabot*.[36]

### The Chabot Case

Dr. Boudewijn Chabot was a psychiatrist who, in 1991, supplied lethal drugs to his patient, Ms. Hilly Bosscher, at her request. Bosscher consumed the drugs in the presence of the psychiatrist, another physician, and a friend, while Bach was playing in the background. She died shortly after. Dr. Chabot immediately informed the local coroner about the circumstances of the suicide. He was charged with "intentionally assisting another person to commit suicide"—an offense under Article 294 of the Dutch Criminal Code.

Bosscher was 50 years old when she died. Five years before her death, she had lost her father, to whom she was very close. Shortly after, one of her two sons, Patrick, killed himself at the age of 20. At that point, Bosscher began contemplating suicide but decided to remain alive to care for her other son, Rodney. Her marriage, which she characterized as violent and abusive, ended in divorce in February 1990. During this extensive period of significant losses and traumatic experiences, Bosscher had received psychiatric treatment, but that did not ameliorate her situation.

Six months following the divorce, Bosscher's son, Rodney, was hospitalized as a result of a car accident. During his stay, the doctors treating his injuries discovered that he had cancer, which was already in an advanced stage. Rodney died in the spring of 1991, also at the age of 20. That same night, Bosscher tried to kill herself by taking medication she had hoarded over years of psychiatric treatment. When that attempt failed, she turned to the NVVE for help. They referred her to Dr. Chabot.

Dr. Chabot treated Bosscher for approximately five weeks. He also had separate meetings with her sister and brother-in-law. In the course of 24 hours of taped sessions, Bosscher continued to insist on her wish to die and be buried between her sons. When Dr. Chabot proposed to give therapy a try, she refused, claiming that "[a]ntidepressants perhaps will make me feel somewhat better, but . . . mourning my children means to let them go and to become a different person" (Thomasma, 1998, p. 380). Bosscher did not want to feel better; the psychiatrist later explained, "She wanted to remain the person [she] was when [she] was a mother and happy."

Persuaded that the patient would eventually kill herself, likely by violent means, Dr. Chabot agreed to help her die, but first consulted with six other physicians and a Christian ethicist, sharing with them his notes and all pertinent documentation on the case. All of the consulted experts were convinced that Bosscher's determination to die was well considered, that her suffering was enduring and unbearable, and that treatment was futile given her resistance to earnestly engage in it. None of them, however, had personally examined the patient.

On trial, Dr. Chabot invoked the necessity defense: It was his professional opinion that Bosscher was "experiencing intense, long-term psychic suffering that, for her, was unbearable and without prospect of improvement," and it was his duty to alleviate her suffering, irrespective of its origins (Griffiths, 1995, p. 235). The lower court acquitted the psychiatrist, agreeing that the cause of the suffering does not detract from the extent to which suffering is experienced and that nonsomatic suffering by a patient is enough to trigger the "conflict of duties" experienced by the physician. On appeal, the Court of Leeuwarden affirmed the lower court's decision.

On June 21, 1994, however, the Dutch Supreme Court reversed the appellate court's decision and found Dr. Chabot guilty of suicide assistance based on the fact that none of the consulted experts had actually examined Bosscher. No punishment was imposed.

The central holding in *Chabot*, then, was not the validity of medically assisted death in psychiatric cases; instead, the Court further elaborated the "rules of careful practice" to include, in nonsomatic cases, a required in-person consultation by a second doctor. Importantly, however, the High Court agreed that the physical nature of the suffering is irrelevant, that is, a patient's nonsomatic suffering is enough to place a physician in a situation where he or she feels a conflict of duties and is compelled to hasten death absent an alternative. Hence, suffering, and not the cause of suffering, is determinative of the necessity argument.

*Chabot* settled once and for all two important issues: an illness does not need to be terminal nor physical to qualify a patient for medically assisted death. The nature of suffering as a condition to doctor's assistance in dying would be revisited by the Dutch courts in 2001 in *Brongersma*: can a doctor feel compelled to assist in the death of a patient who is not sick, not dying, but is simply tired of living?[37] In other words, if somatic (i.e., physiological) and nonsomatic (i.e., psychological) suffering are legitimate triggers of a "conflict of duties" by a physician, is "existential" suffering also within the purview of medical expertise?

## *The* Brongersma *Case*

Edward Brongersma, a former senator and longtime supporter of aid in dying, was 86 years old when he took a lethal dose of medication provided by his physician, Dr. Philip Sutorius. Following his assistance in Brongersma's suicide, Dr. Sutorius reported that he had acceded to the request because Brongersma was "lonely," experienced "feelings of senselessness," and had a "long-standing wish to die not associated with depression" (Weyers, 2012, p. 58). The absence of a depressive disorder was confirmed by a psychiatrist, whose opinion was sought by Dr. Sutorius. Indeed, by all accounts, Mr. Brongersma was in good health; his physical ailments were minor incontinence and some difficulty walking. His suffering, the patient claimed, stemmed from life itself; he had no family or friends left and as a result felt socially isolated. Brongersma's unbearable and lasting suffering was a result of a loss of his *joie de vivre*—once a socially and intellectually engaged jurist, Brongersma now lived an "empty existence" (van Dam, 2003). In assessing the nature of his patient's suffering, Dr. Sutorius sought the opinion of a psychiatrist, who confirmed the absence of any depressive disorders. He consulted with another physician, known for his reluctance to resort to euthanasia, and the colleague also deemed Brongersma's suffering unbearable, lasting, and with no prospects of improvement.

Upon reporting the death, Dr. Sutorius was prosecuted. His first trial took place in 2000, concomitantly with discussions in the parliament about the bill that would ultimately legalize medically assisted dying in the Netherlands. The lower court acquitted the doctor. The verdict was reversed in 2001, when the appellate court ruled that relieving suffering that does not have a medical cause is not part of the professional duties of doctors. Dr. Sutorius then appealed to the Dutch Supreme Court, which ruled, in 2002, that the justification of necessity in his case does not apply. A physician who furnishes the drugs to an individual, whose suffering is not predominantly due to a "medically classified disease or disorder," but instead stems from disenchantment with life, is acting outside his professional competence. Dr. Sutorius was thus found guilty, but the court imposed no punishment, recognizing that he had acted out of great concern for his patient (Sheldon, 2003).

The prosecution of Dr. Sutorius had the result of curtailing the limits of medical monopoly over the idea of suffering. If one looks at the evolution of the concept in the Dutch context, it becomes obvious that, although there has been a gradual move from an objective measurement of suffering as "physical pain" to a subjective measurement based on psychological symptoms, the linchpin of the legal defense of necessity was always the idea that suffering stemmed from a diagnosable illness. Euthanasia and assisted suicide by physicians have thus constituted a response to illness, be it physical or psychiatric. Being "tired of life" is not an illness and, although it has been argued that it may indeed be the source of intolerable suffering, the Dutch Supreme Court determined that the answer to existential anguish is not to be found in the doctor's saddlebags. Simply put, when suffering is not the result of a medical condition, it falls outside the boundaries of medical expertise and thus outside the doctor-patient relationship. In this scenario, a doctor who is sympathetic to the individual's plight is not acting as his or her doctor due to the absence of a medical diagnosis. Accordingly, the physician cannot claim that he or she has entered into a conflict of duties, which is limited to his or her professional status as a treating physician.

The decision in *Brongersma* was encapsulated in a broader debate that had begun in 1991, when Huibert Drion, a retired Dutch Supreme Court justice, argued in an open letter to a prominent newspaper that doctors should be able to provide elderly people over 75 years old who were "tired of life" with the means to kill themselves (Sheldon, 2004). Known as the *Drion Pill*, his proposal entailed a two-stage process whereby the elderly who are weary of life would take two pills, two days apart (to allow for change of mind), in an effort to die before experiencing decay and dependence. In 1996, the NVVE tried to have the idea legalized through a nonparliamentary bill. That effort failed. Drion's argument was later echoed by Els Borst, a former Dutch Minister of Health. In 2001, shortly after *Brongersma* was decided and just days after the legalization of medically aid in dying through the parliament, she endorsed the idea of a suicide pill for the elderly (CNN, Apr. 14, 2001).

Despite the decision in *Brongersma* and the failed 1996 bill, efforts to decriminalize medically assisted dying in the context of existential suffering have persisted in the Netherlands. Current debate focuses on attempts, primarily by NVVE's advocates, to resuscitate the idea of rational suicide for the elderly who believe that their life is "complete." The advocacy group has recently tried to have the manufacture and distribution of Drion Pills—rebranded by the NVVE as "Last Will Pills"—legalized.[38] There is some evidence of public support for the idea; a 2005 study that 15 percent of the Dutch definitely think a "suicide pill" should be made available for "elderly people who do not want to live any longer" and 32 percent thought that "maybe" it should (Rurup, Onwuteaka-Philipsen, & Van Der Wal, 2005).

Early discussions seemed to suggest that physicians would also favor an expansion of the notion of suffering to include the social ailments frequently associated with aging. For example, in 2004, an advisory commission appointed by the Dutch Medical Association had proposed that "suffering from life," such as the anguish experienced by Senator Brongersma, could fall within the purview of physicians' expertise (Dijkhuis Commission, per NVVE, 2004). However, in 2011, the Dutch Medical Association refuted the commission's advice and, while recognizing that an accumulation of geriatric afflictions such as progressive deterioration may cause unbearable and lasting suffering, stated that doctors must adhere to diagnosing suffering that stems from an actual medical condition (KNMG Position Paper, 2011).

The current debate on "existential suffering" in the Netherlands as basis for expansion of aid in dying is frequently characterized by critics as a step down a "slippery slope" triggered by the codification of euthanasia and physician-assisted suicide practices into law. Enacted in 2002, the "Termination of Life on Request and Assisted Suicide (Review Procedures) Act" was the result of intense legislative debate, in addition to the long *de facto* tolerance of the practice as described earlier. In the next section, we turn our attention to the legislative process surrounding the issue and briefly review the aspects of the Act as it is implemented in the Netherlands today.

## Law on the Books

Although the courts were determinant in shaping the legal permissibility of aid in dying in the Netherlands, since the 1980s attempts to codify the practice also took place in the parliament. As mentioned earlier, the first bill was introduced only a few months before the landmark decision in *Schoonheim*. In spite of the pressure by certain minority leaders, legislative codification faced real political barriers. On the one hand, reflecting the Dutch way of "conflict avoidance" discussed in the introduction to this chapter, the polarizing debate was essentially postponed by political actors through the commission of scientific studies, for instance. On the other hand, political obstruction came in a more direct manner. Since 1917, Dutch conservative confessional parties—later merged into the Christian Democratic Appeal (CDA)—had retained majority control in the parliament. The CDA was responsible for blocking the passage of several proposed bills on aid in dying, including one introduced by the government in 1987, and even when a majority in parliament seemed willing to support them (Gevers, 1992).

In 1993, the Netherlands became the first country to pass explicit legislation referring to termination of life (Ten Have & Welie, 2005). Although aid in dying remained a crime, this bill changed the Dutch Burial Act to require physicians to report deaths as "nonnatural" when their assistance was provided. The law was designed to increase control over the practice of euthanasia and physician-assisted suicide. The physician would report the nonnatural death to the coroner, who would in turn inform the prosecutor. In reviewing the doctor's report, the prosecutor would assess whether the criteria of "due care" established by case law had been followed. If so, the prosecutor would issue a certificate releasing the body for burial or cremation without additional investigation. The law, however, a strange hybrid of penalization (the practice was still not legalized) and mandatory notification, did not reach the expected goal of increasing physician reporting and facilitating procedural scrutiny (Ten Have & Welie, 2005).

By that point, the legislative stalemate on the direct issue of assisted dying had originated two national studies that promoted further understanding of the practice, and the modification of the Burial Act, while maintaining the criminal status of medical aid in dying, represented a first step toward decriminalization. In 1994, the Dutch political landscape changed in an unprecedented way, signaling to proponents that legalization was near. The CDA, for the first time in decades, was not part of the leading political coalition. Instead, the new government, often referred to as the "Purple coalition," was led by the Democrats '66 (D66), the Labor Party (PvdA), and the People's Party for Freedom and Democracy (VVD)—all of which had a social-liberal inclination and had supported the original bill introduced in 1984. To advocates' disappointment, the Purple coalition did not pursue legalization; instead, it commissioned yet another national-level research study.

To keep the pressure on, the NVVE introduced a nonparliamentary proposal in 1996 that would have legalized medical aid in dying as well as the dispensation of lethal medicine for the elderly who were not yet suffering but wished to die for "fear of mental or physical deterioration that has become inescapable and imminent" (Law proposal by the Dutch Association for Voluntary Euthanasia, 1996, as translated by Griffiths et al., 1998, p. 318). That bill failed.

Two years later, with new elections imminent, the D66 put the debate back on the legislative agenda by introducing a bill that proposed to decriminalize medical aid in dying, reflecting the due care criteria that had been delineated through case law. The bill was discussed in the parliament in 2000–2001. Its goal, as stated by proponents and by the ministers of health and justice, was to fill the void of legal uncertainty created by decades of statutory postponement, which, they argued, had created a climate of insecurity among doctors who were in effect involved in patients' deaths but were not reporting their behavior (Griffiths, Weyers, & Adams, 2008). The modification to the Burial Act a few years prior had not resolved the issue, as indicated by the national-level study commissioned by the Purple coalition.

Effective as of April 2002, the bill was accepted by the Dutch parliament's Second Chamber with 40 members voting against it (mostly those affiliated with

**Table 7.1  Policy of Forbearance and the Law on the Books: Comparing the Criteria**

Guidelines for nonprosecution emerging from the Committee of Prosecutors-General and the Dutch Medical Association's position paper, 1982–1984

1. The request by the patient must be voluntary and well considered.
2. The patient's desire to die must be a lasting one.
3. The patient must consider his or her suffering unbearable.
4. The doctor must consult with a colleague.

Requirements by the "Termination of Life on Request and Assisted Suicide (Review Procedures) Act of 2002"

1. The patient's request must be voluntary and well considered.
2. The patient is duly informed of his or her prognosis by the doctor.
3. The patient's suffering is unbearable and no reasonable alternatives exist to alleviate it.
4. The doctor consults with at least one independent physician who examines the patient and gives a written opinion on whether the due care criteria have been met.
5. The doctor exercises due medical care and attention in terminating the patient's life or assisting in his or her suicide.

the CDA) and 104 in favor. The First Chamber approved it with 46 senators in favor and 28 against (Griffiths et al., 2008, p. 35). Although the international community was quick to criticize the law,[39] in reality, the "Termination of Life on Request and Assisted Suicide (Review Procedures) Act of 2002" (hereafter the 2002 Act) did little more than build into the legislative code a practice that had been in effect over a number of years in the Netherlands, as described throughout this chapter (for a comparison, see Table 7.1). In sum, the 2002 Act authorizes aid in dying by physicians in the form of prescribing and/or injecting lethal medication to patients, provided certain "due care criteria" are met, namely, the patient's request for hastened death is well considered and voluntary; the patient is duly informed of his or her prognosis by the doctor; the patient's suffering is unbearable and no reasonable alternatives exist to alleviate it; the doctor acts with due care and attention; the doctor consults with an independent physician who gives a written opinion on whether the due care criteria have been met.

Deaths under the 2002 Act are reported by the aiding doctor to the municipal pathologist, who records the cause as nonnatural. Such reported cases are then referred to one of five "Regional Review Committees" (RCCs). Composed of a lawyer (who acts as a chairperson), an ethicist, and a physician, each RCC investigates whether the cases are indeed in compliance with the criteria delineated earlier. If not, the cases are subsequently referred to prosecutorial authorities. In 2011, nearly 4,000 cases[40] were reported by physicians to the RCCs; four of these were not in accordance with the 2002 Act. Finally, only residents of the Netherlands are eligible to utilize the law and physicians facing patients' requests are not obliged to provide assistance.

**Figure 7.1 Number of Assisted-Death Requests Granted by Dutch Physicians.**

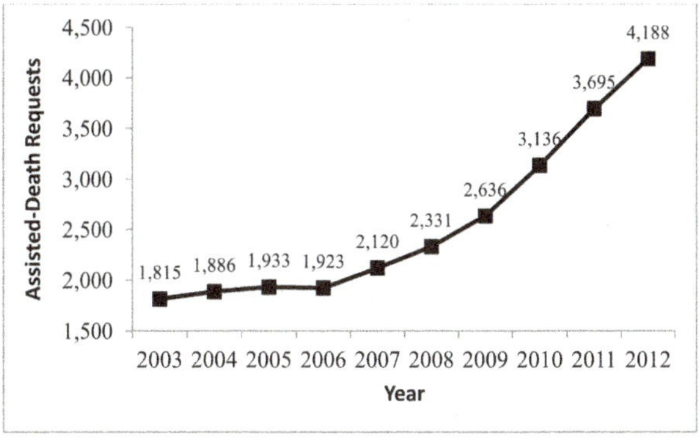

*Source*: Annual Reports, 2003–2012, Regional Euthanasia Review Committees.

Even if, for the most part, the 2002 Act simply codified the practice put forth by 20 years of case law, the new law did tackle certain issues that had not been made explicit by the courts. Of specific importance were the legal contours of informed consent in the context of minors. Although the original bill proposed by the D66 would have allowed parental veto in cases where children, aged between 12 and 18 years, requested aid in dying, the final law defers more broadly to the suffering minors. According to the 2002 Act, children as old as 12 may request euthanasia, but parental consent is mandatory until they reach the age of 16.Minors aged 16–18 years do not need parental approval; however, parents must be involved in the decision-making process (Government of the Netherlands, 2011). Reacting to this change from the original bill, the United Nations' Human Rights Committee expressed "serious concern" about the law in general and this issue, in particular, pointing out its difficulty in "reconcil [ing] a reasoned decision to terminate life with the evolving and maturing capacities of minors" (CCPR Human Rights Commission, 2001).[41]

Over a decade has lapsed since the Dutch formally implemented their physician aid in dying practices. During this time, there has been a steady increase in requests granted by doctors (see Figure 7.1). However, physicians are not legally required to provide lethal help, and it is estimated that 12 percent of patients' requests for help in dying are declined by their doctors (van der Weide, Onwuteaka-Philipsen, & van der Wal, 2005).

The reason for such refusals vary from an objective assessment of the circumstances (e.g., the determination by the physician that the criteria required by law are unfulfilled) to a subjective stance on the issue. In these cases, doctors are not required to refer patients to other physicians who may be willing to help. To address the issue, in 2012, several mobile "Life End Clinics" (*Levenseindekliniek*) were established by the NVVE. Patients whose doctors have refused to grant their request to die can forward their medical records to the clinics' staff.

After reviewing each case, the clinics' doctors and nurses visit with the patient and consult with the original physician, as well as with an independent doctor, to ascertain whether the individual qualifies for help under the provisions of the 2002 Act. If so, the patient receives lethal medication administered or prescribed by the physicians employed by the clinic. Life End Clinics have reported assisting in 32 death requests during its first year; all were found in compliance with the law (Regional Euthanasia Review Committees, 2012). Although advocates believe that the clinics increase access to the law, the KNMG does not endorse the mobile clinics on the grounds that the in-depth understanding of the patient's condition by the long-term attending physician, and the trust that emerges from it, cannot be replicated in a few visits (Jolly, 2012; KNMG, May 11, 2012).

## BELGIUM

In 2002, shortly after the Dutch law permitting doctors to deliberately end a patient's life at his or her request was enacted, Belgium passed a similar legislative bill. Unlike in the Netherlands, however, where a rich case law history shaped public, medical, and legal sentiment and practice about aid in dying over nearly three decades, the debate surrounding the legalization process of euthanasia in Belgium was much shorter and much more polarizing, and did not rely on the direct benefaction of either organized medicine or the criminal justice system. The brief, yet consequential milestones in the decriminalization of aid in dying in the Belgian context are reviewed below, following an overview of that country's health care and political systems.

### Belgium's Political and Health Care Systems: A Brief Overview

With a population of 11 million and an area, roughly the size of Maryland, Belgium has experienced an economic boom in the past 50 years and its gross domestic product (GDP) is among the highest in the world. The country is home to iconic comic strip characters, such as "Tintin" and the "Smurfs," as well as the headquarters of the European Union and NATO. In its early history—Belgium became independent from the Netherlands in 1830—it was a refuge for exiled dissidents, including Karl Marx and Victor Hugo, and home to one of the most influential criminologists of all times, Adolphe Quetelet.

Belgium borders the Netherlands, Germany, Luxembourg, and France. This geographic circumstance has resulted in linguistic and political diversity within the country. Although cultural identities are reconciled under a single federal structure (a parliamentary democracy with a constitutional monarch), Belgium is subdivided into "regions" (Wallonia, Flanders, and Brussels-Capital) and "communities" (Dutch, French, and German), each of which retains some gubernatorial independence. Many aspects of health care fall under the governing authorities of these local communities and regions. Due to its approval through parliamentary process, the law on "euthanasia," however, falls within the federal purview.

The health system in Belgium is mainly organized on two levels, namely, federal and regional, and it is compulsory and universal—about 99 percent of the Belgians have health benefits (Corens, 2007).[42] Although patients pay a fee for services rendered, most of these services are reimbursed at a rate of 75 percent, with individuals footing 25 percent of the cost. Belgians tend to live for a long time—80.5 years on average—and the main causes of death in the country are heart and vascular disorders, cancers, disorders of the respiratory system, and unnatural causes of death (e.g., accidents and suicide; Corens, 2007). Most elderly Belgians die in hospitals. However, at least one study has shown a decrease in hospital deaths for this population over time accompanied by an increase in nursing home deaths (Houttekier et al., 2011).

Delivery of health services in Belgium is primarily a private business. Doctors are typically self-employed and there are three practicing physicians per 1,000 population (World Health Organization, 2011). This ratio is higher than many other developed countries, including the United States, where there are about 2.4 practicing physicians per 1,000 inhabitants.

Since the early 1900s, health care in Belgium has been increasingly managed through "mutual sick funds" (or *mutualités*). These mutual sick funds, grouped into five national-level associations, are nongovernmental and nonprofit organizations that have historically aligned with the religious and political "pillars"[43] of the Belgian culture. Together, the two largest ones—*Mutualité* Chrétienne and *Mutualité* Socialiste—insure three-quarters of the population (Schokkaert & Van de Voorde, 2005).

Religion and health care have traditionally been intertwined in Belgium, not only through the mutual sick funds but also with respect to the pastoral delivery of care for the sick in that country. In 1843, for instance, a travel guide written for British individuals seeking to relocate to Belgium describes a hospital in Geel as "one of the cleanest and best regulated establishments I ever beheld. It is kept up by fourteen Sisters of Charity, who receive twenty sick patients, besides a few lunatics, for whom separate rooms are built in the very nice garden attached to the Hospital" (Addison, 1843, p. 289).[44] Today, a majority of the 215 Belgian hospitals remain linked to religious charitable orders either directly or through associations. Hospitals are allowed to develop their intramural policies with respect to end-of-life measures, such as withdrawal of life support and "euthanasia."

The most important regulatory institution of the Belgian medical profession is the "Order of Physicians" (*Ordre des Médecins*), established in 1938. To be allowed to practice medicine in Belgium, a physician must be registered with the Order. Although this Belgian professional association, unlike its Dutch counterpart, did not directly support the legalization of aid in dying, its "Code of Medical Deontology" (*Code de Déontologie Médicale*) has changed over time to reflect the legal status of the practice. For example, in 1975 the Code determined that "deliberately causing the death of a patient, whatever the motivation, is a criminal act" (Ordre des Medecins, 2014). In 1992, a cautionary clause against suicide assistance was added: "The doctor cannot deliberately cause the death of a patient or help a patient commit suicide" (Ordre des Medecins, 2014). Finally, in 2006 the same article was broadened to include general advice about end-of-life measures that may be available once a terminal condition is diagnosed. Therefore, the Code now declares that for any requests related to end of life, the doctor should explain which initiatives can be taken (such as the appointment of a health proxy) and should record the patient's wishes regarding certain interventions, including advance directives regarding euthanasia (Ordre des Medecins, 2014).[45] It is relevant to note that although Belgian physicians had little influence on the passage of the "2002 Act on Euthanasia," research has shown that they now generally endorse the practice (Smets et al., 2011).

## 1960s–1990s: Two Precursor Cases and the Inception of Activism

In 2014, the world's attention turned to Belgium as that country expanded its assisted death law to include children without age limits. As it will be discussed later in this chapter, this aspect of the Belgian law is one of its most controversial. Some 50 years before, however, Belgium had already been the stage of yet another scandalous case of altruistic infanticide. The "Thalidomide Homicide" (*Time Magazine*, Nov. 16, 1962), as it was dubbed by the American press, took place in Liege. Newspaper and magazine reporters, as well as cinematographers from around the globe, descended to the historic town in the east of Belgium to recount the tragic story of a mother who admitted to killing her week-old baby with a mixture of milk, honey, and barbiturates.

On May 22, 1962, around two in the morning, Mrs. Suzanne Vandeput, a 24-year-old typist, gave birth to a little girl in a Belgian Catholic clinic. Corinne, blonde like her mother, weighed only six pounds. She lacked both arms, and her anus was malformed and misplaced. Corinne's deformities had been caused by "Softenon" (the Belgian trade name for thalidomide), a drug taken by her mother during pregnancy to ease morning sickness.

As soon as she was born, the baby was taken away by the delivering doctor and a nurse. Vandeput did not see Corinne until four days later. In the meantime, Vandeput's mother and sister, along with the baby's father, pled with the hospital staff to put an end to the child. But they refused. When they left the maternity clinic to take Corinne home, Vandeput, along with her husband, her mother, her sister, and brother-in-law, stopped by Dr. Jacques Casters's office and procured a prescription for barbiturates. Dr. Casters was the family physician who had prescribed thalidomide to Vandeput. At night, Vandeput asked to be left alone with the baby. Corinne was dead the next morning.

Vandeput called the police and described what she had done. She was charged with murder, whereas her husband, mother, sister, and Dr. Casters were charged as accomplices. What ensued was a week-long trial that incited "sympathy for the defendants throughout Belgium and Europe" (UPI, 1962). The defense declared that the accused felt pity for a "hopelessly condemned and wretched human thing who faced a prospective existence without a glimmer of human happiness" (UPI, 1962). A parade of expert witnesses was brought in to show the horrors that affected the thalidomide victims like Corinne. The coroner who signed the baby's death certificate explained at the trial that "had he been aware of the situation surrounding Corrine's death, he would have declared her death to be 'natural' " (Haquin & Stephany, 2005, p. 138; my translation). The courtroom broke out in applause.

Sympathy for Vandeput, her family, and the doctor who furnished the lethal prescription was such that at one point the judge ordered the courtroom to be cleared "to stop the shouted demands to free the defendants" (*Rome News-Tribune*, Nov. 11, 1962). After deliberating for "one hour and fifty minutes," the all-male jury acquitted the accused (*The Miami News*, Nov. 15, 1962). Thousands celebrated on the streets. When Dr. Casters drove through his neighborhood after leaving the courthouse, "fireworks exploded," "wild cheering broke out," and the doctor was carried by the crowd to his house while he "was bombarded with flowers" (Roth, 1962).

Ten years after the Thalidomide Homicide, another mercy killing case emerged from Belgium. Suzanne Picquereau, who suffered from cerebral sclerosis, was put to death by her husband. Seventy-four-year-old Jean Picquereau had been Suzanne's main caregiver for three years. Once her illness began causing her unbearable pain and a mental breakdown, Mr. Picquereau decided to kill his wife of 40 years. He turned himself to the police after strangling her. Following a short trial, Picquereau was acquitted (*L'Impartial*, Jan. 15, 1972).

Although these two cases pushed the debate about "mercy killing" to the forefront of Belgian (and international) newspapers, they did little to advance legalization of assisted death. In both cases, the principal defendants were not physicians, and it is plausible to infer that some degree of compassion by jurors muddled their factual decision making.[46]

It was not until 1982 that the first advocacy organizations seeking decriminalization of assisted death were established in Belgium. Two such groups were launched simultaneously: a Flanders-based organization, *Recht Op Waardig Sterven* ("Right to Die with Dignity," RWS for short) and another, *L'Association pour le Droit de Mourir dans la Dignité* ("The Association for the Right to Die with Dignity," ADMD for short), based in Brussels.

In the beginning, efforts by activists from the RWS and ADMD were restricted to patients' right to refuse treatment, the dissemination of living wills, and educational campaigns about end-of-life issues. From 1984 until the mid-1990s, the organizations' focus shifted to providing active support to actual decriminalization of the issue. In that period, a few bills were advanced by parliamentary members of different parties without success.[47]

## 1990s–2002: The Passage of the Belgian 2002 Act on Euthanasia

From the mid-1990s onward, the movement pro-legalization gained some momentum in Belgium. In 1993, an Advisory Committee on Bioethics composed of politicians and multidisciplinary experts was launched and, in 1997, it published a report concerning the issue of aid in dying. The report laid out four quite distinct options, ranging from a straightforward decriminalization to maintenance of the prohibitive *status quo*. Although the Committee did not reach a consensual position, it did urge "the authorities to encourage a broad democratic debate on this issue among the main players concerned and, more widely still, among all citizens" (Belgian Advisory Committee on Bioethics, 1997.

Following the Committee's advice, the Belgian Senate held a debate on the matter that same year. Again, no consensus was reached. Political members of the Christian-Democratic party, while accepting the idea of doctors invoking the "necessity" defense after reporting their involvement to authorities, opposed any direct legislative modification that would sanction the practice outright. Additionally, those affiliated with the Flemish Block (*Vlaams Blok*), a far-right political party, refused permissive changes of any kind.

The political balance of power would shift in 1999, however, when, much like in the Netherlands, for the first time in 40 years, the Christian-Democrats were out of power and a new coalition comprising liberals, socialists, and the Green Party took charge in Belgium. Historically, several members of the new coalition now in government had sought legalization of medically assisted death.[48]

Moreover, a contemporaneous public opinion poll indicated that 80 percent of Belgians supported legislation for aid in dying in certain circumstances (*La Libre Belgique*, Oct., 1999, cited in Adams, 2011). These developments were accompanied by the publication of the first scientific study assessing the incidence of aid in dying practices among physicians in Belgium (Mortier et al., 2000). While restricted to one city—Hasselt, in Flanders—and finding that euthanasia and physician-assisted suicide were relatively rare, the study revealed that in 3.3 percent of cases physicians had administered lethal drugs without patients' consent, hinting at the need for regulation or, at a minimum, for continued debate.

Taken together, all of these developments—i.e., the arrival of the new, more sympathetic government, along with the first advisory report by the Bioethics Commission, public support for the issue, and the backing of scientific evidence that the debate merited attention—suggested that the time was finally ripe for regulation and that a political and social window of opportunity had presented itself in Belgium. Although not without extensive debate, in merely two years since its introduction in the parliamentary agenda, the "Act on Euthanasia of May 28th, 2002" (hereafter the Belgian 2002 Act) was approved in the Senate and in the Chamber of Representatives and signed by the Belgian King.

## Rights and Requirements under the Belgian 2002 Act

*Euthanasia*, defined by the Belgian law as "the intentional termination of life at the individual's request," is allowed only when the patient's suffering is unbearable and cannot be alleviated otherwise, and only if performed by a physician. A doctor, in turn, can decline to participate on grounds of conscience or for medical reasons, and in such cases he or she must explain to the patient (or designated proxy, if the patient is unconscious) the reasons for his or her refusal. When the physician refuses to participate for medical reasons, he or she must note the rationale in the patient's records.

In Belgium, the patient's request must be "voluntary," "considered," and "durable," that is, must be made repeatedly in the course of several discussions, and should not result from external pressure. Also, it should be expressed in writing. However, in cases where the patient is unable to write the request himself or herself—due, for instance, to physical disability—another individual (who has no material interest in the patient's death) can draft the request instead. Records must be made as to why the patient personally did not write the request and who ultimately did so, and a physician must be present when the request is drafted by a third party.

Requests can be revoked at any time and can also be made in advance. In the latter cases, advance directives regarding euthanasia work in the same manner as other end-of-life decisions in that they must be signed in the presence of two witnesses, one of whom should not have any material interest in the ensuing death. A representative (or representatives) for the patient can be named in the directive, and that person should inform the physician about the patient's preferences. Although they can be drafted at any time, advance directives only allow for legal euthanasia if they have been written fewer than five years before the patient has become incapable of expressing his or her wishes.

Patients requesting euthanasia do not need to be terminally ill. However, different requirements are in place when natural death is imminent versus situations where the patient is not expected to die in the near future. For patients whose death is impending, the doctor evaluating the request must consult another, independent physician who will, in turn, review relevant medical records, examine the patient, and report in writing his or her assessment.[49] In cases where death is not immediately foreseeable, a third doctor (a psychiatrist, if the request originates from a nonsomatic illness) must also be involved, and an interval of at least one month must be observed between the written request and the termination of the patient's life.

## Euthanasia in Belgium and the Netherlands: Three Divergent Aspects

For the most part, the Belgian law mirrors that of neighboring Netherlands. However, three aspects make it unique. Like the Dutch, the Belgian 2002 Act prescribes that the patient seeking to be terminated should be suffering unbearably and that this suffering cannot be otherwise alleviated. However, although the patient's suffering can have a psychiatric or a physical origin, the Belgian 2002 Act is distinct from the law in the Netherlands in that it explicitly states that the unbearable suffering must be due to "illness or accident." This clause effectively rules out cases of "existential suffering" such as *Brongersma*, discussed earlier.[50]

A second, startling difference between these "Low Countries" is that in Belgium any consideration of "physician-assisted suicide" is omitted from the legislation. Therefore, although the 2002 Act establishes the legal boundaries of when and how a physician may inject a patient with lethal substances, it does not directly address the situations where a patient may wish to ingest the drugs himself or herself. From the point of view of a patient's autonomy, the latter would be preferable than the former, and it would have been desirable to build it into the law. Reflecting on this paradox, other scholars have pointed out that this may have been the result of legislative compromise (Griffiths et al., 2008). Specifically, during the debate that preceded the passage of the 2002 Act, opponents of the practice framed physician-assisted suicide to be murder on request, and proponents avoided it altogether in order to preserve the viability of the law, even if it only included euthanasia. The distinction was addressed again after the 2002 Act had been enacted, first by the Order of Physicians and later by the Federal Control and Evaluation Commission—the body that oversees the practice of euthanasia in Belgium. In sum, these two institutions settled on accepting the equivalency of these two means of physician involvement, provided the procedures laid out in the 2002 Act are also observed when the physician merely assists in the patient's suicide. Accordingly, mandatory reports produced every two years, which document the incidence of medically assisted deaths in the country, include both practices. As Figure 7.2 illustrates, granted assisted-death requests by Belgian physicians have increased

**Figure 7.2 Number of Assisted-Death Requests Granted by Belgian Physicians.**

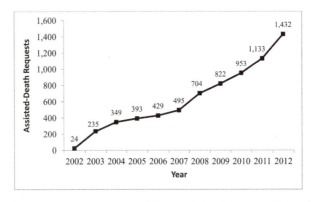

*Source*: Belgian Euthanasia Evaluation Commission, 2012 (http://www.worldrtd.net/news/belgium -publishes-2012-numbers).

from 24 when the law was first enacted to 1,432 after 10 years. Most patients are over 60 years old and suffer from cancer.

Finally, a third aspect of the Belgian law differentiates it from the Dutch experience. In the Netherlands, requests from minors, as discussed earlier, can be honored, provided certain conditions are met. Accordingly, Dutch children as young as 12 years may request euthanasia; however, parental consent is mandatory until the child patient reaches the age of 16. Minors aged 16–18 years do not need parental approval; however, parents must be involved in the decision-making process (Government of the Netherlands, 2011). In Belgium, however, a 2014 legal reform lifted the age restrictions of the Belgian 2002 Act. That change and other contemporary debates surrounding the practice of hastened death in Belgium are discussed in the next section.

## Contemporary Debates in Belgium Surrounding the Practice of Hastened Death

Originally, the Belgian 2002 Act had allowed for medically assisted deaths exclusively for individuals aged 18 years or older. Recently, however, the boundaries of the Belgian law permitting the involvement of doctors in hastening death have expanded to lift the age restrictions. Approved in the parliament in February 2014 and subsequently enacted by King Philippe, Belgian physicians, with parental consent expressed in writing, can accede to a request for assisted death from minor patients of any age, provided they demonstrate a "capacity for discernment" verified by a psychiatrist or a psychologist. The amended law excludes requests where the child's suffering stems from nonsomatic conditions.

Although the expansion of the Belgian law to include children is not without controversy, with domestic criticism emerging primarily from religious organizations, a contemporaneous survey commissioned by *La Libre* (a Catholic and conservative newspaper published in French) revealed that three-quarters of the Belgians approved the euthanasia of incurably ill minors (*La Dernière Heure*, Oct. 2, 2013). A similar number would also endorse an amendment of the 2002 Act to include adults suffering from dementia.

Beginning with the Thalidomide baby case, Belgium's experience with assisted death often has captured the attention of the international media. Recently, the legal expansion to include minors has unleashed many aggrieved headlines. In reality, however, the debate to include children as eligible patients under the Belgian 2002 Act was not novel—and treatment of the issue by the international media largely failed to put it in context. Discussions had emerged first during the hearings preceding the enactment of the law, and again in 2004 and 2006 through the introductions of two legislative proposals.

The main argument posed by proponents was the fact that the 2002 Act, as originally enacted, was in stark contrast to the treatment of minors in another Belgian law that covers end-of-life issues. Namely, the "Law on Patient's Rights" provides that minor patients who are deemed capable of assessing their situation should be involved in other major end-of-life decisions, such as refusing consent to medical treatment (Article 12(2), in Nys, 2010). Additionally, and in accordance with the "Law on Patient's Rights," the "Code of Medical Deontology" (Article 96) expressly states that physicians treating minors must involve their patients in all end-of-life decisions, depending on the minor's age, maturity, and nature of the intervention in question. The inclusion of minors in 2014, therefore, was seen as correcting the legal discrepancy on the treatment given to that age group by these different end-of-life laws.

Contemporary discussions about hastened death in Belgium focus on two additional issues. In 2012, Belgium was the first country to allow one of its prison inmates to pursue aid in dying. The prisoner, who was convicted of two murders, had been incarcerated for 20 years and was terminally ill. Other inmates have since requested to be euthanized, including one individual who has spent substantial amounts of time in solitary confinement within psychiatric wings in the Belgian correctional system, waiting for treatment for his violent sexual urges (*The Globe and Mail*, Jan. 1, 2014). Clearly, hastening the deaths of inmates has serious ethical implications, and in a sense it creates a twisted version of death penalty by request. This is further complicated by the fact that the correctional system in Belgium struggles with overcrowding and inadequate treatment of its mentally ill population (Vandevelde et al., 2011). Certain advocates, however, have supported the idea of "voluntary euthanasia" as the "last frontier in prison reform" (Nitschke & Stewart, 2005, p. 35). At present, nothing in Belgian law precludes its prisoners from pursuing that path, provided they meet the eligibility requirements set forth by the country's 2002 Act.

Another salient point in the current Belgian debate is the issue of organ harvesting following physician-assisted and physician-performed deaths. In 1986, Belgium enacted an organ donation law based on "presumed consent," that is, deceased individuals are assumed to be potential donors in absence of explicit opposition to donation before death. Relatives are also consulted before the harvesting procedure begins and may object to it, thereby halting the process. Although Belgium, compared to other nations, traditionally has achieved high rates of donors per million inhabitants, the number of effective donors is decreasing, because donors are more often medically unsuitable for donation due to their age and ill health (Eurotransplant, 2013).

It is in that context that one should reflect about the implications of post-euthanasia organ harvesting in Belgium. Although the majority of the individuals procuring hastened death are cancer-ridden, and cancer patients are not eligible to donate their organs, euthanasia patients whose suffering stems from psychological reasons or neurological/muscular illnesses may be eligible, if their organs are deemed suitable. A few studies have been conducted to assess the pragmatic and the ethical repercussions of this practice. Notably, surgeons at a university-affiliated hospital in Leuven found that the condition of the lungs extracted from those who were euthanized was superior to those harvested from people who died in an accident (Raemdonck et al., 2013). Typically, deaths resulting from accidents can traumatize the individual's lungs in what is called the *agonal* phase, when a prolonged struggle to breathe take place. That is not the case when lethal injections are duly performed. In line with this finding, yet another study pointed out that the "potential in Belgium ... could be substantial," as the "percentage of patients with debilitating neurologic disease with their request for euthanasia granted" is not negligible (Ysebaert et al., 2009, p. 586).

In March 2009, Luxembourg was the last of the Benelux countries to decriminalize physician aid in dying under certain conditions. In comparison with the Netherlands, and even with Belgium, the process by which aid in dying became permissible in Luxembourg was very brief. Fundamentally achieved as a result of the efforts of two activists, the legal development was politically and religiously contentious, despite strong public support.

## LUXEMBOURG

One of the smallest nations in Europe, the "Grand Duchy of Luxembourg" is about two-thirds the size of Rhode Island and is home to half a million people—only half of whom are economically active (European Observatory on Health Care Systems, 1999). It borders Belgium, Germany, and France. Three languages—Letzeburgesch (a German dialect, which is the national language), French (the main language of official documents and legislation), and German—are officially used in the country; in addition, English, Portuguese, and Italian are also widely adopted. Luxembourg's GDP is among the world's highest and its population also sits atop international rankings for literacy (International Monetary Fund, 2014).

In 2012, life expectancy at birth for Luxembourgers was 81 years for men and women (OECD, 2014). Access to health care in the country is free and universal, and there are nearly three doctors per 1,000 inhabitants (OECD, 2014). The leading causes of death among Luxembourgers are circulatory diseases (cardiovascular and cerebrovascular diseases) and cancer (Eurostat, 2010).

Although Luxembourg is a secular state, its population is chiefly Roman Catholic. A constitutional monarchy, Luxembourg is headed by a "Grand Duke," who, up until the legalization of aid in dying in that country, enjoyed a greater degree of legislative power. How that changed in the context of the legalization of aid in dying in Luxembourg is explored next.

### Church and State: The Brief, Yet Contentious, Legalization Process in Luxembourg

With roughly 900 members at present, the Association for the Right to Die with Dignity—Luxembourg (*L'Association pour le Droit de Mourir dans la Dignité— Lëtzebuerg*) was founded in 1988 by Henri Clees, a medical doctor (L'Association pour le Droit de Mourir dans la Dignité—Lëtzebuerg, 2014). In its first 15 years, the

Association had an international presence,[51] but did little to advance legalization in Luxembourg.

In 2002, Jean Huss and Lydie Err, both members of the parliament and founders of the Luxembourger Association for the Right to Die with Dignity, introduced a bill that would have shielded physicians from prosecution if they assisted terminally ill patients die under certain predefined conditions. The Err/Huss bill was narrowly defeated, blocked primarily by members of the conservative Christian Social People's Party (*Chrëschtlech Sozial Vollekspartei*; CSV henceforth).[52]

In 2004, right before national elections were held, Huss and Err organized a petition for the decriminalization of euthanasia, which gathered about 3,000 signatures and was accompanied by a concerted media campaign (*World Right to Die News*, 2008). Simultaneously, the new government, a coalition between the CSV and the Socialist Party, put forth a new proposal dealing exclusively with palliative care, which would establish the availability of such care for terminally ill individuals.

In 2008, the palliative care proposal and an amended version of the Err/Huss bill were debated and a parliamentary vote ensued. The palliative care bill was unanimously approved.[53] The Err/Huss bill, however, sparked intense debate and strong opposition by those from the CSV party. The bill ultimately passed, but the margin was narrow: 30 votes in favor, 26 votes against, and 3 abstentions (L'Association pour le Droit de Mourir dans la Dignité —Lëtzebuerg, 2008). Only one member of the CSV supported the proposed law—generating outrage in her party colleagues, who demanded her expulsion (The Nathaniel Centre for Bioethics, 2009).

Although no sanction was imposed on that CSV member, the political turmoil was far from over. At that point, the euthanasia law, although approved by the parliament, still lacked the constitutionally required royal avowal in order to be enacted. Luxembourg's Grand Duke Henri, a devout Roman Catholic, refused to back the law, for "reasons of conscience" (Israely, Dec. 12, 2008). He called on the parliament to change the constitution and strip him of veto powers if the euthanasia law were to proceed. The last time a Luxembourger monarch had defied the will of democratically elected representatives was in 1912, when Grand Duchess Marie-Adélaïde refused to sign a bill that would have curtailed the role of Catholic priests in the education system. She eventually agreed to enact the law under increased public pressure (Péporté, Kmec, Majerus, & Margue, 2010).

Luxembourg Prime Minister Jean-Claude Juncker, head of the CSV and strong opponent of the Err/Huss bill, albeit sympathetic to the Grand Duke's "problems of conscience," publicly voiced his belief that "if the parliament votes in a law, it must be brought into force" (*Spiegel Online International*, Dec. 4, 2008). Contemporary polls echoed his opinion: 60 percent of Luxembourgers disapproved of the monarch's withholding of royal assent; furthermore, 70 percent backed the euthanasia law (Associated Press, 2008). The result was an overwhelming vote by lawmakers to amend the constitution and reduce the Grand Duke's role to a purely ceremonial one.

Luxembourg's "Euthanasia and Assisted Suicide Law of 16 March 2009" is in many aspects very similar to the Belgian law, especially with regard to the duties of the performing physician, the nature of the patient's request, and the reporting of cases. However, unlike the other Benelux countries, the Luxembourg law is restricted to terminally ill adults.

In the first two years after the law was enacted, five individuals were granted their request to die with the help of a physician (Commission Nationale de Contrôle et d'Evaluation, 2009–2010, p. 4). Fourteen requests were then granted between 2011 and 2012. Most patients were over 60 years old and suffered from cancer.

In contrast to certain American jurisdictions where "physician-assisted suicide" is legal, it could be argued that the Benelux countries offer a model of extreme medicalized death, with doctors going beyond the prescription to the actual injection of lethal substances. In Chapter 8, we explore the opposite model, where the role of nonphysicians is indispensable.

## NOTES

1. Not since the 1950s has the word *euthanasia* garnered as much political purchase by its opponents in the United States as it has just recently, with the unveiling of *H.R. 3200, America's Affordable Health Choices Act of 2009*. The Act, also known as *Obamacare*, became controversial due (among other things) to its provision on Medicare reimbursement for end-of-life counseling to be provided by doctors to patients 65 years and older (Section 1233). Such counseling, which may occur every five years, should the patient so choose, includes discussions about drawing up a living will or planning for hospice treatment.

At the height of the debate surrounding the "Obamacare" law, Republicans and conservatives, as well as pro-life organizations, invoked the "slippery slope" argument that the Act was the first step toward involuntary euthanasia of vulnerable populations. This argument, as the reader will see, has been invoked persistently throughout the history covered here. Former Governor Sarah Palin, for example, suggested on her Facebook page that her own "parents or [her own] baby with Down Syndrome will have to stand in front of Obama's 'death panel' so his bureaucrats can decide, based on a subjective judgment of their 'level of productivity in society,' whether they are worthy of health care" (Farber, 2009).

The recent discussion about the possible implications for Obama's proposed health care reform as it is related to Medicare and informed choices at the end of life is only one example of how a thorough analysis of end-of-life decision making cannot overlook the political context upon which any legalization attempt is contingent. More than a set of innocuous partisan exchanges, the controversy generated by the Act captured the public eye just a few weeks shy of oral arguments on *Baxter v. Montana*, heard by that state's Supreme Court in the height of the debate on health care reform.

2. They are also not novel. In 1989, the Hastings Center reported on how the American lay and medical press abound with inaccurate accounts about the process in the Netherlands (Rigter, 1989) Among the examples of such misrepresentation of facts were the following excerpts, closely aligned with those propagated by Santorum:

"In The Netherlands," one of the articles suggests, "There's evidence that patients are avoiding health care facilities because of this fear (of being sneaked upon by a doctor)" (Rigter, 1989, p. 31). Another argues: "There is clear evidence that active voluntary euthanasia has been clinically extended (in The Netherlands) to include involuntary active euthanasia at family request, and secret involuntary active euthanasia by both physicians and nurses."

3. Unlike the United States, where a rights-based judicial tradition is prevalent, in the Dutch legal system constitutional judicial reviews are banned; accordingly, individuals cannot assert their constitutionally guaranteed human rights if their action would result in review of parliamentary or primary legislation (see dr Vries, 2004, for a discussion).

4. Others have covered more exhaustively all aspects of that history, as well as subsequent assessments of the utilization of the law (see, e.g., Griffiths et al., 1998).

5. This formal, systematic application of discretion is a Dutch tradition (*gedoogbeleid*) observed in relation to many legal issues, such as the sale and use of marijuana. Legalization of marijuana consumption had not taken place until 1992. However, although these acts were still forbidden by law, in 1976 the Dutch adopted a formal written policy of nonenforcement for violations involving possession or sale of up to 30 g of cannabis (MacCoun & Reuter, 1997).

6. In addition to this notion of "pragmatic tolerance," scholars have pointed out several characteristics of the Dutch society that may have contributed to the legalization of medical aid in dying in the Netherlands (see, e.g., Griffiths, Bood, & Weyers, 1998). Of particular importance were the following developments taking place in the 1960s and 1970s: the secularization of the Dutch society, which gradually undermined the status of traditional institutions, particularly the Catholic Church; the weakening of death as taboo, which, has been argued, happened in the Netherlands more rapidly than in the rest of the Western world (Kennedy, 2002); the rejection of medical technology in futile cases; and individualization (Weyers, 2006).

7. Prior to the prosecution of Dr. Berman, the issue of killing on request occupied the Dutch courts in 1908 and 1910. Both cases involved laymen who shot their girlfriends at their request (Griffiths et al., 1998).

8. The first time when Dutch courts faced the issue of "passive euthanasia" was in the case of Ms. Mia Versluis, who was in permanent vegetative state for five years following a mishap during an operation. Versluis's plight generated intense debate on the limits of medical treatment. In the spring of 1966, Versluis, then 21 years old, had a surgery under complete anesthesia to have a growth removed from her heel. Her heart failed during the operation and she was resuscitated but lapsed into a coma. She was supported by a ventilator that kept her alive. By the fall of 1966, the anesthesiologist who was involved in the surgery and had continued to care for Versluis proposed to the patient's family that the artificial respirator be removed, which would inevitably lead to her death. The family filed a complaint against the doctor, who was ultimately fined for engaging in behavior that undermines confidence in the medical profession. The court also ruled that when termination of life support is considered, there must be consultation with other physicians. Versluis's lingering death made the Dutch "extremely anxious" about the life-sustaining interventions that could keep patients between life and death (Ten Have & Welie, 2005, p. 9).

9. Throughout the 1970s, Baroness Adrienne Van Till-D'Aulnis de Bourouill wrote a series of influential works differentiating murder, active euthanasia, and removal of

life-sustaining equipment in medicolegal terms (see, e.g., de Bourouill, 1975). Through her work, she helped frame the legal, ethical, and medical boundaries of the issue. She was a cofounder of NVVE and a board member of the World Federation of Right-to-Die Societies.

10. Dutch Roman Catholic priest and ethicist Paul Sporken, for example, defended that the categorical prohibition of euthanasia is not justified: "There are extremely rare cases [when] active euthanasia could be allowed ... where the patient, himself, decides to short[en] his own dying process" (Simon, Bob, Jan. 4, 1974).

11. Jan Hendrik Van den Berg was a psychiatrist who, in 1969, published a book proposing that human life should not always be extended by technological means and that in certain cases the doctors should actively bring about patients' deaths. In discussing what he calls a "new ethic" of medicine, Van den Berg recounts several medical cases—accident victims, children affected by Downs' syndrome, thalidomide and spina bifida defects, and the infirm old—where life should be shortened in order to avoid prolonged suffering or futile existence. He justifies his position thus: "It does sound quite barbarous for the doctor to kill his patient. It is unfamiliar. It seems improper. But it is also improper to force a suffering patient ... to continue to vegetate. That must be made uncommon. It is always barbarous" (Van den Berg, 1978 [English translation], p. 64).

12. To provide an example, in the late 1950s, 24% of Dutch men and women were "unchurched," that is, did not claim to be members of any organized religion, whereas in 1991 the proportion had increased to 57% (Lechner, 1996, p. 254). By 2004, some 64% of Dutch respondents claimed that they did not belong to any churches (Lechner, 2012, p. 130). By contrast, in the United States, the number of "religiously unaffiliated" remained below 10% from the 1970s through the early 1990s; today, at its highest, the proportion is 18% (Liu, 2012).

13. The facts of the case recounted here rely on a translation of the opinion in *Postma* published in English 15 years after the case was decided (Netherlands Jurisprudence, 1987).

14. Testimony by a witness in the case suggested that the medical director had previously made certain statements that led Dr. Postma to believe that he endorsed her actions. According to the witness, the director had said "that we are stuck with that damn law from the 1800s, and that he himself had also done that kind of thing on several occasions" (Netherlands Jurisprudence, 1987, p. 441).

15. Article 293 states, "A person who takes the life of another person at that other person's express and earnest request is liable to a term of imprisonment of not more than twelve years or a fine of the fifth category" (Rayar et al., 1997).

16. In its opinion, the Court agreed with the conditions set forth by the medical inspection, except the requirement that the patient is terminal. The Court reasoned that it knew of "many cases of incurable illness or accident-caused disability combined with serious physical and/or mental suffering where the patient is otherwise healthy and can continue living in this state for years. It is not the Court's view that such suffering should be denied the relief described by the expert witness" (Griffith, Bood, & Weyers, 1998, p. 52).

17. As discussed previously, the doctrine of "double effect" condones the administration of pain-relieving drugs even when the doctor knows that death may ensue. The practice, known as "terminal sedation," is widely accepted. The key distinction in a "double-effect" scenario is the physician's intent: to alleviate pain and suffering and not to bring about immediate death. The court in *Postma* emphasized that the doctor did not

manipulate the medication over the course of time in order to relieve her mother's suffering, but instead injected a lethal dose "all at one time," thereby signaling that her intention was not to pursue a more conservative course of alleviation (Netherlands Jurisprudence, 1987, translated by Walter Lagerwey).

18. *Postma* was widely publicized but was not the only such case to be prosecuted between 1969 and 1980. During this period, there were three other cases, all of which involved family members who killed or assisted in the suicide of their loved ones. All of them were found guilty and imprisoned for relatively short periods of time (Griffiths et al., 1998).

19. Article 294 of the Dutch Penal Code states, "A person who intentionally incites another to commit suicide, assists in the suicide of another, or procures for that other person the means to commit suicide, is liable to a term of imprisonment of not more than three years or a fine of the fourth category, where the suicide ensues" (Rayar et al., 1997).

As discussed above, in addition to the prohibition of "suicide assistance" (Article 294), the Dutch Penal Code also forbids "killing on request" (Article 293). The Code—*Wetboek van Strafretch*, hereafter WvSr—came into force in 1886. Prior to that, although the Netherlands regained independence from the French empire in 1815, the Napoleonic Penal Code had remained in effect. The Napoleonic Code was silent on "killing on request" and "assisted suicide." When the WvSr was drafted, the Commission in charge of the document mirrored a provision from the North German Penal Code (Section 216) that prohibited "killing on request." Additionally, reflecting the statutory trends of the times, the WvSr maintained "suicide" as an immoral, yet noncriminal act, but criminalized the act of assisting in a suicide. For an in-depth discussion of the statutory development of Articles 293 and 294 of the WvSr, see Groenhuijsen and van Laanen (2006).

20. Adelbert Jitta died in 2010, making use of the 2002 Act (The World Federation for the Right to Die Societies, 2010).

21. For example, Ch. J. Enschedé, former member of the Dutch Supreme Court, argued that physician-performed euthanasia and physician-assisted suicide are analogous to the practice of abortion and as such should constitute a medical exception. For an overview of his and other legal scholars on the use of "medical exception" as a legitimate defense in medical aid in dying, see Elders and Woretshofer (1992).

22. In *Pols*, for example, a psychiatrist presented the "medical exception" defense to the Dutch Supreme Court, defending that her behavior was justified because she had "acted in accordance with the demands of appropriate professional practice" (Bostrom & Lagerwey, 1987, p. 445). Dr. Pols had furnished Seconal to a 73-year-old woman suffering from multiple sclerosis, and when that did not cause her death, the psychiatrist injected the woman with a lethal dose of morphine. The High Court affirmed that certain medical interventions do not fall under criminal law. However, it reasoned that aid in dying, unlike a surgery to remove an appendix, was not consensually conceived "common medical practice." The doctor was found guilty of "killing on request."

23. In *Death and Medical Power*, Ten Have and Welie (2005, p. 187) provide a summary of the types of cases that inspired the Dutch Penal Code drafters to include Articles 293 (killing on request) and 294 (assisted suicide) among its proscriptions. For instance, a case decided in 1859 involved a young military who, unable to take his bride along to his tour of duty, forged a suicide pact with her. He obtained poison and they both ingested it. She died, but he survived. At trial, he was convicted of poisoning and sentenced to hang to death, but on appeal the Dutch Supreme Court concluded that no culpability or sentence

could be imposed because suicide was not prohibited by law and the Penal Code also did not prohibit assistance in suicide.

24. "Overmacht," literally "overpower," is most commonly translated as *force majeure*.

25. The classic example in Dutch legal history of a conflict of duties that lends itself to a necessity defense emerged in 1923 and involved an optician. The optician owned a shop in Amsterdam, where a city ordinance required shopkeepers to close their business by 6:00 p.m.; failure to do so was a criminal offense. Approached by a customer who needed glasses near closing time, the optician sold the man a pair of spectacles and the transaction took place after 6:00 p.m.. In court, the optician argued that he had faced a dilemma: his duty to obey the city ordinance versus his duty, as an optician, to help the man to be able to see. The court agreed with the optician, determining that the violation of the city ordinance attained a higher good and no other viable alternatives were available to him at the time (dr Vries, 2004).

26. For a discussion of Glanville Williams's legacy on the formulation of necessity as a potential defense in aid in dying, see Lewis (2013).

27. He also argued that his action was not a substantial violation of the law; although successful in the lower court, this line of defense was subsequently rejected by the appellate and Supreme courts.

28. The KNMG defended that in a pluralistic society there should remain room for a standpoint contrary to physician aid in dying as well as to one in favor of it. The organization's approach in publicizing its view was a pragmatic one; its doctors were faced with requests by patients, and, absent legal clarification, the KNMG sought to advance some professional guidance for those who felt that they could not decline their patients' requests. By seeking to establish pragmatic guidance, and not to take a moral stance on the issue, the KNMG avoided the schism it had experienced a few years prior, when it expressed its support for decriminalization of abortion. On that occasion, several physicians who believed that terminating a life is contradictory to their fundamental duties left the KNMG to form another association, the "Dutch Physicians' League." In the 1990s, the League had about 600 affiliated doctors, whereas the KNMG had 25,000 (Hendin, 1998, p. 113).

29. In 1992, the KNMG revised its policy to include another requirement, that is, that a written record be submitted to the appropriate agencies regulating death.

30. Dr. Admiraal, whom others would dub "Holland's leading euthanasia practitioner" (Marker et al., 1991, p. 294), later explained that each one of his patients always thanked him at their final moment (Cliness, 1986). Dismissing their gratitude as unnecessary, Dr. Admiraal reasoned that it was his "duty" to obliterate their suffering and offered a sensitive account of the dying process: "These moments are very decent ...We cry and it's good for the family to see the doctor cry at losing a friend, losing a human being."

31. To inform its recommendations, the Commission executed a comparative survey of legislation, case law, and relevant legal literature; consulted with medical and legal experts; compiled data on attitudes toward aid in dying and its prevalence and number of requests; and held public hearings (Gevers, 1987, p. 165).

32. According to Leenen (2001, p. 128), opinion polls show that acceptance of aid in dying facilitated by doctors increased substantially: in 1975, two years after the conclusion of *Postma*, 52.6% of those surveyed approved of the practice, whereas in 1998, two years before the legalization by parliament, 88% of the Dutch supported the practice.

33. The Catholic Church and other Christian religious organizations and institutions for the most part opposed the emergence of medically assisted death as a policy in the Netherlands. For a sample of their counterlegalization arguments unfolding between the 1980s and 2001, see Kohnen and Schumacher (2002).

34. Other such empirical studies were carried out in 1995 and 2001. For a succinct explanation of the findings of these three investigations, see Cohen-Almagor (2004).

35. The "1993 Burial Act" is an example of this regulatory effort. It is further discussed subsequently.

36. In 1993, the KNMG had suggested that in certain psychiatric cases where the patient has no prospect of improvement, medically assisted dying may be desirable (Commissie Aanvaardbaarheid Levensbeëindigend handelen, *Discussienota Hulp bij zelf-doding bij psychiatrische patiënten*, Utrecht, KNMG 1993).

37. Although Dr. Philip Sutorius helped his patient die in 1998, the decision in *Brongersma* had not been reached until 2001, after the Termination of Life on Request and Assisted Suicide (Review Procedures) Act had passed.

38. There is no single Drion Pill or Last Will Pill. Advocates explained that these terms have become metaphors for "freedom for the aged to depart from life based on what the future still may have to offer, and after balanced thought and in a legally appropriate way" (NVVE, 2010). Hence, their attempts of legalizing rational suicide for the elderly refer in effect to a combination of medications that would be dispensed to those "tired of life" or whose life is "completed."

39. *Time Magazine*, for instance, while recognizing that the Netherlands has not yet "completely become Hemlockland," characterized the new law as "creepy" (Cloud, 2001).

40. Specifically, in 2011 the RCCs were notified of 3,695 acts of termination of life on request. Of these, 3,446 were cases of active termination of life by physician, 196 cases were "physician-assisted suicides," and 53 cases involved a combination of the two. The 2011 data suggest an increase of 18% in granted requests in comparison with 2010 (Regional Euthanasia Review Committees, 2011).In 2003, the first report prepared by the RCCs because the 2002 Act went into effect revealed 1,815 notifications of termination of life by physicians. Of these, 1,626 cases were active termination of life by physician, 148 cases of physician-assisted suicides, and 41 cases involved a combination of the two. Eight cases were deemed in noncompliance with the Act that year (Regional Euthanasia Review Committees, 2003).

41. Relatedly, in certain extreme circumstances, Dutch physicians are also allowed to terminate, deliberately, the lives of newborn infants who are suffering unbearably and without prospect of improvement. In these cases, parental consent is required, and the "due care" criteria apply, as well as the "nonnatural death" notification procedure. Prior to the enactment of the 2002 Act, Dutch courts had ruled on two cases involving newborns to whom medical aid in dying had been provided. In the first case, the physician ended the life of an infant born with spina bifida. The second case involved a newborn who had trisomy 13. Both doctors were acquitted. A national survey conducted in the 1990s revealed that each year between 15 and 20 newborns are euthanized in the Netherlands (Verhagen & Sauer, 2005). Dr. Eduard Verhagen, who has medically induced the deaths of several doomed infants, expressed that their dying is "beautiful in a way . . . It is after they die that you see them relaxed for the first time" (Holt, 2005).

42. In 1900, only 3.4% of Belgians had some form of health insurance (Schepers, 1993).

43. "Pillars" are a set of close organizations held together by a common cultural orientation (see Therborn [1989] for in-depth discussion).

44. Geel would later become one of the European hubs for the treatment of mentally ill patients, spearheading a therapeutic model of deinstitutionalization of such patients. Painter Vincent van Gogh's father tried to have him sent to Geel for treatment in 1879.

45. These are my translations. The multiple versions of the Code in French can be found in http://ordomedic.be/fr/code/index.

46. The first prosecutions of Belgian doctors for their direct involvement in hastening patients' deaths took place only in 2000, as discussed later in this chapter. As such, there was no case history testing the legitimacy of "necessity" as a line of defense.

47. In 1984, Congressman Edgar d'Hose introduced the first bill, followed, in 1988, by Edouard Klein. In 1995, another bill, this one filed by MM. Boutmans, Moureaux, Lozie, and Bacquelaine, was proposed but also failed (Sénat de Belgique, Session de 2000–2001).

48. Concomitantly, the Advisory Committee on Bioethics issued a second report, this one providing advice on termination of life for noncompetent patients and the legal status of "living wills" (Belgian Advisory Committee on Bioethics, "Opinion no. 9 of 22 February 1999 concerning active termination of the lives of persons incapable of expressing their wishes"). Unlike the previous report, this one made apparent the ideological oppositions surrounding the issue and was in a sense illustrative of the polarized legislative debate that would ensue.

49. Getting a second opinion, and a third in the cases of nonsomatic suffering, may prove difficult. Although doctors involved in this process are required to review medical records and examine the requesting patient, often traveling to do so, their work is not remunerated. In 2013, the Belgian government was devising a payment scheme to fill this gap, by which such physicians would be paid €160.00 (roughly US$215.00) per consult (LegalWorld, 2013). In the Netherlands, similar services are remunerated at a rate of €330.00 (or US$443.00).

50. In comparison with its Dutch counterpart, the legal boundaries of the practice are better delineated in the Belgian law. However, controversial cases continue to emerge, making it clear that the issue is far from settled, particularly when patients' suffering is nonsomatic. For instance, in 2011, two 45-year-old twin brothers were euthanized. They had been deaf all of their lives, but a recent diagnosis of incurable glaucoma prompted their request to die. In 2013, a transsexual was helped die after a series of failed sex-change operations. Both cases involved one physician, Dr. Wim Distelmans. Dr. Distelmans, an oncologist by training, was an early proponent of legalization in Belgium and served as chair of the committee assigned to regulate the practice of euthanasia in that country when it became legal. Today, he is under investigation by that same committee after two complaints were filed against him by relatives of patients whom he helped die and who question whether the legal procedures were followed.

51. For example, in 1998, the 12th International Conference of the World Federation of the Right to Die Societies was convened in Switzerland. In that meeting, a document, later known as the "Zurich Declaration on Assisted Dying," was drafted by Dr. Clees and signed by other doctors. The "Zurich Declaration" stated the medical professionals' support "for the right of competent, adult patients, who are suffering severely, to seek [their] assistance in hastening death, if this should be their enduring request" (The World Federation of the Right to Die Societies, 1998).

52. Nowadays, the CSV describes itself as follows: "The CSV is the heir of a tradition of political Catholicism and has traditionally been the most socially conservative of the three major parties. The party still favours a strong role for religion in public life and religious classes in school but the party now supports same-sex marriage and euthanasia" (Terry, 2014).

53. The law on palliative care also established time off work, so individuals can spend time with their terminal parents (Centeno et al., 2013). The law was enacted in 2009; in 2010, Luxembourg's first hospice, "Haus Omega," was founded.

# 8

# Laymen and Altruism: Assisted Death in Switzerland

THE LEGALITY OF AID IN DYING in certain American states and in the Benelux countries, as discussed in the previous pages, has been based on the presumption of a central, practically exclusive role for physicians. In all of those jurisdictions, the ability to legally assist in one's death—by prescribing the lethal drugs or effectively injecting them—is afforded exclusively to the medical profession.[1]

This *medicalized* model of assisted death stands in sharp contrast to Swiss law on the subject, according to which such assistance may be given by laypersons, provided their motivation is altruistic. Therefore, anyone in the country can, in principle, assist someone in killing himself or herself and not be afraid of prosecution, if he or she is not acting self-interestedly. Since the Swiss Criminal Code was implemented in 1942, *assisted suicide* by laypersons has been legal in that country. Here, I recount the development of this unique legal situation and describe the practice as it is implemented today.

## THE LEGAL ORIGINS OF THE *SWISS MODEL*

Switzerland is a small yet affluent country, with most of its 8 million inhabitants living on the plateau that stretches between the Alps and the Jura Mountains. Founded in the thirteenth century, the nation has undergone many political changes throughout its history. Its current organization—a centralized federal government uniting 26 semi-autonomous cantons—was effected in 1848, when a new Constitution was promulgated.[2]

The constitutional reform that took place in 1848 was later accompanied by a revision of the criminal and civil codes, which, a contemporaneous author explained, had until then "remained as they had been of old, defective and encumbered with the rust of middle ages" (Vieusseux, 1840, p. 267). Carl Stooss, professor of law at the University of Bern at the time, was commissioned to draft new criminal and penal codes that would supplant the archaic ones. Published in 1893, his "Basic Principles of Swiss Criminal Law"[3] set forth many of the provisions of what later became the Swiss Criminal Code ("Strafgesezbuch," or StGB), including the regulation of suicide assistance.

By the end of the nineteenth century the cultural and social understanding of suicide had moved from a sinful act to be condemned to a mental health issue to be prevented.[4] This shift was reflected, for instance, in the contemporaneous American law, where suicide itself became decriminalized. However, as we have seen, assisting or abetting suicide for the most part remained a crime in the United States at the time via either common law proscription or state law.

A similar debate took place in Switzerland during the legal reform of the late 1800s. In his 1893 draft, Professor Stooss reasoned that in most cases suicide is due to a mental disorder and as such it is an act that calls for "compassion instead of punishment" (Stooss, 1893, p. 15; my translation). Participation of third parties in assisting or inciting suicide, however, did not fall under that rationale and should therefore remain legally proscribed, as it had always been in several Swiss cantons. The extant cantonal laws construed assistance in suicide as complicity in an offense (in this case, self-murder or suicide). Because suicide itself was not to be criminalized, those who aided or incited suicide could not be deemed complicit in an offense that would no longer exist. Thus, specific provisions against assisted suicide would have to be created, and the punishment suggested by Stooss was imprisonment ranging from three months to one year (Guillod & Schmidt, 2005).

As legal reform proceeded in Switzerland, a committee of experts was appointed to review Stooss's proposed laws. While the committee did not question that suicide assistance should indeed remain a punishable offense, a debate arose among the experts as to whether a blanket prohibition did not, in effect, overextend the intent of the law. An argument was made that in certain situations, those assisting one's suicide were guided by honorable motives.

Specifically, Ernst Hafter, a prominent criminal law professor, proposed that only when the assistor acted in a self-interested manner should his or her behavior be punished. Hafter suggested, among other hypothetical scenarios, that "it is contrary to justice to punish the helper who strengthens the resolve of an incurably ill man who has decided to take his own life, and provides him with the means to do so" (Swiss National Advisory Commission on Biomedical Ethics, 2005, p. 28).

The exception proposed by Hafter was not undisputed, as other committee members pointed to the difficulty in establishing whether the motives of the assistor were, in fact, altruistic. However, as reform moved forward, Hafter's view prevailed and, in 1942, when the Swiss Criminal Code was finally adopted, it contained the following:

Article 115—Inciting and assisting suicide: Any person who *for selfish motives* incites or assists another to commit or attempt to commit suicide is, if that other person thereafter commits or attempts to commit suicide, liable to a custodial sentence not exceeding five years or to a monetary penalty. (StBG, 1937; translation provided by the Federal Authorities of the Swiss Confederation for information purposes only; my emphasis)

While the Swiss Criminal Code has been revised multiple times since it was enacted, the altruistic exception built into Article 115 remains in effect. Remarkably, although the example of assistance given to an "incurably ill man" was used to construe circumstances in which the behavior should be condoned, the debate itself—and ultimately the law—did not refer to assistance by a doctor. Additionally, despite Hafter's characterization in his scenario of the suicidal person as "incurably ill," Article 115 does not mention any medical precondition as a requirement. The result therefore is that assistance in one's suicide can be furnished by laypersons in Switzerland, provided the assistor does not stand to benefit from the death.

Even though suicide assistance is allowed in Switzerland, mercy killing is not. Accordingly, in contrast to Article 115, Article 114 of the StBG establishes that

> Article 114—Homicide at the request of the victim: Any person who *for commendable motives, and in particular out of compassion for the victim*, causes the death of a person at that person's own genuine and insistent request is liable to a custodial sentence not exceeding three years or to a monetary penalty. (StBG, 1937; translation provided by the Federal Authorities of the Swiss Confederation for information purposes only; my emphasis)[5]

The clear distinction in Swiss law, therefore, is between causing a death—which is prohibited—and merely assisting in another's suicide—which is permitted provided the assistor does not act self-interestedly.

## CURRENT PRACTICE: THE ROLE OF NONPROFIT ORGANIZATIONS

It was in this somewhat legally permissive context that, in 1982, 40 years after Article 115 was enacted, two organizations were founded in Switzerland whose primary goals were to provide direct assistance to those who wanted to die. Until the early 1990s, the organizations were exclusively dedicated to distributing living wills and suicide manuals. In 1992, they began openly assisting members in hastening their deaths.

The two original organizations, *Exit Deutsch Schweiz* (henceforth Exit) and *Exit Association pour le Droit de Mourir dans la Dignité Suisse Romande* (henceforth Exit ADMD), have since been joined by four others, *EXInternational*, founded in 1998; *Dignitas*, established in 1998; *Lifecircle/Eternal SPIRIT*, founded in 2011; and *SterbeHilfe Deutschland*, founded in 2012. Together, these six groups have at least 80,000 members and are the primary way in which Swiss and foreigners obtain aid in dying in that country.[6] Routinely, opinion polls suggest that 80 percent of the Swiss approve of the practice (Falconer, 2010).

In 2012, the Swiss Federal Statistical Office published the first ever national report on aid in dying, which covered cases between 1998 and 2009. According to the report, in 1998, almost 50 deaths in Switzerland happened with the assistance of these organizations. In 2009, nearly 300 cases were registered—or roughly 5 out of every 1,000 deaths in the country. Women and those suffering from cancer were the largest groups to seek help in dying (Federal Statistical Office, 2012). A study conducted by Swiss researchers found that the number of assistances by these organizations had reached approximately 600 in 2013 (Gauthier, Saskia, Mausbasch, Reisch, & Bartsch, 2014).

A person who wishes to hasten his or her death may approach one of these organizations and formally request their assistance in writing. "Accompanied suicide," or "assisted voluntary death," as two of the nonprofits put it, will be performed if certain conditions are met. Each of these organizations has their own prerequisites, which are diverse and have changed over time. Minors and those incapable of discernment, however, are universally excluded.

For the most part, those seeking assistance must be a member of the organization. Membership fees are annual or *for life*, and vary from gratis to €2,000.00 (or US$2,600.00). Discounts are offered to retirees, and some associations will reimburse the fee if the assistance takes place (Gauthier et al., 2014). While a few organizations charge to accompany the suicide (as much as U.S. $11,000.00), others offer their assistance at no cost. Because, to be legal, assistance must not be motivated by selfish interests, these organizations are charitable and the assistors are unpaid volunteers. Volunteers are mostly clergymen, nurses, and social workers.

In most cases, notwithstanding the omission of health criteria from Article 115, the self-imposed rules of these organizations dictate that documentation must be presented to show that the individual is terminally ill, or is experiencing unbearable physical or psychological suffering, or is severely disabled, or has an incurable disease that will ultimately lead to poor quality of life (such as multiple sclerosis or dementia). Medical records are typically reviewed by a doctor affiliated with the organization, who will ascertain whether terminal illness, severity of disability, or degree of suffering meets the self-imposed guidelines of the organization. Often, the cooperating physician—and if possible the family physician—will have one or two discussions with the individual. If the records are found to be sufficient evidence of a qualifying illness or disability, a prescription is issued and a date is set for the expedited death, which may take place on the organizations' premises, at the individual's home, in a rented apartment, or in certain nursing homes and hospitals.[7]

Prior to furnishing the lethal medication, the organization's volunteer will ask the individual if he or she remains determined to die. If the answer is positive, the individual takes medication to prevent nausea so that he or she does not vomit the lethal drug. Sodium pentobarbital is usually mixed with water, and the lethal mixture is taken by the individual in the presence of an *end-of-life attendant* and any others invited by the individual. For those who cannot swallow, the drugs are self-delivered via catheter directly to the stomach or through an IV (as long as the individual opens the valve himself or herself, these methods are legal). All deaths assisted by the organizations are reported to the police and a criminal investigation ensues to ensure that the assistance was legally provided.

A step-by-step summary of the procedures followed by Exit, the largest of the six Swiss organizations, is presented in Figure 8.1. These procedures are the result of a bilateral agreement negotiated in 2009 with the prosecutor of the Canton of Zurich, where the organization operates. The basis of the agreement was a consensus on the need to make the practice more transparent and to regulate the dispensation of sodium pentobarbital (the substance used by the organization) (S.W.I., 2009). Dignitas, the other organization that operates in the Canton of Zurich, did not sign the agreement. One year later, the Swiss Federal Court declared the arrangement null and void, reasoning that "the issue of human life was so important that it fell exclusively under federal jurisdiction" (S.W.I., June 16, 2010). Despite the ruling, Exit continues to abide by the procedures.

Because these guidelines are self-imposed, the involvement of physicians by these organizations at any stage of the process is strictly voluntary. Moreover, some have actively resisted such involvement where possible, to the point that

**Figure 8.1 Exit Deutsche Schweiz's Procedures of Suicide Assistance for Members**

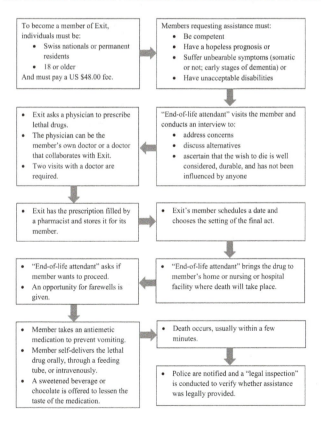

medical involvement in assisted death procedures, in Switzerland, though common, is not ubiquitous. Practically, if drugs are to be used to end a life, then, inasmuch as the drugs used are controlled substances, they must be prescribed by a doctor. Finding a physician who is willing to prescribe the lethal drugs can be difficult, particularly in cases where suffering is nonsomatic (Lewy, 2011). Consequently, assistance provided by the organizations has involved other means, which do not require drugs or a prescription and consequently circumvent the need for a physician altogether.

At least one organization—EXInternational—has consistently sought to bypass the involvement of physicians. Pastor Rolf Sigg, the director of EXInternational, "is opposed to doctors carrying out any form of euthanasia, believing that the task is more suited to specially trained operatives" (Humphry, 2001, p. 11). In 2008, meanwhile Dignitas, a Zurich-based aid in dying organization, began using nonmedical means of assistance in hastened deaths. The organization's action was prompted by statements by the medical director of the Canton of Zurich, who suggested publicly that a physician willing to provide a lethal prescription should meet the individual requesting aid in dying more than once. Although there was nothing legally binding about the cantonal medical director's statement, Dignitas perceived it as potentially restrictive and sought alternatives to pharmaceutical substances to be used by their members. "We needed to send a signal to authorities that we aren't reduced to using only sodium pentabarbitol," Ludwig Minelli, director of Dignitas, instructed in an interview by the *Wall Street Journal* (Ball & Mengewein, 2010).

Dignitas's solution was oxygen deprivation through the inhalation of helium. In these cases, the individual is provided with a mask, which he or she must place over the nose, and through which helium flows.[8] Such a dying process effectively *demedicalizes* aid in dying in that physicians are uninvolved in it, but some worry that it may seem distasteful to those witnessing it. In an interview to The *Atlantic*, Mr. Minelli described the process as "not nice to see. . . . Muscles are agitated. Eyes open wide and close. . . . And if you are not well informed you might mistake this for a terrible struggle against death, which it's not" (Falconer, 2010). "It's just the same when you cut the head off a chicken," he added.

It must be stressed that most of the assistances provided by these organizations follow self-imposed procedures that are not all that different from the way aid in dying is practiced, for instance, in the American states. In other words, in Switzerland it would be perfectly legal to hand a loaded gun to an individual who wants to die and watch him or her pull the trigger, in the same manner that it is perfectly legal to watch someone expire as he or she inhales helium through a mask. More often than not, however, assistors do not resort to a gun and only infrequently do they resort to helium. Handing a cup filled with sodium pentobarbital prescribed by a doctor is the means of choice adopted by most of the charitable organizations. As such, physicians in the Swiss model have a limited yet absolutely crucial role in the way aid in dying is implemented in that country.

## RECENT ATTEMPTS AT LEGAL CHANGE

Since the 1970s, several attempts have been made to change Articles 114 and 115 of the StBG. Most significantly, in 1999, a task force established by the Swiss Federal Council issued a report in which a majority of its members argued for decriminalization of mercy killing under some circumstances. The group of experts proposed an amendment to Article 114, which would have included the following:

> If the perpetrator has brought about the death of a person suffering in his/her health from an incurable illness which is in its terminal phase, and this with the intent of bringing an end to his/her unbearable and irremediable sufferance, the competent authority will renounce taking legal action, sending the person to court, or imposing a punishment. (Exit Association pour le Droit de Mourir dans la Dignité Suisse Romande, n.d.)

Although the report had no legal force, it contributed to advancing the debate in the media and within the political arena. Also furthering these discussions was the prosecution and subsequent conviction of Roger Andermatt, a Swiss nurse who killed 22 nursing home patients (Reuters, 2005). In his confession, Andermatt explained he had acted out of "sympathy, compassion, empathy, and salvation of the people involved" (*The Guardian*, Sep. 12, 2001). He also claimed that "he had been overwhelmed by caring for the people involved [and in] some cases he felt relieved, somehow liberated, after the person had died."

In 2001, amidst the controversy, Franco Cavalli, an oncologist and then member of the Swiss parliament, introduced a parliamentary initiative seeking to grant immunity from prosecution to physicians who had actively hastened a patient's death upon his or her request. Modeled after the Dutch model presented in the previous chapter, the "Cavalli Initiative" sought to increase transparency in a practice that, he argued, already happened and of which the nursing home killings were just "the tip of the iceberg" (*Neue Zürcher Zeitung*, Dec. 12, 2001). Concomitantly, another member of the parliament, Dorle Vallender, introduced an opposing parliamentary initiative, this one seeking to restrict suicide assistance as allowed in Article 115 and to prohibit physicians from prescribing lethal drugs. The Swiss parliament rejected both proposals.

More recently, other attempts to revise the Criminal Code either to clarify the regulation of or to ban the practice of assisted suicide altogether have been made, but without success. Between 2006 and 2011, the Swiss Federal Council once again entertained the pros and cons of revising of the Criminal Code in relation to assisted suicide. Ultimately, it concluded that "such an amendment to [the] criminal law would have various drawbacks," including that "it could officially legitimise assisted suicide organisations, which could provide people with an incentive to take up their services" (Swiss Federal Office of Justice, 2014). Referenda in Zurich to ban assisted suicide altogether or at a minimum to impose a residency requirement also failed to pass. In 2011, for example, 85 percent of

voters in that part of Switzerland opposed a ballot initiative to outlaw suicide assistance, while 78 percent opposed a proposed restriction to make it illegal to foreigners (BBC News, May 15, 2011). In 2013, another bill drafted to regulate and
supervise suicide assistance was rejected by Zurich's local government.

While Articles 114 and 115 of the Swiss Criminal Code remain in force, they
are far from definitive—many of the practical aspects of assisted death are not
addressed in the criminal law. For instance, the distinction between Articles
114 and 115 is, as discussed previously, essential; to be legal, the ultimate
death-precipitating action must be *self-inflicted*. Albeit crucial, the line distinguishing aid and action may be, in practice, difficult to discern, particularly in
cases where the individual seeking death uses an intravenous device or gastric
catheter to absorb the lethal substance.[9] To shield themselves from possible prosecution, many of the organizations routinely videotape the final act to record that
the death was precipitated by the individual and not by a third party.

The law also is silent on whether foreigners should be excluded. As a result,
four of the six organizations[10] have provided assistance to individuals who reside
in countries where the laws on this matter proscribe the practice. A recent pilot
study by Swiss researchers estimates that between 150 and 200 suicide assistances performed by these organizations each year involve foreigners, most of
whom are Germans, followed by British, French, and Italian citizens (Gauthier
et al., 2014, p. 3). Twenty-one Americans have sought help from Swiss organizations between 2008 and 2012. "At least in the UK," the researchers claim, "going
to Switzerland has become a euphemism" for the practice (p. 1).

Equally importantly, Article 115 does not explicate what constitutes "selfish
motives." Traditionally, gains in the form of material benefits had been tacitly
understood as the criterion for establishing "selfish motives." However, in 2003,
charges were brought against a Swiss psychiatrist whose assistance in a suicide
was deemed to be motivated by self-interest, albeit of nonfinancial nature. The
psychiatrist, Peter Baumman, had assisted in the suicide of a severely depressed,
60-year-old wheelchair-bound woman, and the event was broadcast on a German-
Swiss TV channel. Baumman was not compensated, nor did he stand to profit
materially in any direct way from the documentary. However, the court found that
the doctor's participation in the documentary and its subsequent broadcast established that his assistance was not altruistic and was instead motivated by his "desire
for publicity." On appeal, he was later cleared of the crime, but the outcome of the
case did not help shed light on what can be construed as "selfish."

Finally, the law does not specify whether the wishful suicide has to be terminally ill, or what, if any, are the possible sanctions for physicians who prescribe
the lethal substances particularly when death is not imminent. This uncertainty
has at a minimum a chilling effect on physicians who prefer not to be involved.

As a result of this and other legal gray areas, the Swiss courts and the
European Court of Human Rights (henceforth ECtHR) have been called upon
to weigh in and provide more clarity regarding the boundaries of the practice in
Switzerland. Most notably, in 2013, the ECtHR ruled that Swiss law is not clear

## Text Box 8.1 European Convention on Human Rights

## "ARTICLE 8

### Right to respect for private and family life

1. Everyone has the right to respect for his private and family life, his home and his correspondence.
2. There shall be no interference by a public authority with the exercise of this right except such as is in accordance with the law and is necessary in a democratic society in the interests of national security, public safety or the economic wellbeing of the country, for the prevention of disorder or crime, for the protection of health or morals, or for the protection of the rights and freedoms of others."

Council of Europe, *European Convention for the Protection of Human Rights and Fundamental Freedoms, as amended by Protocols Nos. 11 and 14*, 4 November 1950, ETS 5, available at: http://www.refworld.org/docid/3ae6b3b04.html. Accessed September 16, 2014.

enough as to when assisted suicide is permitted. The court held that, as such, it violated Article 8 of the European Convention on Human Rights (see Text Box 8.1). The judgment, which is under appeal, was delivered in a case brought by Alda Gross, an elderly Swiss woman who was not terminally ill, but who was "unwilling to continue suffering the decline of her physical and mental faculties" (European Court of Human Rights, *Gross v. Switzerland*, n 67810/10, §6).

After a failed suicide attempt, Ms. Gross sought to die with the help of physicians, but she was unable to find a doctor willing to prescribe her a lethal dose of medication. One of the physicians from whom she had sought help was a psychiatrist who later testified that Ms. Gross was mentally competent, and her wish to die was reasoned, enduring, and well considered. However, although he did not object to Ms. Gross being prescribed a lethal dose of medications, the psychiatrist refrained from issuing the prescription himself. Ms. Gross turned to several other doctors, all of whom declined to help.

Her doctors explained that because Ms. Gross was not suffering from a clinical illness, they felt that issuing a prescription would violate their code of professional medical conduct as posited by the Swiss Academy of Medical Sciences (henceforth, SAMS). The guidelines issued by SAMS (Text Box 8.2) are not legally binding, but may serve to define the duty of diligence in criminal or civil proceedings. One of the physicians consulted by Ms. Gross said she would be willing to entertain the request if Ms. Gross's attorney could guarantee that she would not be sanctioned by SAMS. When the attorney replied that there was no such guarantee, the physician declined to become involved.

---

### Text Box 8.2 Medical-Ethical Guidelines of the Swiss Association of Medical Sciences

#### "4. The limits of medical intervention

Respect for the patient's wishes reaches its limit if the patient asks for measures to be taken that are ineffective or to no purpose, or that are not compatible with the personal moral conscience of the doctor, the rules of medical practice or the applicable laws.

#### 4.1. Assisted suicide

According to Article 115 of the Penal Code, helping someone to commit suicide is not a punishable offence when it is done for unselfish reasons. This applies to everyone.

With patients at the end of life, the task of the doctor is to alleviate symptoms and to support the patient. It is not his task to directly offer assistance in suicide, he rather is obliged to alleviate any suffering underlying the patient's wish to commit suicide.

However, in the final phase of life, when the situation becomes intolerable for the patient he or she may ask for help in committing suicide and may persist in this wish.

In this borderline situation a very difficult conflict of interests can arise for the doctor. On the one hand assisted suicide is not part of a doctor's task, because this contradicts the aims of medicine. On the other hand, consideration of the patient's wishes is fundamental for the doctor-patient relationship. This dilemma requires a personal decision of conscience on the part of the doctor. The decision to provide assistance in suicide must be respected as such.

In any case, the doctor has the right to refuse help in committing suicide. If he decides to assist a person to commit suicide, it is his responsibility to check the following preconditions:

- The patient's disease justifies the assumption that he is approaching the end of life.
- Alternative possibilities for providing assistance have been discussed and, if desired, have been implemented.
- The patient is capable of making the decision, his wish has been well thought out, without external pressure, and he persists in this wish. This has been checked by a third person, who is not necessarily a doctor.

The final action in the process leading to death must always be taken by the patient himself."

*Source:* Swiss Academy of Medical Sciences. 2005. *Care of Patients in the End of Life, Medical-Ethical Guidelines of the SAMS.* Basel, Switzerland: SAMS. www.samw.ch.

---

Ms. Gross then turned to the Swiss health authorities. She claimed that it would be unreasonable to expect her to continue searching for a physician who would be willing to give her a prescription and she requested that the Health Board of Zurich provide her 15 mg of sodium pentobarbital so she could end her life. The Health Board rejected her request. They reasoned that the state was not obliged "to provide a person who wished to end his or her life with the means of suicide of their choice" (*Gross v. Switzerland*, n 67810/10, §13).

Ms. Gross appealed the decision of the Health Board and subsequently also appealed unfavorable judgments by several Swiss courts, whose rationale to deny her request was similar to the original ruling. Resorting to the ECtHR, she complained that by denying her the right to decide by what means and at what point her life would end, Swiss authorities breached her "right to respect for private and family life" (see Text Box 8.1). The court agreed; "Without in any way negating the principle of the sanctity of life," it posited that "in an era of growing medical sophistication combined with longer life expectancies, many people are concerned that they should not be forced to linger on in old age or in states of advanced physical or mental decrepitude which conflict with strongly held ideas of self and personal identity" (*Gross v. Switzerland*, n 67810/10, §58).

Specifically, and without taking a stance on whether Ms. Gross should be given the sodium pentobarbital, the ECtHR held that Swiss law, while providing the possibility of obtaining a lethal dose of a drug on medical prescription, did not provide sufficient guidelines clarifying the boundaries of this right. The majority wrote, in its opinion, that

> [t]he Court considers that the uncertainty as to the outcome of her request in a situation concerning a particularly important aspect of her life must have caused the applicant a considerable degree of anguish. The Court concludes that the applicant must have found herself in a state of anguish and uncertainty regarding the extent of her right to end her life which would not have occurred if there had been clear, State-approved guidelines defining the circumstances under which medical practitioners are authorised to issue the requested prescription in cases where an individual has come to a serious decision, in the exercise of his or her free will, to end his or her life, but where death is not imminent as a result of a specific medical condition. (*Gross v. Switzerland*, n 67810/10, §66)

Although Alda Gross's case is under appeal and a definitive judgment has yet to be made by the ECtHR's Grand Chamber, a succession of other cases before that court have gradually specified the boundaries of a "right to assisted suicide" (for an in-depth analysis, see Puppinck & de La Hougue, 2014). While the matter in *Gross* was the lack of clarity of the Swiss law, litigation has emerged from other European countries where the practice is banned altogether. Since 2000, individuals from France, United Kingdom, Germany, Spain, and Italy, who were seeking help in expediting death, have brought their pleas to the ECtHR.[11] The debate is likely to continue in and out of the courtrooms.

## NOTES

1. Indeed, when laypersons get involved in enabling a suicide, their assistance might carry grave punitive consequences. One of the earliest relevant cases in the United States

helps illustrate the point. Decided by the Michigan Supreme Court in 1920, this case involved a 36-year-old farmer, Frank Roberts, whose wife, Katie, was suffering from multiple sclerosis. She was bedridden, and "her body was considerably wasted," as her doctor explained at trial (*People v. Roberts*, 211 Mich. 187). Katie had tried to kill herself with carbolic acid one year before and had remained "desirous of dying." At her request, Mr. Roberts mixed *paris green* (a poison containing arsenic) with water and placed the cup on a chair next to the bed where his incurable wife lay. She drank the mixture and died a few hours later.

As far as the records show, there was nothing in Frank Roberts's case that suggested he had been motivated by anything other than his compassion for his suffering wife—he had cared for her devotedly throughout her illness. The court, however, disagreed. "It is beyond my comprehension," said the judge, "how a human being of normal conditions at least, or apparent normal conditions, can commit such a crime as you have in this case" (*People v. Roberts*, 211 Mich. 187). The court added: "It doesn't make any difference whether she had that intention or not of committing suicide. You are a principal, under the law of the state, to committing the crime of murder. It was, indeed, an inhuman and dastardly act" (*People v. Roberts*, 211 Mich. 187). Mr. Roberts was found guilty of "murder by means of poison" and sentenced to prison "for the period of [his] natural life, at hard labor, and in solitary confinement" (*People v. Roberts*, 211 Mich. 187).

The harsh punishment rendered to Roberts is even more striking when one considers how similar the circumstances surrounding his acts are to the way *assisted suicide* takes place in Switzerland. It is very likely Roberts's case would not have been pursued by Swiss authorities.

2. The 1848 Constitution has been revised several times.

3. The original title of Stooss's draft is "Die Grundzüge des schweizerischen Strafrechts, im Auftrage des Bundesrathes vergleichend."

4. For more on this, see Chapter 3.

5. The reference to "compassion for the victim" was added in 1989 in order to make Article 114 more in line with the idea of unselfish motives present in Article 115 (Guillod & Schmidt, 2005).

6. Membership figures are available on each of these associations' Web sites. However, it is unclear how many members Lifecircle/Eternal SPIRIT and StHD + SterbeHilfe Deutschland have or how often they have provided aid in dying.

7. Renting an apartment to be used for aid in dying has proven complicated. For example, in 2007, Dignitas had secured a rental in an affluent condominium complex near Lake Zurich. Neighbors complained that "[n]obody wants to live next door to an apartment where you know somebody is going to die every day" (*Chicago Tribune*, Dec. 2007). Because each assisted death is treated in Switzerland as unusual, a thorough investigation must be conducted every time a member of these organizations dies in the apartment. Hence, the local coroner, a mortician, and police must visit the scene. As a result, aggrieved tenants have successfully evicted Dignitas from several apartment buildings. Dignitas has also used hotel rooms but ceased it after threats of a lawsuit.

8. The use of a plastic bag (*suicide bag* or *exit bag*) to deliver helium and hasten death had been widely divulged much before Dignitas entertained it as an option. Between 1991 and 2002, three editions of a "#1 New York Times bestseller" titled "Final Exit, The Practicalities of Self-Deliverance and Assisted Suicide for the Dying" by Derek Humphry detailed a step-by-step guide on how to build the apparatus. Interestingly,

Dignitas chose a mask—instead of a bag—to deliver the lethal gas. In 2010, a study published in the *Journal of Medical Ethics*, detailed four assisted deaths in which helium was used by members of Dignitas. The study points out that the choice of a mask was for aesthetic reasons and that a *hood* (or bag) decreases opportunities of leaks.

9. Take the example of a 44-year-old Swiss woman who, as a result of a severe stroke, became bound to a wheelchair, could not speak intelligibly, and, because she was unable to swallow, received nourishment exclusively through a catheter inserted directly to her stomach. Her husband, a technician, built a device that allowed the woman to administer liquids through the catheter with minimal effort. Four years after the stroke, having experienced no improvement, she asked for help to die. Confronted with the request, her physician prescribed a lethal dose of pentobarbital. Using the device built by her husband and in the presence of her husband and an aid in dying volunteer, the woman administered the drugs through the catheter. An investigation ensued and the case was deemed compatible with the provisions of Article 115. The fact that the woman had used a medically inserted catheter to self-deliver the drugs was not enough to implicate the prescribing physician as an agent of her death. She was the one who, according to the witnesses present, ultimately activated the device (for details of the case, see Bosshard, Jermini, Eisenhart, & Bar, 2003)

10. Exit and Exit ADMD are the only ones that require members to be Swiss nationals or permanent residents.

11. See, for example, *Lambert and Others v. France* (no. 46043/14), *Pretty v. United Kingdom* (no. 2346/02), *Haas v. Switzerland* (no. 31322/07), and *Koch v. Germany* (no. 497/09).

# PART 3

## Conclusion

# 9

# Epilogue

JACOB ("KOBUS") SIMON was born in Germany in 1845. "A devoted member of the Roman Catholic Church," he came to the United States when he was 31 years old, eventually establishing residence in Morton, Minnesota, where the round-house for the Minneapolis and St. Louis Railway was located. He died in 1906, at age 57, of pneumonia, at his home, surrounded by his wife and five of his six children—one had been "called away" 11 months before (Ancestry.com, 2005).

Simon's obituary reflects many facts of typical American life and death at the turn of the nineteenth to the twentieth century—the onset of European migration on a large scale; the expansion westward facilitated by the train tracks; his young child's death; his own death at a "young" age; its cause, the "Winter Plague"; his deathbed, his own. Today, Americans die differently—older, sicker, primarily in healthcare institutions.

Since Simon's death, Americans have also incrementally refined their end-of-life decision-making. These various choices include changes in burial decisions (the nineteenth-century need for a *safety coffin*, the twenty-first-century ability to ship your ashes to space)[1] as well as legal and medical ones (from a *last will* to a *living will*, accompanied by healthcare proxy appointments). More recently, for those residing in Oregon, Washington, and Vermont, and to some extent Montana and New Mexico,[2] decision-making while dying has also come to include the hastening of death via ingestion of lethal drugs prescribed by a physician.

Also in the timeframe between Simon's birth and now, dying has moved from a supernatural experience to a somatic one, placing physicians firmly at the moribund patient's bedside. Dying has become an "illness," death, a "medical event," and assisted death a "treatment" (Youngner, Arnold, & Schapiro, 2002; Capron, 1995). For as long as we have relied on medicine and physicians to prolong life, alleviate pain, and keep death at bay, death and medicalization have gradually and increasingly gone hand-in-hand. Concomitantly, the profession of medicine has moved from an undesirable career to a powerful lobbying group—at times, arguably "the most powerful lobbying group in the country" (Weissert & Weissert, 2012).

However, as doctors achieved their professional "golden age" in the mid- to late 1950s, so did the techno-medicalization of death, resulting in the indiscriminate sustention of life beyond any reasonable expectation of survival. At that point, the "medicalization of death" pendulum started to swing backward. Thus, especially in the past 50 years or so, aspects of the process of death and dying have gradually become demedicalized—particularly patients' ability to choose withdrawal of life-sustaining treatment, the development of palliative care, the rise of the natural death movement, and an increasingly eloquent claim for patient autonomy and patients' access to information. But this "pendulum," so to speak, has never made a wholesale shift back to a natural, demedicalized death. Such a swing, it has been argued, would be "unrealistic" (Ost, 2010).

Just as medicine has become pervasive in the arena of death and dying, it is persistent in the *American way* of death with assistance. The model of aid in dying available in the states where the practice is legal draws heavily on a medical framework. The enabler is a doctor. The means by which death is invited is a drug. The reason that qualifies a patient to make the option is medically defined: a terminal prognosis and a certain level of unbearable physical pain. Indeed, in this country, almost all of the assisted-death legalization efforts discussed throughout this book have relied on a medical framework, mimicking by and large the main characteristics developed by Anna Hall and her supporters back in 1906, when the *chloroform bills* were drafted.[3]

Yet, paradoxically, physicians are precisely the ones who, as professionals, have posed and continue to pose a significant obstacle to the decriminalization of this model of death with assistance. Although physicians have appeared from time to time either supporting the decriminalization or in fact admitting to having assisted their patients in securing a *painless* death, the *American Medical Association* and most state-level medical organizations adamantly oppose the practice. Often, organized medicine invokes modern translations of the *Hippocratic Oath* as a shield[4] and argues that the role of physician as a *healer* is incompatible with hastened death.[5] Equally often, their official opposition is persuasive.[6]

Additionally, physicians in practice can preempt patients' exercise of the law by refusing participation. There has been an increase in physician participation since the implementation of *Death with Dignity* acts in Oregon and Washington. However, the number of doctors willing to prescribe lethal medication is not only very small but also typically concentrated in urban centers.[7] In Montana, for instance, following the court decision that shielded participating physicians from prosecution in 2009, patients who wanted doctor's assistance in acquiring the medication had difficulty locating physicians who would prescribe the drugs. One of them, Janet Murdock, a 67-year-old woman from Missoula dying of ovarian cancer, issued a statement to the media, charging Montana doctors of disrespecting her "decision to choose aid in dying" and to die "a peaceful, dignified death in keeping with [her] values and beliefs" (Appel, 2009).[8]

With these premises in mind, it is useful to question why physician participation has come to be seen as necessary and/or sufficient in assisted death in the United States and, through international comparisons, whether alternatives, refinements, or redefinitions of the role doctors play are possible. My concluding remarks therefore focus on comparing the different degrees or physician involvement implicit in the alternative assisted-dying models discussed throughout the book and considering whether each has advantages or disadvantages. Especially instructive are examples from European countries, including those discussed in Chapters 7 and 8, which have decriminalized death with assistance or debated its legal limits in recent years. In examining these models, I will focus primarily on the assistor/enabler of death and the means employed by the person seeking assistance.

## AN APPLE A DAY? ASSISTED DEATH AND PHYSICIAN INVOLVEMENT

In terms of physician involvement, instances of assisted death range, conceivably, from lawful mercy killings (where a layperson is permitted to kill without any physician assistance) to active euthanasia (where a physician is licensed to actively accelerate death).[9] The former is an instance of demedicalized assisted death; the latter a fully medicalized instance. In between lie instances where laypersons or physicians may be involved in, but are not empowered directly to precipitate, death. Accordingly, the following gradation can be described:

| (−) | | Medicalization | | (+) |
|---|---|---|---|---|
| Mercy killing by layperson | Layperson-assisted death | Multidisciplinary assisted death model | Physician-assisted death | Mercy killing by physician |

### Assessing the Nonmedicalized Approach

As discussed previously, there have been a number of highly publicized cases where a layperson, typically a relative or close friend, killed a dying loved one in unbearable suffering (for instance, the Shakers' case, per Chapter 4). Although media interest in such cases peaked in the first half of the twentieth century, mercy killings continue to happen in the United States and elsewhere.[10] Also, as discussed previously, the criminal justice system has treated these cases with lenience; however, it tends to do so mostly when a *diminished capacity* defense is invoked.[11] Because the establishment of *insanity* requires medical endorsement, one scholar has argued that this equally medicalizes the mercy killer's behavior "thus providing . . . sympathetic legal response with a cloak of respectability" (Ost, 2010, p. 519).

The legal conundrum posed by the discrepancy between the act of *murder* implicit in mercy killings and its relative tolerance by jurors and judges has been discussed at length elsewhere. In the United Kingdom, for instance, a 1979 Criminal Law Revision Committee considered differentiating the practice from murder. After a "long period" of discussions, however, the committee ruled against creating a *mercy killing* offense, "reluctantly [reaching] the conclusion that it would not be possible to find a satisfactory definition of 'mercy killings' " because any such definition would have to rest on motive (Lawton, 1979, p. 461). Unlike intent, the commission argued that motive cannot "be inferred from a person's overt acts," and although a family member may give the impression that they are acting altruistically, it is possible that other, more sinister motives are at play.[12]

Besides the difficulty in detecting possible self-interested motives, mercy killings by relatives/friends raise a series of issues, such as consent (as in the case of Carol Paight's killing of her father, described in Chapter 4). Additionally, because relatives and other nonprofessional caregivers are not generally accustomed to the death process and are emotionally attached to the dying individual, they may feel a "sense of obligation" to honor a loved one's request and to do so prematurely (Biggs, 2007). In turn, and in line with a *diminished capacity* defense, family and friends' own judgment may be tainted by the exhaustion that often accompanies the round-the-clock care-giving duties of a sick individual.[13]

All of these concerns are also involved in what I have termed layperson-*assisted* death. Because the circumstances surrounding such cases are typically kept secret—precisely to avoid prosecution—instances in which a relative or friend *enables* a terminally ill person in hastening his or her death have received much less attention by the media. There are, however, remarkable public accounts by laypersons that helped a dying relative hasten death. In 1957, for example, *Time Magazine* reporter Lael Tucker Wertenbaker published *Death of a Man*, the first memoir of the kind, describing how she helped her cancer-ridden husband kill himself. More recently, California attorney John West published a similar narrative, recounting how he assisted the deaths of both of his parents when they asked for his help (West, 2009).

Perhaps most salient at present, however, are cases taking place in relation to what has become known as *suicide tourism*, particularly to Switzerland. As discussed in Chapter 8, Switzerland is the only country where there is no residency requirement in legal assisted death. Craig Ewert, an American professor living in England, was one of the many foreigners who took advantage of this opportunity. At 59 years and suffering from Lou Gehrig's disease, Ewert went to Switzerland to die. His death was televised in the United Kingdom and his journey was documented by PBS (Zaritsky, 2010). His wife, Mary, accompanied him on the trip and was at his bedside until the end.

In many cases where an individual elects to travel to Switzerland with the same purpose as Ewert's, his or her health has deteriorated such that family members or friends are asked to help with the logistics—like Mary did. Potentially in those situations these relatives/friends could be prosecuted for aiding in a suicide, depending on the law in their country of origin. In the United Kingdom, one who is found guilty of such an offense (*aiding and abetting suicide*) could face up to 14 years in prison. By 2009, the English and Welsh director of public prosecutions (DPP)[14] had refrained from prosecuting over 100 cases where family members had assisted terminally ill patients in their trip to Switzerland to end their lives (Sturcke, 2009). Much like the mercy killing cases described in Chapter 4, in that country discretion to prosecute had no clear legal guideline.

In 2009, Debbie Purdy, a British woman suffering from multiple sclerosis, asked Britain's high court to rule on whether her husband, Omar Puente, would be arrested and prosecuted upon his return from Switzerland if he chose to accompany her on her final journey to that country. She claimed that a clear procedure informing prosecutorial discretion was needed. The court agreed that the law as such was disparate in its application and required that a detailed list of conditions be outlined by the DPP. A report was published in 2010, and among the many factors discouraging prosecution were the following: a clear, voluntary, informed decision by the dying individual to hasten death; the compassionate nature of the assistor's involvement; and the reluctant encouragement or assistance by the individual in the face of the dying person's determination to hasten death.[15]

## Assessing the Medicalized Approach

Although the pursuit of decriminalization of assisted death could take place by legal reform via redefinition of *mercy killing* as a separate offense from murder, as the British entertained in the late 1970s, or via clarification of prosecutorial discretion, as in Purdy's case, the preference in the United States and elsewhere has instead been to create pathways for assisted death that do not include the active involvement of or assistance by laypersons at all. While these medicalized approaches may provide some assurance of avoiding the pitfalls that accompany nonmedicalized approaches (i.e., the difficulty of determining intent and the potential for abuse), the question of whether assistance by physicians guarantees the achievement of *death with dignity* is more complex.

In the Netherlands, Belgium, and Luxembourg, physicians have the most permissive license to hasten patients' deaths, as they are allowed personally to inject intravenously doses of sodium thiopental, a sedative that induces coma, and then a lethal dose of pancuronium, a muscle relaxant that stops breathing when administered in certain amounts.[16] Doctors' mere assistance in hastened death (by furnishing lethal prescription to be taken by the patient) is also permitted in these three countries—just as it is in the few American states that allow it.

For critics of this most extremely medicalized model of hastened death, the practice raises issues similar to *mercy killing by laypersons*. Because the physician, and not the patient, is performing the final act, the opportunity for coercion and abuse is greater.[17] Additionally, in this model, physicians are indubitably afforded greater power over the patient such that the principle of true autonomy in controlling one's death may be at risk. In the Netherlands, where official statistics distinguish cases of *active euthanasia* from mere *suicide assistance*, the former cases are more frequent. Researchers have attributed this disparity to physicians' desire to control the act of ending life (Rietjens, van Tol, Schermer, & van der Heide, 2009). A more charitable view would attribute it to doctors' desire to avoid unforeseen difficulties more likely to occur when patients take the drugs orally themselves, or to ensure successful death when patients are too physically weak to ingest the medication themselves (Groenewoud et al., 2000). Conversely, critics of the model that allows physicians to prescribe the medication but not administer it, as it is practiced in the United States, argue that patients who are terminally ill and yet not able to swallow the medication are not given equal access to the law (see Chapter 5 for a brief discussion).[18]

Although the less-medicalized models of hastened death (by laypersons) enjoy certain kinds of informal legal tolerance, most cases where assisted death has actually been legally sanctioned require physician involvement. Instances of such sanctioning have propagated in recent years both within the United States (from Oregon to Washington and to Vermont, and also the cases in Montana and New Mexico) and abroad (in the Netherlands, Belgium, and Luxembourg; currently under appeal in Canada). Even where such legal approval is granted, however, ethical ambivalence among doctors vis-à-vis their role—with some equating the practice to the violation of professional integrity and others arguing that refusal of helping patients die is tantamount to "abandonment" (Angell & Lowenstein, 2013)—exists. Moreover, an apparent difficulty in obtaining access to physicians willing to take part in the practice (as in Montana, per earlier discussion) is also evident. These obstacles therefore represent complications in assisted death implementation distinctive to medicalized models.

## FINDING THE BALANCE FOR PHYSICIAN ASSISTANCE IN DEATH

Fully medicalized models of assisted death require physicians' involvement in total oversight and coordination of diverse tasks. These include, at least in the United States, (a) diagnosing the problem, (b) ascertaining the prognosis, (c) assessing competence, (d) ruling out depression as a motive, (e) providing the means (i.e., the prescription), (f) coaching individuals through the dying process, and (g) reporting postmortem data.

Although (a) through (d)[19] undoubtedly reflect the perceived necessity of physician involvement in that country (where assisted death is after all limited to the terminally ill patients who choose to expedite the dying process and who have no other means to precipitate their own deaths that they find palatable), we must ask whether physicians are the most appropriate professionals to execute (e) and (f). These aspects of the process are vital to ensure what has become known as a *dignified* death and its regulation. In what follows, I take a closer look at alternatives to doctors' involvement in these tasks, with a focus on their license to prescribe lethal medication and their ability to be of service in a more holistic view of the dying process.

### Of Guns, Bridges, and Self-Starvation: Doctors as Prescription Gatekeepers

As mentioned in Chapter 4, it was not until the passage of the *Harrison Tax Act* (HTA) in 1914 that potent pharmaceuticals came to be more strictly regulated by the government, and their prescription became exclusively a physicians' chore. The HTA was one of the first laws drafted to regulate the dispensation of addictive drugs for legitimate medical purposes. It was followed by many others, including the *Controlled Substances Act* (CSA) enacted by Congress in 1970.

In the early 2000s, after the implementation of Oregon's *Death with Dignity Act*, then attorney general John Ashcroft issued an interpretive rule,[20] charging that *physician-assisted suicide* was not a legitimate medical purpose and that any physician administering federally controlled drugs with that objective would be in violation of the CSA. Joined by a physician, a pharmacist, and several terminally ill patients, the State of Oregon filed a challenge to Ashcroft's rule. Eventually, that suit was entertained by the Supreme Court (*Gonzales v. Oregon*, 546 U.S. 243, 2006), which ruled that the attorney general could not use the CSA to prohibit doctors from prescribing regulated drugs for use in compliance with the *Death with Dignity Act*.

In addition to physicians' potential refusal to take part in the *Death with Dignity Act* creating obstacles for patients choosing that option, their position as legal kingpins only compounds the problem. In theory, a few have argued, prescriptions need not come from physicians in assisted deaths. Prokopetz and Lehmann (2012, p. 98), in a recent article published by the *New England Journal of Medicine*, proposed "the development of a central state or federal mechanism to confirm the eligibility of patients' requests, dispense medication, and monitor demand and use." This outsourcing of duties would obviate the need for physician involvement beyond usual care.[21] Defenders of the current model, however, have criticized this proposal, arguing that it would establish an "intrusive bureaucracy" (Angell & Lowenstein, 2013).

The discussion about physicians as gatekeepers to lethal medication, of course, rests on the assumption that drugs are the preferred method of hastening death. This is interesting because pain, which initially justified physicians' expanded dominion over death, is no longer the top reason cited by those who elect hastened death. As discussed in Chapter 6, philosophical concepts of autonomy and life enjoyment lead the ranking. It is possible that this persistent pharmacopoeiac fascination is still justified, however. Indeed, a pill that kills—rather, several of them crushed and mixed with water—works fairly quickly; is mostly effective;[22] confers upon the process an aura of peacefulness, as if the patient drifted into a deep sleep; and allows loved ones to be gathered at the bedside for a final goodbye.

The pill solution, unlike a dive from a bridge, the use of a gun, helium gas, $CO_2$, or the "Exit Bag" plan, is not considered distasteful, violent,[23] or isolating by most people. These other widely available forms of "hastening death" may also result in botched events, with the result that a terminally ill person spends his/her last days with yet other problems besides their disease. Botching may be less likely with physician assistance. There has been, however, increased support for a partially demedicalized solution for expediting death in the last stages of the dying process within the United States: patient's voluntary stopping eating and drinking (VSED). With VSED, patients who are otherwise physically capable of feeding/drinking make the conscious decision to discontinue all oral intake in order to be "allowed to die" as a result of either dehydration or some other intervening complication (Bernat & Gert, 1993).

Besides being legal, which of course it is, VSED by patients fulfills the principle of autonomy, imposes no burdens or dangers to others, and when done with adequate palliative care can provide a peaceful death (Bernat & Gert, 1993; Quill, Lo, & Brock, 2008). Refusing nutrition and hydration is a natural process and one that often happens in the final stages of many illnesses (McCue, 1995). Most importantly, it does not require the direct participation of physicians and it is an option in effect, currently, in all 50 American states. Critics of this model, however, point out the considerable resolve required of patients who chose this death, as it may go on for several days or even weeks (Faber-Langendoen & Karlawish, 2000).

## Midwives[24] of the Dying Process?

Scholars have argued that physicians might not be the best professionals to accompany and oversee the patient throughout the death process and that the post-prescription task should be left primarily to clergy and social workers, with minimal physician participation (Faber-Langendowen & Karlawish, 2000).

Those who advocate this view highlight, for example, the spiritual dimensions of the death process. Although there has been a well-documented decrease in support for organized religion in the United States, one in five Americans consider themselves "spiritual but not religious" (Pew Forum on Religion and Public Life, 2012). This suggests that dying, for a number of people, may invoke questions on issues beyond what to expect physically. In contrast, yet not surprisingly, a survey of American doctors has found that while most patients seem to their physicians to "look to God for strength, support, and guidance," physicians themselves instead try to "make sense of the situation and decide what to do without relying on God" (Curlin, Lantos, Roach, Sellergren, & Chin, 2005). How such differences shape the clinical encounter is unknown (as the study's authors admit), but they do invite consideration of including clergy and other spiritual leaders in a collaborative model of assisted dying. Moreover, a recent study of British doctors revealed that doctors who describe themselves as nonreligious (agnostic/atheist) are twice as likely to report having engaged in terminal sedation (Seale, 2010).

Although "house call medicine" is making a comeback (American Medical News, 2011), especially to address the needs of an aging population, doctors traditionally have seen their patients outside their homes. Their inability to observe family dynamics due to physicians' relative distance from the dying patient for most of the death process has also encouraged scholars to suggest expanding the participation of social workers in aid in dying practices (Faber-Langendoen & Karlawish, 2000). A close observation of family dynamics, they argue, would help ascertain whether coercion is in place or whether the true motive by patients seeking to hasten death finds its genesis in fear of burdening loved ones or financial hardship.

This multidisciplinary model of assisted death, which involves physicians at points where they are really needed, but also includes other professionals, such as social workers and clergy, falls in between the two extremes of death hastened by (or with the help) of loved ones and death precipitated by physicians. Currently, it is employed in Switzerland. Although the legal history of the Swiss way of "team-assisted" death differs from that of the other European nations and the United States, Switzerland's practice has been hailed as a model to be emulated (Ziegler, 2009).[25] It promotes better oversight (all assisted deaths are investigated in Switzerland) and some degree of demedicalization (nearly all deaths happen at home and although physician participation remains crucial in practice, it is not required and is limited to self-imposed requirements by the nonprofit organizations), and reduces ethical conflict among doctors (as it reduces physician participation and increases patient assessment by the multidisciplinary team). At the time of writing, Canada's high court is considering the legality of hastened death for terminally ill patients and the Swiss model is favored by one of the petitioners (the Farewell Foundation for the Right to Die) on the basis that it "successfully regulates assisted dying without imposing a general supervisory role on the medical profession" (*Carter v. Canada*, 2012). The Canadian high court will hear arguments in the fall of 2014.

While this trend to partial demedicalization may seem viable to some, others have argued that a wholesale shift toward total demedicalization is "unrealistic" (Ost, 2010). There may be some truth to that. In Ireland, 59-year-old former law professor Marie Fleming challenged the country's prohibition on assisted suicide on the basis that it breached her personal autonomy rights under the Irish constitution and the European convention on human rights. Fleming, suffering from multiple sclerosis, needs help in dying as she has little to no mobility. She wanted the court to allow her to pursue a nonmedical death (by breathing nitrogen), with her husband's assistance, and with assurance that he would not be prosecuted. In April 2013, she lost the case without further chance to appeal.

## CONCLUDING REMARKS

The previous pages recounted over 100 years of the medicalization of assisted dying, a subsequent shift toward demedicalization, and its decriminalization in some jurisdictions. While a few ethicists and "euthanasiasts" see death with physician's assistance as a sign of progress in patients' autonomy, others beg to differ. Thomas Szasz, one of the pioneer architects of "medicalization of society," has fiercely opposed state- and medicine-sanctioned suicide (Szasz, 2011). For Szasz, the decision to die is not a medical problem, but instead the exercise of one's conscious and deliberate choice that should leave no room for the state or for the doctor.

Regardless of its shape, momentum is building for proponents of assisted death. Domestically, between the "1906 chloroform bills" and early 1990s Supreme Court cases advocates did not have much reason for optimism, but the passage of the *Death with Dignity Act* in Oregon and its successful implementation has served prolegalization organizations well. Engaged in what they called an "Oregon plus one equals fifty" strategy, aid in dying nonprofits have secured decriminalization a decade later in Washington, followed by the Montana court decision in *Baxter*, the governor's blessing in Vermont, and a lower court decision in New Mexico that, if upheld, will guarantee a *right to aid in dying* under that state's constitution.[26] The discussion, it is only logical to expect, will continue in the chambers, at the bedside, in the courts, and in the ballots—here and elsewhere.

## NOTES

1. Fear of being buried alive was not unfounded in the nineteenth century and American ingenuity solved the problem by creating *safety coffins*. New Jersey inventor Franz Vester patented the first such vault in 1868. His patent application describes it as an "Improved Burial Case" and depicts a coffin with a bell attached to its exterior and a rope tied to the bell accessible from inside (Clark, 2004). If the individual regained conscience, he/she could easily get the outsiders' attention by sounding the alarm. If men of the past feared being trapped alive, today's dying individuals may wish to send their ashes to space to "experienc[e] the zero gravity environment" and then return safely home (Celestis, Inc., n.d.). For an additional fee, a "portion of cremated remains [can be launched] into Earth orbit, onto the lunar surface or into deep space."

2. As discussed previously, it is important to distinguish the legal boundaries of this practice in the American context. While there are three U.S. states that have made physician-assisted death explicitly legal, two others have court rulings that may have opened the door to the practice but are not as definitive. Legislatures in Oregon, Washington, and Vermont have enacted laws to allow their residents to obtain a prescription for lethal medication if they are terminally ill. In Montana, the state Supreme Court ruled that physicians who help a person end his or her own life will not be subject to trial for homicide (*Baxter v. Montana*, 2009). In 2014, a New Mexico lower court ruled that under the state's constitution, terminally ill individuals who are mentally competent have the "right to aid in dying" (*Morris v. Brandenberg*, 2014). This decision, currently under appeal, may apply statewide, if upheld.

3. Exceptions, of course, are the mercy killing cases related in Chapter 4. However, even then, when the accused was a physician (Dr. Hermann Sander), advocates seemed particularly interested, claiming this was a "true test" of the issue (see Chapter 4).

4. Steven Miles (2005) demonstrates, cogently, how history offers no evidence that the Oath spoke to an ancient debate on "euthanasia" or "assisted suicide." Interestingly, the Oath was not always offered to graduate medics; in 1928, for instance, only 24 percent of medical schools administered the Hippocratic Oath (Tyson, 2001). After the passage of the *Death with Dignity Act* in Oregon, the Physicians for Compassionate Care Foundation (n.d.), a group of doctors opposing the practice, crafted a revised Oath and made the new version available for download from their website. Their "Pledge to my patients" states: "I will never give a deadly drug to anyone, even if asked, nor will I suggest suicide."

5. That role is preserved in cases of terminal sedation since the physician's intent is not to kill. This principle of double effect is discussed in Chapter 3.

6. The American Medical Association's *amicus brief* submitted to the Supreme Court in the companion cases of *Glucksberg* and *Quill* was seemingly persuasive in that the opinions by various judges mentioned this issue referring to the brief. Because the profession is ambivalent on this matter, physicians have called for a revision of their position and an adoption of "studied neutrality" by their associations (see Quill & Cassell, 2003; Tallis, 2012).

7. As discussed in Chapter 6, during the years in which the Death with Dignity Act has been in effect in Oregon, the state has seen an increase of doctor participation: from 14 prescribing the drugs in 1998 to 62 in 2011. An equivalent trend is observed in Washington, where 53 physicians enabled their patients to "die with dignity" in 2009, while 80 of them did so in 2011. Although the percent increase in participation is noteworthy, the number of physicians assisting in these deaths is relatively small, considering, for instance, that in 2011 over 6,500 primary care doctors and over 17,500 physicians overall were in practice in Washington.

8. Following the Montana court ruling, the state's medical association issued a policy statement opposing the legal decision: "The Montana Medical Association does not condone the deliberate act of precipitating the death of a patient ... and does not accept the proposition that death with dignity may be achieved only through physician-assisted suicide" (Baklinski, 2009). Unable to find assistance, Janet Murdock died of voluntary starvation (Appel, 2009).

9. It is important to note that I would also include here the practice of *terminal sedation* (the hastening of death in accordance with a double-effect doctrine). Because it is legal, however, I choose not to draw attention to it.

10. One example was the killing of 81-year-old Virginia Sander by her husband, George, 84 years old, in 2013. Virginia Sander had been suffering from multiple sclerosis for decades and had also developed gangrene on a foot. Before she was shot, she asked her husband: "Is it going to hurt?" He replied she would not feel a thing and pressed the trigger. At trial, the prosecutor recommended not sending Sander to prison. The judge ordered two years of unsupervised probation. He then remarked that his decision "tempers justice with mercy" (Skoloff, 2013).

11. Alternative defenses articulated by the mercy killer, such as *necessity*, have been rejected by foreign courts, such as Canada's. When invoked by physicians, it has been accepted as legitimate, for instance, in the Netherlands. In the mid-1980s, the Dutch Supreme Court, in *Schoonheim*, reasoned that notwithstanding the prohibition of the practice in the *Penal Code*, a physician was able to invoke the defence of necessity when confronted with a conflict between his or her duties to preserve life, on the one hand, and to relieve suffering, on the other. If, faced with such conflict, the physician chose a course

of action that was objectively justifiable, he or she was not guilty of an offense. The court held that the criteria for accepting the defence of necessity were to be derived from medical-ethical opinions formulated by the medical profession. For details, see Grubb, Laing, McHale, & Sir (2010).

12. See Chapter 8 for a discussion on the implications of altruistic motives in the Swiss context.

13. This burden on caregivers impacts those caring for cancer patients even more acutely (Bevans & Sternberg, 2012). Given the prevalence of that disease among those who legally resort to assisted death in Oregon and Washington (per Tables 6.1 and 6.2, Chapter 6), this disproportionate effect seems relevant.

14. The Director of Public Prosecutions (DPP) is the office or official charged with the prosecution of criminal offenses in several jurisdictions around the world. In England and Wales, the director is appointed by the attorney general for those two jurisdictions.

15. The report and full list of guidelines can be read here: http://www.cps.gov.uk/publications/prosecution/assisted_suicide.html

16. This is distinct from all American jurisdictions that permit aid in dying; here, patients have to ingest the medication themselves, as discussed at length in Chapter 6.

17. However, no evidence of such abuse has been found. See, for example, Battin et al. (2007) comparing data on "euthanasia" in the Netherlands to "physician-assisted suicide" as practiced in Oregon and Washington.

18. I do not wish to propose that the European practice is better or worse than the American one. Difference in access to health care in these two regions as well as different dynamics in doctor–patient relationships here and there are but two crucial issues that may justify *euthanasia* in one place and *assisted suicide* in another. I defer a discussion on these and cultural aspects for the future.

19. In the Netherlands, Belgium, and Switzerland, where a terminal diagnosis is not required, (a) and (b) are not necessary. However, the notion of *unbearable suffering* that cannot be alleviated otherwise is part of physicians' task.

20. "Interpretative rules" are issued by an administrative agency—in this case the U.S. government—to clarify or explain existing laws or regulations—in this case, Oregon's *Death with Dignity Act*. An interpretative rule does not attempt to create a new law or modify existing ones. The rule only provides clarifications or explanations to a statute or regulation.

21. A similar proposal was made by Jacob Appel, in 2011, whereby he suggests that the state "scrap its general requirement for physician-issued prescriptions in cases of terminal illness, instead providing both drugs and instructions directly to dying individuals or their families." Appel also suggested the state hire a handful of publicly salaried physicians whose primary responsibility would be to offer palliative services, including lethal prescriptions, to the terminally ill. This would minimize patients' shopping around for a sympathetic physician as they cope with their dying process.

22. But see notes to Table 6.1.

23. A similar sentiment may be present in the medicalization of execution methods in carrying out death penalties, particularly in terms of protocols for physician participation.

24. The term *midwife* used in this context is Quill's (2001).

25. For more on the Swiss model of assisted death, see Chapter 8.

26. The "Oregon plus one . . ." slogan was developed on the assumption that Oregon is not a trend-setting state and therefore at least one more state would be required to serve as the tipping point for victory (Marker, 2008).

# References

## REFERENCE WORKS

Ballantyne, John William. 1907. "Euthanasia." In *Green's Encyclopedia and Dictionary of Medicine and Surgery*. Chicago: W.T. Keener & Co.

Chambers, William. 1904. "Euthanasia." In *Chambers's Etymological Dictionary of the English Language: Pronouncing, Explanatory, Etymological*, 161. London and Edinburgh: W. & R. Chambers, Limited.

*Law Notes*. 1912. Northport, Long Island, New York: Edward Thompson Co.

O'Brien, Jodi. 2009. *Encyclopedia of Gender and Society*. Thousand Oaks, CA: Sage.

Rapalje, Stewart, and Robert Linn Lawrence. 1883. *A Dictionary of American and English Law: With Definitions of the Technical Terms of the Canon and Civil Laws. Also, Containing a Full Collection of Latin Maxims, and Citations of Upwards of Forty Thousand Reported Cases, in Which Words and Phrases Have Been Judicially Defined or Construed...* Jersey City, NJ: F. D. Linn & Co.

Unspecified. 2009. "Euthanasia." In *Merriam-Webster Online*. Online Edition. http://www.merriam-webster.com/.


## SCHOLARLY PUBLICATIONS AND REPORTS

Adams, Maurice. 2011. "Euthanasia: The Process of Legal Change in Belgium: Reflections on the Parliamentary Debate." In *Regulating Physician-Negotiated Death*, edited by Albert Klijn, Margaret Otlowski, and M. J. Trappenburg, 29–47. s'Gravenhage: Elsevier.

Alexander, L. 1949. "Medical Science under Dictatorship." *The New England Journal of Medicine* 241 (2): 39–47. doi:10.1056/NEJM194907142410201.

The American Law Institute. 1980. Model Penal Code and Commentaries (Official Draft and Revised Comments), Part II, Definition of Specific Crimes, §210.0 to 213.6. Philadelphia, PA: The American Law Institute.

American Medical Association. 1885. "The Moral Side of Euthanasia." *Journal of the American Medical Association* 5 (14): 382–83.

American Medical Association. 2000. *Code of Medical Ethics: 2000–2001.* 14th ed. Chicago: AMA. http://www.ama-assn.org/ama/pub/physician-resources/medical -ethics/code-medical-ethics/opinion206.shtml.

Anderson, Oscar E., Jr., and Harvey W. Wiley. 1958. *The Health of a Nation.* Chicago: University of Chicago Press.

Anderson, Russell H. 1959. "The Shaker Community in Florida." *Florida Historical Quarterly* 38 (1): 29–44.

Angell, Marcia, and Edward Lowenstein. 2013. "Redefining Physicians' Role in Assisted Dying." *New England Journal of Medicine* 368 (5): 485–86.

Anonymous. 1987. "Final Report of the Netherlands State Commission on Euthanasia: An English Summary." *Bioethics* 1 (2): 163–70.

Anonymous. 1988. "A Piece of My Mind. It's Over, Debbie." *JAMA* 259 (2): 272.

Appel, Jacob M. 2004. "A Duty to Kill? A Duty to Die? Rethinking the Euthanasia Controversy of 1906." *Bulletin of the History of Medicine* 78 (3): 610–34.

Appel, Jacob M. 2007. "A Suicide Right for the Mentally Ill?" *A Swiss Case Opens a New Debate* 37 (3): 21–23. The Hastings Center Report. http://www.thehastingscenter. org/Publications/HCR/Detail.aspx?id=814.

Appel, Jacob M. 2009. "Big Sky Dilemma: Must Doctors Help Their Patients Die?" *The Huffington Post,* September 2. http://www.huffingtonpost.com/jacob-m-appel/big-sky-dilemma-must-doct_b_275034.html.

Ashhurst, John. 1896. "Surgery before the Days of Anesthesia." *The Boston Medical and Surgical Journal* CXXXV (16): 378–80.

Bachman, Jerald G., Kirsten H. Alcser, David J. Doukas, Richard L. Lichtenstein, Amy D. Corning, and Howard Brody. 1996. "Attitudes of Michigan Physicians and the Public toward Legalizing Physician-Assisted Suicide and Voluntary Euthanasia." *New England Journal of Medicine* 334 (5): 303–9. doi:10.1056/NEJM199602013340506.

Back, Anthony L., Jeffrey I. Wallace, Helene E. Starks, and Robert A. Pearlman. 1996. "Physician-Assisted Suicide and Euthanasia in Washington State. Patient Requests and Physician Responses." *JAMA: The Journal of the American Medical Association* 275 (12): 919–25.

Baker, Robert B., Arthur L. Caplan, Linda L. Emanuel, and Stephen R. Latham, eds. 1999. *The American Medical Ethics Revolution.* Baltimore, MD: The Johns Hopkins University Press.

Barak, Gregg. 2000. *Crime and Crime Control: A Global View.* Westport, CT: Greenwood Press.

Battin, Margaret P. 2008a. "Safe, Legal, Rare? Physician-Assisted Suicide and Cultural Change in the Future." In *Giving Death a Helping Hand: Physician-Assisted Suicide and Public Policy. An International Perspective,* edited by Dieter Birnbacher and Edgar Dahl, 2008 edition, 37–48. Dordrecht: Springer.

Battin, Margaret P. 2008b. "Terminal Sedation: Pulling the Sheet over Our Eyes." *The Hastings Center Report* 38 (5): 27–30.

Battin, Margaret P., Heide, Agnes van der, Ganzini, Linda, Wal, Gerrit van der, and Onwuteaka-Philipsen, Bregie D. 2007. "Legal Physician-Assisted Dying in Oregon and the Netherlands: Evidence Concerning the Impact on Patients in 'Vulnerable' Groups." *Journal of Medical Ethics* 33 (10): 591–97. doi:10.2307/27719957.

Behuniak, Susan M., and Arthur G. Svenson. 2002. *Physician-Assisted Suicide: The Anatomy of a Constitutional Law Issue.* Lanham: Rowman & Littlefield Publishers.

Berg, Jan Hendrik van den. 1978. *Medical Power and Medical Ethics.* New York: W. W. Norton & Company.

Bernat J. L., and Gert. B. 1993. "Patient Refusal of Hydration and Nutrition: An Alternative to Physician-Assisted Suicide or Voluntary Active Euthanasia." *Archives of Internal Medicine* 153 (24): 2723–31. doi:10.1001/archinte.1993.00410240021003.

Bernstein, C. A., J. G. Rabkin, and H. Wolland. 1990. "Medical and Dental Students' Attitudes about the AIDS Epidemic." *Academic Medicine: Journal of the Association of American Medical Colleges* 65 (7): 458–60.

Betz, Michael, and Lenahan O'Connell. 2003. "Changing Doctor-Patient Relationships and the Rise in Concern for Accountability." In *Health and Health Care As Social Problems*, edited by Peter Conrad and Valerie Leiter, 317–30. Lanham, Md.: Rowman & Littlefield.

Bevans, Margaret, and Esther M. Sternberg. 2012. "Caregiving Burden, Stress, and Health Effects Among Family Caregivers of Adult Cancer Patients." *JAMA* 307 (4): 398–403. doi:10.1001/jama.2012.29.

Bierce, Ambrose. 1911. *The Collected Works.* New York and Washington: Neale Pub. Co.

Bierce, Ambrose. 2012. *The Devil's Dictionary.* Mineola, NY: Dover Publications.

Biggs, Hazel. 2007. "Criminalising Carers: Death Desires and Assisted Dying Outlaws." In *Death Rites and Rights*, edited by B. Brooks-Gordon, F. Ebtehaj, J. Herring, M. H. Johnson, and M. Richards, 58–74. Oxford, UK: Hart.

Billings, J. Andrew, and Susan D. Block. 1996. "Slow Euthanasia." *Journal of Palliative Care* 12 (4): 21–30.

Blackstone, Sir William, and David Mitchell Aird. 1873. *Blackstone Economized: Being a Compendium of the Laws of England to the Present Time. In Four Books, Each Book Embracing the Legal Principles and Practical Information Contained in the Respective Volumes of Blackstone, Supplemented by Subsequent Statutory Enactments, Important Legal Decisions, Etc.* London, UK: Longmans, Green, and Co.

Blendon, R. J, U. S. Szalay, and R. A. Knox. 1992. "Should Physicians Aid Their Patients in Dying?: The Public Perspective." *JAMA* 267 (19): 2658–62. doi:10.1001/jama.1992.03480190102042

Boehm, Gustav. 1898. "The Right to Commit Suicide." *The Medico-Legal Journal* 16 (1): 79–82.

Bold, Richard J., Philip D. Schneider, Vijay P. Khatri, and James E. Goodnight Jr. 2001. "Resident Experience and Opinions about Physician Assisted Death for Cancer Patients." *Archives of Surgery* 136 (1): 60–64. doi:10.1001/archsurg.136.1.60.

Bond, John, and Lynne Corner. 2004. *Quality of Life and Older People: Rethinking Ageing.* Berkshire, UK: Open University Press.

Bosshard, G., D. Jermini, D. Eisenhart, and W. Bär. 2003. "Assisted Suicide Bordering on Active Euthanasia." *International Journal of Legal Medicine* 117 (2): 106–8. doi: http://dx.doi.org/10.1007/s00414-002-0346-3.

Bostrom, Barry, and Walter Lagerwey. 1987. "The High Court of the Hague Case No. 79065, October 21, 1986." *Issues in Law and Medicine* 3: 445–46.

Bourouill, Adrienne Van Till-D'Aulnis de. 1975. "How Dead Can You Be?" *Medicine, Science and the Law* 15 (2): 133–46. doi:10.1177/002580247501500208.

Boyle, Joseph. 2004. "Medical Ethics and Double Effect: The Case of Terminal Sedation." *Theoretical Medicine and Bioethics* 25 (1): 51–60.

Brandt, Richard B. 1975. "The Morality and Rationality of Suicide." In *A Handbook for the Study of Suicide*, edited by S. Perlin, 61–76. New York: Oxford University Press.

Brinton, D. G., ed. 1879. "The Doctrine of Euthanasia." *The Medical and Surgical Reporter*, The Medical and Surgical Reporter, xli (November): 478–81.

Brown, Ron M. 2001. *The Art of Suicide*. London, UK: Reaktion Books.

Buchanan, Joseph R., and T. V. Morrow, eds. 1849. *The Eclectic Medical Journal*. Cincinnati: W.M. Phillips and Company.

Burgess-Jackson, Keith. 1982. "The Legal Status of Suicide in Early America: A Comparison with the English Experience." *Wayne Law Review* 29: 57.

Burnham, John C. 1997. "American Medicine's Golden Age: What Happened to It?" In *Sickness and Health in America: Readings in the History of Medicine and Public Health*, edited by Judith W. Leavitt and Ronald L. Numbers. University of Wisconsin Press.

Burt, Robert. 2004. *Death is That Man Taking Names: Intersections of American Medidine, Law and Culture*. Berkeley: University of California Press.

Caddell, David P., and Newton, Rae R. 1995. "Euthanasia: American Attitudes toward the Physician's Role." *Social Science & Medicine* 40 (12): 1671–81. doi:10.1016/0277-9536(94)00287-4.

Canetto, Silvia S., and Janet D. Hollenshead. 2000. "Older Women and Mercy Killing." *Omega* 42 (1): 83–99.

Capron, Alexander Morgan. 1995. "Constitutionalizing Death." *Hastings Center Report* 25 (6): 23–24. doi:10.2307/3527837.

Cassedy, James H. 1964. "Muckraking and Medicine: Samuel Hopkins Adams." *American Quarterly* 16 (1): 85–99. doi:10.2307/2710829.

Caton, Donald. 1985. "The Secularization of Pain." *Anesthesiology* 62 (4): 493–501.

Caton, Donald. 1999. *What a Blessing She Had Chloroform: The Medical and Social Response to the Pain of Childbirth from 1800 to the Present*. New Haven, CT: Yale University Press.

Center for Workforce Studies. 2011. *2011 State Physician Workforce Data Book*, 61. Association of American Colleges. https://www.aamc.org/download/263512/data/statedata2011.pdf.

Centers for Disease Control and Prevention. n.d. *Leading Causes of Death, 1900–1998*. Atlanta, GA: National Center for Health Statistics. http://www.cdc.gov/nchs/data/dvs/lead1900_98.pdf.

Chang, Hui Ming. 1999. "Cancer Pain Management." *Medical Clinics of North America* 83 (3): 711–36. doi:10.1016/S0025-7125(05)70131-0.

Christianson, Eric. 1976. *Individuals in the Healing Arts and the Emergence of a Medical Community in Massachusetts, 1700-1794: A Collective Biography*. Unpublished Ph.D. diss., University of Southern California.

Christianson, Eric. 1997. "Early American Medicine." In *Sickness and Health in America: Readings in the History of Medicine and Public Health*, edited by Judith Walzer Leavitt and Ronald L. Numbers, 45–71. University of Wisconsin Press.

The Chronicle: A Weekly Journal, Devoted to the Interests of Insurance, Manufacturers and Real Estate. 1875. "Suicide and Life Insurance." *The Chronicle* 16 (24): 372–74.

Clark, Rusty. 2004. *West Springfield, Massachusetts: Stories Carved in Stone*. West Springfield, MA: Dog Pond Press.

Clarke, Edwin, and L. S. Jacyna. 1992. *Nineteenth-Century Origins of Neuroscientific Concepts*. University of California Press.

Cohen, Alan B., and Ruth S. Hanft. 2004. *Technology in American Health Care: Policy Directions for Effective Evaluation and Management*. Ann Arbor: University of Michigan Press.

Cohen, Jonathan S., Stephan D. Fihn, and Edward J. Boyko. 2000. "Attitudes Toward Assisted Suicide and Euthanasia among Physicians in Washington State." *New England Journal of Medicine* 331 (July 1994): 89–94.

Cohen-Almagor, Raphael. 2002. "Why the Netherlands?" *The Journal of Law, Medicine & Ethics* 30 (1): 95–104. doi:10.1111/j.1748-720X.2002.tb00725.x.

Cohen-Almagor, Raphael. 2004. *Euthanasia in the Netherlands: The Policy and Practice of Mercy Killing*. Dordrecht; Boston: Kluwer Academic Publishers.

Colby, William H. 2002. *Long Goodbye: The Deaths of Nancy Cruzan*. Carlsbad, CA: Hay House, Inc.

Cole, Carolyne P. 1993. *A History of the Shaker Community at Narcoossee, Florida, 1894–1916* (M.A., American Studies). Tampa, FL: University of South Florida.

Collester, Donald, Jr. 1977. "Death, Dying and the Law: A Prosecutorial View of the Quinlan Case." *Rutgers Law Review* 30 (2): 304–28.

Commissie Aanvaardbaarheid Levensbeëindigend handelen. 1993. *Discussienota Hulp Bij Zelfdoding Bij Psychiatrische Patiënten*. Utrecht: KNMG.

Commission Nationale de Contrôle et d'Evaluation de la loi du 16 mars 2009 sur l'euthanasie et l'assistance au suicide. 2011. *Premier rapport à l'attention de la Chambre des Députés (Années 2009 et 2010)*. Luxembourg: Ministère de la Santé.

Commission Nationale de Contrôle et d'Evaluation de la loi du 16 mars 2009 sur l'euthanasie et l'assistance au suicide. 2013. *Deuxième rapport à l'attention de la Chambre des Députés (Années 2011 et 2012)*. Luxembourg: Ministère de la Santé.

Conrad, Peter. 1975. "The Discovery of Hyperkinesis: Notes on the Medicalization of Deviant Behavior." *Social Problems* 23: 12–21.

Conrad, Peter. 2007. *The Medicalization of Society: On the Transformation of Human Conditions into Treatable Disorders*. Baltimore, MD: Johns Hopkins University Press.

Conrad, Peter, and Joseph W. Schneider. 1992. *Deviance and Medicalization: From Badness to Sickness*. Expanded Edition. Philadelphia, PA: Temple University Press.

Coombs, R. H., and Powers, P. S. 1975. "Socialization for Death: The Physician's Role." In *Toward a Sociology of Death and Dying*, edited by L. Lofland, 15–36. Beverly Hills, CA: Sage Publications Ltd.

Crosby, A. E., Han, B., Ortega, L. A. G., Parks, S. E., and Gfroerer, J. 2011. *Suicidal Thoughts and Behaviors Among Adults Aged ≥18 Years, United States, 2008–2009*, 1–22. Morbidity and Mortality Weekly Report No. 60. Washington: Centers for Disease Control and Prevention. http://www.cdc.gov/mmwr/preview/ mmwrhtml/ss6013a1.htm?s_cid=ss6013a1_w.

Crutchfield, Nikki J. 2008, December 19. *To Succeed of Not to Succeed How Do Political Influences, Culture, and Demographics of a State Afffect the Passing of Physician Assisted Suicide Initiatives?* Ph.D. diss., Auburn University, Auburn, Alabama.

Curlin, Farr A., John D. Lantos, Chad J. Roach, Sarah A. Sellergren, and Marshall H. Chin. 2005. "Religious Characteristics of U.S. Physicians." *Journal of General Internal Medicine* 20 (7): 629–34. doi:10.1111/j.1525-1497.2005.0119.x.

Van Dam, Hans. 2003. "Uitspraak Euthanasie Historische Vergissing." *TROUW*. January 2. http://www.trouw.nl/tr/nl/4324/Nieuws/archief/article/detail/1778167/ 2003/01/02/Uitspraak-euthanasie-historische-vergissing.dhtml.

Death with Dignity National Center. n.d. *The Road to Success in Washington: A Historical Timeline of the Washington Death with Dignity Act.* Death with Dignity National Center. http://www.deathwithdignity.org/media/uploads/WashingtonDWDTimeline 120408.pdf.

Department of Human Services, Oregon Health Division. 1999. *Death with Dignity Act Annual Report: The First Year's Experience.* Portland, OR: Oregon Health Division, Center for Disease Prevention and Epidemiology.

Department of Human Services, Oregon Health Division. 2000. *Oregon's Death with Dignity Act: The Second Year's Experience.* Portland, OR: Oregon Health Division, Center for Disease Prevention and Epidemiology.

Department of Human Services, Oregon Health Division. 2001. *Oregon's Death with Dignity Act: Three Years of Legalized Physician-Assisted Suicide.* Portland, OR: Oregon Health Division, Center for Disease Prevention and Epidemiology.

Department of Human Services, Oregon Health Division. 2002. *Fourth Annual Report on Oregon's Death with Dignity Act.* Portland, OR: Oregon Health Division, Center for Disease Prevention and Epidemiology.

Department of Human Services, Oregon Health Division. 2003. *Fifth Annual Report on Oregon's Death with Dignity Act.* Portland, OR: Oregon Health Division, Center for Disease Prevention and Epidemiology.

Department of Human Services, Oregon Health Division. 2004. *Sixth Annual Report on Oregon's Death with Dignity Act.* Portland, OR: Oregon Health Division, Center for Disease Prevention and Epidemiology.

Department of Human Services, Oregon Health Division. 2005. *Seventh Annual Report on Oregon's Death with Dignity Act.* Portland, OR: Oregon Health Division, Center for Disease Prevention and Epidemiology.

Department of Human Services, Oregon Health Division. 2006. *Eighth Annual Report on Oregon's Death with Dignity Act.* Portland, OR: Oregon Health Division, Center for Disease Prevention and Epidemiology.

Department of Human Services, Oregon Health Division. 2007. *Oregon's Death with Dignity Act: 2006.* Portland, OR: Oregon Health Division, Center for Disease Prevention and Epidemiology.

Department of Human Services, Oregon Health Division. 2008. *Oregon's Death with Dignity Act: 2007.* Portland, OR: Oregon Health Division, Center for Disease Prevention and Epidemiology.

Department of Human Services, Oregon Health Division. 2009. *Oregon's Death with Dignity Act: 2008*. Portland, OR: Oregon Health Division, Center for Disease Prevention and Epidemiology.

Department of Human Services, Oregon Health Division. 2010. *Oregon's Death with Dignity Act: 2009*. Portland, OR: Oregon Health Division, Center for Disease Prevention and Epidemiology.

Department of Human Services, Oregon Health Division. 2011. *Oregon's Death with Dignity Act: 2010*. Portland, OR: Oregon Health Division, Center for Disease Prevention and Epidemiology.

Dowbiggin, Ian. 2002. "'A Rational Coalition': Euthanasia, Eugenics, and Birth Control in America, 1940–1970." *Journal of Policy History* 14 (03): 223–60. doi:10.1353/jph.2002.0017.

Dowbiggin, Ian. 2003. *A Merciful End: The Euthanasia Movement in Modern America*. New York: Oxford University Press.

Dowbiggin, Ian. 2005. *A Concise History of Euthanasia: Life, Death, God, and Medicine*. Lanham, MD: Rowman & Littlefield Publishers, Inc.

Durkheim, Emile. 2006 [1897]. *On Suicide*. London: Penguin Books, Ltd.

Ekland-Olson, Sheldon. 2013. *Life and Death Decisions: The Quest for Morality and Justice in Human Societies*. New York: Routledge.

Elders, J. L. M., and J. Woretshofer. 1992. "Euthanasia in the Netherlands: Current Court Decisions and Legislation." In *International Perspectives on Aging*, edited by George J. Alexander, 209–40. Martinus Nijhoff Publishers.

Elliotson, John. 1843. *Numerous Cases of Surgical Operations without Pain in the Mesmeric State: With Remarks upon the Opposition of Many Members of the Royal Medical and Chirurgical Society and Others to the Reception of the Inestimable Blessings of Mesmerism*. Philadelphia: Lea and Blanchard.

Emanuel, Ezekiel J. 1994a. "Euthanasia. Historical, Ethical, and Empiric Perspectives." *Archives of Internal Medicine* 154: 1890–901.

Emanuel, Ezekiel J. 1994b. "The History of Euthanasia Debates in the United States and Britain." *Annals of Internal Medicine* 121 (10): 793–802.

Emanuel, Ezekiel J., Diane L. Fairclough, Elisabeth R. Daniels, and Brian R. Clarridge. 1996. "Euthanasia and Physician-Assisted Suicide: Attitudes and Experiences of Oncology Patients, Oncologists, and the Public." *Lancet* 347: 1805–10.

Emanuel, Ezekiel J., Diane L. Fairclough, Brian C. Clarridge, D. Blum, E. Bruera, W. C. Penley, L. E. Schnipper, and R. J. Mayer. 2000. "Attitudes and Practices of U.S. Oncologists Regarding Euthanasia and Physician-Assisted Suicide." *Annals of Internal Medicine* 133 (7): 527–32.

Emanuel, Linda, and Leigh. B. Bienen. 2001. "Physician Participation in Executions: Time to Eliminate Anonymity Provisions and Protest the Practice." *Annals of Internal Medicine* 135: 922–24.

European Observatory on Health Care Systems. 1999. *Health Care Systems in Transition: Luxembourg*. AMS 5001890. World Health Organization.

Faber-Langendoen, Kathy, and Karlawish, Jason H. T. 2000. "Should Assisted Suicide Be Only Physician Assisted?" *Annals of Internal Medicine* 132 (6): 482–87. doi:10.7326/0003-4819-132-6-200003210-00010.

Federal Statistical Office. 2012. *Assisted Suicide and Suicide in Switzerland*. 14 Health. Cause of Death Statistics 2009. Neuchatel: Federal Department of Home Affairs.

Feldmann, T. B., R. A. Bell, J. J. Stephenson, and F. E. Purifoy. 1990. "Attitudes of Medical School Faculty and Students toward Acquired Immunodeficiency Syndrome." *Academic Medicine: Journal of the Association of American Medical Colleges* 65 (7): 464–66.

Field, Marilyn J. 2009. "How People Die in the United States." In *Decision Making Near the End of Life: Issues, Developments, and Future Directions*, edited by James L. Werth and Dean Blevins. New York: Routledge.

File, Thom, and Kominski, Robert. 2009. *Dependency Ratio in the United States: A State and Metropolitan Area Analysis*. U.S. Census Bureau. http://www.census.gov/hhes/well-being/files/Dependency%20Ratios%20in%20the%20United%20States.pdf.

Findley, I., and G. Chamberlain. 1999. "ABC of Labour Care. Relief of Pain." *BMJ (Clinical Research Ed.)* 318 (7188): 927–30.

Fletcher, Joseph F. 1954. *Morals and Medicine*. Boston: Beacon Press.

Foucault, Michel. 1973. *The Birth of the Clinic: An Archaeology of Medical Perception*. Translated by A.M. Sheridan. New York: Pantheon Books.

Freidson, Eliot. 1988. *Profession of Medicine*. Chicago: University of Chicago Press.

Gailey, Elizabeth A. 2003. *Write to Death: News Framing of the Right to Die Conflict, from Quinlan's Coma to Kevorkian's Conviction*. Westport, CT: Praeger.

Ganzini, Linda, Elizabeth R. Goy, and Steven K. Dobscha. 2008. "Why Oregon Patients Request Assisted Death: Family Members' Views." *Journal of General Internal Medicine* 23 (8): 1296–96. doi:10.1007/s11606-008-0542-z.

Ganzini, L., H. D. Nelson, T. A. Schmidt, D. F. Kraemer, M. A. Delorit, and M. A. Lee. 2000. "Physicians' Experiences with the Oregon Death with Dignity Act." *New England Journal of Medicine* 342 (8): 557–63. doi:10.1056/NEJM200002243 420806.

Gardner, Booth. 2008. "Dear Friend." www.spokesmanreview.com/media/pdf/20080429_fundraisingletter.pdf.

Garman, E. T., and Raymond E. Forgue. 2007. *Personal Finance*. Boston: Houghton, Mifflin and Company.

Garrett, Valery. 1998. "The Last Civil Right? Euthanasia Policy and Politics in the United States, 1938-1991." Ph.D. diss., University of California: Santa Barbara, CA.

Gauthier, Saskia, Julian Mausbach, Thomas Reisch, and Christine Bartsch. 2014. "Suicide Tourism: A Pilot Study on the Swiss Phenomenon." *Journal of Medical Ethics*, August, medethics – 2014–102091. doi:10.1136/medethics-2014-102091.

Gawande, Atul. 2012. "Two Hundred Years of Surgery." *New England Journal of Medicine* 366 (18): 1716–23. doi:10.1056/NEJMra1202392.

Gerber, Elisabeth R. 1999. *The Populist Paradox: Interest Group Influence and the Promise of Direct Legislation*. Princeton, NJ: Princeton University Press.

Gevers, J. K. M.. 1987. "Legal Developments Concerning Active Euthanasia on Request in the Netherlands." *Bioethics* 1 (2): 157–62.

Gevers, J. K. M. 1992. "Legislation on Euthanasia: Recent Developments in The Netherlands." *Journal of Medical Ethics* 18 (3): 138–41.

van Gijn, J,, and D, J, Nieuwkamp. 2002. "William Osler and the 'chloroforming' of men over 60: a media outcry in 1905." *Nederlands tijdschrift voor geneeskunde* 146 (51): 2489–93.

Gomes, Barbara, Natalia Calanzani, Marjolein Gysels, Sue Hall, and Irene J. Higginson. 2013. "Heterogeneity and Changes in Preferences for Dying at Home: A Systematic Review." *BMC Palliative Care* 12 (1): 7. doi:10.1186/1472-684X-12-7.

Gordijn, B. 2001. "Regulating Moral Dissent in an Open Society: The Dutch Experience with Pragmatic Tolerance." *The Journal of Medicine and Philosophy* 26 (3): 225–44. doi:10.1076/jmep.26.3.225.3013.

Grattet, Ryken, Valerie Jenness, and Theodore R. Curry. 1998. "The Homogenization and Differentiation of Hate Crime Law in the United States, 1978 to 1995: Innovation and Diffusion in the Criminalization of Bigotry." *American Sociological Review* 63 (2): 286–307. doi:10.2307/2657328.

Griffiths, John. 1995. "Assisted Suicide in the Netherlands: The Chabot Case." *The Modern Law Review* 58 (2): 232–48. doi:10.1111/j.1468-2230.1995.tb02006.x.

Griffiths, John, Alex Bood, and Heleen Weyers. 1998. *Euthanasia and Law in the Netherlands*. Amsterdam: Amsterdam University Press.

Griffiths, John, Heleen Weyers, and Maurice Adams. 2008. *Euthanasia and Law in Europe*. 2nd edition. Oxford, UK; Portland, Or: Hart Publishing.

Groenhuijsen, M. S., and Floris van Laanen. 2006. *Euthanasia in International and Comparative Perspective*. Nijmegen: Wolf Legal Publishers.

Groenewoud, J. H., Agnes van der Heide, Bregji D. Onwuteaka-Philipsen, Dick L. Willems, Paul J. van der Maas, and Gerrit van der Wal. 2000. "Clinical Problems with the Performance of Euthanasia and Physician-Assisted Suicide in The Netherlands." *New England Journal of Medicine* 342 (8): 551–56. doi:10.1056/NEJM 200002243420805.

Grubb, Andrew, Judith Laing, Jean McHale, and Ian K. Sir. 2010. *Principles of Medical Law*. Oxford: Oxford University Press.

Hafner, Katie. 2012. "In Ill Doctor, a Surprise Reflection of Who Picks Assisted Suicide." The New York Times, August 11, sec. Health/Money & Policy. http://www.nytimes.com/2012/08/12/health/policy/in-ill-doctor-a-surprise-reflection-of-who-picks-assisted-suicide.html

Haines, Herb. 1989. "'Primum Non Nocere': Chemical Execution and the Limits of Medical Social Control." *Social Problems* 36 (5): 442–54.

Hallenbeck, James. 2003. *Palliative Care Perspectives*. New York: Oxford University Press.

Halper, Thomas. 2000. "Accommodating Death." In *The Philosophy of Medicine: Framing the Field*, edited by Hugo Tristram Engelhardt. Springer.

Hapenney, Sandra S. 2011, August. "Appeal to Conscience Clauses in the Face of Divergent Practices among Catholic Hospitals." Ph.D. diss., Baylor University, Waco, TX.

Haquin, Rene, and Pierre Stephany. 2005. *Les grands dossiers criminels en Belgique*. Tielt: Lannoo Uitgeverij.

Hendin, Herbert. 1998. *Seduced by Death: Doctors, Patients, and Assisted Suicide*. New York: W. W. Norton & Company.

Henk, A. M. J. Ten Have, and Jos V. M. Welie. 2005. *Death and Medical Power: An Ethical Analysis of Dutch Euthanasia Practice*. Maidenhead, UK: Open University Press.

Van der Heide, Agnes, Bregje D. Onwuteaka-Philipsen, Mette L. Rurup, Hilde M. Buiting, Johannes J. M. van Delden, Johanna E. Hanssen-de Wolf, Anke G. J. M. Janssen, et al. 2007. "End-of-Life Practices in the Netherlands under the Euthanasia Act." *New England Journal of Medicine* 356 (19): 1957–65. doi:10.1056/NEJMsa071143.

Henry, Vincent E. 1995. "The Police Officer as Survivor: Death Confrontations and the Police Subculture." *Behavioral Sciences & the Law* 13 (1): 93–112.

Himmelstein, David U., and Steffie Woolhandler. 1998. "The Silence of the Doctors." *Journal of General Internal Medicine* 13 (6): 422–23. doi:10.1046/j.1525-1497 .1998.00125.x.

Holbrook, Stewart Hall. 1959. *The Golden Age of Quackery*. New York: Macmillan.

Holmes, Oliver W. 1911. *Medical Essays*. Boston: Houghton, Mifflin and Company.

Hoyert, Donna L., Elizabeth Arias, Betty L. Smith, Sherry L. Murphy, and Kenneth D. Kochanek. 2001. *Deaths: Final Data for 1999*. vol. 49 no. 8. National Vital Statistics Reports. Hyattsville, MD: Center for Disease Control and Prevention.

Hughes, John C. 2010. *Booth Who? A Biography of Booth Gardner*. 1st ed. Olympia, WA: Washington State Legacy Project.

Hume, David. 2005. *On Suicide*. UK: Penguin.

Humphry, Derek. 2001. "Swiss Assisted Suicide Branching Out." *Voluntary Euthanasia Society of New South Wales Newsletter*, November.

Humphry, Derek. 2002. *Final Exit: The Practicalities of Self-Deliverance and Assisted Suicide for the Dying*. 3rd ed. New York: Delta.

Humphry, Derek. 2005. *The Good Euthanasia Guide: Where, What, and Who in Choices in Dying*. Junction City, OR: ERGO Bookstore.

Humphry, Derek, and Ann Wickett. 2003. *Jean's Way*. Junction City, OR: Norris Lane Press/ERGO.

Illich, Ivan. 1975. *Medical Nemesis*. New York: Pantheon.

Imber, Jonathan B. 2008. *Markets, Morals & Religion*. New Brunswick, NJ: Transaction Publishers.

Induru, Raghava R., and Lagman, Ruth L. 2011. "Managing Cancer Pain: Frequently Asked Questions." *Cleveland Clinic Journal of Medicine* 78 (7): 449–64. doi:10.3949/ccjm.78a.10054.

Initiative and Referendum Institute. 2001. *Statewide Initiatives Usage: Washington.* Initiatives and Referendums Institute. http://www.iandrinstitute.org/New%20IRI %20Website%20Info/I&R%20Research%20and%20History/I&R%20at%20the %20Statewide%20Level/Usage%20history/Washington.pdf.

Initiative and Referendum Institute. 2013. *Initiative Use*. Los Angeles: USC Gould School of Law. http://www.iandrinstitute.org/IRI%20Initiative%20Use%20%282013-1 %29.pdf.

International Monetary Fund. 2014. "Report for Selected Countries and Subjects." *Report for Selected Countries and Subjects*. http://www.imf.org/

Irons, Peter. 2006. *A People's History of the Supreme Court: The Men and Women Whose Cases and Decisions Have Shaped Our Constitution*. rev. ed. New York: Penguin Books.

Israely, Jeff. 2008. "Luxembourg's Monarch Steps Back On Euthanasia Bill." *Time Magazine*, December 12. http://content.time.com/time/world/article/0,8599,1865 825,00.html.

Jansen-van der Weide, Marijke C., Bregje D. Onwuteaka-Philipsen, and Gerrit van der Wal. 2005. "Granted, Undecided, Withdrawn, and Refused Requests for Euthanasia and Physician-Assisted Suicide." *Arch Intern Med* 165, no. 15 (August 8): 1698–1704.

Jones, Jeffrey M. 2004. *Tracking Religious Affiliation*. Washington, DC: Gallup, Inc. http://www.gallup.com/poll/12091/tracking-religious-affiliation-state-state.aspx.

Jonsen, Albert R. 2003. *The Birth of Bioethics*. New York: Oxford University Press.

Kamisar, Yale. 1958. "Some Non-Religious Views against Proposed Mercy-Killing Legislation." *Minnesota Law Review* 42: 969.

Kane, Harry Hubbell. 1881. *Drugs That Enslave: The Opium, Morphine, Chloral and Hashisch Habits*. Philadelphia: Presley Blakiston.

Kemp, N. D. A. 2002. *Merciful Release*. New York: Manchester University Press.

Kennedy, Duncan. 1858. *A Clergyman's Idea of a Model Physician: An Address Delivered at the Commencement, Albany Medical College*. Albany, NY: Munsell & Rowland.

Kennedy, James C. 2002. *Een Weloverwogen Dood (A Well-Considered Death)*. Amsterdam, Netherlands: Bert Bakker.

Kennedy, James C. 2012. "The Lateness of the Dutch Euthanasia Debate and Its Consequences." In *Physician-Assisted Death in Perspective*, edited by Stuart J. Youngner and Gerrit Kimsma, 3–20. Cambridge, UK: Cambridge University Press. http://dx.doi.org/10.1017/CBO9780511843976.005.

Ketting, Evert. 1982. "Contraception and Fertility in the Netherlands." *International Family Planning Perspectives* 8 (4): 141. doi:10.2307/2948134.

Kevorkian, Jack. 1991. *Prescription -Medicide: The Goodness of Planned Death*. Buffalo, NY: Prometheus Books.

Kiernan, Jas. G. 1892. "Suicide." *The Medical Standard* 12 (3): 61–64.

Kirtley, Bill. 2011. "The Right Time and the Right Place: Washington and Montana Adopt Death with Dignity." *National Social Science Journal* 35 (1): 99–104.

Kmietovicz, Zosia. 2002. "R.E.S.P.E.C.T.—Why Doctors Are Still Getting Enough of It." *BMJ: British Medical Journal* 324 (7328): 11.

KNMG. 1996. *Euthanasia in the Netherlands—A Vision on Euthanasia*. Utrecht: KNMG.

KNMG. 2011. *The Role of the Physician in the Voluntary Termination of Life-Position Paper*. Utrecht: KNMG.

Knippenberg, Hans. 1998. "Secularization in the Netherlands in Its Historical and Geographical Dimensions." *GeoJournal* 45 (3): 209–20. doi:10.1023/A:1006973011455.

Koenig, H. G. 2000. "Religion and Medicine I: Historical Background and Reasons for Separation." *International Journal of Psychiatry in Medicine* 30 (4): 385–98.

Kohnen, P., and G. Schumacher. 2002. *Euthanasia and Human Dignity: A Collection of Contributions by the Dutch Catholic Bishops' Conference to the Legislative Procedure, 1983–2001*. Utrecht: Peeters.

Kübler-Ross, Elisabeth. 1969. *On Death and Dying: What the Dying Have to Teach Doctors, Nurses, Clergy, and Their Families*. 1st ed. New York: Scribner.

Kushner, Howard I. 1991. *American Suicide: A Psycocultural Exploration*. New Brunswick, NJ: Rutgers University Press.

Laine, Christine, and Frank Davidoff. 1996. "Patient-Centered Medicine: A Professional Evolution." *JAMA* 275 (2): 152–56.

Lavi, Shai J. 2003. "Euthanasia and the Changing Laws of the Deathbed: A Study in Historical Jurisprudence." *Theoretical Inquiries in Law* 4 (2): 729–761.

Lavi, Shai J. 2005. *The Modern Art of Dying*. Princeton, NJ: Princeton University Press.

Lavigne-pley, Claire, and Louise Lévesque. 1992. "Reactions of the Institutionalized Elderly Upon Learning of the Death of a Peer." *Death Studies* 16 (5): 451–61. doi:10.1080/07481189208252591.

Lechner, Frank J. 1996. "Secularization in the Netherlands?" *Journal for the Scientific Study of Religion* 35 (3): 252–64.

Lechner, Frank J. 2012. *The Netherlands: Globalization and National Identity.* Routledge.

Leenen, H. J. J. 1987. "Euthanasia, Assistance to Suicide and the Law: Developments in the Netherlands." *Health Policy* 8 (2): 197–206. doi:10.1016/0168-8510(87)90062-5.

Leenen, H. J. J. 2001. "The Development of Euthanasia in the Netherlands." *European Journal of Health Law* 8 (2): 125–33. doi:10.1163/15718090120523457.

Lewis, Milton J. 2007. *Medicine and Care of the Dying.* Oxford: Oxford University Press.

Lewy, Guenter. 2011. *Assisted Death in Europe and America: Four Regimes and Their Lessons.* Oxford; New York: Oxford University Press.

Livingston, S. B. 1895. "Suicide and Reactionary Legislation in New York." *Counsellor (New York Law School Law Journal)* 4: 91.

Lundberg, George D. 1988. "'It's over, Debbie' and the Euthanasia Debate." *JAMA* 259, no. 14 (April 8): 2142–43. doi:10.1001/jama.1988.03720140062036.

MacCoun, Robert, and Peter Reuter. 1997. "Interpreting Dutch Cannabis Policy: Reasoning by Analogy in the Legalization Debate." *Science* 278 (5335): 47–52. doi:10.1126/science.278.5335.47.

MacDonald, Arthur. 1903. *Statistics of Crime, Suicide, Insanity, and Other Forms of Abnormality: And Criminological Studies in Connection with Bills to Establish a Laboratory for the Study of the Criminal, Pauper and Defective Classes.* Washington, DC: Government Printing Office.

Macdonald, Lyn. 2000. *1915: The Death of Innocence.* Baltimore, MD: Johns Hopkins University Press.

Machado, Calixto. 2007. *Brain Death.* New York: Springer Publishers.

Marzen, Thomas J., Mary K. O'Dowd, Daniel Crone, and Thomas J. Balch. 1985. "Suicide: A Constitutional Right." *Duquesne Law Review* 24: 1.

Marzuk, P. M., H. Tierney, K. Tardiff, et al. 1988. "Increased Risk of Suicide in Persons with AIDS." *JAMA* 259 (9): 1333–37. doi:10.1001/jama.1988.037200900 23028.McCue, J. D. 1995. "The Naturalness of Dying." *JAMA* 273 (13): 1039–43. doi:10.1001/jama.1995.03520370081041.

Mcdougall, Jennifer F., and Maratha Gorman. 2008. *Euthanasia: A Reference Handbook.* Santa Barbara, CA: ABC-CLIO.

McIntosh, John L. (for the American Association of Suicidology). (2012). *U.S.A. suicide: 2009 official final data.* Washington, DC: American Association of Suicidology, dated January 12, 2012, downloaded from http://www.suicidology.org.

McKinlay, John B., and Lisa D Marceau. 2002. "The End of the Golden Age of Doctoring." *International Journal of Health Services: Planning, Administration, Evaluation* 32 (2): 379–416.

Meier, Diane E., Carol-Ann Emmons, Sylvan Wallenstein, Timothy Quill, R. Sean Morrison, and Christine K. Cassel. 1998. "A National Survey of Physician-Assisted Suicide and Euthanasia in the United States." *New England Journal of Medicine* 338, no. 17 (April 23): 1193–1201.

Meisel, Alan, and Kathy L. Cerminara. 2009. *The Right to Die: The Law of End-of-Life Decisionmaking.* 4th ed. New York: Aspen Publishers.

Mercadante, S. 1999. "Opioid Rotation for Cancer Pain: Rationale and Clinical Aspects." *Cancer* 86 (9): 1856–66.

Miles, Steven H. 2005. *The Hippocratic Oath and the Ethics of Medicine.* 1st ed. Oxford: Oxford University Press.

Morrell, M. A. 1877. *Our Work for Christ among His Suffering People, a Book for Hospital Nurses*. Oxford and Cambridge: Rivingtons.

Mortier, Freddy, Luc Deliens, Johan Bilsen, Marc Cosyns, Koen Ingels, and Robert Vander Stichele. 2000. "End-of-Life Decisions of Physicians in the City of Hasselt (Flanders, Belgium)." *Bioethics* 14 (3): 254–67. doi:10.1111/1467-8519.00195.

Munk, William. 1887. *Euthanasia; Or, Medical Treatment in Aid of an Easy Death*. London and New York: Longmans, Green, and co.

Netherlands Jurisprudence. 1987. "Euthanasia Case Leeuwarden-1973." Translated by Lagerwey Walter. *Issues in Law & Medicine* 3: 439.

Newport, Frank. 2004. *A Look at Americans and Religion Today*. Washington, DC: Gallup, Inc. http://www.gallup.com/poll/11089/Look-Americans-Religion-Today.aspx.

NVVE. 2010. *Completed Life: What Are We Talking about? Questions and Answers*. Amsterdam, Netherlands: NVVE.

Nicol, Neal, and Harry Wylie. 2006. *Between the Dying and the Dead: Dr. Jack Kevorkian's Life and the Battle to Legalize Euthanasia*. 1st ed. Madison: University of Wisconsin Press.

Nicolaidis, Christina. 2006. "A Piece of My Mind. My Mother's Choice." *JAMA* 296 (8): 907–8. doi:10.1001/jama.296.8.907.

Nitschke, Philip Haig, and Fiona Stewart. 2005. *Killing Me Softly: Voluntary Euthanasia and the Road to the Peaceful Pill*. Camberwell: Penguin Group (USA) Incorporated.

Nitschke, Philip, and Fiona Stewart. 2006, September 1. *The Peaceful Pill Handbook*. Waterford, MI: Exit International US.

Nye, Robert A. 2003. "The Evolution of the Concept of Medicalization in the Late Twentieth Century." *Journal of the History of the Behavioral Sciences* 39 (2): 115–29. doi:10.1002/jhbs.10108.

Nys, Herman. 2010. *Medical Law in Belgium*. Alphen aan den Rijn: Kluwer Law International.

OECD. 2014. *Statistiques Sur La Sante 2014: Comment Le Luxemburg Se Positionne?*. http://www.oecd.org/luxembourg/oecd-health-statistics-2014-country-notes.htm.

Ohio General Assembly, House of Representatives. 1907. *Journal of the House of Representatives, Regular Session, Seventy-Seventh General Assembly of the State of Ohio, 1906*. Springfield, Ohio: The Springfield Publishing Company.

Oken, Donald. 1961. "What to Tell Cancer Patients: A Study of Medical Attitudes." *JAMA* 175, no. 13 (April 1): 1120–28.

Oliver, Michael. 1996. *Understanding disability*. Basingstoke: Palgrave Macmillan.

Oregon Public Health Division. 2013. *Oregon's Death with Dignity Act, 2012*. Oregon Public Health Division. Public.health.oregon.gov/ProviderPartnerResources/EvaluationResearch/DeathwithDignityAct/Documents/year15.pdf.

Ost, Suzanne. 2010. "The De-Medicalisation of Assisted Dying: Is a Less Medicalised Model the Way Forward?" *Medical Law Review* 18 (4): 497–540. doi:10.1093/medlaw/fwq025.

Otlowski, Margaret. 2000. *Voluntary Euthanasia and the Common Law*. Oxford: Oxford University Press.

Papper, Emanuel M. 1995. *Romance, Poetry, and Surgical Sleep: Literature Influences Medicine*. Westport, CT: Greenwood Press.

Parsons, Talcott. 1951. *The Social System*. Glencoe, IL: Free Press.

Pascalis, Felix. 1826. "Remarks on the Theory of Pain." *American Medical and Surgical Journal* 1: 79–89.

Percival, Thomas. 1849. *Medical Ethics; Or, A Code of Institutes and Precepts, Adapted to the Professional Conduct of Physicians and Surgeons: To Which Is Added an Appendix; Containing A Discourse on Hospital Duties; Also Notes and Illustrations*. 3rd ed. London: John Henry Parker.

Patients Rights Council. 2005. *Assisted Suicide & Death with Dignity: Past, Present & Future - Part I*. Patients Rights Council. http://www.patientsrightscouncil.org/site/rpt2005-part1/.

Patterson, James T. 1989. *The Dread Disease: Cancer and Modern American Culture*. Cambridge, MA: Harvard University Press.

Pearlman, R. A., C. Hsu, H. Starks, A. L. Back, J. R. Gordon, A. J. Bharucha, . . . M. P. Battin. 2005. "Motivations for Physician-Assisted Suicide." *Journal of General Internal Medicine* 20 (3): 485.

Pellegrino, Edmund D., and David C. Thomasma. 1988. *For the Patient's Good: The Restoration of Beneficence in Health Care*. 1 edition. New York: Oxford University Press.

Pernick, Martin S. 1994. *A Calculus of Suffering: Pain, Professionalism, and Anesthesia in Nineteenth-Century America*. New York: Columbia University Press.

Pew Research Center. 2011. *The Generation Gap and the 2012 Election*. Washington, DC: Pew Research Center for the People and the Press. http://www.people-press.org/2011/11/03/the-generation-gap-and-the-2012-election-3/.

Péporté, Pit, Kmec, Sonja, Majerus, Benoit, and Margue, Michel. 2010. *Inventing Luxembourg: Representations of the Past, Space and Language from the Nineteenth to the Twenty-First Century*. Leiden: Kononklijke Brill NV.

Pitts, Jesse. 1968. "Social Control: The Concept." In *International Encyclopedia of Social Sciences*, edited by David Sills. Vol. 14. New York: MacMillan Publishing Co., Inc.

Prokopetz, Julian J. Z., and Lehmann, Lisa S. 2012. "Redefining Physicians' Role in Assisted Dying." *New England Journal of Medicine* 367 (2): 97–99. doi:10.1056/NEJMp1205283.

Public Policy Polling. 2012. *Obama Holds Modest lead in MA*. Raleigh, NC: Public Policy Polling. http://www.publicpolicypolling.com/pdf/2011/PPP_Release_MA_082212.pdf#page=2.

Puppinck, Gregor, and Claire de La Hougue. 2014. "The Right to Assisted Suicide in the Case Law of the European Courtof Human Rights." *The International Journal of Human Rights* 18 (7/8): 735–55. doi:10.1080/13642987.2014.926891.

Quill, Timothy E. 1983. "Partnerships in Patient Care: A Contractual Approach." *Annals of Internal Medicine* 98 (2): 228–34. doi:10.7326/0003-4819-98-2-228.

Quill, Timothy E. 1991. "Death and Dignity. A Case of Individualized Decision Making." *The New England Journal of Medicine* 324 (10): 691–94. doi:10.1056/NEJM199103073241010.

Quill, Timothy E. 2001. *A Midwife through the Dying Process: Stories of Healing and Hard Choices at the End of Life*. Baltimore, MD: Johns Hopkins University Press.

Quill, Timothy E. 2007. "Legal Regulation of Physician-Assisted Death—The Latest Report Cards." *New England Journal of Medicine* 356 (19): 1911–13. doi:10.1056/NEJMp078061.

Quill, Timothy E., and Christine K. Cassel. 2003. "Professional Organizations' Position Statements on Physician-Assisted Suicide: A Case for Studied Neutrality." *Annals of Internal Medicine* 138 (3): 208–212.

Quill, Timothy E., Bernard Lo, and Dan W. Brock. 2008. "Palliative Options of Last Resort: A Comparison of Voluntarily Stopping Eating and Drinking, Terminal Sedation, Physician-Assisted Suicide, and Voluntary Active Euthanasia." In *Giving Death a Helping Hand*, edited by D. Birnbacher and E. Dahl, 49–64. Springer Netherlands.

Rayar, L, Stafford Wadsworth, Mona Cheung, J. A. W. Lensing, and Grat van den Heuvel. 1997. *The Dutch Penal Code*. Littleton, CO: Rothman.

Reeves, Aaron, David Stuckler, Martin McKee, David Gunnell, Chang Shu-Sen, and Sanjay Basu. 2012. "Increase in State Suicide Rates in the USA during Economic Recession." *The Lancet* 380 (9856): 1813–14.

Regional Euthanasia Review Committees. 2003. *Annual Report - 2003*. The Hague, Netherlands. http://www.euthanasiecommissie.nl

Regional Euthanasia Review Committees. 2011. *Annual Report - 2011*. The Hague, Netherlands. http://www.euthanasiecommissie.nl.

Regional Euthanasia Review Committees. 2012. *Annual Report - 2012*. The Hague, Netherlands. http://www.euthanasiecommissie.nl.

Regionale Toetsingscommissies Euthanasie. 2011. *Euthanasia: Q and A–Review Procedures*. The Netherlands. www.euthanasiecommissie.nl/Images/qa-euthanasie-engels-2011_tcm52-33857.pdf.

Rejali, Darius M. 2007. *Torture and Democracy*. Princeton, NJ: Princeton University Press.

Richards, Timothy, William Allender, and Di Fang. 2013. "Media Advertising and Ballot Initiatives: The Case of Animal Welfare Regulation." *Contemporary Economic Policy* 31 (1): 145–62. doi:10.1111/j.1465-7287.2011.00292.x.

Rietjens, Judith A. C., Donald G. van Tol, Maartje Schermer, and Agnes van der Heide. 2009. "Judgement of Suffering in the Case of a Euthanasia Request in The Netherlands." *Journal of Medical Ethics* 35 (8): 502–507.

The Right Hon Lord Justice Lawton. 1979. "Mercy Killing: The Judicial Dilemma." *Journal of the Royal Society of Medicine* 72: 460–61.

Rigter, Henk. 1989. "Euthanasia in the Netherlands: Distinguishing Facts from Fiction." *The Hastings Center Report* 19 (1): S31.

Rodick, Giza. 2007. "Dr. Death: Jack Kevorkian and the Right-to-Die Debate." In *Crimes and Trials of the Century*, edited by Steven Chermak and Frankie Bailey, 101–22. ABC-CLIO, Westport, CT: Greenwood Press.

Romer, Christina. 1986. "Spurious Volatility in Historical Unemployment Data." *Journal of Political Economy* 94 (1): 1–37.

Roscoe, Lori A., Julie E. Malphurs, L. J. Dragovic, and Donna Cohen. 2000. "Dr. Jack Kevorkian and Cases of Euthanasia in Oakland County, Michigan, 1990–1998." *New England Journal of Medicine* 343 (23): 1735–36. doi:10.1056/NEJM200012073432315.

Rosenberg, Charles E. 1995, March 1. *The Care of Strangers: The Rise of America's Hospital System*. Baltimore, MD: Johns Hopkins University Press.

Rurup, Mette L., Bregje D Onwuteaka-Philipsen, and Gerrit Van Der Wal. 2005. "A 'Suicide Pill' for Older People: Attitudes of Physicians, the General Population, and Relatives of Patients Who Died after Euthanasia or Physician-Assisted Suicide in

The Netherlands." *Death Studies* 29 (6): 519–34. doi:10.1080/07481180590 962677.

Russell, Olive Ruth. 1977. *Freedom to Die*. New York: Human Sciences Press.

Samuels, Suzanne U. 2004. *First among Friends: Interest Groups, the U.S. Supreme Court, and the Right to Privacy: Interest Groups, the U.S. Supreme Court, and the Right to Privacy*. ABC-CLIO, Westport, CT: Praeger.

Schepers, Rita. "The Belgian Medical Profession and the Sickness Funds: The Collectivization of Health Care (1900-1945)." In *Curing and Insuring: Essays on Illness in Past Times: The Netherlands, Belgium, England, and Italy, 16th-20th Centuries: Proceedings of the . . . of the Faculty of History and Arts)*. Hilversum: Verloren.

Scherer, Jennifer M., and Rita James Simon. 1999. *Euthanasia and the Right to Die: A Comparative View*. Lanham: Rowman & Littlefield.

Schneider, Joseph W., and Peter Conrad. 1985, June 26. *Having Epilepsy*. Philadelphia: Temple University Press.

Schoonman, Merel Kristi, Ghislaine José Madeleine Wilhelmien van Thiel, and Johannes Jozef Marten van Delden. 2013. "Non-Physician-Assisted Suicide in The Netherlands: A Cross-Sectional Survey among the General Public." *Journal of Medical Ethics*, December, medethics–2013–101736. doi:10.1136/medethics-2013 -101736.

Seale, Clive. 2010. "The Role of Doctors' Religious Faith and Ethnicity in Taking Ethically Controversial Decisions during End-of-Life Care." *Journal of Medical Ethics* 36 (11): 677–82. doi:10.1136/jme.2010.036194.

Seppala, Marvin D. Seppala, and Mark E. Rose. 2010. *Prescription Painkillers: History, Pharmacology, and Treatment*. Center City, MN: Hazelden Publishing.

Sharpe, Virginia Ashby, and Alan I. Faden. 1998. *Medical Harm: Historical, Conceptual and Ethical Dimensions of Iatrogenic Illness*. Cambridge, UK: Cambridge University Press.

Sheldon, Tony. 2003. "Being 'Tired of Life' Is Not Grounds for Euthanasia." *BMJ: British Medical Journal* 326 (7380): 71.

Sheldon, Tony. 2004. "Huibert Drion." *BMJ: British Medical Journal* 328 (7449): 1204.

Shryock, Richard Harrison. 1960. *Medicine and Society in America: 1660-1860*. Ithaca, NY: Cornell University Press.

Simonds, Wendy, Barbara Katz Rothman, and Bari Meltzer Norman. 2007. *Laboring on: Birth in Transition in the United States*. CRC Press.

Simpson, James Young. 1847. *Answer to the Religious Objections Made against the Employment of Anesthetic Agents in Midwifery and Surgery*. Edinburgh: Sutherland & Knox.

Simpson, James Young. 1848. "Account of a New Anaesthetic Agent, as a Substitute for Sulphuric Ether in Surgery and Midwifery." *Buffalo Medical Journal* 3: 561–67.

Singer, Peter. 1983. Sanctity of Life or Quality of Life? *Pediatrics* 72, no. 1 (July 1): 128–29.

Slome, Lee R., Thomas F. Mitchell, Edwin Charlebois, Jeffrey Moulton Benevedes, and Donald I. Abrams. 1997. "Physician-Assisted Suicide and Patients with Human Immunodeficiency Virus Disease." *New England Journal of Medicine* 336 (6): 417–21. doi:10.1056/NEJM199702063360606.

Smets, Tinne, Joachim Cohen, Johan Bilsen, Yanna Van Wesemael, Mette L. Rurup, and Luc Deliens. 2011. "Attitudes and Experiences of Belgian Physicians Regarding

Euthanasia Practice and the Euthanasia Law." *Journal of Pain and Symptom Management* 41 (3): 580–93. doi:10.1016/j.jpainsymman.2010.05.015.

Smith, Wesley J. 2004. "Assisted Suicide in Oregon: Piercing the Myth of Compassion." In *Suffering and Dignity in the Twilight of Life*, edited by B. Ars and É. Montero, 71–86. The Hague, Netherlands: Kugler Publications.

Sneiderman, Barney, and Marja Verhoef. 1995. "Patient Autonomy and the Defence of Medical Necessity: Five Dutch Euthanasia Cases." *Alberta Law Review* 34: 374–395.

Starr, Paul. 1984, June 5. *The Social Transformation of American Medicine: The Rise of a Sovereign Profession and the Making of a Vast Industry*. New York: Basic Books.

Stein, Stephen J. 1994. *The Shaker Experience in America: A History of the United Society of Believers*. New Haven: Yale University Press.

Steinbrook, Robert. 2008. "Physician-Assisted Death—From Oregon to Washington State." *New England Journal of Medicine* 359 (24): 2513–15. doi:10.1056/NEJMp0809394.

Stephens, Ronald L. 1995. "Reviews and Notes." *Annals of Internal Medicine* 122 (4): 320.

Stijn Vandevelde, Veerle Soyez, Tom Vander Beken, Stefaan De Smet, Anka Boers, and Eric Broekaert. 2011. "Mentally Ill Offenders in Prison: The Belgian Case." *International Journal of Law and Psychiatry* 34 (1): 71–78.

Stooss, Carl. 1893. *Die Grundzüge des schweizerischen Strafrechts: im Auftrage des Bundesrathes vergleichend*. Basel, Switzerland: von H. Georg.

Stover, John F. 1997. *American Railroads*. Chicago, IL: University of Chicago Press.

Strachey, Lytton. 1948. *Eminent Victorians: Cardinal Manning, Florence Nightingale, Dr. Arnold, General Gordon*. G.P. Putnam's Sons.

Strate, John, Timothy Kiska, and Marvin Zalman. 2001. "Who Favors Legalizing Physician-Assisted Suicide? The Vote on Michigan's Proposal B." *Politics & the Life Sciences* 20 (2): 155.

Sutherland, John. 1989. *The Stanford Companion to Victorian Fiction*. Stanford, CA: Stanford University Press.

Swiss Academy of Medical Sciences. 2005. *Care of Patients in the End of Life, Medical-Ethical Guidelines of the SAMS*. Basel, Switzerland: SAMS. www.samw.ch.

Swiss National Advisory Commission on Bioethical Ethics. 2005. *Assisted Suicide*. Opinion no.9/2005. Bern, Switzerland: Swiss National Advisory Commission on Biomedical Ethics (NEK0CNE).

Szasz, Thomas S. 1970. *The Medicalization of Everyday Life. Selected Essays*. Syracuse, NY: Syracuse University Press.

Szasz, Thomas S. 1977. *The Theology of Medicine: The Political-Philosophical Foundation of Medical Ethics*. Syracuse, NY: Syracuse University Press.

Szasz, Thomas S. 1984. *The Myth of Mental Illness, Revised Edition*. HarperCollins.

Szasz, Thomas S. 2011. *Suicide Prohibition: The Shame of Medicine*. Syracuse, NY: Syracuse University Press.

Tallis, Raymond. 2012. "Our Professional Bodies Should Stop Opposing Assisted Dying." *BMJ* 344 (June 13): e4115–e4115. doi:10.1136/bmj.e4115.

Task Force on Life and the Law. 1994. *When Death is Sought: Assisted Suicide and Euthanasia in the Medical Context*. New York: New York State Department of Health.

Temin, Peter. 1979. "The Origin of Compulsory Drug Prescriptions." *Journal of Law and Economics* 22 (1): 91–105.

Testa, Nicole. 1998. "Sentenced to Life? An Analysis of the United States Supreme Court's Decision in Washington v. Glucksberg." *Nova Law Review* 22: 821.

Therborn, G. 1989. "Pillarization and Popular Movements: Two Variants of Welfare State capitalism—The Netherlands and Sweden." In *The Comparative History of Public Policy*, edited by Francis Geoffrey Castles. New York: Oxford University Press, Incorporated.

Thomas, Eliza L. S. 1855. "Inaugural Thesis on the Propriety of Anaesthetic Agents in Surgical Operations." Philadelphia, PA: Female Medical College of Pennsylvania.

Thomasma, David C. 1998. *Asking to Die: Inside the Dutch Debate about Euthanasia: Inside the Dutch Debate About Euthanasia*. Springer.

Thomasson, Melissa A., and Jaret Treber. 2008. "From Home to Hospital: The Evolution of Childbirth in the United States, 1928–1940." *Explorations in Economic History* 45 (1): 76–99.

Thorson, J. A., and F. C. Powell. 1994. "A Revised Death Anxiety Scale." In *Death Anxiety Handbook*, edited by R. A. Neimeyer, 31–43. Washington, DC: Taylor & Francis.

Thorwald, Jurgen. 1957. *The Century of the Surgeon*. Second Printing. New York: Pantheon Books.

Timmermmans, Arco, and Gerard Breeman. 2012. In *Morality Politics in Western Europe: Parties, Agendas and Policy Choices*, edited by Isabelle Engeli, Christoffer Green-Pedersen, and Lars Thorup Larsen, 35–61. Houndmills, Basingstoke, Hampshire: Palgrave Macmillan.

Timmermans, Stefan, and Hyeyoung Oh. 2010. "The Continued Social Transformation of the Medical Profession." *Journal of Health and Social Behavior* 51 (1 suppl): S94–106. doi:10.1177/0022146510383500.

Tresidder, H. J., ed. 1871. "Birmingham Skepticism." *The London Quarterly Review* 36: 310–31.

Tucker, Kathryn L. 2008. "In the Laboratory of the States: The Progress of Glucksberg's Invitation to States to Address End-of-Life Choice." *Michigan Law Review* 106 (June): 1593–1611.

Turner, Frank M. 1978. "The Victorian Conflict between Science and Religion: A Professional Dimension." *Isis* 69 (3): 356–76. doi:10.2307/231040.

United States Bureau of the Census. 1975. *Historical Statistics of the United States, Colonial Times to 1970*. Washington: U.S. Department of Commerce, Bureau of the Census.

Urman, Richard, Wendy Gross, and Beverly Philip. 2011. *Anesthesia Outside of the Operating Room*. New York: Oxford University Press.

Verhagen, Eduard, and Pieter J.J. Sauer. 2005. "The Groningen Protocol — Euthanasia in Severely Ill Newborns." *New England Journal of Medicine* 352 (10): 959–62. doi:10.1056/NEJMp058026.

Vieusseux, André. 1840. *The History of Switzerland: From the Irruption of the Barbarians to the Present Time*. London, UK: Society for the diffusion of useful knowledge.

dr Vries. Ubaldus. 2004. "A Dutch Perspective: The Limits of Lawful Euthanasia." *Annals of Health Law* 13 (2): 365–92.

Wacker, Grant. 2000. *Religion in Nineteenth Century America*. New York: Oxford University Press.

Wald, Patricia. 1997. "Looking Forward to the next Millennium: Social Previews to Legal Change." *Temple Law Review* 70: 1085–1121.

Warren, John Collins. 1848. *Etherization; with Surgical Remarks.* Boston: Ticknor & co.

Washington Secretary of State. 2008, November 26. Initiative Measure 1000 Concerns Allowing Certain Terminally Ill Competent Adults to Obtain Lethal Prescriptions. *Washington Secretary of State—Kim Wyman.* Accessed May 27, 2013. http://vote .wa.gov/results/20081104/Initiative-Measure-1000-concerns-allowing-certain -terminally-ill-competent-adults-to-obtain-lethal-prescriptions.html.

Washington Secretary of State. 2012. *Top 25 Initiatives Based on the Number of Signatures Filed.* Washington Secretary of State. http://www.sos.wa.gov/_assets/ elections/Top-25—-update-10-9-12.pdf.

Washington State Department of Health. 2009. *Instructions for Physicians and Other Medical Certifiers for Death Certificates: Compliance with the Death with Dignity Act.* Washington State Department of Health. http://www.doh.wa.gov/portals/1/ Documents/5300/DWDAMedCertifier.pdf.

Washington State Department of Health. 2011. *2011 Death with Dignity Act Report*, 12. Washington State Department of Health. http://www.doh.wa.gov/portals/1/ Documents/5300/DWDA2011.pdf.

Washington State Department of Health. 2012. *Death Tables by Year—Washington State Dept. of Health.* Accessed May 28, 2013. http://www.doh.wa.gov/DataandStatistical Reports/VitalStatisticsData/DeathData/DeathTablesbyYear.aspx.

Washington State Department of Health. 2013. *Washington State Injury and Violence Prevention Guide*, 35–40. No. DOH 530-090. Washington State Department of Health. http://www.doh.wa.gov/portals/1/Documents/2900/DOH530090Suic.pdf.

Watt, Jeffrey Rodgers. 2004. *From Sin To Insanity: Suicide In Early Modern Europe.* Ithaca: Cornell University Press.

Weiss, E. 1949. "The Psychosomatic Concept in General Medical Practice." *Pennsylvania Medical Journal (1928)* 52 (7): 692–97.

Weissert, William G., and Carol S. Weissert. 2012. *Governing Health: The Politics of Health Policy.* Baltimore: Johns Hopkins University Press.

Wendte, Charles William. 1927. *The Wider Fellowship; Memories, Friendships, and Endeavors for Religious Unity, 1844–1927.* Boston: The Beacon Press, Inc.

Wertenbaker, Lael Tucker. 1957. *Death of a Man.* New York: Random House.

Wertz, Richard W., and Dorothy C. Wertz. 1989. *Lying-in.* New Haven, CT: Yale University Press.

West, John. 2009. *The Last Goodnights: Assisting My Parents with Their Suicides.* Berkeley: Counterpoint.

Weyers, Heleen. 2001. "Euthanasia: The Process of Legal Change in the Netherlands-The Making of the 'Requirements of Careful Practice'." In *Regulating Physician-Negotiated Death*, edited by Albert Klijn, Margaret Otlowski, and M. J. Trappenburg, 11–28. The Hague: Elsevier.

Weyers, Heleen. 2012. "The Legalization of Euthanasia in the Netherlands: Revolutionary Normality." In *Physician-Assisted Death in Perspective: Assessing the Dutch Experience*, edited by Stuart Youngner and Gerrit Kimsma, 34–68. New York: Cambridge University Press.

Williams, Glanville. 1958. *The Sanctity of Life and the Criminal law.* London, UK: Faber.

Williams, Glanville Llewelyn. 1961. *Criminal Law: The General Part.* London: Stevens.

Williams, Samuel D. 2008 [1870]. "Euthanasia." In *Essays by Members of the Birmingham Speculative Club*, edited by Birmingham Speculative Club, 210–37. Charleston: BiblioBazaar, LLC.

Winslow, Forbes. 1895. "Suicide as a Mental Epidemic." *Journal of the American Medical Association* XXV (12): 471–76.

Winter, Alison. 1998. "Mesmerism and the Introduction of Surgical Anesthesia to Victorian England." *Engineering and Science* 61 (2): 30–37.

Winter, Alison. 2000. *Mesmerized: Powers of Mind in Victorian Britain*. Chicago: University of Chicago Press.

Wolf, Jacqueline H. 2009. *Deliver Me from Pain: Anesthesia and Birth in America*. Baltimore: Johns Hopkins University Press.

Wood, William R., and John B. Williamson. 2003. "Historical Changes in the Meaning of Death in the Western Tradition." In *Handbook of Death and Dying*, edited by Clifton D. Bryant, 14–24. Thousand Oaks: Sage Publishers.

Yandell, D.W., and H.A. Cottell, eds. 1896. *American Practitioner and News: A Bi-Weekly Journal of Medicine and Surgery*. Vol. 21–22. Louisville: American Practitioner and News Pub. Co.

Youngner, Stuart J., Robert M. Arnold, and Renie Schapiro. 2002. *The Definition of Death: Contemporary Controversies*. Baltimore: The Johns Hopkins University Press.

Ysebaert, D., G. Van Beeumen, K. De Greef, J.P. Squifflet, O. Detry, A. De Roover, M.-H. Delbouille, et al. 2009. "Organ Procurement after Euthanasia: Belgian Experience." *Transplantation Proceedings* 41 (2): 585–86. doi:10.1016/j.transproceed.2008.12.025.

Zelizer, Viviana A. 1978. "Human Values and the Market: The Case of Life Insurance and Death in 19th-Century America." *American Journal of Sociology* 84 (3): 591–610. doi:10.2307/2778256.

Ziegler, Stephen J. 2009. "Collaborated Death: An Exploration of the Swiss Model of Assisted Suicide for Its Potential to Enhance Oversight and Demedicalize the Dying Process." *The Journal of Law, Medicine & Ethics* 37 (2): 318–30. doi:10.1111/j.1748-720X.2009.00375.x.

The Zoist. 1851. *A Journal of Cerebral Physiology & Mesmerism and Their Applications to Human Welfare*. Vol. 8. London: Hippolyte Baillière Publisher.

Zola, Irving K. 1972. "Medicine as an Institution of Social Control." *The Sociological Review* 20 (4) (November): 487–504.

## LEGAL CASES, BILLS, BALLOT INITIATIVES, AND OTHER LEGAL DOCUMENTS

*Act of Belgian Parliament on Euthanasia*, Belgium 2002 (Parliament Document no. 50K1488).

*Ballot Measure 16*, Oregon, 1994.

*Ballot Measure 51*, Oregon, Special Election 1997.

*Baxter et al. v. State*, 224 P.3d 1211 (Mont., 2009).

*Baze v. Rees*, 128 S.Ct. 1520 (U.S. Ky., 2008).

Brief of the American Society of Anesthesiologists as Amicus Curiae in Support of Neither Party, *Baze v. Rees*, 128 S.Ct. 1520 (2008). (No. 07-5439), available at http://www.law.berkeley.edu/clinics/dpclinic/LethalInjection/LI/documents/bazebriefs/ASA.pdf.

Brief for Montana Residents with Disabilities and Autonomy, Inc. as Amici Curiae Supporting Plaintiffs, Baxter v. Montana, MT DA 09-0051 (2009) (no. ADV-2007 -787), 2009.

*Carter v. Canada* (2012 BCSC 886).

*Compassion in Dying v. State of Washington*, 850 F. Supp. 1454 (W.D. Wash., 1994).

*Compassion in Dying v. State of Washington*. 850 F. Supp. 1454 (Dist. Court, W.D. Wash., 1994).

*Compassion in Dying v. State of Washington*. 49 F.3d 586 (U.S. Court of Appeals, 9th Circuit, 1995).

*Compassion in Dying v. State of Washington*. 79 F. 3d 790 (Court of Appeals, 9th Circuit, 1996).

*Controlled Substances Act*.

*Cruzan v. Director, Missouri Dept. of Health*, 110 S.Ct. 2841 (U.S. Mo., 1990).

*Death with Dignity Act*, Oregon, 1994/1998.

Dutch Penal Code

*Gonzales v. Oregon*, 126 S.Ct. 904 (U.S., 2006).

*Griswold v. Connecticut*, 85 S.Ct. 1678 (U.S. Conn., 1965).

*Harrison Tax Act*.

*H.B. 145*, Ohio, 1906 (Introduced by Mr. Hunt, by request).

*H.R. 3200, America's Affordable Health Choices Act*, 2009.

*Humane and Dignified Act*, California Ballot Initiative (1986).

*In re Quinlan*, 355 A.2d 647 (N.J., 1976).

*Iowa Code § 707A.2 [1996]*.

*La. Rev. Stat. 14:32.12 [1995]*.

*Lee v. Oregon*, 891 F. Supp. 1439 (D. Or., 1995).

*Md. Ann. Code Art. 27, §416 [1999]*.

*Mich. 1931 PA 328, MCL 750.329a [1998]*.

*Morris v. Brandenberg*, D-202-CV-2012-02909 (N.M. 2d Jud. Dist., Jan. 13, 2014).

*Natural Death Act*, California, Sec. 7186 (1976).

*Nev. Rev. Stat. § 449.670 (2)*.

*Ohio H.B. 145 (1906)*.

Ordre des Medecins. 2014. "*Code de Déontologie Médicale-Index-Ordre Des Médecins-Ordomedic.*" http://ordomedic.be/fr/code/index/E.

*People v. Roberts*, N.W. 178. (Mich., 1920).

*Planned Parenthood of Southeastern PA v. Casey*, 505 U.S. 833 (1992)

*Quill v. Vacco*, 80 F.3d 716 (2nd. Cir. 1996)

*Quill v. Koppell*, 870 F. Supp. 78 (S.D.N.Y., 1994).

*R (Nicklinson) v. Ministry of Justice* EWCA Civ 961 (2013), MHLO 65 (2013).

RCW 70.245, 2008, Washington State.

*Repouille v. U.S.,* 165 F.2 153.

*R.I. Gen. Stat. Tit. 11, ch. 60 [1996]*.

*Roe v. Wade*, 93 S.Ct. 705 (U.S. Tex., 1973).

*S.B. 5596*, Washington.

*S.C. Code Ann. §16-3-1090 [1998]*.

*Schoonheim* (Dutch Supreme Court, 27 November 1984, N.J. 1985, No. 106).

*Sénat de Belgique. 2001. "Document législatif n° 2-244/22." Sénat de Belgique. http://
    www.senate.be/www/webdriver?MIval=/publications/viewPub.html&COLL=S&LEG
    =2&NR=244&VOLGNR=22&LANG=fr.*
Swiss Penal Code, Article 115.
StBG. 1937. http://www.legislationline.org/documents/section/criminal-codes. (Accessed
    January 2015).
*Termination of Life on Request and Assisted Suicide (Review Procedures) Act,*
    Netherlands, 2001.
*Termination of Life on Request and Assisted Suicide Review Procedures Act,* The
    Netherlands, 2002 (26 691, no. 137 of the 2000-2001 Parliamentary Session).
*Turner v. State, 108 S. W. 1139 (1908).*
*Utah Code § 75-2a-122 (2).*
*Va. Code Ann., § 18.2-76.3, 18.2-76.4 [1998].*
*Vacco v. Quill,* 117 S.Ct. 2293 (U.S. N.Y., 1997).
*Washington Initiative 119* (1991).
*Washington Initiative 1000* (2008).
*Washington v. Glucksberg,* 117 S.Ct. 2258 (U.S. Wash., 1997).
Zaremski, Miles J. 2008. American College of Legal Medicine Policy on Aid in Dying:
    Resolution Approved by the Executive Committee and the Board of Governors.
    ACLM. http://www.aclm.org/resources/amicus_briefs/.

## NEWSPAPERS AND OTHER MEDIA ARTICLES

The Advertiser. 1925. "The Problem of the Inevitable." *The Advertiser,* February 20, 13.
American Medical Association. 2008, October 27. "Polls Show Washington Voters Favor
    Physician-Assisted Suicide - amednews.com." *American Medical News.* http://
    www.amednews.com/article/20081027/profession/310279971/6/.
Associated Press. 1908. "Takes Three Kinds of Poison to End Life." *Los Angeles Herald,*
    January 1.
Associated Press. 1937. "Mercy Death Measure Proposed in Nebraska." *The Reading
    Eagle,* February 2.
Associated Press. 1950. "Carol Paight's Thoughts Turn to Romance." *Lewiston Evening
    Journal,* February 8.
Associated Press. 1958. "Court Frees Mercy-Killing Chicago Man." *Freeport Journal-
    Standard,* December 31.
Associated Press. 1991. "Grand Jury To Consider Case of Doctor-Assisted Suicide."
    *Associated Press Archive,* June 17.
Associated Press. 2008. "Luxembourg Strips Monarch of Legislative Role." *The Guard-
    ian,* December 11, World news. http://www.theguardian.com/world/2008/dec/12/
    luxembourg-monarchy.
Ball, Deborah, and Julia Mengewein. 2010. "Assisted-Suicide Pioneer Stirs a Legal Back-
    lash." *Wall Street Journal,* February 6, Business. http://online.wsj.com/articles/
    SB10001424052748703414504575001363599545120.
Bergner, Daniel. 2007. "Death in the Family." *New York Times,* December 2. http://www
    .nytimes.com/2007/12/02/magazine/02suicide-t.html?pagewanted=6&_r=1.

The Berkshire Evening Eagle. 1950. "Pulpit Battle Goes on over Mercy Killing." *The Berkshire Evening Eagle*, January 9.

The Berkshire Evening Eagle. 1950. "Jurors' Remarks on Mercy-Killing, Religion Released by Judge as Sander Panel Is Filled." *The Berkshire Evening Eagle*, February 23.

Blair, William M. 1958. "Humane Appeals Swamp Congress." *New York Times*, May 4.

The Brookshire Times. 1949. "Mercy Billing: Has Advocates." *The Brookshire Times*, January 28.

Bruni, Frank. 1996. "Court Overturns Ban in New York on Aided Suicides; U.S. Court Clears Way for Doctors in New York to Aid in Some Suicides." *The New York Times*, April 3, N.Y. / Region. http://www.nytimes.com/1996/04/03/nyregion/court-overturns-ban-new-york-aided-suicides-us-court-clears-way-for-doctors-new.html.

Carman, Diane. 2012. "Assisted Suicide: New Mexico Court Asked to Redefine the Term." *The Denver Post Online*, August 19. http://www.denverpost.com/opinion/ci_21331135/court-asked-redefine-term-assisted-suicide.

The Citizen. (Honesdale, Pa.) 1908–1914, September 22, 1911, Image 6. (1911, September 22), 6.

Cliness, Francis. Special to The New York Times. 1986. "Dutch Are Quietly Taking the Lead in Euthanasia." *New York Times*, October 31.

Cloud, John. 2001. "A License to Kill? Critics Say a Dutch Euthanasia Law Goes Too Far." *Time Magazine*, April 22.

CNN.com - Dutch Minister Favours Suicide Pill - April 14, 2001." 2014. Accessed February 27. http://edition.cnn.com/2001/WORLD/europe/04/14/netherlands.suicide/.

CNN. 2008. Local Exit Polls - Election Center 2008 - Elections & Politics from CNN.com. Accessed May 28, 2013. http://www.cnn.com/ELECTION/2008/results/polls/#val=WAI01p1.

Davies, Stanley. 1925, May 31. Scientists have new plan for dealing with morons: segregation and sterilization found ineffective, experts hope to train feeble-minded for useful lives — Discoveries at Letchford, XX7. New York, NY.

Davis, Chester. 1950. "'Mercy Doctor': Euthanasia Colors Murder Case against Idealist Physician; Won't Be Defense." *Indiana Evening Gazette*, February 7.

Doward, Jamie. 2009. " 'Dr Death' Sells Euthanasia Kits in UK for £35." *The Observer*, March 29. http://www.guardian.co.uk/society/2009/mar/29/assisted-suicide-doctor-philip-nitschke.

Editorial Article 3. 1897. No Title. *New York Times*, July 15.

Ertelt, Steven. 2008a. "Spokesman's Son, Disability Groups Oppose Washington Assisted Suicide Prop." *Lifenews.com*, June 16. Accessed May 27, 2013. http://archive.lifenews.com/bio2484.html.

Ertelt, Steven. 2008b. "Washington Poll Finds Strong Support for Assisted Suicide Ballot Proposal." *Lifenews.com*, August 15. Accessed May 27, 2013. http://archive.lifenews.com/bio2549.html.

Ertelt, Steven. 2013. "Montana Defeats Bill to Protect People from Assisted Suicide | LifeNews.com." *Lifenews.com*, April 15. Accessed May 27, 2013. http://www.lifenews.com/2013/04/15/montana-defeats-bill-to-protect-people-from-assisted-suicide/.

The Evening World. (New York, NY) 1887–1931, September 23, 1911, Night Edition, Image 1. (1911, September 23). http://chroniclingamerica.loc.gov/lccn/sn8303 0193/1911-09-23/ed-1/seq-1/#date1=1911&index=0&rows=20&words=Barnes +chloroformed+Earl&searchType=basic&sequence=0&state=&date2=1911&prox text=earl%2Bbarnes%2Bchloroform&y=8&x=15&dateFilterType=yearRange &page=1.

Exit Association pour le Droit de Mourir dans la Dignite' Suisse Romande. 2008. "Luxembourg Parliament Backs Legalising Euthanasia." December 19.

Exit Association pour le Droit de Mourir dans la Dignite' Suisse Romande. 2008. "Luxembourg Parliament Backs Legalising Euthanasia." December 19.

Falconer, Bruce. 2010. "Death Becomes Him." *The Atlantic*, March. http://www .theatlantic.com/magazine/archive/2010/03/death-becomes-him/307916/?single _page=true.

Farber, Daniel. 2009. "Palin Weighs In on Health Care Reform." *Political Hotsheet*, August 8. http://www.cbsnews.com/8301-503544_162-5226795-503544.html.

Frankham, Jonquil. 2008. "Health Care Providers in Washington State Refuse to Perform Assisted Suicide | LifeSiteNews.com." *LifeSiteNews*. November 7. http://www .lifesitenews.com/news/archive/ldn/2008/nov/08110707.

France, David. 1997. "This Doctor Wants to Help You Die." *New York Magazine*, January 13.

The Globe and Mail. 2014. "Belgian Rapist's Plea for Euthanasia Stirs Debates on Mental Health and Right to Die." *The Globe and Mail*. January 1. http://www.theglobe andmail.com/news/world/belgian-rapists-plea-for-euthanasia-stirs-debates-on -mental-health-and-right-to-die/article16157723/.

Gonzaga University. 2011. "Honor Roll 2010–2011." *Gonzaga-The Magazine of Gonzaga University*, November 17. http://issuu.com/gonzaga/docs/gmag-honor-roll-2011/1.

Gross, Jane. 1997. "Quiet Doctor Finds a Mission in Assisted Suicide Court Case." *The New York Times*, January 2. N.Y. / Region. http://www.nytimes.com/1997/01/02/ nyregion/quiet-doctor-finds-a-mission-in-assisted-suicide-court-case.html.

Hamilton, Chloe. 2013. "Hafner, Katie. 2012. "In Ill Doctor, a Surprise Reflection of Who Picks Assisted Suicide." The New York Times, August 11, sec. Health/Money & Policy. http://www.nytimes.com/2012/08/12/health/policy/in-ill-doctor-a-surprise-reflection-of-who-picks-assisted-suicide.html.

Hilton, Bruce. 1987. "As Funds For Elderly Dry Up, Mercy Killing Rises." *San Francisco Examiner*, January 25.

Holt, Jim. 2005. "Euthanasia for Babies?" *The New York Times*, July 10. *Magazine*. http:// www.nytimes.com/2005/07/10/magazine/10WWLN.html.

The Iola Register. 1885. "Painless Death: The Practice of Euthanasia Discussed by Physicians." *The Iola Register*, October 9.

Jenkins, Austin. 2008. "Unlike Father, Unlike Son: The Gardners Are Split on 'Death with Dignity.'" *Crosscut.com*, January 11. Accessed May 27, 2013. http://crosscut.com/ 2008/01/11/elections/10636/Unlike-father-unlike-son-The-Gardners-are-split-on/.

Jolly, David. 2012. "Push for the Right to Die Grows in the Netherlands." *The New York Times*, April 2, Health. http://www.nytimes.com/2012/04/03/health/push-for-the -right-to-die-grows-in-the-netherlands.html.

Kentucky Irish American. 1906. "Would Legalize Murder." *Kentucky Irish American*, January 27.

The Keowee Courier. 1879. "Euthanasia." *The Keowee Courier*, April 17.

Kissimmee Valley Gazette. 1911. "Conscious of No Crime." *Ocala Evening Star*, September 4. http://ufdc.ufl.edu/UF00075908/04266/1x?vo=31&vp=0,140.

Kupfer, David. 2003. "Martin Sheen Interview." *The Progressive*. July. http://www.progressive.org/mag_intvsheen.

Kurtzleben, Danielle. 2011. "Baby Boomer Retirements Bring Challenges to Cities and Localities." June 14. Accessed February 25, 2013. http://www.usnews.com/news/best-cities/articles/2011/06/14/baby-boomer-retirement-bring-challenges-to-cities-and-localities—the-challenge-of-baby-boomer-retirement.

La Derniere Heure. 2013. "Les Belges Acceptent L'euthanasie Des Enfants." *DH.be*. October 2. http://www.dhnet.be/actu/sante/les-belges-acceptent-l-euthanasie-des-enfants-524b93823570bed7dba298ff.

L'Impartial. 1972. "Euthanasie: Un Acquittement." *L'Impartial*, January 15.

Los Angeles Herald. 1906. "Euthanasia." *Los Angeles Herald*, January 14.

Los Angeles Times. 1988. "AMA Rebuffs Grand Jury in Mercy Killing Admission." *Los Angeles Times*, February 17.

Maguire, Daniel C. 1974. "Death, Legal and Illegal - 74.02." *The Atlantic Monthly— Online*, February. Magazine. Accessed April 1, 2011. http://www.theatlantic.com/past/politics/abortion/mag.htm.

The Marion Daily Mirror. 1911. "Opinions of Governors Concerning the Two Florida Quakers Charged with Murder Differ Widely." *The Marion Daily Mirror*, September 14.

The Mathews Journal. (Mathews C.H. [Court House]) 1903–1937, September 21, 1911, Image 7. 1911, September 21. http://chroniclingamerica.loc.gov/lccn/sn95067647/1911-09-21/ed-1/seq-7/#date1=1911&index=0&rows=20&words=HER+KILL+PRAYED+WOULD&searchType=basic&sequence=0&state=&date2=1911&proxtext=%22prayed+that+they+would+kill+her%22&y=6&x=25&dateFilterType=yearRange&page=1.

Miller, Nora. 2005. "USATODAY.com - My Husband Died with Dignity." *USA Today*, October 3. Editorial/Opinion. http://usatoday30.usatoday.com/news/opinion/editorials/2005-10-03-death-with-dignity-edit_x.htm.

The New York Times. 1893. "Mrs. Tyndall's Fatal Error; She Tells How She Gave Prof. Tyndall the Chloral Dose." *The New York Times*, December 25.

The New York Times. 1895. "Suicide To End Misery: Favored By Gustave Boehm Before The Medico-Legal Congress. Right Of Doctors To Kill Patients Some Lawyers Hold That The Physicians Should Take Life To Relieve Hopeless Cases. Hypnotism And Crime Also Discussed Dr. Forbes Winslow's View On Self-Destruction Considered As A Mental Epidemic.," *The New York Times*, September 6.

The New York Times. 1910. "Warns Catholics Of Christian Science: Archbishop O'Connell of Boston Calls 100 Physicians Into Conference Against the Cult." *New York Times*, May 15.

The New York Times. 1911. "Shakers Justify Killing Sister: Did Right, Say Man and Woman of Florida Colony Held on Murder Charge. Dead Woman Consumptive Gave Her Chloroform at Her Request to End Her Sufferings, They Assert — Their Deed Defended." *New York Times*, September 14..

The New York Times. 1911. "Tells of Killing Invalid: Consumptive, Woman Shaker Says, Had Entreated Her Aid." *New York Times*, September 16..

The New York Times. 1911. "Shakers Acted Openly: Use of Chloroform to Put Sister Out of Pain Approved by Colony." *New York Times*, September 17..

The New York Times. 1911. "Hold Shaker Elder for 'Sister's' Death: Jury Finds Gillette Committed Murder When He Chloroformed Sadie Marchant. In Jail without Bail Elizabeth Sears, Also Accused of 'Assisting Sister Sadie Out of Life,' Under $2,000 Bail." *New York Times*, September 21. New York, NY, United States.

The New York Times. 1913. "Mayor Hunt's Achievements." *New York Times*, September 24.

The New York Times. 1924. "Woman Gives $20,000 to the Smithsonian: Original Will, at Institution, May Be Needed to Ascertain Miss Anna Hall's Wishes." *New York Times*, December 24.

The New York Times. 1946. "Noxon's Sentence Commuted to Life: Governor Says Special Circumstances Warranted Mercy for Convicted Child Slayer." *New York Times*, August 8.

The New York Times. 1946. "Anesthesia's Centenary." *New York Times*, October 16.

The New York Times. 1949. "Stamford Lenient In Cancer Killing: City's Leaders Analyze Case of Young Daughter Who Shot Doomed Police Sergeant." *New York Times*, September 26.

The New York Times. 1949. "Service in Stamford for Slain Policeman." *New York Times*, September 27.

The New York Times. 1949. "Mercy Killer' Sent to Bridgeport Jail." *New York Times*, October 2.

The New York Times. 1949. "Mercy Killing' Inquest: Daughter Attends Hearing in Case of Stamford Police Sergeant." *New York Times*, October 12.

The New York Times. 1950. "'Mercy' Case Doctor Returns to Practice." *New York Times*, January 1.

The New York Times. 1950. "Neighbors Uphold Doctor On 'Mercy': 90 % of Them Sign Petition to Aid Dr. Sanders as 2 Pastors Also Give Him Their Support." *New York Times*, January 2.

The New York Times. 1950. "Group Will Seek Mercy-Death Law: Euthanasia Society Will Ask New Hampshire Act Over Dr. Sander Murder Case Petitions for Doctor Cited Case Called Help to Cause." *New York Times*, January 3.

The New York Times. 1950. "Sander Is Indicted in 'Mercy Killing'." *New York Times*, January 4.

The New York Times. 1950. "Doctor Indicted in Woman's 'Mercy' Slaying Threatened With Loss of License to Practice." *New York Times*, January 5.

The New York Times.1950. "Innocence Is Plea of 'Mercy' Doctor." *New York Times*, January 6.

The New York Times. 1950. "Mercy or Murder?" *New York Times*, January 8, 128.

The New York Times. 1950. "New England Sifts 'Mercy' Pros, Cons: Euthanasia Head Tells Boston Forum the Law Lags, While Preachers Differ on Sander Calls Euthanasia Widespread." *New York Times*, January 9.

The New York Times. 1950. "'Mercy Killing' Trial Is Scheduled Feb. 20." *New York Times*, January 12.

The New York Times. 1950. "Physician Enables Incurables to Die: Provides Patients with Drug, Warning it is Lethal, He tells Euthanasia Meeting Practice Common, He Says Society, Backing Dr. Sander, Plans Big Rally- 'Another Scopes Case' Predicted Sander Visit Described A 'Scopes Trial' Predicted." *New York Times*, January 18.

The New York Times. 1950. "Girl Mercy Slayer to Plead Insanity: Plan of Defense Outlined as Trial of Miss Paight Opens in Bridgeport Court Mother, Brother in Court First Juror Is Chosen." *New York Times*, January 25.

The New York Times. 1950. "11 Jurors Picked In 'Mercy' Killing: Trial of Connecticut College Girl for Father's Murder May Start Today." *New York Times*, January 26.

The New York Times. 1950. "Miss Paight 'Calm' after Shooting: But Was 'Hysterically Crying' Later, Jury is Told as Trial in 'Mercy' Killing Opens on Duty in Chart Room Physician on Stand Found Her Staring." *New York Times*, January 27.

The New York Times. 1950. "Girl Held Not Sane at Time of Killing: Dead Man's Doctor Testifies for Miss Paight—Told Her Father Would Die Soon Say's She Was Hysterical Deviation From Normal." *New York Times*, January 28.

The New York Times. 1950. "Mrs. Paight Tells of Mercy Killing: Says Daughter Was Not Sane in Slaying Her Ill Father, Whom She Adored Cancer Only Family Trouble Shook Shrieking Daughter Says Girl Was Not Sane." *New York Times*, February 1.

The New York Times. 1950. "Psychiatrist Finds Miss Paight Insane: Dr. C. E. Moore Testifies She Had No Recollection of Shooting Her Father." *New York Times*, February 2, 22.

The New York Times. 1950. "Miss Paight Denies Memory of Killing: College Girl Breaks Down on Stand during Questioning in Mercy Death Trial." *New York Times*, February 3.

The New York Times. 1950. "Testimony Ended in "Mercy" Killing: Psychiatrist Says Miss Paight Was Sane—Jury May Get Case Late Tuesday Examined Her 5 Times Refers to Girl's Actions." *New York Times*, February 4.

The New York Times. 1950. "Carol Paight Acquitted as Insane at Time She Killed Ailing Father: Carol Paight Acquitted as Insane at Time She Killed Ailing Father Temporary Insanity Accepted Presentation of Verdict Judge Discusses 'Mercy.' " *New York Times*, February 8.

The New York Times. 1950. "Not Guilty." *New York Times*, February 12.

The New York Times. 1950. "Mercy Death Trial Begins Tomorrow: Names of Prospective Jurors Kept Secret." *New York Times*, February 19.

The New York Times. 1950. "First Nine Jurors, All Men, Chosen: Mercy Doctor Arriving For Trail In New Hampshire." *New York Times*, February 21.

The New York Times. 1950. "State Not to Ask Death for Sander: Juror Excused." *New York Times*, February 22.

The New York Times. 1950. "Sander Jury Visits the Scene of Death: Jury Selected for the Sander 'Mercy Killing' Trial in Manchester." *New York Times*, February 23.

The New York Times. 1950. "Sheriff Testifies Sander Told Him He Took Life 'in a Weak Moment'." *New York Times*, February 24.

The New York Times. 1950. "Sander Aide Backs State's Death Case: Librarian Confirms Testimony That 'Mercy Killer' Knew He Violated Law." *New York Times*, February 25.

The New York Times. 1950. "4th Witness Heard Against Dr. Sander: Medical Library Aide Says Defendant Admitted His Air Injections Killed Patient" *New York Times*, March 1

The New York Times. 1950. "Sander Hints Plea of 'Somatic Death'" *New York Times*, March 2.

The New York Times. 1950. "Defense Opens Case, Says Sander Will Testify Air Followed Death." *New York Times*, March 3.

The New York Times. 1950. "$6,000 Is Donated To Sander Defense: Author Says 700 Contributions for 'Mercy Death' Physician Have Been Received One of Many Friends." *New York Times*, March 5.

The New York Times. 1950a. "Dr. Sander Denies He Killed Patient; Says Mind Snapped" *New York Times*, March 7.

The New York Times. 1950b. "Textual Excerpts From Testimony of Dr. Sander at His Trial." *New York Times*, March 7.

The New York Times. 1950. "Church Hospitals Exclude Sander: Two Catholic Institutions Bar 'Mercy Case' Doctor—Charge Filed in Medical Society." *New York Times*, March 21.

The New York Times. 1950. "Brother Convicted In "Mercy" Killing: Pennsylvania Jury Rules Out Insanity Plea in Cancer Case —Manslaughter Is Verdict State Contention Upheld Crime Is Called 'Planned' New Meeting on Sander Due It's Cherry Blossom Time In Nation's Capital." *New York Times*, April 8.

The New York Times. 1950. "Sander Is Stripped Of Medical License." *New York Times*, April 20.

The New York Times. 1950. "Medical Group Deals New Blow to Sander." *New York Times*, April 21.The New York Times. "Dr. Sander Expects to Resume In June: His Lawyer Says Revocation of License is Considered a 2-Month 'Suspension.'" *New York Times*, April 26.

The New York Times. 1950. "Carol Ann Paight Married." *New York Times*, September 18.

The New York Times. 1984. "Dutch Court Acts on 'Right To Die': Justices Order Appellate Panel to Reweigh Decision to try Physician as a Criminal." *New York Times*, November 28.

The New York Times. 1991. "Doctor Says He Gave Patient Drug to Help Her Commit Suicide," March 7.

The New York Times. 1992. "David Goldstein: Lawyer, 93." *New York Times*, February 29, 30.

The New York Times. 1993. "There's No Simple Suicide." *New York Times*, November 14. Accessed May 27, 2013. http://www.nytimes.com/1993/11/14/magazine/there-s-no-simple-suicide.html?pagewanted=all&src=pm.

The New York Times. 1994. "AIDS Patients Seek Solace in Suicide But Many Risk Added Pain in Failure." *The New York Times*, June 14. http://www.nytimes.com/1994/06/14/science/aids-patients-seek-solace-in-suicide-but-many-risk-added-pain-in-failure.html?pagewanted=all&src=pm.

The New York Times. 1999. "Statement From Judge to Kevorkian," April 14, U.S. http://www.nytimes.com/1999/04/14/us/statement-from-judge-to-kevorkian.html.

The New York Times. 2012. "In Ill Doctor, a Surprise Reflection of Who Picks Assisted Suicide." *New York Times*, August 11. http://www.nytimes.com/2012/08/12/health/policy/in-ill-doctor-a-surprise-reflection-of-who-picks-assisted-suicide.html.

Nuland, Sherwin. 2004. "Appreciation: Dr. Elisabeth Kubler-Ross." *Time Magazine*, September 6. http://www.time.com/time/magazine/article/0,9171,995057,00.html.

Ostrom, Carol M. 1994a. "Facing Death, Three Challenge State Ban On Assisted Suicides." *The Seattle Times*, January 25.

Ostrom, Carol M. 1994b. "Right-To-Suicide Group Files New York Lawsuit." *The Seattle Times*, July 22.

Philadelphia Press. 1905. "Kill the Suffering Urge Women of the Humane Society." *Philadelphia Press*, October 12.

Porter, Russell, Special to the New York Times. 1950. "Mercy Death Trial Begins Tomorrow: Names of Prospective Jurors kept Secret—Dr. Sanders Faces Prison, Hanging Faces Life Imprisonment Two-Thirds of City Catholic Jury to be Locked Up Cancer Listed as Death Cause Lethal Injection Doubted." *New York Times*, February 19.

Posthumus, Niels. 2012. "Rick Santorum Denkt Nederland Te Kennen: Grootschalige Bejaardenmoord." *Nrc.nl*. February 18. http://www.nrc.nl/nieuws/2012/02/18/rick-santorum-gedwongen-euthanasie-in-nederland/.

The Racine Journal -Times. 1935. "Doctors Question 'Confession' of New England 'Mercy Death.'" *The Racine Journal -Times*, November 20.

Reuters. 2005. "Swiss Nurse Is Sentenced for 22 Murders." *The New York Times*, January 29, International / Europe. http://www.nytimes.com/2005/01/29/international/europe/29swiss.html.

Reuters. 1952. "'Mercy'-Killing Doctor Has Bigger Practice." *New York Times*, March 13. http://search.proquest.com/docview/112529376/abstract/141D17EED6114D61746/3?accountid=14166.

Roberts, Annabel. 2013. "Faced with Blindness, Deaf Twins Choose Euthanasia." *NBC News*, January 14. Accessed May 28, 2013. http://worldnews.nbcnews.com/_news/2013/01/14/16507519-faced-with-blindness-deaf-twins-choose-euthanasia.

Robison, Jim. 1993. "Shakers Planted Colony, Pineapples Here." *Orlando Sentinel*, May 30. http://articles.orlandosentinel.com/1993-05-30/news/9305290789_1_flagler-pineapples-shakers.

Rosenbaum, Ron. 1991. "Angel of Death: The Trial of the Suicide Doctor." *Vanity Fair*, May 1. http://www.vanityfair.com/magazine/archive/1991/05/jack-kevorkian199105.

Roth, Edwin. 1962. "Cheers, Tears Support Thal Trial Acquittal Verdict." *The Miami News*, November 15.

Royce, Caroline H. 1906. "Evil of Euthanasia Talk: Its Effect Very Bad on Many Who Are Ill, Old, or Friendless." *New York Times*, March 12.

The San Francisco Call. 1896. "Whether 'Tis Nobler in the Mind to Suffer the Slings and Arrows of Outrageous Fortune, or to Take Arms against a Sea of Trouble." *The San Francisco Call*, August 2.

The San Francisco Call. 1906. "Prolonging Life." *The San Francisco Call*, January 14.The Seattle Times. 1990. "Initiative Campaigns Gaining Momentum." *The Seattle Times*, October 14. http://community.seattletimes.nwsource.com/archive/?date=19901014&slug=1098171.

The Seattle Times. 1991. "Gardner Wants Abortion, Aid-In-Dying Votes." *The Seattle Times*, January 23. http://community.seattletimes.nwsource.com/archive/?date=19910123&slug=1262181.

The Seattle Times. 1991. "Small Donations Push Death-With-Dignity Initiative Near Record." *The Seattle Times*, July 18. http://community.seattletimes.nwsource.com/archive/?date=19910718&slug=1295070.

The Seattle Times. 1994. "Rothstein's Ruling Too Late to End Suffering Of 'Jane Roe'," May 4.

The Seattle Times. 1995. "Assisted-Suicide Bill is Offered in State Senate." *The Seattle Times*, January 25. http://community.seattletimes.nwsource.com/archive/?date=19950125&slug=2101323.

The Seattle Times. 1995. "Thibaudeau Bests Anderson's Choice for His Seat — State Senate." *The Seattle Times*, September 20. http://community.seattletimes. nwsource.com/archive/?date=19950920&slug=2142628.

The Seattle Times. 1998. "More Disclosure Sought in Oregon Assisted Suicides." *The Seattle Times*, March 30. http://community.seattletimes.nwsource.com/archive/? date=19980330&slug=2742499.

The Seattle Times. 1996. "State Will Ask Supreme Court to Rule on Assisted-Suicide Law." *The Seattle Times*, March 25.

The Seattle Times. 2006. Doctor-Aided Suicide Backed. *The Seattle Times*, January 27. http://community.seattletimes.nwsource.com/archive/? date=20060127&slug=suicide27m.

The Seattle Times. 2008. "Doctors Divided on Assisted Suicide." *The Seattle Times*, September 22. http://seattletimes.com/html/localnews/2008194843_death22m.html.

The Singapore Free Press. 1925. "Sister Killed by Request." *The Singapore Free Press and Mercantile Adviser*, March 25, 14.

Sheldon, Lurana W. 1906a. "Euthanasia: Another Argument in Favor of Quick Death of Hopeless Sufferers." *New York Times*, February 9.

Sheldon, Lurana W. 1906b. "Euthanasia: Lurana W. Sheldon Replies to the Critics of Her Views." *New York Times*, February 18.

Silver, Roy. Special The NewYork Times. 1974. "Jury is Told Doctor Acquitted Killing." *New York Times,* January 26.

Silver, Roy. Special the *NewYork Times*. 1974. "Physician Acquitted in Patient's Death: Jury on L.I. Reaches Verdict in Less Than an Hour Physician Acquitted in Death of Patient." *New York Times*, February 6.

The Singapore Free Press. 1925. "Sister Killed by Request." *The Singapore Free Press and Mercantile Adviser*, March 25.

Skoloff, Brian. 2013. "George Sanders, Arizona Man, Gets Probation in Mercy Killing." *Huffington Post*, March 30. Accessed May 18, 2013. http://www.huffingtonpost.com/2013/ 03/30/george-sanders-probation_n_2983996.html.Spiegel Online International. 2008. "Euthanasia Controversy: Grand Duke of Luxembourg Will Lose his Veto." *Spiegel Online*, December 4. http://www.spiegel.de/international/europe/euthanasia -controversy-grand-duke-of-luxembourg-will-lose-his-veto-a-594398.html.

Simon, Bob. 1974. *CBS Evening News with Walter Cronkite*. CBS.

The Spokane Press. 1906. "Bill to Legally Kill Incurables in Iowa," March 17.

The Sun. 1885. "Making Death Painless." *The Sun*, August 23, sec. Page 3.

Sturcke, James. 2009. "Multiple Sclerosis Patient Takes Assisted Suicide Case to House of Lords." *The Guardian*, June 2. http://www.guardian.co.uk/society/2009/jun/02/ assisted-suicide-debbie-purdy-lords.

S. W. I. 2009. "Agreement to Regulate Assisted Suicide." *SWI Swissinfo.ch*. July 10. http://www.swissinfo.ch/eng/agreement-to-regulate-assisted-suicide/7502620.

The Syracuse Journal. 1938. "Mother Poisons Girl, 9, Then Attempts Suicide." *The Syracuse Journal*, January 18.

Tinckom-Fernandez, W. G. 1925. "Euthanasia Doctrine Still has Advocates: Four Recent Cases Revive Discussion of Ancient Practice of Putting Incurables to Death." *New York Times*, March 22.

Time Magazine. 1929. "France: Euthanasia." *Time*, November 18. http://www.time.com/ time/subscriber/article/0,33009,738052,00.html.

Time Magazine. 1935. "Medicine: The Right to Kill." *Time*, November 18.

Time Magazine. 1935. "Medicine: The Right to Kill (Cont'd)." *Time*, December 2. http://content.time.com/time/magazine/article/0,9171,848263,00.html.

Time Magazine. 1950. "New Hampshire: The Law of God." *Time*, January 16. http://content.time.com/time/magazine/article/0,9171,811719,00.html.

Time Magazine. 1950. "Connecticut: For Love or Pity." *Time*, February 6. http://content.time.com/time/magazine/article/0,9171,811801,00.html.

Time Magazine. 1950. "Trials: Similar To. . .murder." *Time*, March 6.

Time Magazine. 1950. "The Press: Not Since Scopes?" *Time*, March 13. http://content.time.com/time/magazine/article/0,9171,812151,00.html.

Time Magazine. 1950. "New Hampshire: Not Guilty." *Time*, March 20. http://content.time.com/time/magazine/article/0,9171,858718,00.html.

Time Magazine. 1962. "Medicine: Thalidomide Homicide." *Time*, November 16. http://content.time.com/time/magazine/article/0,9171,829419,00.html.

Time Magazine. 1973. "The Law: Implications of Mercy." *Time*, March 5. http://content.time.com/time/subscriber/article/0,33009,903906,00.html.

The Times Dispatch. 1911. "Held for Wilful [*sic.*] Murder." *The Times Dispatch*, September 21. http://chroniclingamerica.loc.gov/lccn/sn85038615/1911-09-21/ed-1/seq-1/#date1=1911&index=4&rows=20&words=MURDER+Shaker&searchType=basic&sequence=0&state=&date2=1913&proxtext=shaker+murder&y=11&x=15&dateFilterType=yearRange&page=1.

Tomlinson, Augustus. 1906. "Euthanasia in Practice: Sad Failure of a Sincere Effort to Relieve a Believer's Pain.," January 29.

"Topics of the Times." 1906. *New York Times*, February 3.

Tracy, G.S. 1906. "Is it Ever Right to Speed the Departing Sick?" *New-York Daily Tribune*, January 21.

New-York Daily Tribune. 1906. "Is it Ever Right to Speed the Departing Sick?" *New-York Daily Tribune*, January 21.

New-York Daily Tribune. 1906. "Compulsory Killing." *New-York Daily Tribune*, March 11.Turner, Joe. 2008. "Dan Evans and Ralph Munro Are Co-chairs of Republicans for I-1000, Support "Death with Dignity" - Political Buzz." *Tacoma News Tribune*, September 10. Accessed May 28, 2013. http://blog.thenewstribune.com/politics/2008/09/10/dan-evans-and-ralph-munro-are-co-chairs-of-republicans-for-i-1000-support-death-with-dignity/.

United Press. 1937. "Youth Killed by His Father to Save Him from Illness Was Making Good Recovery." *Montana Butte Standard*, July 24.

United Press. 1938. "Mercy Killer Asks Leave to Go to Funeral." *The Milwaukee Journal*, October 3, sec. PAGE 1.

United Press. 1939. "Loved the Imbecile Son They Killed." *The Wisconsin State Journal*, May 10.

United Press. 1950. "College to Help Carol Graduate." *The Day*, February 8.

United Press. 1950. "Delivers Next Babies, Mothers Pray Sander." *Brooklyn Daily Eagle*, February 23.

United Press. 1950. "Acquitted in Mercy Death." *The Pittsburg Press*, May 23.

United Press. 1952. "U.N. Asked to Sanction Mercy Deaths." *The Berkshire Eagle*, March 26.

United Press. 1953. "Father Slays Daughter in 'Mercy Death.'" *Prescott Evening Courier*, September 7.

UPI. 1958. "Husband Freed in Mercy Death of Ailing Wife." *The Deseret News & Telegram*, December 31.

UPI. 1962. "Mercy-Killer, Four Others Cleared as Court Crowd Roars Approval." *Rome News-Tribune*, November 11.

The Washington Times. (Washington [D.C.]) 1902–1939, September 13, 1911, Last Edition, Image 4. 1911, September 13, 4.

The Washington times. (Washington [D.C.]) 1902–1939, December 02, 1911, Final Edition, Image 14. 1911, December 2, 14.

Wlach, Jennifer. 2002. "Med School in History: The 1980s | The Chronicle." *Duke University, The Chronicle*. February 21. http://m.dukechronicle.com/articles/2002/02/21/med-school-history-1980s.

World Right to Die News. 2008. "[Right_to_die] Luxemburg to Try Again to Pass Euthanasia Law." *The World Federation of Right to Die Societies*, February 15. http://lists.opn.org/pipermail/right-to-die_lists.opn.org/2008-February/002616.html.

"25 Books That Leave a Legacy." 2007. *USA Today*, April 9. http://www.usatoday.com/life/top25-books.htm.

## OTHER SOURCES

American Academy of Hospice and Palliative Medicine. 2007. *Position Statements: Physician-Assisted Death*. February 14. http://www.aahpm.org/positions/suicide.html.

American Medical Association. n.d. "1921 to 1940." *American Medical Association-Timeline, 1921 to 1940*. http://www.ama-assn.org/ama/pub/about-ama/our-history/timelines-ama-history/1921-1940.page?

American Medical News. 2011. "Health System Reform Expected to Boost House Calls." *American Medical Association-amednews.com*, March 1. Accessed May 20, 2013. http://www.amednews.com/article/20110103/business/301039975/1/.

Ancestry.com. 2005. "Simon, Jacob (Kobus) (1845–1906) Obituary-Simon-Family History & Genealogy Message Board-Ancestry.com." *Ancestry.com*, September 7. Accessed May 29, 2013. http://boards.ancestry.com/surnames.simon/671/mb.

Appel, Jacob M. 2009. "Big Sky Dilemma: Must Doctors Help Their Patients Die?" *Huffington Post*, May 25. http://www.huffingtonpost.com/jacob-m-appel/big-sky-dilemma-must-doct_b_275034.html.

Baklinski,Thaddeus. 2009. "Montana Doctors Refuse to Participate in Assisted Suicide | LifeSiteNews.com." *LifeSiteNews*, April 7. Accessed May 16, 2013. http://www.lifesitenews.com/news/archive/ldn/2009/apr/09040705.

Ballotpedia.org. 2012a. "Washington 'Death with Dignity Act,' Initiative 1000 (2008)." *Ballotpedia*, June 14. Accessed May 29, 2013. http://ballotpedia.org/wiki/index.php/Washington_%22Death_with_Dignity_Act%22,_Initiative_1000_(2008).

Ballotpedia.org. 2012b. "Washington Aid-in-Dying, Initiative 119 (1991)." *Ballotpedia*, June 19. Accessed May 27, 2013. http://ballotpedia.org/wiki/index.php/Washington_Aid-in-Dying,_Initiative_119_%281991%29.

Ballotpedia.org. 2012c, October 22. "Loren Parks." *Ballotpedia*. Accessed May 29, 2013. http://ballotpedia.org/wiki/index.php/Loren_Parks.

Ballotpedia.org. 2013. "Washington 1914 Ballot Measures." *Ballotpedia*, February 9. http://ballotpedia.org/wiki/index.php/Washington_1914_ballot_measures.

Belgian Advisory Committee on Bioethics. 1997. "Opinion No. 1 of May 12, 1997, Concerning the Advisability of a Legal Regulation on Euthanasia." http://www.sante .belgique.be.

Belgian Advisory Committee on Bioethics. 1999. "Opinion No. 9 of 22 February 1999 concerning active termination of the lives of persons incapable of expressing their wishes." http://www.sante.belgique.be.

Carroll, Joseph. 2006. "Public Continues to Support Right-to-Die for Terminally Ill Patients. Opinion Polls." *Gallup*, June 19. http://www.gallup.com/poll/23356/ Public-Continues-Support-RighttoDie-Terminally-Ill-Patients.aspx.

Carroll, Joseph. 2007. *Public Divided over Moral Acceptability of Doctor-Assisted Suicide*. Princeton, NJ: Gallup, Inc. http://www.gallup.com/poll/27727/ public-divided-over-moral-acceptability-doctorassisted-suicide.aspx.

Celestis, Inc. n.d. *Memorial Spaceflights-Launch Ashes into Space-Space Burial-Funerals in Space - Unique Post Cremation Option*. Accessed May 18, 2013. http://www. celestis.com/.

Centeno Carlos, Juan Jose Pons, Thomas Lynch, Oana Donea, Javier Rocafort, and David Clark. 2013. "Atlas of Palliative Care in Europe 2013. Cartographic Edition." *Atlas of Palliative Care in Europe 2013*. http://issuu.com/universidaddenavarra/docs/ atlas_europa_edic_cart.

The Center for Information & Research on Civic Learning and Engagement. 2010. Millennials are on par with boomers in voter turnout. *CIRCLE—Tufts University*. http:// www.civicyouth.org/millennials-are-on-par-with-boomers-in-voter-turnout/.

Centers for Disease Control and Prevention. n.d. "Vital Statistics Online." *Centers for Disease Control and Prevention*. http://www.cdc.gov/nchs/data_access/Vitalstats online.htm.

Centers for Disease Control and Prevention. 2012. "Data Access - Health Data Interactive." Accessed December 30. http://www.cdc.gov/nchs/hdi.htm.

Clark, Brian. 1993. *Whose Life Is It Anyway?* UK: Heinemann.

Clinton, William J. April 30, 1997. "Statement on Signing the Assisted Suicide Funding Restriction Act of 1997," Online by Gerhard Peters and John T. Woolley, *The American Presidency Project*. http://www.presidency.ucsb.edu/ws/? pid=54070.

Compassion and Choices. 2013. "Expanding Choice State by State | Compassion & Choices." *Compassion and Choices—Choice and Care at the End of Life*, January 4. Accessed May 28, 2013. http://www.compassionandchoices.org/2013/01/04/ expanding-choice-state-by-state/.

Compassion and Choices. n.d. "Compassion & Choices Volunteer Opportunities." *Compassion and Choices—Choice and Care at the End of Life*. Accessed May 28, 2013. https://community.compassionandchoices.org/sslpage.aspx?pid=364.

Compassion and Choices of Washington. 2009, Spring. "Mission Accomplished!" *C&C Connection* (10). http://compassionwa.org/wp-content/uploads/2012/09/spr09 -newsletter.pdf.

Compassion and Choices of Washington. 2012, Winter. "Hospital 'Alliances' Threaten Patient Choice." *C&C Connection* (16). http://compassionwa.org/wp-content/ uploads/2012/09/16news.pdf.

Compassion in Dying. n.d. "Connections, Issue 5." *TheBody.com.* http://www.thebody
.com/content/art16645.html.

Compassion in Dying. 1997. "Connections, Special Edition, Issue 8." *TheBody.com*
. http://www.thebody.com/content/art16647.html.

Concern for Dying (Association). Fall 1990. "Concern for Dying Newsletter."

D66. 1984. "D66.nl - Wessel-Tuinstra Dient Initiatiefvoorstel in over Euthanasie." *D66.nl.*
http://site.d66.nl/9359000/1/j9vvi0vj881cqtt/vhdkcdswcz28?ctx=vhddruu7q8tw.

Economic Modeling Specialists International. 2010. "Interactive Map: Maine Has Highest
Concentration of Baby Boomers." *EMSI | Economic Modeling Specialists Intl.*
Accessed May 29, 2013. http://www.economicmodeling.com/2010/09/08/
interactive-map-maine-has-highest-concentration-of-baby-boomers/.

Eurostat-European Commission. 2010. "File:Causes of Death — Standardised Death
Rate, 2010 (per 100 000 Inhabitants) YB14 II.png - Statistics Explained." *Causes
of Death—Standardised Death Rate, 2010 (per 100,000 Inhabitants).* http://epp
.eurostat.ec.europa.eu/statistics_explained/index.php/File:Causes_of_death_%E2
%80%94_standardised_death_rate,_2010_(per_100_000_inhabitants)_YB14_II.png.

Eurotransplant Region | Eurotransplant." 2013. Accessed October 18. http://www
.eurotransplant.org/cms/index.php?page=et_region.

*Euthanasia Educational Fund*, February 13, 1970.

Euthanasia Society of America, Minutes of First Annual Meeting, January 26, 1939

followthemoney.org. n.d. *YES ON I 1000 | Follow the Money.* Accessed May 29, 2013.
http://www.followthemoney.org/database/StateGlance/committee.phtml?c=3263.

Exit Association pour le Droit de Mourir dans la Dignite' Suisse Romande. n.d. "Outline
of the Campaign to Decriminalise Active Euthanasia in Switzerland." http://
www.exit-geneve.ch/.

Exit Association pour le Droit de Mourir dans la Dignite' Suisse Romande - Lëtzebuerg.
2014. "ADMD-L | Association Pour Le Droit de Mourir Dans La Dignite'–Lëtze-
buerg A.s.b.l." March 17. http://web403u1.site.lu/?lang=en.

Gallup, Inc. 2011, May 31. "Doctor-Assisted Suicide Is Moral Issue Dividing Americans
Most." *Gallup Politics.* Accessed May 27, 2013. http://www.gallup.com/poll/
147842/doctor-assisted-suicide-moral-issue-dividing-americans.aspx.

Gallup, Inc. 2012. "Honesty/Ethics in Professions." *Gallup.* November. http://www
.gallup.com/poll/1654/honesty-ethics-professions.aspx#4.

Government of The Netherlands. 2011. "Euthanasia, Assisted Suicide and
Non-Resuscitation on Request - Euthanasia - Government.nl." Issue. September 4.
http://www.government.nl/issues/euthanasia/euthanasia-assisted-suicide-and-non
-resuscitation-on-request.

GovTrack.us. n.d. "Bills and Resolutions—GovTrack.us." *GovTrack.us.* Accessed
May 29, 2013. http://www.govtrack.us/congress/bills/.

Grossman, Howard. 1997. "As I See It." *Haverford College.* Fall. http://www.haverford
.edu/publications/fall97/asiseeit.html.

Gurwitt, Rob. 2012. "Baby Boomers' Impact on Elections." *Governing the States and
Localities*, September. Accessed May 28, 2013. http://www.governing.com/
generations/government-management/gov-baby-boomer-impact-on-elections.html.

Heisel, William. 2009. *Q&A with Cassie Sauer: Hospitals and Washington State's 'Death
with Dignity Act' | Reporting on Health.* Accessed February 28, 2013. http://www

.reportingonhealth.org/blogs/qa-cassie-sauer-washington-state%E2%80%99s-%E2%80%9Cdeath-dignity-act%E2%80%9D-poses-quandary-hospitals.

*Hemlock Quarterly 24*, July 1986.

*Hemlock Quarterly 32*, July 1988.

Hensley, Scott. 2012. "Americans Support Physician-Assisted Suicide for Terminally Ill." *NPR.org*, December 28. Accessed May 27, 2013. http://www.npr.org/blogs/health/2012/12/27/168150886/americans-support-physician-assisted-suicide-for-terminally-ill.

International Task Force. 1996–2009. Assisted Suicide & Death with Dignity: Past, Present & Future - Part I. *InternationalTaskForce.org: Addressing Euthanasia, Assisted Suicide, Advance Directives, Disability Rights, Pain Control and More.* http://www.internationaltaskforce.org/rpt2005_I.htm.

Junge, Daniel. 2009. *The Last Campaign of Governor Booth Gardner.* Documentary, Short.

KNMG. 2012. "KNMG Blijft Kritisch over Levenseindekliniek." *KNMG Blijft Kritisch over Levenseindekliniek.* May 11. http://knmg.artsennet.nl/Nieuws/Nieuwsarchief/Nieuwsbericht/KNMG-blijft-kritisch-over-Levenseindekliniek.htm.

LegalWorld. 2013. "Médecins Rémunérés Pour Donner Un Deuxième Avis En Cas D'euthanasie." April 16. http://www.legalworld.be/legalworld/content.aspx?id=63664&LangType=2060.

Liu, Joseph. 2012. "'Nones' on the Rise." *Pew Research Center's Religion & Public Life Project.* October 9. http://www.pewforum.org/2012/10/09/nones-on-the-rise/.

Marker, Rita. 2008. "Oregon Plus One" Equals Fifty?" *The Human Life Review* (Summer). www.humanlifereview.com/index.php/archives/26-2008-summer/14-qoregon-plus-oneq-equals-fifty.

The Nathaniel Centre for Bioethics. 2009. "Interview with Professor Erny Gillen, Moral Theologian and Bioethicist from Luxembourg." November. http://www.nathaniel.org.nz/component/content/article/16-bioethical-issues/bioethics-at-the-end-of-life/195-interview-with-professor-erny-gillen-moral-theologian-and-bioethicist-from-luxembourg.

National Archives and Records Administration, Office of the Federal Register. 1999. *Public Papers of the Presidents of the United States, William J. Clinton, 1997, Book 1, January 1 to June 30, 1997.* Government Printing Office.

Nederlandse Vereniging voor Vrijwillige Euthanasie (NVVE) 2004. "Nvve-English - Call to Allow 'Suffering from Life' Mercy Killings." http://www.wilsverklaring.nl/nvve-english/pagina.asp?pagkey=72150.

Nederlandse Vereniging voor Vrijwillige Euthanasie (NVVE). 2013. "40 Jaar NVVE 1973-2013." *Relevant.*

Patients Rights Council. 2013. "Washington | Patients Rights Council." *Patients Rights Council: Addressing Euthanasia, Assisted Suicide, Advance Directives, Disability Rights, Pain Control and More.* Accessed May 28, 2013. http://www.patientsrightscouncil.org/site/washington/.

The Pew Forum on Religion and Public Life. 2012, October 9. *'Nones' on the Rise.* Accessed May 20, 2013. http://www.pewforum.org/Unaffiliated/nones-on-the-rise-religion.aspx#spiritual.

Physicians for Compassionate Care Education Foundation. n.d. Accessed May 21, 2013. http://www.pccef.org/.

Pope Pius XII. Encyclical Letter. 1943. "Mystici Corporis Christi: Encyclical of Pope Pius XII on the Mystical Body of Christ to Our Venerable Brethren, Patriarchs, Primates, Archbishops, Bishops, and Other Local Ordinaries Enjoying Peace and Communion with the Apostolic See, Section 4.1.2." http://www.vatican.va/holy _father/pius_xii/encyclicals/documents/hf_p-xii_enc_29061943_mystici-corporis -christi_en.html.

Pope Pius XII. 1957. Address to an International Congress of Anesthesiologists. *L'Osservatore Romano*, November 25.

van Raemdonck Dirk, A. Neyrinck, W. Coosemans, H. Decaluwe, P. De Leyn, P. Nafteux, H. Van Veer, and G.M. Verleden. 2013. "Lung Transplantation with Grafts Recovered from Euthanasia Donors." In Birmingham: European Society of Thoracic Surgery.

Swiss Federal Office of Justice. 2014. "Assisted Suicide: Strengthening the Right of Self-Determination-FDJP." *Swiss Federal Department of Justice and Police.* https:// www.bj.admin.ch/bj/en/home/aktuell/news/2011/ref_2011-06-29.html.

Tyson, Peter. 2001. "NOVA | The Hippocratic Oath Today." *WMHT—PBS*, March 7. Accessed May 29, 2013. http://www.pbs.org/wgbh/nova/body/hippocratic-oath -today.html.

CCPR Human Rights Commission. 2001. "United Nations Human Rights Website - Treaty Bodies Database-Document-Concluding Observations/Comments-Netherlands." *United Nations-CCPR.* August 27. http://www.unhchr.ch/tbs/doc.nsf/0/dbab71d01e 02db11c1256a950041d732?OpenDocument&Highlight=0,euthanasia.

U.S. Social Security Administration. n.d. "Social Security History." *The Evolution of Medicare: The Second Round, 1927 to 1940.* http://www.ssa.gov/history/ corningchap2.html.

UW Medicine. n.d. Northwest Hospital & Medical Center. *I-1000, The Death with Dignity Act.* Accessed May 28, 2013. http://www.nwhospital.org/visitorinfo/dda.asp.

Washington State Hospital Association. 2011. "Washington Hospital Fast Facts." *WSHA.* Accessed May 28, 2013. http://www.wsha.org/fastfacts.cfm.

Terry, Chris. 2014. "Christian Social People's Party (CSV)." *Demsoc Europe.* May 6. http://europe.demsoc.org/2014/05/06/christian-social-peoples-party-csv/.

Valley General Hospital. 2009. "Policies of Valley General Hospital." February 2. valleygeneral.com/about_us/Death_Dignity.pdf.

The World Federation of Right to Die Societies. n.d. "What is the Difference between Assisted Dying and Euthanasia?" *WFRTDS.* Accessed May 28, 2013. http://www .worldrtd.net/qanda/what-difference-between-assisted-dying-and-euthanasia.

The World Federation of Right to Die Societies. 1998. "Declarations on Assisted Dying." http://www.worldrtd.net/declarations-assisted-dying.

The World Federation of the Right to Die Societies. 2010. "In Memoriam Adelbert Josephus Jitta." July 6. http://www.worldrtd.net/news/memoriam-adelbert -josephus-jitta.

Vonnegut, Kurt. 1968. *Welcome to the Monkey House: A Collection of Short Works.* New York: Delacorte Press.

Zaritsky, John. 2010. *The Suicide Tourist.* WGHB/FRONTLINE with Point Grey Pictures, Inc. http://www.pbs.org/wgbh/pages/frontline/suicidetourist/etc/credits.html.

# Index

Waiting periods, for WDDA, 116–22

*Wall Street Journal,* 186

Warren, John C., 25

Washington: *Death with Dignity Act* and, 109–11; donations for "Yes on I-1000" campaign, 108–9, 112; I-119 in, 105–38; medically assisted death in, 107–8; Roman Catholics in, 109; suicide rates in, 109; use of DDA in, 117–18; via ballots and bills, 109

Washington Assessment of Student Learning (WASL), 108

*Washington Death with Dignity Act* (WDDA). *See* WDDA

Washington's *Initiative 1000 (I-1000),* 96, 105–38; aftermath of, 114–22; age and state of mind, 114–15; fate of, 112; residency, 114; resistance to, 111

Washington State Public Health Association, 111

*The Washington Times,* 47

*Washington v. Glucksberg,* 78, 79

WASL. *See* Washington Assessment of Student Learning (WASL)

WDDA, 114; death certificates under, 121; deaths at private residences, 123; diagnosis and prognosis for, 114–15; pain as a motive in, 124; prohibited medical terms and words under, 121; requests for, 116–22; rescissions for, 116–22; residency requirement for, 114; safeguards to patients, 121–22; self-administration for, 114–15; waiting periods for, 116–22

Wendte, Charles W., 31

WFRDS. *See* World Federation of Right to Die Societies (WFRDS)

*When Death Is Sought: Assisted Suicide and Euthanasia in the Medical Context,* 84

Wicks, Brian, 112

Willful murder, 47

Williams, Glanville, 66

World Federation of Right to Die Societies (WFRDS), 82

Worley, Lloyd, 58

Wyman, Louis, 60

Zola, Irving, 11

# About the Author

GIZA LOPES, PhD, is a postdoctoral associate at the School of Criminal Justice, University at Albany, New York. Fluent in several languages, she has published extensively on diverse topics of crime and justice.

1-16